THE OHIO RIVER VALLEY SERIES

Rita Kohn and William Lynwood Montell
Series Editors

Towns & Villages
OF THE
Lower Ohio

DARREL E. BIGHAM ~

THE UNIVERSITY PRESS OF KENTUCKY

Publication of this volume was made possible in part
by a grant from the National Endowment for the Humanities.

Editorial and Sales Offices: The University Press of Kentucky
663 South Limestone Street, Lexington, Kentucky 40508-4008

02 01 00 99 98   5 4 3 2 1

Library of Congress Cataloging-in-Publication Data
Bigham, Darrel E.
   Towns and villages of the lower Ohio / Darrel E. Bigham.
     p.   cm. — (Ohio River Valley series)
   Includes bibliographical references and index.
   ISBN 0-8131-2042-X (acid-free paper)
     1. Ohio River Valley—History, Local. 2 City and town life—
   Ohio River Valley—History. I. Title. II. Series.
   F516.B54   1997
   976.9—dc21   97-30247

Manufactured in the United States of America

For Polly

Contents

Illustrations follow page 178

Figures and Maps

Figures

Maps

Series Foreword

The Ohio River Valley Series, conceived and published by the University Press of Kentucky, is an ongoing series of books that examine and illuminate the Ohio River and its tributaries, the lands drained by these streams, and the peoples who made this fertile and desirable area their place of residence, of refuge, of commerce and industry, of cultural development, and, ultimately, of engagement with American democracy. In doing this, the series builds upon an earlier project, "Always a River: The Ohio River and the American Experience," which was sponsored by the National Endowment for the Humanities and the humanities councils of Illinois, Indiana, Kentucky, Ohio, Pennsylvania, and West Virginia, with a mix of private and public organizations.

The Always a River project directed widespread public attention to the place of the Ohio River in the context of the larger American story. This series expands on this significant role of the river in the growth of the American nation by presenting the varied history and folklife of the region. Each book's story is told through men and women acting within their particular place and time. Each reveals the rich resources for the history of the Ohio River and of the nation afforded by records, papers, and oral stories preserved by families and institutions. Each traces the impact the river and the land have had on individuals and cultures and, conversely, the changes these individuals and cultures have wrought on the valley with the passage of years.

As a force of nation and as a waterway into the American heartland, the Ohio and its tributaries have touched us individually and collectively. This series celebrates the story of that river and its valley through multiple voices and visions.

Towns and Villages of the Lower Ohio brings forward a long-neglected part of our American regional story. Based on thorough, impeccable research, this book takes us into the eras of big dreams and exuberant dreamers for whom every bend in the river conjured up economic promise. Here we meet the people who established a myriad of places along the new nation's waterway to riches and fame. Here we relive their triumphs and disappointments. Here we walk with our history in process, making deals, measuring corporate limits, and sometimes manipulating facts to boost enterprise. Here we grasp the realities between place and promise and celebrate names absent and extant on current maps of the flat-plained corridor from the Salt River's entry to the Mississippi's flow. Here we encounter the Ohio of Audubon and Lincoln and the Trail of Tears.

RITA KOHN
WILLIAM LYNWOOD MONTELL

Preface

The roots of this book are quite deep. Having grown up along a major river, the Susquehanna, I have always had special interest in the ways that rivers shape communities, and vice versa. A seminar in antebellum America that I had thirty years ago at the University of Kansas kindled appreciation for the vagaries of river town development. John G. Clark, seminar director, sparked my desire to someday explore the topic in depth. My coming to the University of Southern Indiana, a brand-new university in Evansville, the lower Ohio's largest city, was fortuituous in that regard. Most of my work before 1990, though, focused on the African and German American settlement of southwestern Indiana.

Little did I know that a superb opportunity would arise in the late 1980s with the Always a River project of the six state humanities councils bordering the Ohio. Led by the indefatigable Rita Kohn, then of the Indiana Humanities Council, this initiative produced *Always a River: The Ohio River and the American Experience,* edited by Robert L. Reid (Bloomington: Indiana University Press, 1991). I had the opportunity to contribute an essay on the economic consequences of the Ohio to this anthology. From the AAR undertaking also emerged a series on the Ohio Valley edited by Rita Kohn and Lynwood Montell of Western Kentucky University. They invited me to write a book on settlements on the lower Ohio, a project which seemed at the time a fairly easy extension of the research I had completed for the 1991 anthology.

I was soon disabused of that notion, as additional reading made me aware of the rich resources on the varied stories of the lower Ohio. Some places, because of size, institutional resources, and historians' attention, possess a wealth of resources for research. Many communities do not, for the same reasons, but size alone does not guarantee an abundance of historical records. Surprisingly, Evansville has yet to be the subject of a comprehensive and reliable history.

I have many people to thank for their assistance, especially those always considerate and helpful librarians at the Indiana State Library, the Indiana Historical Society, the Evansville–Vanderburgh County Public Library, and the University of Southern Indiana. The staff at the Kentucky Room of the Owensboro–Daviess County Public Library were generous with time and suggestions, as were their counterparts in other town libraries, especially in Metropolis and Paducah. Special thanks are due Lyn Martin and Carol Bartlett of Evansville's Willard Library and to Gina Walker, who manages special collections in the USI Library.

USI's granting me another sabbatical during the 1994-95 academic year freed me from classes and most administrative work for about half a year so that I could complete research and begin writing this book. Bob Reid, vice president for academic affairs at USI as well as a superb historian, has been unswerving in his support.

Most of all, I am grateful to Polly, my wife, for her steadfast and loving support of my work over the past thirty-plus years. I offer this book as a modest form of appreciation to her.

Introduction

In late November 1996, a large steel manufacturer from Ohio announced plans to construct a billion-dollar edifice on rolling land just northwest of Rockport, Indiana. The facility would employ over four hundred in positions paying on the average $50,000 annually, beginning in 1998. When asked why the company had chosen this location, officials stressed access to the Ohio River. Material for processing would be shipped to the plant via the river, and barges would take away much of the completed product to manufacturers of automobiles and appliances. The river would also supply huge amounts of water for processing the steel. Ironically, days earlier, the *Evansville Press* reported that the bankrupt Tell City Chair Company had been sold, bringing to an ignoble end the city's largest employer, a nationally renowned manufacturer founded in 1865.

To those conversant with the continuing importance of the lower Ohio River and with the ebb and flow of economic activity in the region, such events were not surprising. To most, though, this area is a remote, obscure place in which little, if anything, of importance has occurred since the mid-nineteenth century. Sometimes another aspect of regional continuity—flooding—reminds residents of the river's awesome power and alerts outsiders to the region's existence. That occurred in March 1997, when the river attained its highest level since 1964. Evansville, Henderson, Owensboro, and Paducah—the region's largest cities—are the most familiar, but even they are often misplaced. Evansville, for instance, is often confused with Evanston, a northern suburb of Chicago. Other places, with names like Cairo, Metropolis, Enterprise, and Rome, suggest that their founders' reach far exceeded their grasp. Most—including Joppa, Hamletsburg, Magnet, and Fredonia—have always been tiny settlements. Many once promising sites have long since disappeared, such as Morvin's Landing, Coffman's Landing, Owen's Ferry, as well as America, Trinity, Boston, Mineral City, and Grand Pier.

These locales offer a microcosm of the history of the United States and its ideas of westward expansion, linear progress, human perfectibility, continental mastery, and material reward. They offer many ways of thinking about how and why success (and failure) occur, as well as how we define success.

Many settlements bore the surname of their founder or patron—Hawesville and Leavenworth, for example. This linked the fortunes of town speculators with community and regional development. To promote growth, other founders honored national heroes through such names as Mount Vernon and Tell City. Paducah and Shawneetown venerated Native Americans. Some names reflected area resources or features—for instance, Mound City and Quarry in Illinois and Cannelton in Indiana. Still others bonded themselves with ancient cities— Cairo and Joppa in Illinois, and Rome, Indiana. America and Metropolis bespoke the most grandiose dreams of all.

Because these communities were created to make money, they participated in the drama of regional and national development. Our images of growth, expansion, and destiny have encouraged us to focus on larger places elsewhere and to ignore these smaller locales. As Oscar Handlin noted, however, every county and municipality demonstrates the benign influences of geography and popular character on growth. There is another side to the picture—modest achievements as well as failure, stagnation, and decline—which is more difficult to explain. Too often, we have attributed progress or the lack thereof to impersonal geographic or economic forces.[1]

The object of this study is the corridor nearly 350 miles long downriver from the Falls of the Ohio located between Louisville, Kentucky, and Clark and Floyd Counties, Indiana and the towns and villages on either side of it to the mouth of the Ohio at Cairo, Illinois. Twenty-four counties (eleven in Kentucky, seven in Indiana, and six in Illinois) lie along it. After the first fifty miles or so below the Falls, dramatic bluffs give way to fairly flat terrain. Within this region are important navigable tributaries—the Green, Wabash, Cumberland, and Tennessee. Along much of the corridor, often flooded and inaccessible in the spring, is rich bottomland, always a source of substantial income to those with the resources and the patience to farm it. The passageway possesses many mineral and natural resources—salines and fluorspar in southern Illinois, coal and petroleum in Indiana and Kentucky, and hardwoods like ash, hickory, and walnut in all three states. Portions offer only the hardiest a living, because the absence of glaciation meant thin topsoil—a dramatic contrast not only to the farmers of the river bottomlands but also to those who settled the prairies to the north and the black belt regions to the south.[2]

With the exception of the Kentucky Bluegrass, settlement along the lower Ohio River began after the Revolution ended. As the nation's first interstate highway, bringing people and goods to the West, the Ohio sparked a variety of transportation and technological strategies, such as the Erie Canal, to exploit western trade. Cincinnati and Louisville were on the cutting edge of national growth. Even after its golden age had passed, the Ohio continued to play a vital role in regional, national, and international affairs.

Yet along this common artery, enormous differences existed in the ways people built their communities, made their livings, and conducted their daily affairs. The Ohio was a physical barrier that divided free and slave labor, and the legacy of that divergence continued to be felt many decades after the Civil War. Largely because of slavery, relatively few immigrants settled on the Kentucky side of the river, where Tidewater and Upper South peoples predominated. North of the river lived more people whose roots were in New England, the Middle Colonies, Germany, or the British Isles. The absence of bridges until the late 1880s reinforced cultural and social differences. The Ohio also separated forms of economic activity, with staple cash crops, chiefly tobacco, dominating the south shore. Railroad freight rate differentials reinforced those differences. With conspicuous exceptions, economic diversification was far more advanced on the northern shore.

Political decisions fostered as well as reflected divergence. The Ordinance of 1785 and the Northwest Ordinance of 1787 offered residents north of the Ohio the nation's first bill of rights, the certainty of land titles, the promise of public education, and the absence of slave labor. Territorial and state governments exhibited the political cultures of their early settlers—a county-based, almost patriarchal system in Kentucky and southern Illinois and a township-based government in Indiana reflecting New England patterns. Territorial and state governments gave differing (although always small) amounts of power to local officials. Early state government in the Old Northwest actively promoted state and local transportation projects. Political cultures within states also varied. For instance, most southern Illinois and Indiana communities frowned on public funding of infrastructure and education because of their cost and threat to laissez-faire society. By contrast, Evansville—with its large numbers of Yankee and Middle States settlers—was far more supportive of market capitalism and public education. Within Kentucky, the strong Tidewater heritage in Henderson and Union Counties contrasted sharply with Paducah's more diverse roots.

Settlers along the lower Ohio River created a distinctive culture by blending their various heritages. The most powerful was that of the Upper South, the intertwined Cavalier, Borderlands, and Transappalachian cultures that followed Kentuckians who crossed the Ohio and settled in Illinois and Indiana. Yankee ideas and institutions permeated some of the larger communities. Nineteenth-century newcomers, mostly from northern Ireland and southern Germany, also added special elements to regional folkways.[3]

This region poses important questions, the most obvious of which is how and why a major city of the size of Cincinnati or Chicago did not emerge there. Promoters of Cairo—the contemporary of Illinois's other "dream city," Chicago—certainly thought otherwise. Elevation and/or location created other "perfect" sites, such as Cannelton, Henderson, Paducah, and Smithland. Evansville, with much less natural advantage, became the dominant metropolis, although it would be smaller than many cities to the north. Evansville's growth merits much more careful exploration by historians. Other than Cincinnati, no northern community on the Ohio experienced such success *after* the coming of railroads, when most Ohio River settlements, such as Madison and New Albany, stagnated or declined.

By standards of founders and historians, many settlements failed. We need to learn much more about these places. The prevailing view is that railroads led to the eclipsing of river trade and thus to the decline of settlements. Many of these sites, though, continued to be important in their immediate vicinity well into the early twentieth century. Their "demise" had many causes, especially the "good roads" movement, the automobile and the truck, the vehicular bridge, and the changed shopping, entertainment, and educational patterns that accelerated in the 1920s. Many river communities did not decline or dry up even after those changes.

The lower Ohio contains many unpretentious hamlets, villages, and towns. It also possesses numerous cases of that unique American phenomenon, the ghost town. In the sorting-out process, some clearings in the thick forests along the Ohio became permanent settlements. Some, in turn, became landings for rivercraft or ferries. A portion of these emerged as small market centers. Over time, a few evolved into towns, and only a handful of these became cities. By the eve of World War I, only Evansville was a radial center or metropolis—a dominant commercial, manufacturing, and cultural center for a large region.[4]

Communities in the lower Ohio have received little attention from academic historians. Monographs on the histories of the three states and articles in the *Illinois Historical Journal,* the *Indiana Magazine of History,* and the *Register of the Kentucky Historical Society,* for instance, rarely examine the region and its villages and towns. Most of this limited historical literature deals with the antebellum period, a reflection of the notion that history ceased to exist with the coming of the railroads.[5]

Fortunately, we have some useful historical literature on town building. In 1945, for example, Francis P. Weisenburger explored factors that led to the urbanization of the Midwest.[6] Several scholars have suggested that study of smaller communities discourages both a preoccupation with success stories and an idealized image of village and town life.[7] Others have increased our appreciation for stages of community life: that relatively few villages and towns have crossed an urban threshold from an agrarian, rural phase to a commercial, industrial phase. William Cronon's study of Chicago and its hinterlands encourages us to understand that most towns were marketplaces a long time, but only some became metropolises. These regions varied in size, but the process was similar.[8]

A community cannot be understood without reference to its region. David Goldfield portrayed antebellum southern towns, for instance, as agrarian settlements built on staple crops and biracialism. Jon Teaford's examination of Old Northwest cities stresses their "interior mentality." Timothy Mahoney has stated that moving "to a new town in the West and [tying] one's life and career to its destiny was to acquire . . . a lesson in the dynamics of power within a regional urban economy."[9]

Settlements were also shaped by internal dynamics. Community building, for instance, often reflected competing visions. Newcomers, whether from the Northeast or from northwestern Europe, helped to reshape local visions and strategies, and out of this emerged a linkage of cultural values, such as local pride and boosterism, with a social structure that allowed different minorities to mark off the boundaries to their entering and leaving such a "community of limited liability." Coming to grips with internal and external dynamics made the difference between a place growing or becoming one of "the countless thousands of failures and false prophecies in small towns and ghost towns."[10] Vandalia, which was the capital of Illinois from 1819 to 1839, had plenty of boosterism but not enough consistency about its future. Promotionalism was a basic element in community growth, but leaders responded differently. The most successful in the antebellum Midwest, Chicago and Indianapolis, accepted a coherent, realistic vision for their cities.[11]

Historical study of these processes on the lower Ohio is unfortunately quite thin. Richard Wade's *The Urban Frontier* examines only a portion of the Ohio River valley and concludes that the urban pattern of the West was established, with few exceptions, by 1800. His argument for the centrality of the town in Ohio River valley development, though, remains compelling. "In the context of this relationship with the outside world," he declared, "western towns developed their basic economic structures." Despite a common setting, "their responses to it varied. Peculiar locations, resources, and historic origins precluded uniformity and produced important differences."[12]

The only scholarly examination of the lower Ohio River valley is Charles E. Conrod's 1976 dissertation in economics. Given its location and its natural resources, he asserts, the lower Ohio should have produced "cities of note," but "its cities are by and large not very prosperous." How could a region with theoretically excellent transportation facilities, a central location to midwestern population centers, good raw materials, and large cities only on its fringe not become what it should have been? Conrod identified four elements of growth—trade, manufacturing, early start, and exogenous forces—and concluded that neither a single factor nor a combination of factors sufficed to produce a major city in the region. The advantages that the region possessed, moreover, were more apparent than real.[13]

Conrod's study is narrowly focused, and it minimizes humans: their ideas, ideals, frailties, and cultures. The elements of luck and accident are also absent. Communities are created not by forces but by human beings. Community building involves chance, ungrasped opportunities, and unplanned events. Conrod's assumption that the region should have produced a great metropolis is problematic. Given the rapid development of more northerly portions of the Old Northwest after 1815, the degree of urbanization along the lower Ohio was surprisingly high.[14]

State and local histories dealing with the lower Ohio River present another problem. According to Richard Wade, they are "abundant in that each town has its own history written many times . . . largely by amateur historians who have brought both affection and insight to the study of their own communities." They are "usually unsystematic and often 'dated' by the circumstances of their publication." Professional historians, by contrast, have generally concentrated on a particular aspect of a single city's development.[15]

A comprehensive analysis includes factors occurring outside and inside communities. Among the former were such elements as the flow of population, the creation and growth of markets, the countless decisions made by businesses and governments, the consequences of the setting, the reports of the settlement's promise by travelers, the impact of national or international crises such as the Great War, the natural and agricultural resources of the region, or the quality of competition from other settlements. Among the latter, probably the most essential were its leaders' vision and their ability to respond favorably to external challenges: the will and the resources to adapt and their willingness to welcome newcomers, among others. These reflected social and cultural attributes.

Change and continuity also can be explored through apparent and real advantages. Site, for example, was a necessary but insufficient condition for growth. Having what appeared to be an ideal location guaranteed nothing. Such physical challenges as flooding and seepage and such social problems as external control of the town's lands and government obviated exploitation of the site's advantage. Fort Massac, Illinois, was situated in an ideal location, but the main current of the river lay on the bend opposite the fort, thus minimizing the threat of its guns and discouraging subsequent commercial development. All successful communities were located on a portion of the river, usually a bend, where the main current flowed by it. Ideally the site was also high enough to weather seasonal flooding. Yet Henderson, Kentucky, described by many early travelers as the lower Ohio's ideal location, was eclipsed over time by places with much less locational advantage.[16] Brandenburg, Mount Vernon, and Newburgh possessed flood-free elevations, but had a somewhat similar experience. Many settlements were ideally located for reaching markets, but only a few were able to do that. What mattered was community leaders' imagining distant markets for their products, generating the means of getting them there, attracting human and financial capital, or obtaining governmental and business support for transportation and site improvement.

Similarly, the region's agricultural and natural resources ensured less than the willingness and the ability to do something with these assets. One illustration was the desire of state governments in Illinois and Indiana in 1836-37 to invest heavily in major transportation projects. Similarly, the presence of slavery in Kentucky and free labor in Indiana and Illinois made for striking differences in the levels of enterprise on either side of the river.

Timing and luck were also important. Examples include the decision of a group of investors elsewhere to build a railroad near or through one's settlement, or a legislative agreement to place a state-supported transportation project in or near one's town (e.g., selecting Evansville as the terminus of the Wabash and Erie Canal in 1834). A fire or flood could devastate a seemingly thriving community and lead to decline or ruin.

Whether one explores external and internal factors or realities and possibilities, however, ultimately no single element explains the unique character of community development. Settlement and development reflected the intermingling of many factors.

This work is designed as an introduction to oft-ignored places in a little-studied part of the country. Each community's story is different, but often narratives overlap. Through the specific and the shared narratives, a story of a region emerges. Comparing and contrasting communities in three states that share a common Main Street, the Ohio, the study begins with the formative years in the late eighteenth century and concludes shortly after World War I, when the metropolis and consumerism were well under way. The internal combustion engine and mass culture had begun to make profound changes in the region, and for many the Ohio would no longer be the center of community life. By the end of the decade, the riverway itself was forever altered by vehicular bridges and federally constructed locks and dams. Despite all of this, the patterns of community life and intraregional relationships continued to reflect long-established traditions.

This work has four chronologically defined parts. The first explores the events up to the admission of Illinois to statehood in 1818. The second treats the period generally known as the transportation revolution, 1815-1850. The third covers the era of the Civil War, the hegemony and decline of the passenger steamboat, and the rise of railroads and industry (1850-1880). The last examines the lower Ohio during the formation age of the industrial city, the creation of a national urban market, and the rise of the metropolis, 1880-1920. In each section, a brief review of population trends is followed by a lengthy description of development in river communities. At the end of each major section the reader is offered an analysis of patterns of change and continuity.

Ultimately, the enormous variety in the form and function of lower Ohio River settlements, which shared many economic and cultural ties, is a phenomenon to be celebrated as well as explained. Landscape and place reveal much about the continuing importance of the Ohio River and the interrelationship between its resources and its people.[17] By looking at this distinctive region of the United States, and in the process discovering the similarities and differences along one river corridor, we gain access to the essence of the American dream.

PART 1 ∾

Lower Ohio River Settlements before 1820

1 ~

Hamlets and Villages

Fernand Braudel has observed that "the history of a people is inseparable from the country it inhabits" and that "a country is a storehouse of dominant energies whose seeds have been planted by nature, but whose use depends on man." Few rivers illustrate that as vividly as the Ohio. Its strategic location, navigability, and natural resources strongly influenced the economic development of the region through which it flows. The Ohio was America's first western thoroughfare, and its tributaries extended the economic influence of the Ohio well beyond its borders. Climate and geology combined with location to make the Ohio a major source of agricultural products, forest and mineral resources, and manufactured goods.[1]

In what is now Kentucky, the lower Ohio defines, east to west, the northern boundaries of three distinctive areas. The largest is the Pennyroyal, some 12,000 square miles east of the Tennessee River and west of the Eastern Mountains and Coal Fields. Its broad plains produce an ample amount of grain and tobacco. It also possesses cavernous sinks and ravines that cut through the layers of limestone. The Pennyroyal encircles the Western Coal Field, a 4,500 square-mile region which yields much tobacco as well. To the west of the Pennyroyal lies the Jackson Purchase, an area 2,400 miles square defined by theTennessee, the Ohio, and the Mississippi. A relatively flat region of little consequence until the purchase of these Chickasaw hunting lands in 1818, the section would subsequently be noted for cotton production as well as cypress and other "Deep South" features.

These three areas possess important navigable tributaries—the Tennessee, the Cumberland, and the Green. They contain some important mineral resources besides coal: iron ore in Livingston County, fluorspar in Crittenden and Livingston Counties, oil and gas in Meade, Henderson, and Breckinridge Counties, and tile clay in Meade County.[2]

Similar geological diversity can be found across the river. Just below the Falls, Indiana is traversed by the Knobstone Escarpment, the state's most prominent topographic feature. This separates southeastern Indiana from the unglaciated central part of southern Indiana. This "Driftless Area" displays steep hills and narrow valleys, sinkholes, lost streams, caves, abundant limestone, and thin topsoil. To its west is the Wabash Lowland, which displays "a general, plainlike structure with stream valleys filled with silt and glacial deposits. It contains the best lands in the southern part of the state and is underlaid with valuable coal [and petroleum] deposits." Southern Indiana is generally not agriculturally rich, and bottomlands in the Driftless Area tend to be narrow. Most of the area was once covered with hardwood forests. Mineral resources are generally limited to limestone, coal, and petroleum. Only the Wabash River on the state's western border provides a navigable waterway to the interior. Topography made east-west road building difficult.[3]

Illinois's Ohio River counties possess the least geological diversity. Much of the territory lies in the Ohio Bottomlands, a low, poorly drained strip of land. The last period of glaciation did not touch this area. It is separated from the Central Upland, a coal-rich area which dominates much of southern Illinois to the north, by the Shawnee Hills or Ozark Plateau, a rugged region extending eastward from the Mississippi through the northern portions of the river counties. Rich in hardwoods and clear streams, this is the most variegated and picturesque portion of southern Illinois. Mineral resources are more plentiful here: chiefly fluorspar and iron ore in Hardin County. Neither the Bottomlands nor the Shawnee Hills possess coal of commercial significance. Eastern Gallatin County lies at the intersection of the southeastern portion of the Central Upland and the southern edge of the Wabash slope. Salines here were an important mineral resource in the early 1800s. There are no navigable waterways to the inland. Flooding is a perennial threat at the mouth of the Wabash. Rugged terrain, as in Indiana, thwarted east-west transportation improvements.[4]

The settlement of the lower Ohio was from the outset the product of nature and culture. Nature provided, for instance, avenues for travel into the region. The most vital at first was Boone's Wilderness Trail, which extended from the Cumberland Gap in southeastern Kentucky to the Bluegrass region via buffalo trails connecting salines that Indian and white hunters enhanced. A buffalo trace extending from the Falls to Vincennes on the Wabash provided another means of accessing the West, as did trails from Shawneetown to Kaskaskia on the Mississippi. Long before Europeans came, a series of distinctive settlements emerged. The most advanced was the Mississippian, where farmers erected flat-topped temple mounds that provided the focal point for trade and government. The largest on the lower Ohio was a village near Evansville now known as Angel Mounds.

The relationship between these prehistoric peoples and the historic Native Americans has never been explained. By the early 1700s, though, Shawnees

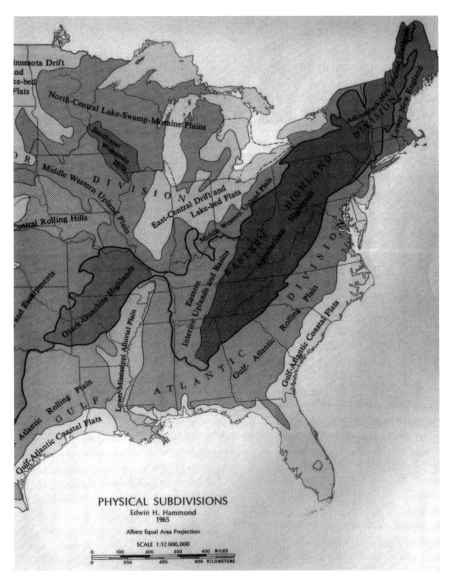

PHYSICAL SUBDIVISIONS
Edwin H. Hammond
1965

Albers Equal Area Projection

SCALE 1:17,000,000

Physical Subdivisions: Lower Ohio. This map clearly shows the differences in the landforms of the upper South and lower Midwest that converge on the lower Ohio. Most of southern Indiana and southern Illinois (and a portion of Kentucky that comprises Henderson and Union counties to the west and Meade and Hardin to the east) is part of the Middle Western Upland Plain. The central part of southern Indiana that is usually labeled the Driftless Area (unglaciated) is part of the Eastern Uplands and Basins, which includes a portion of Kentucky's Ohio border as well as a small amount of Illinois's Ohio border. The Gulf-Atlantic Rolling Plain extends northward into the Purchase region west of the Tennessee River and into a portion of Illinois's Ohio border that includes Cairo (United States Department of the Interior, U.S. Geological Survey, *National Atlas of the United States of America* [Washington, 1970], 61) resided in southwestern Ohio and southeastern Indiana, the Wea and the Piankashaw band of Miamis on the lower Wabash, the Illini in the Mississippi valley, and the Chickasaws and Cherokees to the southwest and southeast, respectively, of present-day Kentucky.[5]

Beginning with LaSalle's explorations in the late 1670s, the Ohio linked French interests in the New World. Seeking to protect trade routes between Quebec and Louisiana, the French erected a series of posts and mission stations, including Fort Ascension (upriver from Metropolis, Illinois) and Post Vincennes. The contest for control of the Ohio valley exploded after the Ohio Company of Virginia received a royal grant in 1749. After the subsequent military conflict, the French and Indian War, Britain gained title to France's western claims east of the Mississippi.[6]

Over the next thirty years the British, and then the Americans, attempted to develop strategies for controlling the Indians while placating land-hungry whites. Cartographers' reports of the Ohio River's navigability and abundant resources fed those appetites. Population pressures forced the British to open the region south of the entire Ohio River to white settlement in 1768. The upper Ohio River valley followed suit. In the early 1770s, Virginians settled what would in 1776 become Virginia's County of Kentucky, defeating in the process efforts by Richard Henderson and his Transylvania Company to create a proprietary colony. Henderson was, however, compensated with a generous land grant. Young George Rogers Clark of Kentucky helped the United States to secure the Transappalachian West in the 1783 peace treaty with Great Britain. Clark and other Revolutionary War veterans received land warrants in recognition of their service. Much of western Kentucky and southern Illinois were set aside as a military reserve.

Americans assumed the Ohio River would be the north-south boundary between rapidly growing Kentucky and the Indians of the Northwest, but they lacked the power to back up that claim. The greatest achievements of the weak Confederation government of the 1780s were the Ordinance of 1785 and the Northwest Ordinance of 1787. For the territory north of the river, these ordinances established the rectilinear, township-based survey, set aside public lands for common schools, forbade slavery, guaranteed basic citizenship rights through a republican form of government, and created a process whereby territories and states were formed and governed.[7]

South of the Ohio, continued conflicts among the former colonies regarding land claims and strong Native American opposition to colonization prevented the establishment of similar plans. Kentuckians followed the old English metes and bounds system of surveying, which depended on natural features. Combined with often overlapping claims through military warrants, this made land titles insecure. In addition, early settlers had been nurtured in the political culture of Virginia and North Carolina, where the county, not the town, was the basic unit of government, and a strong agrarian tradition minimized the role of government. Most early settlers had also grown up in a slave society. Although there was much evidence of discomfort with the institution, and most whites did not own slaves, slavery became a fundamental part of Kentucky's society. In short, the Ohio River divided two ways of looking at land development and human labor.[8]

Settlement in the Ohio valley expanded from the late 1780s onward, although Native Americans' hostility limited settlement in the north and west, where only a few squatters "broke the stillness of a forest solitude that existed much as it had before the first English settlement on the continent."[9] Despite efforts of the Northwest Territory's infant government, established at Marietta in 1788, the region remained dangerous, and Indian raids into Kentucky were common. Hence a line of forts was established in the Ohio valley, including Fort Massac (the former Fort Ascension) in Illinois country. Travel on the Ohio continued to be less secure than on the Wilderness Trail. Population growth south of the Ohio led to Kentucky's admittance to the Union in June 1792, the first state west of the Appalachians. Tennessee followed four years later.[10]

A series of successful American military and diplomatic ventures in 1794-95 boosted development not only in Kentucky but also north of the Ohio. The Louisiana Purchase of 1803 strengthened American access to New Orleans and gave the nation control over the lands west of the Mississippi.

Rapid growth of the eastern portion of the Northwest Territory prompted its separation (1800) and subsequent admission as the state of Ohio. The remainder became the Indiana Territory. From its capital at Vincennes, Governor William Henry Harrison negotiated eight treaties between 1803 and 1809 that opened what is now southern Indiana as well as much of present-day Illinois and southern Wisconsin to American settlement. Strong resistance from an Indian confederation led by the charismatic Shawnee chief Tecumseh and his brother, the Prophet, followed Harrison's efforts, but the Indians' resistance came to naught with the Battle of Tippecanoe in the fall of 1811 and Tecumseh's death in 1813. The westward expansionism that followed the War of 1812 led to a series of treaties ceding most of the remainder of the Old Northwest to Americans. Population growth to the west and the north, in the meantime, had led to the creation of Michigan Territory in 1805 and Illinois Territory in 1809.[11]

White settlement on the lower Ohio ensued. By the second war with Britain, some settlements had become villages and towns. Pioneers often floated down the Ohio in flatboats, settling at the mouths of tributaries and other promising sites. However crude, these settlements offered a degree of stability for business and government not found to the interior.[12]

Early travelers on the lower Ohio, though, noted the sparseness of development. One navigator in 1797 claimed to have spied only thirty families in four hundred miles. General Victor Collot, who explored the region between March and December 1796 on behalf of the French ambassador, declared that navigation below the Falls was good in all seasons. He observed a small settlement of eight to ten families at Yellow Bank (Owensboro) and a cluster of hunters at Red Bank (Henderson). Having only recently occupied this high ground—which Collot thought the best site on the lower Ohio for a fort—these almost naked "foresters" subsisted on game and fish. He also saw three families at the mouth of Highland Creek, just downriver, and a small wooden fort between the mouths of the Cumberland and the Tennessee. Regarding Fort Massac, occupied during the previous two years by a hundred-man American garrison, he thought its military value was minimal, since the main river channel flowed against the bank opposite the fort. Because the fort was situated at the terminus of two roads into the Illinois country, however, the site had future importance. Collot recorded no other settlements thence to the Mississippi.[13]

Zadok Cramer, whose guidebook for boatmen, *The Navigator*, appeared only a few years later, revealed how inchoate settlement was. In his seventh edition (1811), for instance, he reported no downriver settlements between the Falls and Henderson. The only other place he mentioned was Smithland, where he thought residents enjoyed good health and a lively business downriver as well as up the Cumberland.[14]

The 1814 edition, the first published after the great earthquake and the first steamboat on the Ohio, offered evidence of further advancement. As before, the first place described below Louisville was Henderson, which he noted possessed a commanding view of the river and comprised thirty houses and "two stores indifferently supplied," two long tobacco warehouses, a post office, a jail, and a courthouse. He also recognized Shawneetown, a place with thirty "indifferent cabin-roofed homes," only two of which were shingled. There were a few "indifferent taverns" and several dram shops there, and nearby was the United States saltworks. Cave-in-Rock was briefly noted as a crossing point to Illinois. Surprisingly, Smithland was described as little more than a farm: "[The founder] is not the first who has got disappointed in the attempt to grow towns in a forest," Cramer declared presciently. Fort Massac was unsuited as a fort or a settlement because swamps and stagnant waters lay to its north. Nothing remained, he said, of Wilkinsonville, just downriver, which had been a station for General James Wilkinson's troops in 1801.

At the mouth of the Ohio, there was "a pretty good landing place on the right [north] side." A Colonel Bird, who resided on the west bank of the Mississippi, had a temporary warehouse there. Someone offering reliable supplies, he added, would be paid well—an anticipation of the many dreamlike schemes for the future city of Cairo. He added ominously that the high-water mark on trees there suggested annual flooding to at least sixteen feet. What a pity, he declared, for the meeting place of two of the world's greatest rivers.[15]

Settlement was a sifting process for migrants with varying resources and degrees of determination. They encountered a mix of nationalities, economic organizations, and religious associations. Distinctive patterns of life and settlement emerged. The urban center of the Transappalachian West, as Malcolm Rohrbough has written, was the small town. Some flourished, and others did not. Zadok Cramer identified some of the reasons: elevation, water supply, access to market, and leadership.[16]

Between 1791 and 1819, nine states were added to the Union, including seven from the Ohio River valley. The dramatic expansion of this region far exceeded the nation's rate of growth. By 1820, shortly after Illinois's admission, the Ohio River valley represented almost a quarter of the nation's population. Sixteen of the present-day counties on the lower river were organized by 1820. The four oldest (Harrison in Indiana and Breckinridge, Hardin, and Henderson in Kentucky) accounted for well over half of the corridor's population.

One promoter, George Imlay, wrote glowingly of the prospects for settlers: "all the variegated charm which color and nature can produce, here in the lap of elegance and beauty."[17] Such romanticized accounts fed the population stream that flowed down the Ohio. So did newspapers, whose proprietors and editors often had a personal stake in the new lands. Successes in military campaigns against Native Americans added to this current, as did word of mouth. Also contributing were river boatmen, first on canoe and pirogue and then on barge, flatboat, and keelboat, who not only made material contributions in their pioneering commercial enterprises but provided social, cultural, and psychological links between the Americas on either side of the Appalachians.

The sizes, shapes, and functions of river settlements varied, but at the time of Illinois's admission to the Union, most were little more than primitive clearings offering basic services. Few were platted or incorporated. But they represented the cutting edge of westward movement.[18]

Kentucky's river communities below the Falls illustrated that. In 1800, almost all Kentuckians dwelled in the north central portion of the state. The treaties of 1794-1803 stimulated growth to the west, reflected in the formation of Livingston (1797), Henderson (1798), and Breckinridge (1800) Counties.

The population "take-off" there and to the north did not occur, however, until 1815-18, following William Henry Harrison's and Andrew Jackson's victories over the British and Indians, Jackson's treaty with the Chickasaw in 1818, and the rapid rise of Louisville, Lexington, and Cincinnati. During this transition, Union (1811) and Daviess (1815) Counties were formed.[19]

Land claims, however, created a major obstacle to growth and helped to strengthen support for the methods used north of the Ohio. The state's land law of 1792 reflected Virginia's. A four-step process was required, culminating in the issuance of a land patent, but each phase was complicated, and litigation was voluminous and protracted. Warrants had been issued extravagantly, especially to veterans, and holders identified their tracts by natural features or buildings. County surveyors generally lacked the necessary skills. Given the absence of comprehensive or accurate maps, much land was "'shingled over' with successive layers of patents, providing still further grounds for litigation."[20]

Notwithstanding these lingering problems, federal military and diplomatic successes stimulated Kentucky's expansion, and state government offered its own encouragement. The Kentucky constitutions of 1792 and 1799 and the legislatures of the Commonwealth offered fundamental protection for property and established a framework for the creation and powers of local government. Because of the power of conservative rural interests, though, Kentucky gave far less authority to towns and made taxation far more difficult than Illinois and Indiana, forcing towns to secure legislative approval for most activities. Local governments commonly provided law and order, licensed gristmills and sawmills, fixed prices of services offered by local taverns, and laid out and maintained roads. In 1792 the General Assembly established a warehouse inspection law, an especially important development for river communities. Reflecting its Virginia roots, Kentucky legislatures also made its rivers public thoroughfares. To keep taxes down, it required men and boys above the age of sixteen living near a river to provide several days' labor annually to maintain and improve channels. The 1818 General Assembly voted $40,000 to improve the Cumberland and Green Rivers, among others, and created a board of internal improvements to oversee the project.[21]

The political culture of early Kentucky offered a distinctive flavor to local government. Until the Constitution of 1850, for example, the governor appointed the justices of the peace, who constituted the county courts, the basic fiscal, legislative, and judicial unit of local government. The justices, in turn, ruled their charges like small fiefdoms. Counties were liberally created—eventually 120—and they were often named for local politicos whose cronies were chiefly interested in perpetuating their power. As in the Tidewater, the county seat was the center of the Kentucky universe. There one received government favors, drank free whiskey at election times, took one's wife on market days, heard campaign speeches, or bought gadgets and patent medicine. The most important events were court days, when men came to town to listen to florid oratory, race their horses, get tipsy, or conduct court business.

Kentucky was also a low-tax state that treated highway development as a private responsibility. Although early state government purchased large amounts of stock in most of the major tollway companies and regulated tolls, the legislature abolished this agency in the 1850s, abandoning state obligations for highway construction and maintenance until the twentieth century. Almost every mile of Kentucky roads by the time of the Civil War was a private tollway. Not surprisingly, the state's roads were also generally poor. No road in the lower Ohio valley was macadamized—graded and covered with crushed stone. Such roads from Henderson, Paducah, and Wickliffe to the Tennessee border were constructed much later. And most roads were local, connecting at most two or three settlements. All this made river entrepots relatively more vital in Kentucky than in Illinois and Indiana.[22]

More than eight thousand slaves living in lower Ohio counties in 1820 distinguished Kentucky most sharply from its neighbors.[23] Kentucky's founders protected a system of labor in ways resembling Virginia's. Over time, manumission became more difficult. The 1820s were the peak of slavery in Kentucky, after which it, like other Upper South states, became known for breeding slaves for sale southward. Kentucky slavery was broadly based: 25 percent of all household heads in 1800 owned at least one slave. The proportion of the population that was enslaved was about as high in Henderson and Livingston Counties as it was in the Bluegrass. Although Kentucky slavery was in some respects distinctive, in most respects it resembled that of the Old South. Kentuckians possessed a lively intraregional slave market, for the frontier did not diminish the almost insatiable appetite for cheap labor. Slavery was also not a benign institution in Kentucky.[24]

Settlements along the lower Ohio grew in number and size. The first significant place below Louisville might have been Fort Jefferson, just south of the mouth of the Ohio in what is now Ballard County, but this was one of many "might have beens." Established by George Rogers Clark in 1780, the fort was abandoned by Virginia a year later for economic and military reasons. The most significant upriver was Henderson, namesake of the leader of the Transylvania Company, to which the Virginia legislature had given 200,000 acres between the Green and Ohio Rivers. Before Richard Henderson's death in 1785, members of the company had founded Nashboro (Nashville). Some surviving members subsequently established a community on "Red Banks," where some squatters of English and German descent had settled.[25]

One of those squatters, John Upp, offered an early portrait of this place. Born in Pennsylvania in 1781, Upp came west with his father, Jacob, his mother, Elizabeth Sprinkle, and her father and brothers. First settling near Pittsburgh, the group moved to Louisville, where they dwelled six years. In 1792 Jacob, his father-in-law, and five brothers-in-law came to Red Banks, where they built houses, cleared land, and planted and harvested their crops before returning to Louisville. By the time the group returned with their families, "villains of the first order" had moved there. Nonetheless, they built more permanent structures, including a blacksmith shop. Life there was perilous: John Upp and four others were captured by Potawatomis in the spring of 1793. John and two others escaped after two years' captivity. The two left behind were killed.[26]

These squatters had selected an attractive spot. Surrounding the nicely elevated site, seventy-two feet above the Ohio's low-water mark, was rich farmland, ideal for the types of crops to which the Virginian and North Carolinian Transylvania Company investors were accustomed. General Samuel Hopkins, a Revolutionary War officer and attorney, was engaged as the company's agent. After arranging a survey, he advertised the settlement in Virginia in late 1797.[27]

In 1798, the community of about 170 people became seat of government of a new county, also named for Henderson. Demonstrating the company's propensity toward Tidewater culture, Hopkins established a number of large estates for himself and others, including Henderson's heirs. The only child of a company officer, for example, claimed 32,000 acres. Not surprisingly, the first slaves arrived in the county a year later. The town was laid out with broad streets, a long riverfront, and a central park. Purchasers of town lots were required to build houses at least sixteen feet square within three years. The squatters appear to have departed, some moving upriver about ten miles to establish what became Newburgh. Their removal testified to the perils of not entering a land claim. Squatters were forced by newcomers intent on building stable communities to depart or to register and purchase the land on which they resided.[28]

Henderson County's first task was building roads, and its court required all able-bodied males to assist. Henderson's river access and its location on the Red Banks Trace guaranteed it many travelers and prospective residents. A number of services were created: a tavern (1799), ferries across the Green (1800) and Ohio (1802), a boat repair yard, a steam sawmill (1817), and a bank (1818). Although corn was a major crop, the county was primarily known for its lucrative dark tobacco, as its bottomlands could yield 1,200 to 1,500 pounds of tobacco per acre. In 1801 a state inspection facility was established, requiring area tobacco exports for the New Orleans market to exit through Henderson. A beef inspection station soon followed. A large tobacco warehouse was erected in 1814. The village and surrounding county grew substantially, reaching nearly 11,000 by 1820. Almost a quarter were slaves.

The town was rough-hewn. When he settled there in 1810, the year of its incorporation, John James Audubon encountered a place with about forty log houses and a weedy landing, although "plats of the town showed broad streets and 2 miles of riverfront park and wharves."[29]

Henderson's distinctive heritage was evident in other ways. Horse racing and ring fighting were popular, and three-day elections and court days made the county seat a social and political mecca. Education for the well-to-do was provided through private academies, whereas ordinary people made do with a few months of subscription schooling. Samuel Hopkins and other aristocratic founders enjoyed a lifestyle befitting Virginia planters, which included fine homes in the town and the country. Reflecting its agrarian context, the town of Henderson would remain a small market center, not achieving one thousand residents until the eve of the Civil War.

The number of settlers attracted to the rich lands surrounding Henderson led to the formation of two new counties, Union in 1811 and Daviess in 1815. Like Henderson, they would be overwhelmingly rural and agricultural. Union, across the river from Shawneetown, enjoyed good soil and undulating terrain, seemingly ideal for corn and tobacco. A wealthy landowner married to the granddaughter of General Daniel Morgan engineered the county's separation from Henderson. The county seat, named Morganfield, was located at the intersection of two ancient trails leading to the Ohio: from Russellville on the east to Shawneetown, and from the south to the future Uniontown on the Ohio. Union County relied heavily on slave labor, almost a third of its approximately 3,400 residents in 1820. Most of its pioneers were from Virginia or Kentucky and of English or Scots-Irish ancestry. Many possessed Revolutionary War land warrants. Local elites, as the county's first historian boasted, thought this was a homogeneous society that was liberal, hospitable, and congenial.

One traveler in 1808 reported several houses at the mouth of Highland Creek, apparently the forerunner of Francisburg, chartered by the Kentucky legislature in 1819. Other speculators created a second settlement, Locust Point, on the other side of the creek. The importance of this location as a shipping point was obvious, and competition intensified between these two settlements, which would eventually become Uniontown.[30]

Upriver, east of Henderson, a somewhat different settlement was taking shape. Much of the land in what was then Ohio County was owned by Virginian Joseph H. Daveiss, the U.S. district attorney for Kentucky and brother-in-law of Justice John Marshall. Daveiss moved to the region in 1808 and died three years later in the Battle of Tippecanoe Creek. The new county, organized in 1815 and named in his honor, had over 3,800 residents in 1820. (Through a typographical error in the legislature, it was spelled Daviess.)[31]

Daveiss was not, however, the first settler in the future Owensboro. A squatter had that honor. In 1798 a Virginia-born hunter and adventurer, identified in local histories as Bill Smothers or William Smeathers, built a cabin on a buffalo trace extending into Indiana. That trace intersected the east-west trail to Shawneetown. Both corridors became state roads. The place was initially known as Yellow Banks because of its soil coloration. The countryside was dominated by a dense canebrake that supported an ample population of wild game. In the late eighteenth century, Native Americans had come to the area, especially in the future Spencer County across the river, to raise corn and to plant tobacco, but whites forced them out. Like so many other town pioneers, in 1813 Smeathers left for new adventures to the west. He died in Texas in the late 1830s.

Others came and stayed, and the town prospered, despite widespread litigation over patents. A small market center emerged on the stage line between West Point and Shawneetown. Named Rossborough, after pioneer David Ross, it became the first and only county seat. When the town was surveyed and platted in 1816, the legislature renamed it in honor of Colonel Abraham Owen, who also was killed at Tippecanoe. Wealthy Virginian Robert Triplett arrived in 1817 to settle Ross's estate and returned three years later with a substantial claim of his own; he would become one of the county's most important residents.[32]

By contrast, the future site of Paducah—noted by early travelers as a desirable location on the west bank of the mouth of the Tennessee, twelve miles south of the mouth of the Cumberland and only forty-seven from the Mississippi—would not be developed until the 1830s. Chickasaw claims west of the Tennessee and disputes among heirs over land patents granted to George Rogers Clark and administered by his brother, William, delayed settlement, as did the border dispute between Kentucky and Tennessee and the Panic of 1819.[33]

Timing and vision seemed to be on the side of Smithland, located nearby on the west bank of the Cumberland's mouth. In the region south of the Green River set aside for veterans of the Revolution, the area—originally part of Logan County—grew rapidly. This led to the creation of Livingston County in 1798 (from which nine counties, including Ballard and Crittenden in 1842, would eventually be carved). Eddyville, an interior community on an important road crossing the Cumberland, was named county seat. The county possessed undulating terrain, hilly and broken in places, as well as rich alluvial soils.[34]

Livingston County's strategic location contributed to its being a conduit through which migrants, including many from North Carolina, moved into southern Illinois. Two of the most important crossings were ferries operated by North Carolinians: the Lusks' to future Golconda, and Hamlet Ferguson's opposite downriver Smithland.[35]

Smithland was the earliest and largest of the four Livingston County settlements on the Ohio. The others were Birdsville, Carrsville (opposite future Rosiclare), and Berry's Ferry (opposite Golconda), all organized by 1839. In 1820, it was the sole Kentucky village on the Ohio downriver from Union County, offering many services to rivermen, travelers, and farmers.

Smithland, named for a Pennsylvanian working for a speculator in the 1790s, experienced legal and financial difficulties. After the speculator's departure in 1803, other investors, led by William Croghan, platted an "Upper Smithland" several miles upriver. This place grew more rapidly and became the sole possessor of the name Smithland, known from the outset as a lusty, brawling community. Its first inn was established in 1807. Its trustees issued permits for several ferries and licenses for additional taverns, and several warehouses were built. Boat repair and service facilities were established. The first roads extended to the future Golconda along what is now State Route 137, through Birdsville and Bayou. One traveler in 1807 observed the character and the promise of this place:

Smith Town consists of only five houses. The situation, however, is extremely eligible for further improvement.... Most of the boats descending to New Orleans and Memphis generally make a halt here, either for hams, provisions, boats or repairs. . . . It appears to be a kind of inland port, where run-away boys, idle young men, and unemployed boatmen assemble to engage as hands on board of any boats that may happen to call. . . . You will scarcely believe, that in a place just emerging from the woods, which although advantageously situated, can prosper only by dint of industry and care, and where girdled trees which surround its houses threaten with every storm to crush the whole settlement . . . that a billiard table has been established, which is continually surrounded by common boatmen, just arrived from the Salt Works [Shawneetown], St. Louis, or St. Genevieve, who in one hour lost all the hard-earned wages of a two-months' voyage.[36]

Many other Kentucky communities were created between the Falls and Owensboro before 1820. Hardin County (1793), adjoining Louisville and Jefferson County, spawned a number of counties that possessed Ohio settlements. (The principal towns of this region, Hardinsburg and Elizabethtown, were located on ancient trails far inland.)[37] The most grandiose plan was Ohiopiomingo, listed on a 1794 map between Otter Creek and Doe Run near present Rock Haven. This "most capital township and town" was a promotional scheme of a Pennsylvanian who died in debtors' prison. The town never materialized, even though it was advertised in a four-volume work by William Winterbotham in 1796. (The name survives in a local park.) Virginia war veterans and others formed communities on the east and west banks of the mouth

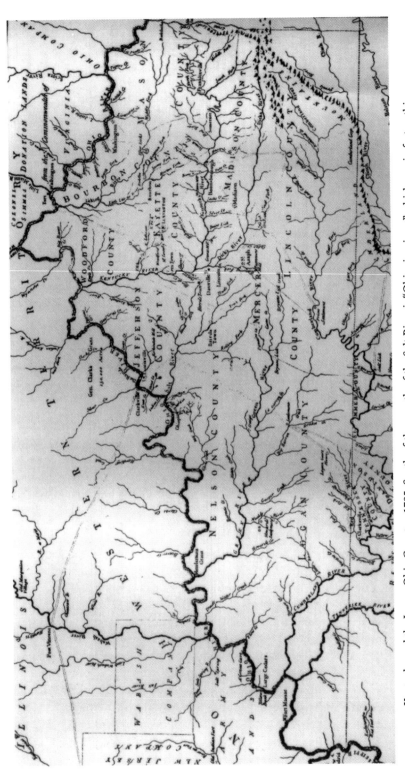

Kentucky and the Lower Ohio Country, 1795. South of the mouth of the Salt River is "Ohiopiomingo," which was in fact nothing more than the dream of a Pennsylvania speculator (Smith, Reid, and Wayland map, Willard Library)

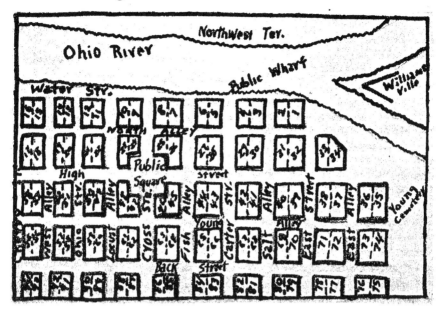

The first town plat of West Point, in Hardin County, Kentucky, in 1796 (Richard Briggs, *The Early History of West Point*)

of the Salt River. The former, Williamsville, was chartered in 1792, but flood waters soon destroyed it. On the west bank, West Point was laid out four years later and its plat was recorded in 1801. A site of 150 acres, it was connected by roads to Elizabethtown and Hardinsburg, and ferries were licensed for the Salt and Ohio Rivers. Zadok Cramer soon noted the presence of settlers in *The Navigator*. Many of the pioneer settlers came from Fayette County, Pennsylvania, on the Monongehela. As Hardin County's borders shrank, West Point would eventually become its principal Ohio River community.[38]

James Young (1767-1849), the village's most prominent landowner, ran both ferries and Young's Inn from 1799 until 1832. He built the first grand home in the village in 1805 and used some of his town lots to encourage religious, educational, and fraternal organizations. West Point businessmen built a lumberyard for steamboats after the War of 1812, and later created repair shops, public warehouses, and a public wharf. The salt works up the Salt River also provided an important export. Local promoters anticipated overtaking Louisville as the major city of the region.[39]

Downriver, several small settlements were established in territory that was originally in Hardin County. State inspection of flour, hemp, and tobacco exports commenced at the mouths of Clover Creek in 1800 and Sinking Creek in 1805, both in newly created Breckinridge County. The former, named Joe's

Landing or Joesport after ferry operator Joe Houston, was incorporated as Cloverport in 1808. Stephensport was much smaller and unincorporated until about 1840. Another inspection station was created upriver at Falling Springs, between Sinking Creek and Salt River, in 1805. This locale became known as Brandenburg Landing and was the main river port of Meade County, carved from Breckinridge in the early 1820s. Breckinridge County enjoyed fertile soil, flood-free elevation, ample drinking water, and much wild game. Long an Indian hunting area, it attracted white hunters such as Squire Boone who, like the squatters at Red Banks, created primitive settlements with such names as Doe River, Otter Creek, and Wolf Creek—the latter the first permanent settlement in what would become Meade County.[40]

Solomon Brandenburg, a hunter and land speculator, purchased land along the river in 1804. His site, dominated by two hills overlooking the river, gave him the opportunity to hunt, fish, and run flatboats. He also secured a license to operate a ferry to Harrison County, Indiana. A few years later the first steamboat, the *Hornet,* was built at his landing, but it proved to be a financial failure. Conflicting land titles plagued this settlement well into the 1820s. Brandenburg sold land across the river to sixteen men, including Frederick Mauck, who organized a settlement bearing his name. Like Bill Smothers and others, Brandenburg subsequently moved on to bigger and better things out west. One of the partners, Joseph Atwell, made a new start in Owensboro.[41]

Other sites emerged in western Breckinridge County. Virginian John Lewis surveyed the land between the Salt and Green Rivers in 1788 and was attracted by its ample bottomland abutting limestone ridges along the river, the slope from the high broken ground of the east to the rolling meadows of the west, the abrupt rise of its cliffs, the tableland overlooking the Ohio, and the lush hardwood forests. Lewis and his bride, armed with claims to thousands of acres, settled at a fort on Yellow Creek in 1799.

The development of this area—which eventually became Hancock County—reflected the interrelationship among culture, environment, and economy. Rich bottomland attracted those with large land grants, whereas the interior was settled by those with smaller claims. (Coal, petroleum, and limestone resources were not exploited until many years later.) Settlers arrived via river or an old wagon road, located on a ridge line that followed a buffalo trace and Indian trail connecting Elizabethtown and Shawneetown (later State Road 144). Lewis eventually owned thousands of acres from the mouth of Yellow Creek to the bend opposite Troy, Indiana. His promising landing, Lewisport, shipped much tobacco and corn.

Cheap, fertile land fed speculators' dreams. Thompson's Ferry, established about 1814 opposite Troy, Indiana, and upriver from Lewisport, was one of numerous historical might-have-beens. A major crossing point, it sent Thomas Lincoln and his young family from Hardin County into the wilds of Indiana. Over time, though, Lewisport and Hawesville would greatly overshadow it.[42]

After 1815 Kentuckians by the thousands crossed the river—to Mauckport and Troy, Indiana, and downriver at Shawneetown, Golconda, and Hamlet's Ferry. The absence of slavery and the security of land claims appealed to them. Yet village and town life on the south bank of the lower Ohio was very much in evidence. Most were small and unincorporated. All reflected the agrarian values of their hinterlands and were enmeshed in a tobacco-slave culture.

Indiana's lower Ohio River communities were also fairly primitive and even more widely scattered. No community was incorporated until the end of the War of 1812. The chief reason was that Indian land cessions proceeded slowly. Even when statehood was granted, the central and northern parts of Indiana were at least two years from being opened to whites.

Land offices opened at Vincennes and Jeffersonville before 1810 created the distinctive pattern of settlement in pre-1815 Indiana. The more rapidly developing area was upriver and slightly downriver of the Falls, a region which thwarted Harrison and his Vincennes supporters' attempts to extend a Tidewater culture into the Old Northwest. Abolishing slavery in the territory, expanding the suffrage, and reducing the powers of the governor, the legislature in 1813 also moved the capital to Corydon. Three years later, delegates to the constitutional convention there agreed to seek statehood and write a constitution. Indiana was admitted to the Union in December.[43]

Before 1816, the many settlements on the Indiana shore were little more than clearings in which lean-tos and crude cabins sheltered hunters. Some were more substantial, offering supplies for passing riverboats and exporting commodities southward. Many were the river terminuses of traces: the Red Banks, from south of Henderson past future Evansville to Vincennes; the Yellow Banks, north from Owensboro to near present-day Stendahl, where it joined with a trail from Rome that extended up the west bank of the White River; and the Buffalo, which extended from Clarksville past Milltown, Haysville, and Petersburg to Vincennes.

In Harrison County, a number of roads led from Corydon to small Ohio settlements. Corydon, though, was the only one platted and organized. Frederick Mauck received a license to operate a ferry fifteen miles due south of the county seat in 1811.[44]

Downriver, along the Ohio shore of the Indiana Territory, settlement was sparse and primitive. In what would become Crawford County, white intrusion was minimal before 1815. That reflected in part the lack of settlement to the south.[45] To the west, in the future Perry and Spencer Counties, the higher level of habitation across the river helped spawn some small settlements before 1811. The largest was the future Troy, on the east bank of the mouth of the Anderson River, where squatters erected dwellings shortly after 1800. Known initially as McDaniel's Landing, the site, with ample nearby timber, attracted Nicholas J. Roosevelt, who purchased land there after passing by in 1811 on the first Ohio steamer. His partner, Robert Fulton, gained title to the land, and Fulton's brother Abraham arrived in 1814 to manage the lumberyard. Pioneer farmers also began to locate along the splendid bottomlands upriver at the horseshoe bend, the future village of Rome, and the site of the future Derby.

Downriver, a group led by Ezekiel Ray gathered at a place soon to become Blount's Landing (later renamed Grandview). Southwest lay a huge bluff overlooking the river. The first cluster of cabins there was called Hanging Rock, after two columnar appendages on the face of the cliff. Arriving in 1807, Daniel Grass changed the name to Mount Duvall, in honor of a Kentucky friend.[46]

A similar motif surfaced just to the west. John Sprinkle, one of squatters at Red Banks, moved upriver to high ground east of Pigeon Creek in 1803. Clearing the land and setting up a blacksmith shop, Sprinkle got around to purchasing it in 1812. In the meantime he had secured a license to operate a ferry to Henderson County. He platted his land as the town of Sprinklesburg and advertised 102 lots for sale in the only newspaper of the region, the *Western Sun* in Vincennes. Typical of town boosters, Sprinkle insisted that no site had a comparable future.[47]

Similar in its origins, but much different in its outcome, was a nearby community with strong connections to Red Banks. Hugh McGary left Henderson with his family in 1803, settling in what would become Gibson County, Indiana. He courted and married Polly Anthony, who had also lived in Henderson. Her father, James, had purchased land for a mill site on Pigeon Creek several miles from its mouth that later became Negley's Mill. The bluff near the mouth of Pigeon Creek was familiar to young McGary, as he had often traveled on the nearby Red Banks Trace. By 1804 the surrounding land had been ceded by Delawares, although wandering bands prevented permanent settlement until 1812. In late March of that year, McGary purchased 441 acres—the present downtown of Evansville—and shortly afterwards erected a primitive cabin there, thus beginning permanent settlement at the site. He gained licenses to run ferries across the river and the creek—McGary's Landing.[48]

Kentucky connections were also evident farther downriver, a few miles from the mouth of the Wabash. The soil there was especially fertile, but abundant game attracted the first permanent white settlers from Kentucky about 1805. The newcomers built a log cabin south of the present landing, but subsequently moved to higher ground upriver. Although they purchased the land, known for about ten years as McFaddin's Bluff, they envisioned little more than a base for hunting. The settlement also served as a flatboat landing and a wood depot. Only about fifteen families resided there in 1815.[49] (A sizable tract of land on the Wabash River, fifteen miles north of McFaddin's Bluff, was purchased in 1814 by George Rapp, a German religious leader who brought hundreds of followers from Pennsylvania to settle in New Harmony. Until they left ten years later, this would be the largest community in the future Posey County.)

Two years after statehood, all six counties on Indiana's lower Ohio had been formed: Warrick (1813), Perry and Posey (1814), and Crawford, Spencer, and Vanderburgh (1818). Harrison County's growth reflected the crossing of upper southerners at Clarksville and Mauck's Landing. Several settlements grew along the Ohio, shipping corn, hay, potatoes, apples, meat, and other products from the southern part of the county downriver and supplying passing rivercraft. Evans's Landing, New Amsterdam, Morvin, and North Hampton were all platted in 1815-16. Other small, unorganized places were founded, chiefly Boston and Bridgeport or Locust Point. New Amsterdam, west of Mauckport, would become the largest and most durable. Most did not survive the mid-nineteenth century. North Hampton, known as a place for drinking, gambling, fighting, and horse racing, was a ghost town by 1860. Morvin's last house was demolished during John Hunt Morgan's raid of July 1863. Boston, below Evans's Landing, was washed away.[50]

Although Mauck's Landing lay near the Brandenburg Ferry and on the principal north-south road to the county seat, east-west traffic on the old buffalo trace north of Corydon carried most of the county's commercial and population development. In addition, the removal of the capital to Indianapolis in 1825 lowered Harrison County's growth rate. The lack of a navigable stream to the Ohio and the annual threat of flooding made matters worse. Harrison County's Ohio hamlets faced a bleak future, according to Edmund Dana, noted western traveler and guide to over 1,300 people seeking western homesteads.

Hope, though, sprang eternal. As in Harrison County, many small settlements were established downriver just before or after statehood. Opposite the northeastern part of Breckinridge County in an area that became Crawford County, two would-be metropolises were created: Fredonia, on a bluff overlooking a picturesque horseshoe bend of the river, and Alton, set on much lower land to the south. Strangely, though, Mount Sterling, eight miles inland and northwest of Fredonia, was selected as the first Crawford County seat. Its limitations, particularly a poor water supply, soon became evident. In 1819, Edmund Dana thought Fredonia, with its view and its healthfulness, was the best town site for fifty miles. That must have pleased Allen Thom, one of two Virginians who laid out the town in 1818, for Dana's reputation was legendary. In 1822 Thom secured the seat of government for his site. The "Fredonia

Road" to the northwest became an important commercial artery. From the outset the site's high elevation was problematic, though, as much labor and capital were required to wrest freight up the long incline from the Ohio. Thom's nemesis was Connecticut-born Seth Leavenworth, who purchased bottomland upriver and platted a town in his name in the summer of 1819. Samuel R. Brown, in his *Western Gazeteer* of 1817, declared that that site, a mile downriver from the mouth of the Blue River, had enormous potential, for he thought the Blue could support a number of mills. Edmund Dana, though, was not especially impressed with the place. Alton was never a threat to either settlement.[51]

To the west, Perry County was carved out of Warrick and Gibson Counties in September 1814. (At the same time, Posey County was created out of the western portion of Warrick.) Troy, platted in March 1815 and named in honor of a North Carolina judge, became county seat. Troy seemed to its investors an ideal location: a major crossing and a port for meal ground at mills up the Anderson, which unfortunately was not a navigable waterway. Troy secured a general store, and pork was packed and shipped southward. Abraham Fulton also supplied wood to steamboats, but his career as town promoter was cut short by accidental death.

Troy's future was seriously jeopardized in January 1818, when the state legislature formed Spencer County out of Warrick and Perry. (At the same time it organized Crawford and Vanderburgh.) Troy thus found itself on the far western corner of its county. The decision reflected the usual complaints about the difficulty of reaching the seat of government, as well as the financial interests of leading citizens and the desire of legislators to strengthen their standing. In March, commissioners authorized by the legislature selected a new seat—on the horseshoe bend, across from Stephensport. Its backers, led by miller Uriah Cummings, laid out a town site and contributed land for a new seat of government. Within a year it was known as Rome—named after either the Italian capital or the New York town where construction on the Erie Canal had begun. Promoters also erected a grand courthouse that resembled Harrison County's. Thus they sounded the "death knell" for Troy's "lofty pretensions."[52]

In the newly created Spencer County, county seat designation was granted Hanging Rock, the largest settlement. Promoters platted a new town site atop the bluff, which they named Rockport, and lots were sold beginning in June 1818. Free whiskey was offered to "sweeten the bids" as well as to make the occasion merry. Many buyers liberally subscribed. A larger cluster of cabins atop the bluff—and a new county courthouse—soon overlooked the dwellings below. Rockport was divided into lower and upper villages. The older portion served as a riverboat landing, and a sawmill was also erected there.

Rockport's future seemed bright. The mainstay of its economy was pork packing and shipping. In 1819 Edmund Dana wrote of the town's "romantic prospect." Rockport's achievements, though, did not dampen the hopes of the early residents of nearby Blount's Landing, which boasted a gristmill, a general store, and a riverboat landing.[53]

Legislative politics produced another fascinating sequence of events to the west. When Warrick County was created in 1813, Hugh McGary, with the help of Indian fighter and legislator Robert M. Evans, had secured the seat of government. In return, he donated one hundred acres for county governance. The first plat named the place Evansville. McGary's achievement was short-lived, though, because the legislature a year later created Perry and Posey Counties from sections of Warrick. This put infant Evansville—still only a plan—in the same predicament as Troy. The seat was moved east to Darlington, which also existed only on paper. (Sprinklesburg was apparently never in the running.) McGary's grant of one hundred acres was returned to him.[54]

County governance and town promotion remained inseparable—and byzantine. Fortuitously, McGary attracted the interest of young Joseph Lane as he was conveying a raft of logs to Henderson. Lane, who worked in the Warrick County clerk's office, eventually became Oregon governor and ran for vice president in 1860. He recalled being impressed with McGary, whose "town" consisted of a crude log structure and a ferry. Lane claimed that he was able to persuade Ratliff Boon, a powerful Warrick County legislator (later lieutenant governor), to help create a new county out of Warrick, Posey, and Gibson. Soon thereafter Evans and James W. Jones, investors in McGary's lots, purchased the remaining unsold land and had a new town plan made. Boon's support contributed to the formation of Vanderburgh County in January 1818—named after a judge of the Northwest Territory. Evansville became its seat, and Boonville became the new Warrick County seat. On a major east-west trail to Vincennes, Boonville soon eclipsed Sprinklesburg. Darlington disappeared, and McGary became the first Vanderburgh County clerk. His log home was the first courthouse.[55]

Incorporated as a town in 1819, Evansville remained small for several years. Morris Birkbeck and Zadok Cramer did not even mention it. Others, however, were enthusiastic. David Thomas's *Travels through the Western Country in the Summer of 1816,* published in 1819, thought the mouth of the "Great Pigeon" formed one of the best harbors beyond Pittsburgh and an ideal crossing point for travelers to Vincennes. Edmund Dana agreed. Traveling through Evansville (probably in June 1818), William Cobbett noted the "little town is rapidly increasing, and promises to be a town of considerable trade."[56]

County seat politics also shaped river community growth in Posey County, whose fertile soil merited praise in many travel accounts. The first county seat was Blackford, about a mile in the interior. The arrival of the Harmonist settlement at Harmonie on the Wabash led to its being moved in May 1817 to Springfield, fifteen miles northward, where Frederick Rapp, business manager of the utopian town, had donated land for the county seat. At about the same time, investors led by Jesse Y. Welborn sought to develop McFaddin's Bluff, platted and renamed in honor of George Washington in 1816. Welborn and eight others purchased about seventy-three acres in the name of the Mount Vernon Company. Welborn was the village's first postmaster and innkeeper.[57]

A somewhat similar cycle of events unfolded to the southwest in Illinois. Approximately 2,500 white settlers were in the southern part of what would become Illinois in 1800, a majority in the "American Bottom" around Kaskaskia and Cahokia on the Mississippi and the rest near Shawneetown on the Ohio. That pattern persisted through formation of Illinois Territory in 1809 and statehood in December 1818. Most of the new state's lands remained in Indian control. Illinois had the dubious honor of possessing the second largest territory and the fewest people.[58]

The same features that made Indiana appealing to upper southerners also applied to Illinois. Settlers' optimism was reflected in names they selected for their communities, many of them "cities" even before a single settler arrived. Land offices were opened at Kaskaskia in 1804 and Shawneetown in 1812. Settlers entered the southern Illinois interior via trails from Shawneetown or Fort Massac on the Ohio or from Vincennes on the Wabash. The pace quickened after 1815. One of the most prominent newcomers was Morris Birkbeck, who arrived at Shawneetown in March 1818 and purchased 1,440 acres of prairie for an English colony about forty-five miles to the north.[59]

When admitted to the Union, Illinois possessed a political culture reminiscent of the Upper South. Its first constitution created a strong legislative branch of government that met only a few months every other year. As in Kentucky, the county was the basic unit of local government, and there was no provision for townships. The people were staunch defenders of traditional rural and agrarian values.[60]

Villages and small towns, nonetheless, spearheaded growth. As in Kentucky and Indiana, early settlers selected lands pragmatically and not necessarily rationally. In addition to a site's healthfulness and available water, they desired low transportation costs, timber for fuel and construction, and a secure and safe foothold, even though it might offer less productive soil. Other factors came into consideration later.[61]

Before 1815, as in Indiana and Kentucky, a number of unorganized encampments had emerged, many formed by squatters. Few grew. The intersection of the Ohio and Mississippi was the most tantalizing spot. For many years the junction was known as Bird's Point, after Virginians who squatted there. The lack of capital and the presence of hostile Chickasaws to the south blocked development.[62]

Upriver, the Fort Massac site also seemed initially to hold great promise. In 1794, American troops rebuilt the French fort, which had been burned by Chickasaws, but after the purchase of Louisiana in 1803 western military headquarters were moved to St. Louis. The fort housed a handful of men and officers on the eve of Tecumseh's uprising against Harrison. Had the Shawnee chief succeeded, Massac might have played a major role in the War of 1812. The fort did receive a large number of trainees from Kentucky and Tennessee in late 1812, but it was small and in poor repair. Two years later the fort was evacuated.[63]

Even more short-lived was Cantonment Wilkinson-Ville (1787-1804), established by General James Wilkinson. An outpost of Massac located at the chain of rocks just downriver, it played a role in blocking a purported scheme to create a Spanish protectorate in the old Southwest. Fort Massac's demise sealed its fate.[64]

More successful was the settlement created about 1808 by James McFarland Sr., who secured a contract to supply beef for the Massac garrison. Four years later he built a tavern, and a water-powered mill was erected. In 1813, he established a ferry service. McFarland's venture was to become the village of Elizabethtown in Hardin County.[65]

Shawneetown was by far the most important early Illinois community on the Ohio. About ten miles from the mouth of the Wabash, it was located at a critical crossing point on the Ohio. Several miles inland were thousands of acres of salines, which had attracted wild animals and Indians for centuries and accounted for the primitive road system in the region. The site also attracted whites, many of whom established hunting bases. Gradually hunter-farmers began to build more permanent residences. A ferry was licensed to Alexander Wilson in 1810, the same year the town was platted. Interest in the salines led the federal government to open a land office there in 1812 and to lease nearly 100,000 acres of salines to private developers. (Later, control passed to the state.) To attract investment, Congress waived the no-slavery provisions of the Northwest Ordinance for labor at the salines. Congress also funded construction of a road to Kaskaskia, which by 1818 was the most important route of travel to the interior. Shawneetown was seat of government for Gallatin County.[66]

Shawneetown anchored a strip of settlement about fifteen miles wide and one hundred miles long, stretching from Saline Creek to the Wabash River. Twelve thousand people resided in that area in 1818. Despite its relatively low elevation and propensity to flood, it was the leading town between Louisville and St. Louis. Land sales flourished, accounting for a third of the territorial sales until the Panic of 1819. One of the three branches of the Bank of Illinois was opened there in 1816. Annual production of salt, destined mostly for New Orleans, reached several hundred thousand bushels. Port status and strategic location encouraged the establishment of attorneys' offices, inns, taverns, and stores stocking such luxuries as silks, wines, and groceries.[67]

One of the new state's two promising settlements, Shawneetown was nonetheless crude and unhealthful. In 1818, it consisted of thirty shoddy wooden structures. It had no courthouse, school, church, or jail. Stagnant water and poor sanitation plagued it: local mosquitoes seemed so "muscular, sprightly, and dissipated [that] they preferred human blood to that of brutes." Before the steamboat, the typically rough and dissolute crewmen from barges and flatboats subjected the place to periodic near-anarchy. Seasonal floods regularly inundated much of the town. Morris Birkbeck, however, likened residents' hope and determination to the Mount Etna region of Sicily, calling it "pertinacious adhesion of the human animal to the spot where it has once fixed itself."[68]

The promise of the place attracted many enterprising residents. One of the most notable was Philadelphian James Hall, a veteran of the War of 1812. After practicing law in Pittsburgh, he moved to Shawneetown in 1820, where he also helped to establish the state's second newspaper and became prosecuting attorney for southern Illinois and circuit judge. Hall was elected state treasurer in 1827 and became the first president of the state's new historical society the following year. In 1833, however, he departed for Cincinnati, where he enjoyed a long banking career.[69]

If Shawneetown was the most advanced community, one needs little imagination to describe the others. The largest was downstream Golconda. In the late 1790s, Major James V. Lusk and thirty or so other Kentuckians with North Carolina roots settled in Livingston County. Lusk operated a ferry there, moving across to Illinois in 1798. After his death in 1803, his widow, Sarah, remarried but continued to operate the ferry, competition for which included one run by her second husband's brother, Hamlet Ferguson, opposite downriver Smithland. Thomas Ferguson, her husband, was one of the county court judges when Pope County was created in 1816; not surprisingly, the judges chose Lusk's Landing, renamed Sarah(s)ville, as county seat. The court also agreed to build a road thence to Hamlet Ferguson's ferry. The town was platted in 1817 and named Golconda, after a city in India. It lacked most amenities, however, possessing only a log cabin courthouse, a jail, and a general store.[70]

Developments before 1820 were not encouraging at what Zadok Cramer's 1802 edition of *The Navigator* called one of the most promising places in the

United States. The third principal meridian intersected this place, where there had seemingly always been some form of habitation. After 1815, the promise of something permanent and grand seemed achievable. In 1817 William Bird entered 318 acres at the Kaskaskia land office. In the same year John Comegys of Baltimore purchased eighteen hundred acres. In January 1818, he and eight others secured from the territorial legislature "An Act to Incorporate the City and Bank of Cairo." Shortly thereafter the new corporation laid out the city in lots to sell at $150 each. The bank, opened at the territorial capital of Vandalia, was to use funds from lot sales to build levees and make other physical improvements. The company's plans foundered, however, because of floods, financial panic (1819), and inadequate capital. The project died with Comegys in 1819. The company did leave a place name, that of the delta city of Egypt, and the region soon became known as Little Egypt. It also left a dream. At the confluence of three states and the head of large steamboat navigation, Cairo offered year-round use because of temperate climate and the character of river channels to the north and east. It could also be the transshipment point for goods.[71]

The creation of grand names for speculative ventures was not limited to Cairo. Some of these places would materialize, but rarely on the scale pictured. Such designs also introduced Americans to the concept of town planning, although urban historian Stanley Schultz notes there was a close link between such proposals and fiction writing.

Interest in the Cairo region did not diminish. The Bird family built a tavern and a store near the mouth in the 1820s, and a woodcutter had a small shop. Six miles up the Ohio, at the mouth of the Cache River, Henry L. Webb founded Trinity, a steamboat landing with a boat store, tavern, and billiard parlor in 1817. Population increases led in March 1819 to the formation of Alexander County, at the time much of the southwestern tip of Illinois. The county was named for William Alexander, a physician, politician, and promoter who became the county's first representative in the Illinois General Assembly. Alexander apparently was agent for four men who had purchased land in the area in 1816.[72]

The first county seat was a raw settlement about twelve miles upriver, where Alexander lived. It had the grand name of America. The first meeting of the county court occurred on June 7, 1819, and like all other pioneer county officials, they began to utilize local government for economic development. As elsewhere, a lofty name belied the toughness of life. When John James Audubon stopped there in November 1820, he saw "a people very sickly, a miserable place altogether." This may have referred to an outbreak of yellow fever that devastated the settlement that year and presaged its short life.[73]

By 1820, three states governed the territory on either shore of the Ohio below the Falls. Only in Indiana, though, were county boundaries fixed. The region was overwhelmingly rural and marginally agrarian, and settlements were small and widely separated. Most, however, seemed to offer enormous promise, especially in the heady days following the end of the war with Britain in 1815.

2 ∾

Patterns of Growth

The hardy souls who created communities on the lower Ohio were part of the stream of pioneers whose efforts to begin anew created a concept of space that washed "relentlessly at the foundations beneath a tottering national hierarchy." New attitudes were breaking loose across the nation because of new relations between enterprise and land. Merchants and settlers alike demanded a "popular politics of choice" that "paralleled the rise of economic self-determination." "Overwhelmingly," notes Robert H. Wiebe, "Americans grasped the power of choice as soon as they spotted it and protected it jealously once they had it."[1]

Newcomers like John James Audubon offered a vivid illustration. Audubon tried unsuccessfully to run a general store in Henderson. Then he tried selling whiskey downriver. Impressed by the first steamboat, the *New Orleans,* he persuaded two newcomers to Henderson, an Englishman and a Scot, to join him in purchasing a keelboat. They added a steam engine and paddle wheels to it, and the *Pike* steamed with its cargo somewhat awkwardly upriver as far as Steubenville. (The eventual sale of the *Pike* was to be Audubon's only successful business venture.)

In the summer of 1816 Audubon and his partners erected a large mill to grind corn and cut wood, purchasing 1,200 acres of forest land to supply the cordwood for the steam engine. Poor demand, however, left the partners deep in debt. Now Audubon owned an idle mill as well as an empty store. In 1819 Audubon met George Keats, a passerby whose brother, the poet John Keats, had asked him to invest his funds in a profitable venture. Audubon convinced Keats that his brother's money should be used to buy a steamboat, which Audubon quickly sold at an apparent profit. Again profit eluded him. He discovered that the buyer's notes were worthless. Enraged, Audubon stabbed the buyer. The man recovered, but Audubon had learned his lesson.[2] Financially ruined, he moved to Louisville and painted portraits until he could establish himself as one of the foremost naturalists of the nineteenth century.

The settlement process was not simply a lottery, as James Hall noted in *The West: Its Commerce and Navigation* (Cincinnati, 1849). Natural advantages, such as elevation, location, quality of soil, healthfulness, and timber resources,

Major Settlements on the Lower Ohio, 1820

1. Trinity
2. America
3. Smithland
4. Golconda
5. Shawneetown
6. Francisburg
7. Mt. Vernon
8. Henderson
9. Evansville
10. Rossborough
11. Rockport
12. Troy
13. Cloverport
14. Rome
15. Fredonia
16. Leavenworth
17. Mauckport
18. Brandenburg
19. West Point / Williamsville

Major Settlements on the Lower Ohio, 1820, based on census data from 1820 and Cowperwaite's map of Indiana (1850), Mitchell's map of Illinois (1837), and Thomas Clark's *Historic Maps of Kentucky* gave some towns a better chance than others. Distance from competition also mattered. The prevailing view then was that successful towns were at least seven miles apart. Pluck, cooperation, vision, and some good fortune also counted. Perhaps most important was the uniting of diverse interests in a common effort. These communities, sometimes unknowingly, were engaged in competition. By 1920, the lower Ohio possessed a hierarchy of urban places: villages, towns, cities, and even one metropolis. Some places that offered great promise in 1820 either stagnated or disappeared. A few appeared later and confounded earlier thinkers' estimates of their prospects. The hierarchy of sites was being formed well before midcentury. In all of this, unpredictability was central.[3]

The economic futures of all settlements were linked to the growth of the early nation-state. These were not feudal towns or fortified mercantile warehouses; they provided basic economic services to their immediate regions, were debt-financed, and promoted economic growth in numerous ways. Investors and local government officials were virtually one and the same—regulating prices of commodities, laying out and maintaining roads, protecting property, and encouraging the growth of financial institutions. The town plan usually preceded actual settlement and in some cases never proceeded further. Town authority, especially in Kentucky, was weak. Merchants controlled town boards, and they undoubtedly shared David Hume's vision of a developing economy in which industry, knowledge, and humanity were intertwined.[4]

Hugh McGary's double log warehouse in Evansville, for example, served for several years as the first county courthouse and as his place of business. One of the earliest decisions of the county commission in 1818 was to set tavern prices in the county. The incorporation of the town of Evansville in March 1819, like gaining county seat status, required considerable influence at the capital. Securing a town charter enabled Evansville to raise tax revenues for rudimentary law and order, a basic condition for successful enterprise. In the same year, the town was granted a post office, also an essential component for commercial activity. Town namesake Robert M. Evans's decision to take up residence there in 1820 was a good omen.

Like all early communities, though, Evansville's future was tenuous. The village of 1819 had about 100 residents. Its crude structures were made of wood. No bricks yet existed in the county. Hugh McGary was plagued by debts. A saltworks proved to be impracticable, and the nearest grain mill was Negley's, to the north on Pigeon Creek, where the English settlement of Mechanicsville seemed to be more promising. Even more up and coming was another English settlement in the northern part of the county, Saundersville. Both were linked to the Birkbeck-Flowers efforts to create an English colony in southern Illinois. Saundersville's star would be bright but short-lived, however, and its plat was vacated by the legislature ten years later.[5]

In these communities, barter was the most common medium for business transactions. Banks existed only in Shawneetown (1816) and Henderson (1818). However inchoate, these places were the foundation upon which an ordered society could be erected, especially if they had been selected as county seats or had received town charters. Often they also served as the locus of organized religious activity. Presbyterians formed Evansville's first congregation, for instance, two years after the town was incorporated. Sunday school, temperance, and other efforts to control local morality surfaced soon after Shawneetown received a charter. Newspapers also were an index of a settlement's promise. The *Evansville Gazette* was established in 1821 and Henderson began publishing its own newspaper two years later.[6]

These early settlements exported the agricultural products and natural resources common to either side of the river: corn, whiskey, pork, tobacco, and hardwood.

Settlers' perspectives were shaped by their origins. Many had roots in Virginia and North Carolina, and their values reflected those of the Upper South. Perhaps the strongest connections were in Livingston County, Kentucky, which spawned not only nine other Kentucky counties but also a substantial number of settlements in southern Illinois. It was not surprising, therefore, that slave labor took hold in Kentucky and that slavery found popular support across the Ohio in territory defined as free.[7]

These places also shared the coarse and, to many foreign observers, barbaric qualities of democratic culture. Thomas Jefferson was widely known to have viewed towns as abnormalities and necessary evils, and according to Robert Wiebe, Charles Dickens's "carefully crafted portrait of a dog-eared pig as democrat epitomized this animal imagery."[8] That Dickens was describing New York City leaves one to wonder what he would have thought of civil society on the lower Ohio. Shawneetown, the most promising in 1820, was notorious for "the riot and license of a Shawneetown Sabbath [which] was a shocking thing to a prim New England bride." In 1822, Shawneetown finally required property owners to remove dead animals and to participate in the construction of wooden sidewalks.[9]

Many elements contributed to community viability. As much as their founders stressed self-help and local boosterism, the growth of these river settlements was more affected by U.S. diplomatic and military achievements and legislative decisions to build roads or canals. Less obvious, but certainly vital, was proximity to ancient trails into the interior. Riverbank settlement on the Kentucky shore, moreover, greatly influenced development to the north. The low level of population growth along the Ohio in Crawford County, Indiana, and the future Massac and Pulaski Counties in Illinois reflected the sparse population across the river.

For everyone, the lower Ohio River was a physical presence and a channel of trade. Healthfulness and elevation of the location were important considerations. So was the reality, even in the early years, that the Ohio exerted profound influence well beyond its boundaries. As acts of the Kentucky legislature in the 1790s revealed, the river prompted strategies to gain greater access to this channel. Pioneer settlers were soon aware of the impact of seasonality and topography. In fall, late winter, and spring, the level of water allowed virtually unhindered transit down the Ohio and thence up the Mississippi to St. Louis as well as down to Memphis and New Orleans. Winter ice and summertime low water limited river transit. In either case, settlers recognized the larger regional and continental implications of these phenomena.

The case of Cairo was especially striking. The land at the mouth of the Ohio seemed ideal for a major city, but Major Stephen H. Long, visiting in 1819, observed three problems: swiftness of the current and lack of a safe and commodious landing site; a propensity to flood; and lack of a place of anchorage for boats of heavy burden. A good nodal position, at a natural break in transport, might not offset a poor harbor and an unhealthy environment.[10]

From 1787 onward, the Ohio River separated not only slave and free labor systems but also governmental institutions with dissimilar origins and characteristics. The presence of slaves had enormous implications at all levels of society. Implicit in the Northwest Ordinance, for which no Southwest equivalent was adopted, was the new concept, as William W. Freehling has argued, that slavery was a problem. Although some slavery was permitted in the Northwest in the early nineteenth century, this gradually ended. Census records for 1820, for instance, reveal that in Gallatin County, Illinois, there were about 300 slaves working in the federally licensed salines. They accounted for most of the state's slaves. In Indiana, all of the river counties below the Falls had 125 slaves in 1820, a legacy of Virginians' efforts at Vincennes to perpetuate planter society in Indiana. In both states, however, these populations were small and dwindling, and the free labor ethos ruled. Slave labor in Kentucky drove poor whites, including Abraham Lincoln's family, across the river into Indiana.[11]

In Kentucky, by contrast, the six river counties included 8,006 slaves in 1820, well over a quarter of whom resided in Henderson County. In Livingston, Henderson, and Union Counties, slaves accounted for 20 to 30 percent of the population. Where blacks were most concentrated, they represented to white paternalists the greatest potential threat to the social order. Slavery required an approach to social order—over whites as well as blacks—which clashed in fundamental ways with the ideal of republican society's limited government and with basic human rights.

Landholding north of the river was facilitated through land offices and a more reliable form of land survey. Squatters like John Sprinkle and Andrew

McFaddin were numerous, of course, and eventually the concept of preemption was accepted. The rectilinear form and the settlement process rooted in the Ordinance of 1785 persisted, however. Lush, open land, free from slave labor competition and indefinite titles, beckoned to thousands. Thomas D. Clark has described Kentucky as "Mother of the West," likening it to the "narrow mouth of a rock-choked cave. . . . [T]he arrow of destiny pointed to the Ohio . . . to the rich lands beyond."[12]

What pushed people onward also mattered. The area south of the river was less amenable to commerce and manufacturing. Early southern towns were small, pastoral places inseparable from the staple-crop economy surrounding them and from the view that agriculture and republican society were intertwined. They also preserved a biracial society. Local government, dominated by planter-merchants, was "a sort of political chamber of commerce." The low level of capital accumulation, with most wealth tied up in slave labor, helped to reinforce a simple, frugal approach to village and town governance. A relatively homogeneous populace, imbued with evangelical Protestant values and committed to slavery, emphasized the need for order and discipline. Public education was virtually nonexistent.

Kentucky's settlements along the Ohio in Kentucky in 1820 reflected that. The Commonwealth's leading towns were Louisville and Lexington. A few small places lay along the Ohio, mostly upriver from the Falls. These two towns exerted disproportionate influence for their size as magnets for speculators and centers for commerce, culture, and education.[13]

The Ohio also divided states and their respective political cultures and structures. The county was the basic unit of local government in Kentucky, as in Virginia. Localistic, agrarian, and anti-urban values persisted well into the twentieth century through it. The center of social order was the county's judges. Not until the early 1850s was the hierarchical system, in which governors appointed county officials, weakened. Popular election of local officials, as well as the availability of the vote to adult white men, was more advanced in the Northwest. Governmental leaders in Indiana and Illinois, while sharing with Kentucky a belief in simple, frugal government, were also more willing to use public resources for transportation and other economic development projects. Admittedly there was a substantial amount of continuity on either side of the river. Yet Kentucky was a slave state rooted deeply in the cultures of the Tidewater and the Upper South. One senses an especially high level of Cavalier values in Henderson and Union Counties.[14]

Nevertheless, the Ohio was no Berlin Wall. The movement of people, commerce, and ideas prevented that from occurring. In addition, there were internal differences in the Northwest as well as within each of the three states.

Southern influence was markedly stronger in southern Illinois, as evidenced by the number of slaves present in 1820, than it was in Indiana. Both Indiana and Illinois created state government that gave predominant power to their legislatures. Both made most local offices elective. Illinois, however, did not establish township government, preferring instead to rest local power on the county as the primary administrative and fiscal unit. Indiana, by contrast, empowered county commissioners to create townships, where trustees became powerful agents in road maintenance, public education, and poor relief.[15]

Indiana and Illinois development differed in several other respects. Topographically, Indiana's Ohio River shore was more varied. The Wabash, and to a lesser extent Pigeon Creek and the Anderson and Blue Rivers, afforded some access to the interior. Illinois's Ohio basin was unglaciated and devoid of ample bottomlands and mineral resources. Interior waterways were nonexistent. From the outset, settlements in Illinois—like its first capital, Vandalia—tended to concentrate far north of the Ohio, in the American Bottom and the Kaskaskia River valley. Settlers arriving at Shawneetown were increasingly drawn to the fertile prairies to the north. To be sure, Indiana's constitution had provided for moving the state capital to a central location, and the Indian treaty of 1818 had secured the region surrounding and north of Indianapolis, the capital after 1825. This accelerated population movement into the interior of Indiana. Yet many of Indiana's Ohio River communities would continue to grow, unlike most of those in Illinois.

State and even county boundaries belied other variations within states—topography, resources, market access, and leadership. In 1820, however, many of these were not readily seen.

Despite such differences, though, in many ways the Ohio linked communities. Cultural geographers, for example, have never located the regional boundary between North and South at the Ohio River. Rather, they have sited it to the north of the river, disagreeing on its northern extent. Stephen S. Birdsall and John W. Florin place what they identify as the division between Deep North and Deep South just above the river counties of Indiana and Illinois. Others go farther north, even as far as the National Road. Whatever the line, the implications of this are enormous. That the Ohio did not divide the Union in 1861 was perhaps the profound illustration of this continuity.[16]

Residents of river communities in Kentucky, Indiana, and Illinois shared many values, including a commitment to limited government. Regardless of their views on slavery, almost all believed blacks to be inferior. The most appealing religious institutions were those nourished by the Great Awakening of the early nineteenth century—Methodist, Baptist, Disciples of Christ, and liberalized Presbyterian. Most residents championed the autonomy and the perfectibility of the individual, the idea of progress, and the obligation of Americans to conquer the West. These were also ethnically homogeneous people. Relatively few white persons settled there whose roots were not British.

Cross-river connections—whether forged in settlement or in commerce—strengthened these ties. Squatters led the way—the Upps and the Sprinkles who arrived at Red Banks and moved on to what became Newburgh, the Anthonys and the McGarys of Henderson and later Evansville, the McAdams family in Jefferson, Harrison, and ultimately Hancock Counties, or the North Carolinians who moved into southern Illinois from Livingston County. Early river traffic also helped to link peoples of the lower valley.

The patterns that were apparent by the time Illinois achieved statehood hinted at a dramatic sorting-out process that was to come. These small, dispersed, and generally insignificant places were well on their way toward becoming an array of communities differing in size, structure, and texture. But this process would be tricky and unpredictable. In 1820 the places with early starts—especially Henderson and Shawneetown—seemed to have the best chances. Evansville and Owensboro had advanced little beyond the fetal stage. Paducah had yet to be conceived. And by 1820 the lush prairie region to the north, fed by the opening of Indian lands and the commencement of the National Road, was already showing signs of soon eclipsing Ohio valley settlements.[17]

PART 2 ∾

The Age of
the Transportation
Revolution, 1815-1850

3 ∿

The Sifting Process Begins

Tapping the wealth of the Transappalachian West was the primary concern of eastern investors following the War of 1812. Technological innovation and legislative subsidies for internal improvements created a transportation revolution. The National Road and the Erie Canal were completed, and steam-powered riverboats entered a golden age at midcentury. Steam applied to rails was already beginning to threaten that, however. Liberalization of land sales created a "land-office business" that reached fever pitch in the mid-1830s. Cheap land and transport fostered a market economy, which promoted commercial agriculture, urbanization, and industries designed to tap the Ohio trade.[1]

Statistical measurements of this growth remain mind-boggling. The number of flatboats passing the Falls of the Ohio in the 1820s doubled, for instance. Kentucky almost doubled in size between 1820 and 1850, but even more astonishing was the fact that Indiana increased by a factor of six and Illinois by a factor of fifteen in the same period. Often overlooked is the fact that the rate of urbanization in this period was unparalleled in American history.[2]

A fundamental aspect of change was the democratization of American culture. Individual self-determination became the national norm. "Leveling authority and dispensing power," writes Robert H. Wiebe, "politicized the routines of white men's everyday lives." Emerging was "a vibrant public process: marching, chanting, disputing, debating, voting." Self-selection prevailed. All one had to do was "get into it. Ask nobody's permission, defer to nobody's prior claim. Just do it."[3]

The lower Ohio was the scene of a gigantic counterclockwise movement of people and products. Newcomers came down the river by flatboat or keelboat. Pork, corn, lumber, and whiskey also traveled downriver, mostly to New Orleans. Finished goods were purchased from the East or from Europe and shipped downriver, usually from Pittsburgh. Canals, steamboats, and later railroads altered this pattern as passengers and freight began to move more easily and cheaply to the north and east. Culture and economic activity gradually diverged on either side of the Ohio, as the northern shore experienced a greater degree of commercial and industrial development.

In Kentucky, five new counties were created along the Ohio: Meade (1824), McCracken (1825), Hancock (1829), Ballard (1842), and Crittenden (1842). Such growth was emblematic of population increase, calls for accessible local government, and factional interests. Rates of growth, however, were uneven. Of the older counties, Hardin remained the largest, although it declined about 12 percent in the 1840s. Of the six counties that had existed in 1820, however, only three—Daviess, Henderson, and Union—exceeded the statewide rate of population growth, 74 percent between 1820 and 1850. Largely because of these three and McCracken County, Kentucky's lower Ohio counties claimed almost 10 percent of the state's populace by 1850, up from 6.5 percent in 1820.[4]

Across the river, Harrison County, the most populous of Indiana's lower Ohio counties in 1820, doubled in size, but dropped to second behind Posey, which trebled in population. Each county, as compared with Kentucky's, experienced substantial growth, but none at or above Indiana's 571.6 percent. Only Vanderburgh came close. By 1850, Vanderburgh and adjoining Warrick had risen to third and fourth place, respectively, among the state's river counties. In share of the state's population only Vanderburgh held its own. These seven dropped, though, to 7.1 percent of the state's population in 1850—less than half that of 1820.

A somewhat similar pattern prevailed in Illinois, where rapid growth of central and northern portions of the state eclipsed that of Ohio River communities. Three new counties were created: Hardin (1839), Massac (1843), and Pulaski (1843). The county with initial superiority, Gallatin, even with a substantial drop in size after 1840 (partially resulting from the formation of Hardin County) remained the most populous. Pope County also lost some of its population in the 1840s with the formation of Hardin and Massac Counties. Alexander County grew most rapidly. By 1850 the second-largest county was Massac. No county approximated the state's rate of growth, 1443.6 percent, however. The region, which represented almost 12 percent of the state's population in 1820, dropped dramatically to 2.5 percent at midcentury. The population increase in the counties existing in 1820 was only 5,500, or 0.7 percent of the state's increase. Indiana counties, all of which existed in 1820, grew to a combined population of 70,538 by 1850, but their share of the total state population dropped from 15 to 7 percent. Kentucky's Ohio River counties, by contrast, accounted for a slightly higher percentage of the Commonwealth's total in 1850 (9.6) than in 1820 (6.5). As in Illinois, though, comparative regional and state growth rates are impossible, as many counties were created after 1820.[5]

The phenomenal growth of territories to the north and west of the Ohio valley suggests that the entire lower Ohio's settlement was ill-timed, destined to be overshadowed. Yet population totals provide a more complex story. Rates

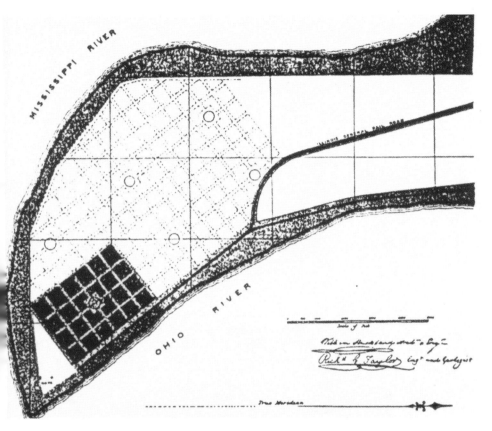

Noted Eastern architect William Strickland, employed by the Cairo City and Canal Company, created this plan for the city of Cairo, Illinois, in 1838 (John Lansden, *History of the City of Cairo* [Chicago, 1910])

of growth were uneven. The Indiana and Kentucky counties with the largest population per square mile also were those with the most substantial growth—chiefly Vanderburgh in Indiana and Daviess, Henderson, and McCracken in Kentucky. Generally the counties with the highest rates of growth possessed the largest settlements. Vanderburgh was the first to have a city charter (1847). With 3,235 residents in 1850, and another 1,441 in the adjoining town of Lamasco, soon to be merged with it, Evansville was by far the largest community. To be sure, these places were smaller than some towns along the Great Lakes and some older upriver settlements. Cincinnati alone had 115,000 residents in 1850. But urbanization was emerging on the lower river and, as else-

Illinois's Ohio Border, 1837 (Mitchell's *Map of Illinois Exhibiting Its Internal Improvements Counties, Towns, Roads, Etc.* [Philadelphia, 1837], Willard Library)

where, a sorting-out process was well under way. The hierarchy of communities in place by 1850, moreover, would be little changed thereafter.

Communities varied in size, composition, and scope of influence. Certain natural advantages—elevation, access to market, regional resources, and water supply—contributed, but something far more important was at work. In ways that were not yet apparent, culture and economic activity shaped these places. Size alone did not make Evansville or Paducah stand out. Who resided there and how they perceived their communities' futures also mattered.

On both sides of the river, Upper Southern culture prevailed. Most of the early settlers of Indiana, for example, came from the southern backwoods. The territory was open from the south, allowing southerners easy access into much of Indiana, but swampy land to the north blocked entry into the more desirable Wabash country. Hence Yankees tended to bypass Indiana "because they could not, or thought they could not, get in," wrote L.C. Rudolph. "Although the state lay directly in the path of the westward-moving thousands, thousands moved westward and never saw it."

Most Hoosier pioneers were poor. Their standards of comfort and equipment were less persnickety than those of the Yankees, for whom moving to the Indiana woods "meant an outlay of hundreds of dollars for horses, a wagon, boat transport, land, cabin, barn, and subsistence, both for the trip and until the first crop could be harvested." If they had money, they bought land. If they did not, they squatted, hoping to buy later when their situation improved. If conditions did not improve, they moved on. They specialized in subsistence farming, and their living habits led many early travelers to describe them as "ignorant, coarse, lazy, [and] lawless." Over time, many historians have romanticized them, but their lives were usually hard. Yet, wrote Rudolph, things were about to change. "Every farmer seemed prepared to draw from his pocket a lithographic city and grant the merest acquaintance the favor of taking a few building lots." Whatever the difficulties, "boundless optimism seemed the mood, and it went with a fierce frontier loyalty that was not anxious for outside counsel." Accompanying this was "the brashness, buoyancy, and confidence of public figures or candidates." Generally their interior roads reflected their rudeness: "general indications of direction to which one returned between mud holes," routes that one traveler described this way:

> The Roads are impassable—
> Hardly jackassable.
> I think those that travel 'em
> Should turn out and gravel 'em.[5]

Despite shared cultural roots, settlements on either side of the river diverged. Slavery was probably the chief reason for that. In 1850, the proportion of slave population in Kentucky's lower river counties ranged from about 13 percent in Crittenden and McCracken Counties to Henderson's 36.1. In Daviess, Henderson, Meade, and Union Counties, the proportion exceeded one-fifth. (The mean for the state was 21.5.) In all but one instance the number of slaves had increased in the previous decade. Slavery, however, was not limited to rural areas. In those towns for which census data was provided in 1850, slavery was numerically more important than in the surrounding countryside: over 15 percent of Paducah's population, 34.7 percent of Owensboro's, and 47.9

percent of Henderson's. The number of urban free blacks, moreover, was small and generally declining, a reflection of the lack of safety and security and the increasingly difficult process of manumission.[6]

North of the river, the number of blacks was miniscule, a reflection of the Northwest Ordinance and the antiblack culture of southern Illinois and southern Indiana, where white residents disliked having blacks around, period. It also mirrored the insecurity of life in river settlements, where slave-catchers roamed at will. Southern Illinois's views on race were unequivocally voiced in the special statewide election of August 1824, to determine whether a constitutional convention would be called to permit slavery. Although the question was voted down statewide, voters in Alexander, Gallatin, and Pope Counties strongly supported the convention. The severe Fugitive Slave Act of 1850 and the prohibition on settlement by free blacks imposed by the revised midcentury Illinois and Indiana constitutions also made residence in river communities extremely hazardous. The Indiana Constitution imposed a fine on anyone employing a black newcomer and also required the existing black population to register with county officials.[7]

Birthplace also distinguished settlements from one another. In 1850, far fewer whites of Illinois and Indiana were natives of their state than their neighbors in Kentucky, where 76 percent were. River counties reflected state trends. Only McCracken approximated the rates across the river. This illustrated the outward flow of Kentucky-born people. The smallest proportions of persons born in their state resided in sites with the most rapid town growth—Alexander, Massac, McCracken, and Vanderburgh Counties. By proportion and numbers, Evansville led the region in residents born outside the Upper South. One of the most distinctive places was Cannelton, Indiana. New England capitalists were prominent in all stages of the community's development before its incorporation in 1852. In fact, Cannelton had the distinction of having the first Unitarian congregation in Indiana, established in 1845.[8]

Growth in some settlements was also fueled by newcomers from abroad. In most communities, immigration was a relatively minor element in river country population, accounting for about 6 percent in Indiana, 4 percent in Kentucky, and 2 percent in Illinois. Vanderburgh County had by far the largest number (4,059) and the highest proportion (35.6 percent) of immigrants in 1850 (see table 3 in Appendix 1). The counties with the next highest percentages were also in Indiana, chiefly Posey (9.5) and Spencer (11.2). Symptomatic of their presence was the formation of a German Catholic parish and a German Lutheran church in Evansville in the 1840s and a number of German Evangelical (Synod of North America) congregations by the early 1850s in Evansville, Newburgh, Rockport, and Cannelton. Evansville had the largest and most ethnically diverse population, although most were from southern Germany. Natives of northern Ireland and England also were prominent.

Gallatin (4.2 percent) and McCracken (6.3 percent) had the largest proportion of immigrants among lower Ohio counties in their states. According to local tradition, Paducah's first Germans arrived accidentally about 1845. Having planned to settle in Indiana, they were forced to land at Paducah because of river ice, and they found the place desirable. A Lutheran congregation was formed shortly thereafter.[9]

As elsewhere, immigrants were indicators of "push" and "pull" factors— economic and political problems in Europe, availability of relatively inexpensive transport from New Orleans or Pittsburgh, assistance from emigrant aid societies, and availability of good, cheap land or jobs.[10]

That most residents were native-born and English-speaking was evident in the 1850 federal census of churches. In Illinois, most congregations were Baptist, Methodist, and Presbyterian. There were no Roman Catholic parishes. There was one Lutheran congregation each in Pope and Pulaski Counties. In Kentucky, a generally similar pattern prevailed, except that no Lutheran organizations were enumerated. Roman Catholics had formed sixteen churches— four each in Daviess and Hardin. Possibly the earliest was St. Stephen's parish in Owensboro, organized about 1838. Most parishioners were English.[11]

In most cases, growth reinforced existing patterns of birthplace. For instance, all of early Owensboro's business and civic leaders were natives of Kentucky or other southern states. The most prominent were entrepreneurs Robert Triplett, a native of Virginia, Tennessean James Weir, and Kentuckian Thomas McCreery. Politically, most aligned themselves with fellow Kentuckian Henry Clay.[12]

A similar pattern existed in Paducah and Henderson. One notable exception in Paducah was James Langstaff (1809-76), who with several other families from New Jersey purchased land near the mouth of the Tennessee in 1847. Jersey, which was later swallowed up by Paducah, was the site of a large gristmill. Langstaff's son George, a Princeton graduate, became one of the town's leading manufacturers, as would another son, Samuel. Henderson's elite in 1850 was limited to Upper Southerners, mostly Virginians and Kentuckians— Alexander Barret, Archibald Dixon, Lazarus Powell, Elijah Worshan, Edmund Starling, and William Soaper.[13]

By midcentury, towns and villages on the lower river varied in size and character. Residents as well as knowledgeable travelers knew that life west of the Falls was hardly uniform.

4 ∽

Perspectives on
Lower Ohio Communities

In the 1830s and 1840s, travelers published detailed descriptions of the lower Ohio River valley. According to John Jakle, they used a hierarchy of concepts—unspoiled wilderness, aboriginal and military life, pastoral notions of early agriculture, and urban images—to describe what they saw. Generally they looked for signs of progress and for diversity amidst the monotony of the riverbanks' landscape.[1]

For example, in his 1825 guidebook, *The Western Pilot*, Samuel Cumings referred to "Brandenburgh's Ferry," Rome, Troy, "Hendersonville," Shawneetown, and Golconda. Evansville was a "very thriving town, situated on the bend of the river" and the point of entry for Vincennes. His 1839 edition included such places as "Mock Port" for the first time. Brandenburg received lavish attention, but Evansville and Henderson were excluded. The 1847 edition named virtually every place along the river, although few were described.[2]

George Conclin's revisions of Cumings in 1848 were the most inclusive and descriptive to date, listing forty-four communities in all. Most were identified as villages, including such relatively new Kentucky places as Concordia, just above Rome, as well as Indiana's Maxville and Batesville, below Troy, and Enterprise, downriver from Rockport. Also appearing for the first time were Kentucky's Raleigh and Caseyville and Illinois's Metropolis and Cairo. Conclin commented freely on their progress or decline. Evansville was said to have a considerable advantage due to elevation and location and was described as a compact community about to build a fine wharf. Paducah's rapid growth was attributed to its vast Tennessee River trade and sharply contrasted with the dilapidation of America and the decline of Caledonia and Trinity. Cairo, the object of considerable speculative enterprise since 1835, received the lengthiest and most negative analysis.[3]

Timothy Flint's *Condensed Geography and History of the Western States* (1828) depicted Evansville as "a village of some consequence" and "the land-

Major Settlements on the Lower Ohio, 1850

1,000 or more residents	Less than 1,000 residents	
1. Paducah	7. Cairo	14. Cannelton
2. Shawneetown	8. Metropolis	15. Hawesville
3. Mt. Vernon	9. Smithland	16. Cloverport
4. Henderson	10. Golconda	17. Leavenworth
5. Evansville	11. Uniontown	18. Mauckport
6. Owensboro	12. Newburgh	19. Brandenburg
	13. Rockport	20. West Point

Major Settlements on the Lower Ohio, 1850, based on census data for 1850 and Cowperwaite's map of Indiana (1850), Mitchell's map of Illinois (1837), and Thomas Clark's *Historic Maps of Kentucky*

ing place for immigrants . . . for the Wabash." John Thurston, a well-to-do Massachusetts store owner and legislator, described Evansville in 1836 as a "flourishing place of only a few years' growth." The proposed canal would make the town "a place of great importance in a few years." He attributed Henderson's lack of enterprise to "soil polluted by slavery."[4]

In 1826 Karl Bernhard, duke of Saxe-Weimar-Eisenach, pictured Mount Vernon as possessing a favorable situation for trade. Its approximately three hundred residents had only frame buildings, but they had a town plan, had built a jail, and were about to complete a courthouse. The place was still fairly crass, however. The roots of felled trees "remain yet in the streets of the town, [and] the woods begin close behind the houses; nay, the latest built were encircled by them."[5]

Karl Postel, writing under the pseudonym Charles Sealsfield in *The Americans as They Are; Described in a Tour through the Valley of the Mississippi* (1828), was absolutely unkind to all things Hoosier. Southern Indiana lacked "sufficient water communication [with the interior], and the inhabitants have no market for their produce." The people lacked money and respectability, largely because of the French around Vincennes and the Kentuckians—"adventurers and idlers of every deception." Troy received special scorn because of residents' indolence and savage appearance. Towns were occupied by "a rude set of people, just emerging from previous bad habits, from whom such friendly assistance as honest neighbors afford, or mutual intercourse and good will, can hardly be expected."[6]

In *Domestic Manners of the Americans*, Mrs. Frances Trollope described Kentucky as having finer scenery and a more fertile, cultivated, and picturesque landscape than the more recently settled northern bank. Most travelers, however, mirrored the comments of Alexis de Tocqueville, who in 1831 contrasted Kentucky's sparsely populated, half-deserted fields and its loitering slaves with the "confused hum" of men busily at work and the elegant dwellings and orderly fields to the north. Work on the northern side was associated with progress and well-being, not with slavery and degradation.[7]

All of the sites originated as boat landings or river crossings. Clusters of dwellings and small businesses catering to travelers, boatmen, and hunter-farmers sprang up at many of these places, which often were ferry crossings. A simple store might only do business if a passing boat chose to stop and trade with the locals or take on fuel. In larger places a general store would supply cloth, tools, salt, sugar, and groceries and ship local produce downriver.

By 1850, many of these spots, generally unplatted and unincorporated, were virtually unchanged. Most were so small that travel accounts rarely if ever mentioned them. Typical were Evans's Landing in Harrison County, Indiana;

The "Prospective View of the City of Cairo," drawn by William Strickland, lithographed by Alfred Hoffy, and printed by P.S. Duval in Philadelphia in 1838 (Special Collections and Archives, Knox College Library, Galesburg, Illinois)

Rock Haven, across the river in Meade County, Kentucky; Bay City, on the Pope-Massac county line in Illinois; Big Bay, Hillerman, Copeland's Ferry (later Joppa), and Davis's Landing (later Brookport), all in Massac County, Illinois; Parkinson's Landing (later Shetlerville) in Hardin County, Illinois; and Ferguson's Ferry (later Hamletsburg) and New Liberty in Pope County.[8]

For pioneer farmers, these places were essential. For settlers, life offered basic challenges—growing food, obtaining clothing and shelter, coping with sickness and injury, and finding time for recreation. This was not the "howling wilderness," though, but a mixture of civilization and barbarism—a land so rich that it civilized them. Newly found wealth from the sale of their products allowed them to purchase cloth and tools in places like Shawneetown, where whiskey and champagne or hides and silks sat side by side in the stores.[9]

Cave-in-Rock, in Hardin County, Illinois, for example—a place notorious for its river bandits—provided a ferry and some basic services for travelers. Crittenden County, Kentucky, formed in 1842 and situated between

Livingston and Union Counties, possessed two tiny river sites, Kirksville and
Ford's Ferry. Located on either side of Cave-in-Rock, these boat landings had
little economic significance. Kirksville, an unorganized settlement in 1800, was
renamed Hurricane Landing after a disastrous windstorm in the 1830s. (In
1884 it would become Tolu, named for a popular hair dressing.) Ford's Ferry
possessed a tavern and was a source of supplies for Marion, the county seat,
twelve miles inland. Its reputation for dishonest dealings with travelers, including robbery and murder, was matched by Cave-in-Rock across the river.
(Not surprisingly, the proprietors of both places met early and violent deaths.)
Dodson's Landing (renamed Rono, then Magnet) in Perry County, Indiana,
situated upriver from Troy, gained a post office in the late 1840s, but was never
platted. It had a lumberyard as well as a general store by 1842 and, shortly
thereafter, a pork-packing facility.

Somewhat larger in size and function were the villages, which were usually platted and sometimes incorporated through the efforts of proprietors who
ran the ferry or the general store and secured a post office. These spots had
perhaps several hundred residents and offered more services than the landings
and ferries. They offered wood for steamboats and food and lodging for travelers. They shipped the produce of the interior. Often they possessed means of
processing those resources—for example, by a grist or a sawmill. Their shops
also served the needs of area residents, whether blacksmithing, carpentry, groceries, or dry goods.

One example in Spencer County, Indiana, was Blount's Landing, later
Grandview, which began as a squatters' settlement downriver from the mouth
of the Anderson River. Platted at midcentury, Grandview offered storage facilities and ferry service and had a gristmill and a general store. An important
export was hoop poles, wood stock for barrels. Upriver, just west of Troy, the
village of Maxville was laid out in 1841 by an entrepreneur who ran a ferry
and offered other services, such as blacksmithing. Maxville packed the meat of
over one thousand hogs annually.[10]

Upriver, Troy managed to survive losing the county seat by offering a number of important services. A ferry operated at this vital crossing point on the
river between Hawesville and Lewisport. Laid out in 1815, within ten years
Troy had about 120 residents and a tavern, a general store, a post office, a
tanyard, a warehouse, two shoemakers, a physician, and a cabinet maker. Incorporated as a town in 1837, it boasted several merchants engaged in trade
with New Orleans. In addition, several potteries were established. Between 1838
and the early 1880s, the Indiana Pottery Company produced jars, vases, jugs,
crocks, pots, pitchers, cuspidors, and mugs for a mostly local market; it also
shipped its goods to Louisville and other river towns in the area. In 1852 Troy

was unsuccessful in its attempt to regain the county seat from its rival, Rome, in a special election.

Rome was little different from Troy. In the late 1820s it possessed a general store, a blacksmith, and a carpenter. Its leading businessman for years was a pork packer, J.W. Ricks. He also sent large quantities of corn, oats, potatoes, horses, and cattle to the South and ran a sawmill and a gristmill. Rome flaunted its wharf and distillery. Incorporated in 1830 and again in 1840, it nonetheless struck George Conclin as a "small, very dilapidated looking place, containing a courthouse, three stores, and a population of three hundred."[11]

Alton, Fredonia, and Leavenworth in Crawford County and New Amsterdam and Mauckport in Harrison County shared similar characteristics. Fredonia, for example, became county seat in 1822 and gained a post office in 1840. It had the county's first hotel (1822), and a few years later exulted in three stores, a tavern, a sawmill, a gristmill, a yard for repairing riverboats, a school, and some carding and spinning machinery. Allen Thom, its chief promoter, sought the southern terminus of the railroad proposed in the 1830s that would connect Indianapolis with the Ohio, but he lost out to Madison. In 1848 Fredonia had about 250 residents.

Fredonia's fate was shaped by more than the lack of a railroad. Rival Seth Leavenworth also failed to secure the rail line, and his community waged relentless warfare on Fredonia. In the 1820s, for instance, one of Leavenworth's supporters sought to have the newly established mail route from New Albany to Princeton bypass Fredonia, but the legislature overruled him. His cousin, Zebulon, who arrived from Connecticut to help him, served for several years in the state legislature and on the county commission. In 1843, with the offer of a free courthouse, county commissioners moved the seat of government to Leavenworth. Its fine landing and its road connections generated extensive trade into the interior through Salem and Paoli. In the late 1840s it was a community of some four hundred residents with stage line connections to Indianapolis and New Albany, a number of businesses, a church, and a newspaper.

New Amsterdam and Mauckport remained small ports for southern Harrison County and entrepots for dry goods and luxuries. Platted in 1815 by Jacob Funk and Samuel McAdams, New Amsterdam was appreciably smaller but noted for its apple brandy. Frederick Mauck, founder of the future Mauckport, was sufficiently ambitious to compete for the southern terminus of the Michigan Road, one of the state's earliest internal improvements projects. Failure to secure that was less important in the site's failure to expand appreciably than the competition from Corydon and east-west trade to the north and the declining numbers of people crossing from Kentucky.[12]

Similar patterns were repeated in the villages of Kentucky and Illinois. West

Point (Hardin County, Kentucky) had grown enough to merit George Conclin's recognition as a thriving village with four stores and a boatyard. In 1829, West Pointers improved access to the interior with the incorporation of the Louisville, West Point, and Elizabethtown Turnpike, a project in which its leading citizen, James Young, was an investor. Young also helped to incorporate the West Point Steam Mill Company. West Point shipped tobacco, pork, corn, and salt. Before the Louisville and Nashville Railroad began providing north-south transportation in the 1850s, West Point was the major entrepot west of Louisville for goods shipped into western Kentucky and Tennessee. West Pointers envisioned overtaking Louisville as the principal city of Kentucky. In 1850, though, it remained a fairly small place, with only six merchants, two traders, and a few clerks among its several hundred residents.

Also enjoying modest success were the Breckinridge County villages of Cloverport and Stephensport. Cloverport had about six hundred residents in 1840. It was connected by road to Hardinsburg, the county seat, and to Bowling Green on the Green River. In addition to tobacco, cannel coal was an important export, especially to England. Brought by track from Bennetsville, coal was also refined into illuminating oil. Stephensport, at the mouth of Sinking Creek opposite Rome, was described in *A New River Guide* as a handsome little village of about two hundred that did considerable shipping of tobacco. Neither place attained great size or importance. The lack of direct road access to Louisville was a factor, as was the marginal economy across the river.[13]

Downriver Lewisport, in western Hancock County, was initially Little Yellow Banks and then Lewis's Landing. Surrounded by rich alluvial soil that produced a heavy tobacco crop, it enjoyed a prime landing site. The wealthiest landowners and the vast majority of slaves in Hancock County resided nearby. Lewisport, though, failed to secure county seat designation when the county was created in 1829, losing out to Hawesville. It also lacked road access to the interior, having as late as 1865 a land connection only with Hawesville to the east. Lewisport gained a post office and was incorporated in 1844, but the town was heavily damaged by fire in 1849.[14]

Three more Kentucky villages to the west—Uniontown, Caseyville, and Raleigh in Union County—resembled Lewisport in size and dependence on tobacco and slavery. The abundant soil of Union County allowed it to produce nearly a half million pounds of tobacco in 1849-50. About 25 percent of the population in 1840 and 1850 were enslaved, and an even higher proportion of slaves resided in the villages. Uniontown was incorporated in 1840 when the legislature decided to merge Francisburg and Locust Point to end their often violent competition. Uniontown shipped the produce of Union, Hopkins, Webster, and Henderson Counties to markets in New Orleans, England, and

Europe. A large warehouse for storing and stemming tobacco was a central feature of the local economy. George Conclin described Uniontown as a thriving town of about three hundred.[15]

Caseyville was established when Nicholas Casey landed his flatboat near the mouth of the Tradewater Rivers in the mid-1820s. While his father and elder brother developed coal deposits inland at De Koven, Casey established a lumberyard, a ferry, a boatyard, and by tradition the first ice house between New Orleans and Louisville. Elected to the Kentucky General Assembly, he was able to secure a corporation in 1837. Casey was a trustee and first magistrate, serving twenty years. George Conclin described Caseyville as a village of about two hundred that exported "stone coal" barged thence on the Tradewater Rivers from mines in what was later Crittenden County. In off-season, miners cut lumber and shipped it to Caseyville, where coal barges were built. The miners also operated small farms in the vicinity. Flooding, though, tempered Caseyville's growth.

Upriver, five miles above Shawneetown, was the third Union County settlement formed in this prosperous time. Raleigh, incorporated in 1851, enjoyed a favorable location: a landing on the river and fine farmland behind it. Between 1840 and 1860, it led the county in grain shipments. By the early 1850s it had three dry goods stores, three warehouses, a hotel, a wagonmaker, and a blacksmith. Unfortunately, it was situated too close to the river and began to experience devastating riverbank cave-ins and flooding.[16]

Despite the relative prosperity of these three villages by midcentury, none was strong enough politically to wrest the seat of government from Morganfield, where it had been since Union County's establishment in 1811.[17]

A cluster of villages also emerged across the river in Illinois. Elizabeth (renamed Elizabethtown in 1840), initially part of Gallatin and Pope Counties, became county seat when Hardin County was formed in 1839. Slightly upriver from Carrsville, since about 1805 it had had a ferry and a tavern run by James McFarland Sr., who also had a contract to supply nearby Fort Massac. In 1830, Elizabeth, named for his wife, gained a post office. Ten years later a son platted the village, which was incorporated in 1857. Elizabethtown exported salt, wheat, corn, potatoes, pork, and pig iron manufactured at interior iron furnaces. Fluorspar was discovered there about 1839, but it would not be a significant export until the early 1900s. Elizabethtown's hotel was a landmark on the river for more than 150 years.[18]

By contrast, Golconda, county seat and the largest settlement in Pope County, had about two hundred residents by 1848. The village, according to *Peck's Gazeteer* in 1837, had twenty dwellings, three stores, a grocery, and two taverns. Its services resembled those of other river villages. By 1850, Golconda also had an attorney, a physician, several teachers, and a number of carpenters, blacksmiths, and wagonmakers. Its location on an ancient trace into Illinois country was also an asset.[19]

The most grandly and redundantly named was Metropolis City, southwest of Golconda and just downriver from Paducah. It was the brainchild of William A. McBane Sr. and James H.G. Wilcox, who had come to Fort Massac as commander in 1806 and owned much of the land in the area. In April 1839, McBane, engineer and merchant, purchased one thousand acres from Wilcox. The two subsequently laid out a town, and in 1840 they began to sell lots. Hoping to attract the Illinois Central Railroad's southern terminus, they were instrumental in the formation of Massac County in 1839 out of Alexander, Johnson, and Pope Counties. (Four years later, Pulaski County was carved from territory to its west.) Incorporated in 1845, Metropolis was promoted as a railroad town with a bridge crossing to Kentucky. (The bridge was not built until 1917.) By 1850 Metropolis had 427 residents. Conclin declared this "a very desirable location."[20]

Metropolis exemplified those places large enough in size and function to be called emerging towns. Their economies were more complex and in some cases sufficiently differentiated to reveal connections to markets that extended far beyond the immediate region. Most also became county seats.

Examples of this on the Indiana shore were Rockport, Newburgh, and Mount Vernon. Rockport grew to slightly over four hundred by 1850, six years after its incorporation. The settlement was noted for its steamboat services, warehouses, and pork packing for plantations in the South and the Caribbean. Local businessmen sought to improve their ties with the interior by incorporating a plank road company in 1850 that would extend northward to Gentryville on the state road connecting New Albany with Princeton. Rockport's commanding position above the river impressed all travelers.[21]

Newburgh resembled Rockport in some respects. Following John Sprinkle's death in 1821, Sprinklesburg possessed a few businesses—a ferry, a tavern, and a pork-packing establishment. In 1829, Abner Luce platted adjacent Newburgh. Eight years later, the Indiana General Assembly merged the two settlements as Newburgh and included in the new town a strip of land between them. By 1850, the town had 526 residents.

Union Bethell and A.M. Phelps ran the town's leading enterprise, the Newburgh Pork House. Bethell carried on a prosperous river trade in local products, especially tobacco, that tied the community via packet boats with Louisville and New Orleans. In 1850, the first shaft coal mine was sunk on Phelps's land east of town, and commercial use, especially by steamboats, grew dramatically. Two newspapers had also been established by then. Newburgh seemed poised to equal, if not surpass, nearby Evansville. At midcentury it was described as a flourishing town with three churches, four stores, three large commercial warehouses, a sawmill, and a gristmill.[22]

Even loftier hopes arose in Mount Vernon, which by 1850 had 1,120 inhabitants. Like Evansville, Mount Vernon's growth was traceable to the efforts of a group of entrepreneurs. Probably the most successful of the young men attracted to this community was William J. Lowry, whose family had come to Posey County from Maryland in 1820. Lowry took up residence in Mount Vernon in 1828, built a lucrative mercantile business, and became the town's leading banker. In the 1860s he would move to Evansville and expand that city's financial institutions.

Mount Vernon's growth was due in large part to the productive soil of the surrounding Wabash lowland. By 1840 another ten settlements had been laid out in interior Posey County, and they were connected by roads to the growing port. Early businesses included a gristmill, a sawmill, a distillery, and a cooperage. Most important was its being named county seat in May 1825. After New Harmony was sold to Robert Owen and George Rapp's community moved to a new site near Pittsburgh, the reason for Springfield's being county seat was diminished. Lowry presided at a special meeting authorized by the legislature in which Mount Vernon was selected. Jesse Welborn donated land for the new county courthouse. Seven years later the town was incorporated. Two weekly newspapers were begun between 1838 and 1848. To enhance local commerce, by 1851 town fathers built a wharf and began laying a plank road to New Harmony.[23]

Several Kentucky communities also grew in size and importance. They ranged in size from Brandenburg (600) to Paducah (2,400+). Their distinguishing characteristic was their dependence on the tobacco-slavery nexus. Deed books of Kentucky's river towns abound in records of slave sales, revolts, and occasional manumissions.

Along the docks and on the steamboats, slaves and owners often worked side by side. After 1850, larger towns, especially Paducah, were important shipping points for slaves sold to the Lower South. Public whippings were common. Slaves violating a 10 P.M. curfew in Henderson, for instance, received a penalty of twenty stripes. Fear of concealed weapons and slave uprisings and escapes plagued white residents. Despite a stronger state fugitive slave law in 1830, the long river border was porous. West of Henderson, where the distance between the river and Tennessee narrowed, flight to free territory was much easier, and whites' fears were greater.[24]

One of the rising stars appeared to be Brandenburg, in the late 1840s as a prosperous community of some six hundred inhabitants situated on a high bluff. By then, however, the town's namesake had long since departed for greener pastures to the west. Most of the county's residents lived on the rich bottom-lands or the rolling countryside nearby. Prominent on the horizon were Brandenburg's 1825 brick courthouse and two churches. The town possessed fourteen stores and groceries and two flour mills and exported a considerable amount of tobacco and corn. The dominant settlement in Meade County, it achieved county seat status through the efforts of its backers, who were able to move it there from Claysville (New Philadelphia), located near Doe Run, in early 1825. The county produced 210,000 pounds of tobacco in 1850 and had a slave population of more than 21 percent. It also harvested 373,000 bushels of corn. Its wealthiest men were eleven farmers whose property accounted for about half of the county's real estate value in that census. Alanson Moreman led the list with property worth $20,000. One merchant in Brandenburg, Richard Graham, came close to matching their wealth with property valued at $12,975. Manufacturing was a small part of the Brandenburg economy, employing ninety-nine men in establishments capitalized at $67,000. The value of products, $519,000, was relatively high because of its flour mills.[25]

Named for Richard Hawes, who donated the land for the county seat when Hancock County was formed in 1829, Hawesville became the major river port for its county. Roads connected it with a number of inland settlements, and it was a convenient crossing point for western travelers. Incorporated in 1836, it had about five hundred residents by 1850, according to *A New River Guide*. Dominating its skyline were the courthouse and two churches. Hawesville also had two schools and ten stores. In addition to tobacco, the area was noted after 1850 for cannel coal, mined in the cliffs behind the town. Residents initially disliked its noxious smoke, and until the 1850s wood was abundant, cheap, and less likely to burn out firebox grates. A writer for *Hunt's Merchant's Magazine* declared in May 1847 that "the mineral power of this region is but little understood."

Hawesville provided a substantial opportunity for two grandsons of Samuel McAdams, an early settler of New Amsterdam, Indiana. George and Samuel arrived in 1832 and soon were among the leading businessmen of the county. They made their fortunes in tobacco speculation, groceries, farming, and coal mining—not in breaking virgin land as their grandfather had done. Their success seemed to corroborate the prevailing Protestant work ethic—and the value of a kin network in the lower valley.[26]

Hancock County's wealth was concentrated in the hands of farmers whose capital was in land and slaves. The most prominent resident of Hawesville in 1850 was Edwin Hawes, Virginia-born farmer and attorney, whose real property was worth $21,200. Five planters owned more than twenty slaves each.

Robert C. Beauchamp was probably the most powerful among them.[27]

Surpassing all these places in size and reach were Henderson, Owensboro, and Paducah. After early problems caused by disputed land claims, Owensboro had grown steadily: 1,215 residents in 1850. This made Owensboro the leading Kentucky port between Louisville and Paducah. Center of a fertile region that produced a whopping 3.4 million pounds of tobacco in the year ending in June 1850 and about 740,000 bushels of corn, Owensboro had thirteen stores and groceries, four churches, two Masonic lodges, an academy, and a new courthouse. The major east-west road between Louisville and Shawneetown offered weekly stage service. The town also enjoyed a number of private tollways to the south.

As in Hancock County, wealthy farmers owned much of the county's land. Richard Barnes Mason, a grandson of George Mason, sold his huge Daviess County holdings in 1822. That land included the town site. A cousin, George, arrived in 1831, establishing a residence on a high bank near the town. He had been deeded some 60,000 acres of Daviess County land. He and five others had estates valued at $180,000 in the mid-1830s. George Mason's estate, worth $27,300, included twenty-one slaves. The largest taxpayer was hot-headed Philip Thompson, Daviess County's first congressman. Moving to Owensboro in 1816, he prospered as attorney, farmer, and tobacco broker. In 1836, when his estate was worth $83,000, he was killed in a duel.[28]

The economy of Owensboro was reflected in its environs. Manufacturing was capitalized at about $221,000, higher than in most lower river counties, and employed 112 workers. Owensboro's major products were tobacco, pork, ground corn and wheat, and whiskey. This pattern prevailed well into the twentieth century.

The most ambitious of the pioneer entrepreneurs was Robert Triplett, who settled in Owensboro about 1820. Son of a Virginia planter, Triplett invested in the first steam-powered sawmill, the first distillery on the river, and most notably Bon Harbor, a few miles west of the town on the river. George Conclin observed in 1848 that Bon Harbor had a woolen mill and a mine less than a mile from the river whence coal was shipped by rail. About 150 persons resided and worked there, making linsey-woolsey and jeans. There was also a small cotton mill. With substantial financial aid from the Barrets of Henderson, Triplett dreamed of a substantial expansion of this early industrial satellite community, including a shipyard, a rolling mill, and a nail factory. Bon Harbor proved, however, to be a financial debacle. Unable to obtain sufficient European capital and suffering from cancer, Triplett had lost most of his Daviess County property by the time he died in Philadelphia in 1853.[29]

Henderson enjoyed superior location on a high bluff downriver from the mouth of the Green, whose navigability promoted export of the town's corn, tobacco, and lumber. The town was also located in one of the state's most fertile counties. At midcentury it had five large tobacco factories and twelve stores as well as four schools and six churches. Its population was 1,775, a substantial increase since 1840. The county's population doubled that of 1840, and the number per square mile was the highest of any Kentucky county beyond the Falls.[30]

Henderson's economy reflected the agricultural wealth of the region. It was the chief tobacco-growing territory of that part of Kentucky and one of the state's leaders. The price per hundred pounds of tobacco more than doubled, to seven dollars, in the 1830s, making its production even more desirable. This was a dark variety used for chewing and for smoking in pipes that was especially prized in England. The town's long-distance trade connections were underscored in the 1840 census, which revealed that it had a commission house capitalized at almost $200,000, by far the most substantial below Louisville. In the year ending June 1, 1850, Henderson produced well over 4 million pounds of tobacco and 331,000 bushels of corn. Manufacturing was fairly limited, however: 174 workers in firms capitalized at about $64,000 producing goods, such as sawed lumber, valued at $85,400. Henderson had groceries, dry goods stores, boat stores, fuel yards, taverns, and inns.[31]

Henderson's growth was striking. In a region that was cash poor, the town was the first to have a bank (1818) and the second to have a newspaper (1823). The next year civic leaders persuaded the legislature to organize a company to dredge and dam the Green River, and in 1837 they obtained a charter for a private turnpike to Hopkinsville that by the 1850s was extended to Nashville (later U.S. 41). The town was on the east-west state-chartered road from the mouth of the Salt River to Morganfield and Shawneetown. The Lodwick brothers organized the region's first packet company in 1843 to provide weekly service to Louisville. In 1844 citizens funded erosion control on the riverfront. Two years later the town board created a municipally owned ferry, connecting it with Evansville. (A highway bridge replaced the ferry in 1932.) And in 1850, while the town's wharf was being paved, local leaders hosted a contingent of Evansville businessmen promoting a railroad from Henderson southward. This Kentucky town was the only one besides Paducah actively planning such a project.[32]

A strong paternalistic elite, many with roots in the Transylvania Company and Tidewater culture, dominated Henderson's development. This coterie included Edmund Lynne Starling, one of the county's wealthiest farmers. Another prosperous farmer was William Soaper, a Virginian who married a grandniece of Richard Henderson and settled there about 1820. Especially prominent were Alexander Buchanan Barret (1811-61), Archibald Dixon (1804-76), and Lazarus Powell (1812-76). Barret, who learned the tobacco trade in his uncle's business in Richmond, came to Henderson in 1833 to expand the firm and subsequently built his own establishment, which his brother John joined. Dixon, a North Carolinian, was a self-taught lawyer and entrepreneur. A Whig, he served as a state legislator in the 1830s, as lieutenant governor in the 1840s, and as president of the 1850 constitutional convention. A year later he ran unsuccessfully for governor, but then was appointed to complete the late Henry Clay's term in the Senate. Dixon's Democratic rival for governor was his former law partner, Powell, a native of Henderson. That two candidates for governor lived in Henderson attested to the town's standing. (Three other Hendersonians would later become governor.)[33]

The wealth of this distinctive group depended on slave labor. On the eve of the Civil War, Barret owned at least 140 slaves in Henderson County and another 94 in Daviess. Dixon owned 124 in Henderson County and 20 in Union. Powell owned 56. Henderson County's nearly 4,400 slaves in 1850 were by far the largest in number and percentage in the counties west of Louisville. Slaves, many of whom worked in the stemmeries, accounted for almost half the population of the town. Such a labor system also scared away immigrants: only 1.3 percent of the county was foreign-born.[34]

Although Paducah was also a part of a slave labor system, the town differed from Henderson and Owensboro in several respects. The site was platted in 1827 by William Clark, western explorer and brother of George Rogers Clark. The delay was due to Chickasaw possession of the area before the Jackson Purchase of 1818 and to legal disputes over Clark's land claims. The Panic of 1819 also slowed land sales in the Purchase region, opened to settlement in 1821. Within twenty-three years, however, Paducah was the largest Kentucky town below the Falls.

George Conclin described Paducah in 1848 as a town of two thousand residents who possessed a fine range of stores and depended on a vast trade up the Tennessee River for their advancement. Paducah enjoyed locational advantages, on the west bank of the mouth of the Tennessee, a natural break in transportation which encouraged commerce and manufacturing. It also possessed a central place advantage over the Purchase and portions of southern Illinois.

Incorporated in 1830, the village became McCracken County seat a year later, replacing Wilmington. In addition to general stores and groceries, it soon had a newspaper (1834), a distillery (1835), a locally owned bank (1837), and a mill (1840). Paducah enjoyed an economic boom in the 1840s because of the timber business and wholesale trade. In 1843 local businessmen created a marine way 350 feet long, connected by a cradle on tracks extending to the river, which was capable of servicing and manufacturing large barges and steamboats. In 1847 a submarine telegraph cable gave the town improved communications upriver. New Jerseyan James Langstaff built a sawmill and a brickyard soon thereafter. Congress, perceiving this as a healthy as well as a thriving place, funded the construction of a marine hospital. Two additional banks were founded between 1845 and 1850. By the early 1850s, moreover, civic leaders were promoting rail connections southward to take advantage of congressional land grants uniting the Ohio with the Gulf.[35]

During the 1840s the economy of Paducah was the most expansive of any of its Kentucky counterparts on the lower Ohio. Agriculture was important, but capital invested in manufacturing establishments was impressive, and about three hundred people were employed. The value of manufactured products— about $653,000 in 1850—greatly exceeded that of agriculture, undoubtedly reflecting the impact of the marine way. Paducah also produced tobacco twists and plugs, cornmeal and flour, railroad ties, rope and cordage, barrel staves, and iron goods. Its chief liability was the sparseness of population and the marginality of the economy in its hinterland.[36]

Paducah diverged in several respects from its upriver neighbors. Slaves represented a much smaller proportion of the population—15.3 percent of the town, slightly above the county's 13.3. There was, moreover, no coterie of patriarchs. More than a third of the residents were not natives of Kentucky and over 6 percent were foreign-born. McCracken was also distinctive in these respects. The business elite resembled in some respects the modernizing ethos of northern towns and cities.[37]

As impressive as Paducah was, from the late 1830s onward visitors described Evansville as the most dynamic of the lower Ohio settlements. Supporting such anecdotal evidence were the census reports of 1840 and 1850. Vanderburgh County's manufacturing and commerce expanded significantly. Capital and labor connected with manufacturing were unrivaled, and commercial enterprises were impressive. One of ten branches of the Second State Bank of Indiana was established at Evansville in 1834, and the private Canal Bank opened in 1850. Commission houses connected local transactions with distant markets. Wholesale dry goods and grocery firms expanded in number and scale. Daily mail service to Mount Vernon and Henderson by river, established in the fall of 1850, complemented existing land service to Terre Haute and the National Road. Telegraph connections to Vincennes were completed in August 1848, allowing residents and steamboat passengers access to the new St. Louis to Philadelphia line opened a year earlier. Two vital transportation projects were also under way—the canal connecting Evansville to Toledo, and the railroad northward that connected with the major east-west rail line between Cincinnati and St. Louis at Vincennes. At midcentury three newspapers—two in English and one in German—were being published; one was a daily. Evansville had more than one hundred stores and warehouses and also claimed the services of fifteen attorneys, sixteen physicians, and thirteen clergymen.

Evansville's development was somewhat similar to other towns. Town founder Hugh McGary, who always lived on the economic edge, left town after his wife's death in the mid-1820s and died in poverty in Tennessee. Before 1834, the town's principal enterprises were blacksmithing, gunsmithing, and tinsmithing; slaughtering of livestock, especially pork; flour and gristmilling; tanning and currying; and cabinet work, crude furniture making, and saw milling. After 1834 they included iron products, hand and farm tools, cabinet-made furniture, planed lumber, flour, beer and whiskey, and bricks and tiles. The *Evansville Gazette* was published between 1821 and 1825. The Whig *Journal*, established as a weekly in March 1834, became a daily in 1847. In the 1840s, new manufacturing establishments produced agricultural implements, boilers, stoves, packed meat, cigars and plugs, woolen textiles, soap, and pottery.

Such changes altered land use. Initially, small factories were situated around Main Street, near the river. In the 1830s and 1840s, they expanded north along Main and along the canal, Pigeon Creek, and the new railroad. Evansville's riverfront became increasingly dedicated to serving rivercraft. The sawmills, the most important of which belonged to John A. Reitz (1845), clustered on Pigeon Creek, where logs were floated from the interior. Green River logs were also important.[38]

Evansville was changing in other distinctive ways. Although workshops remained generally small, employing fewer than seven men, one-third of workers were associated with larger places. One foundry employed more than fifteen men. Steam was used in some manufactures, and although most workers were artisans, a less skilled, wage-earning force was being formed.[39]

Early residents offered a number of explanations for its rise. Most echoed nineteenth-century analysts Joseph P. Elliott and John M. Lockwood. Evansville was a fairly dull place until 1834. Lockwood recalled that few steamboats ever stopped at the village. *Journal* publisher William Town, who arrived in March 1834, was a major catalyst for change. Although he supplemented his income by teaching at the New School Presbyterian Church, Town nonetheless endeared himself by inviting Lockwood and others to celebrate the publication of the first issue by partaking of a barrel of whiskey that had just arrived by steamboat. The legislature's creation of the state bank branch was also a cause for celebration. Nothing matched the great canal dinner of May 1834, which observed the town's designation as terminus of the Central Canal. "Every male citizen of town—also every one of the invited guests from abroad," Lockwood recalled, "was over-set, upset, and reeling, staggering, whooping in the streets as a result of too much wine and whiskey mixed."[40]

Armed with a congressional land grant in 1827, supporters of the Wabash and Erie finally saw construction begin in 1832. Two years later, with strong support from Vigo County, Evansville—not Mount Vernon—was selected as the southern terminus of a connector to it. Construction was advanced with the passage of a massive internal improvements bill in 1836, which promised a statewide system of roads, canals, and railroads. Construction of segments of the fifteen-foot-wide and three-foot-deep channel commenced in Evansville in November 1834, but the Panic of 1837 halted work on state projects and bankrupted Indiana. Antitax Democrats gained control of the state beginning in the early 1840s. The no-debt clause in the constitution of 1851 reflected their views. In 1845, Congress had authorized a huge land grant to aid canal work. Two years later, a private company consolidated the canal companies and resumed construction. (The state had assumed half of its transportation debts and deeded the canal to its creditors.) Completed in 1853, the project was, unfortunately, an economic debacle. The vision of state and local leaders, optimistic and democratic, fell victim to bad timing and bad luck—flooding and vandalism, but mostly state-encouraged railroad construction. Their plans attested to the progressive belief in government's potential for improving the lives of its citizens.[41]

The canal also attracted scores of newcomers and energized commercial and industrial development. In 1837, the Igleheart brothers, for instance, established what would eventually become one of the Midwest's largest flour mills on the canal. In the same year, the adjoining town of Lamasco, at the western end of the canal, was incorporated. John Roelker's foundry was also sited on the canal, and Reitz's sawmill was near its terminus. Town namesake Robert Evans lived long enough (1842) to see the beginning of this new era.[42]

Evansville's elevation and location were important, providing entrepot trade in a fairly large hinterland lacking strong competition and being a break in transportation for goods from the Upper South and the area north and east of the Ohio. As vital were the people like Willard Carpenter who were attracted by the canal, because they believed they could make money in Evansville.

That explained, for example, the high proportion of foreign-born elite— 20 percent in 1850. Two of the most prominent early manufacturers were John A. Reitz and William Heilman. Born in Prussia in 1815, Reitz arrived in 1836 and later built one of the nation's largest hardwood mills. Other investments were built on his lumber fortune. Heilman, a native of Hesse-Darmstadt, built his first foundry in the 1840s with his brother-in-law, Christian Kratz. An able

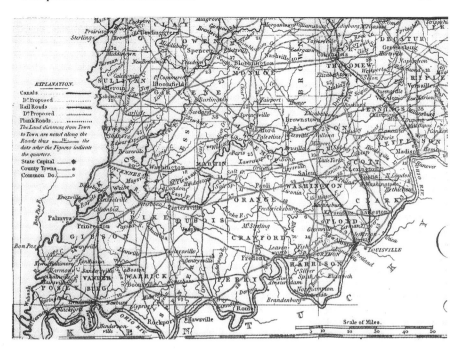

Southern Indiana in 1850 (Philadelphia: Cowperwaite, 1850, Willard Library)

financial manager, Heilman expanded the range and quality of his enterprises.

John Shanklin and Samuel Orr played similar roles. Shanklin, born in Donegal County, Ireland, in 1795, came to America in 1815. After selling hardware in New York and Kentucky, he established a dry goods store in Evansville in 1823 and later became the town's first commission merchant. Irish-born Orr settled in Evansville in 1835 after briefly residing in Pittsburgh. He branched out from groceries to iron production. By the 1850s, Samuel Orr and Company was one of the largest ironmakers west of the Appalachians. Orr also invested heavily in railroads.

John Ingle Jr. came to rural Vanderburgh County from England with his family at age six. After graduating from Princeton, he supported his legal education through cabinet making. Admitted to the bar in 1838, he began a successful career as lawyer and railroad and coal entrepreneur.[43]

The German element in Evansville was especially strong. The first business advertisement in German appeared in the *Journal* of August 1845. In the same year German Township was formed in the northwestern part of the county. Germans also clustered in portions of rural Armstrong and Perry Townships and in Lamasco. Five German-language congregations were established in the 1840s—two Evangelical, one Lutheran, one Methodist, and one Roman Catholic. A weekly newspaper, the *Volksbote,* began in 1851.[44]

Evansville also attracted many natives of the Middle Atlantic and New England states. One of the earliest was Marcus Sherwood, born in Connecticut in 1803, who set out for a new life with his uncle at the age of sixteen. Arriving by flatboat at Evansville in June 1819, the onetime day laborer and flatboat hand amassed probably the city's first great fortune and built its first grand hotel, the Sherwood House. Nathan Rowley (1788-1872), a Vermonter, arrived in the same year and invested in a number of ventures, including the town's first recreational facility, Salt Wells.

The most prominent Yankee was Willard Carpenter, born in Vermont in 1803. One of twelve children, he left home at eighteen to make his fortune. After a series of occupations in New York and Ohio, including working on the Erie Canal, he arrived in Evansville in 1837, two years after a younger brother, A.B. Carpenter, had established a wholesale dry goods and notions firm. He managed to salvage his brother's depression-damaged business; then in 1840 he sold the store and concentrated on speculative investments.

Carpenter became the leading local supporter of the canal: at his own expense he circulated petitions in seventeen states and lobbied legislators in the Northeast for a congressional land grant and financial reorganization. He was also one of the leading investors in the railroad northward. According to Edward White, author of Evansville's first history, *Evansville and Its Men of Mark* (1873), Carpenter was the result of "good old English stock, propagated for generations in New England, and then transplanted to the rich soil of the West, which stimulates all growth and gives rich results where the stock is thrifty and strong."[45] Frederick Jackson Turner would have agreed.

White's book reveals that half of the business and civic elite arrived between 1836 and 1849. Forty percent were natives of the Middle Atlantic or New England states. John Gilbert, who was born in Pennsylvania in 1818 and grew up on his family's farm in Ohio, left home at eighteen for Evansville. After a highly profitable stint as a deerskin and fur agent in the territory west of Evansville, he got into other lines of business, including cattle sales. He made enough money to move to Golconda, where he ran a mercantile establishment and got into the packet business, running boats up and down the Ohio and Tennessee Rivers. Gilbert returned to Evansville in 1872 as a major investor in local banking, insurance, and street railways.

Charles Viele, a native of New York, also came to Evansville at age eighteen in 1836 and clerked for A.B. Carpenter. Four years later, he and another man established a wholesale grocery firm. Considered luxuries by country folk, groceries would become essential to the residents of the many villages and towns in the lower Ohio valley. Viele became one of the most successful wholesalers in the region. He later branched out into other ventures, including textile manufacturing.[46]

John Stuart Hopkins, born in western New York in 1811, moved to Vanderburgh County at age eight. He recalled that "the British and Yankees [had] come in so thick [that] the natives [squatters] became alarmed and entered the lands and paid taxes." As a teen, Hopkins gathered cane brakes, split them, and packed them in barrels for shipment to Pittsburgh, where they were made into "weavers' reeds." Then he started his own factory, selling reeds "to the farmers to weave their jeans and linsies." Subsequently, he established a lumberyard and boat stores business, to which he added a saloon. He sold this and got into the grocery business, making his first thousand dollars in the process. Hopkins, whose formal education was limited to a few months, recalled that "all you had to have then to start [a] grocerie was a barrel of whiskey 1 doz ginger cakes 1 box herring, some molases 1 keg nails 1 kit mackerel crackers tobaco and one Blader of Snuff."

Hopkins bought a canal boat and fitted it out as a storeboat "for a coasting trip." He then took dry goods and groceries downriver, selling them as far south as Natchez. He later ran flatboats to New Orleans and crossed the Appalachians by stage and wagon to secure finished goods. Out of this emerged a successful dry goods business, which he ran for almost thirty years. Hopkins was one of the first investors in the Evansville and Crawfordsville Railroad and was the first president of the Canal Bank. He served as town collector and trustee, was elected to a three-year term as mayor, and served three terms in the Indiana General Assembly.[47]

Numerous other Yankee and Middle States newcomers energized Evansville's development after the mid-1830s. The Chandlers, John and William, natives of New York City, purchased the Whig *Journal*. Connecticut-born Daniel Morgan arrived in 1837, after schooling at Andover and Yale, to practice medicine with the eminent Madison J. Bray, one of the region's most influential men. George B. Walker arrived from New Jersey in 1835 and became a pioneer medical educator as well as a business and civic leader. Horatio Q. Wheeler, born in Maine in 1819 and graduated from Bowdoin College, arrived in 1847 to practice law in partnership with John Ingle. Wheeler became one of the founders of the town's public schools. (He also married a sister of John Stuart Hopkins.) Another of Ingle's associates was attorney Conrad Baker, a Pennsylvanian who arrived in 1841. Brother William, a merchant and Pennsylvania state legislator, came about a decade later. A successful businessman, William Baker would be the city's most active nineteenth-century mayor. Conrad Baker became Indiana's governor in 1867.[48]

Most of this activity, in short, reflected the promise offered by the canal project. Backers of the canal also advocated telegraph, river packet, and railroad projects. It was not, therefore, contradictory for Carpenter, despite later disagreements with Ingle over the railroad's route, to back efforts to construct the Evansville and Illinois, chartered by the legislature in January 1849. Later the E&I extended its line north beyond Princeton to Vincennes and Terre Haute. *That* decision led to a falling out between Carpenter and Ingle, as Carpenter wanted it to follow the canal route to the northeast and Indianapolis.[49]

Vision and risk taking were fundamental to the rise of Evansville, which in January 1847 was incorporated as a city, the first on the lower Ohio. The results were spectacular. By the early 1850s Evansville had packet boat connections with settlements on the Ohio, Wabash, Green, Cumberland, and Tennessee. Huge amounts of local grain, pork and bacon, potatoes, and hay were shipped out, along with an increasing amount of dry goods, groceries, and manufactured items. The coming of rail connections to the north in 1853, the same year as the completion of the canal, added a north and eastward dimension to local trade, which remained predominantly southern. In 1856, the city became a port of entry, with a U.S. customs house, and merchants formed a board of trade. A year later the communities of Evansville and Lamasco united in a special election. Lamasco would remain a distinctive place, the West Side, with a predominantly German, working-class, and heavily Lutheran and Roman Catholic character.[50]

While many places grew, others declined or were, by founders' standards, failures. Still others ceased to exist. Examples of the first were Caledonia, Illinois, Smithland, Kentucky, and Shawneetown, Illinois. The most vivid illustration of the second was Cairo, Illinois, although Cannelton, Indiana, had somewhat similar experiences in its early years. Of the third there were numerous examples—especially America, Napoleon, and Trinity, Illinois.

George Conclin described Caledonia as a collection of a few small houses. According to the federal census of 1850, it had 284 residents, but it had already passed its peak. Within a decade, it was little more than a place on the map, later known as Olmsted. Directly upriver from the future Mound City, it was laid out in the 1830s by James Riddle and John Skiles after America was abandoned. Riddle, a Pennsylvania-born riverboat captain who was one of the region's early New Orleans traders, had promoted America. Henry Webb, once at America, also established a store and warehouse at Caledonia. A guide for emigrants, *Illinois in 1837*, described it as a small community with a post office. In 1843, it became seat of Pulaski County, carved out of Alexander that year. In the same year, North Caledonia was platted in an effort to attract a portion of the proposed Illinois Central Railroad. Caledonia's decline began when the terminus was established at Cairo. After the Pulaski County seat was moved in 1861, Caledonia became another deserted metropolis.[51]

Smithland had been incorporated in 1805. Situated at the Cumberland's mouth and at a major crossing point to Illinois, it appeared to be prospering. It rose to a population of 882 in 1850, enjoying substantial trade on the Cumberland and exporting large amounts of corn, tobacco, and meat.

Largest of about ten small river settlements nearby—Berry's Ferry, Birdsville, and Carrsville, among others—Smithland was powerful enough to become Livingston County seat in 1842, the same year that upriver Crittenden County was created. A year later it was reincorporated. It secured a marine hospital, three short-lived newspapers, a number of drygoods stores, groceries, and other services, a brickyard, an iron fabricating works, and a docking facility for repairing barges and steamboats. The amount of capital invested in manufacturing, the number of workers (131), and the value of products ($84,000) were relatively high. Its riverfront hotels attracted travelers and planters seeking respite from summertime heat in the interior.[52]

Yet things were not what they seemed. The loss of territory and population to Crittenden County in 1842 shrank its tax base. In addition, few newcomers settled there. Almost all residents (98.5 percent) were Kentucky natives, and its population increase was the lowest on the lower river. Only Crittenden had fewer people per square mile by 1850. The comparatively low level of tobacco and corn production and small number of slaves indicated the area's agricultural base was weak. Smithland's population in 1850 would be its apex. Although historians typically blame railroads for river towns' demise, their explanation does not fit this case. Smithland lacked a strong economic basis and was overshadowed by neighboring Paducah.[53]

Shawneetown also reached a midcentury pinnacle, but not necessarily for the same reasons. As late as 1848, visitors described it glowingly. James Hall's *Letters from the West,* published in London in 1828, noted residents' dogged determination to build a town, despite periodic flooding. The map in John Mason Peck's 1831 *Guide for Emigrants* included only it and America, and stated it was a town of six hundred. *Illinois in 1837* repeated Hall's description, adding that this place was no less healthful than more elevated portions of the state. *A New River Guide* in 1848 referred to Shawneetown as a pleasant-looking but flood-prone town of 1,200 that possessed a fine bank and was an important river port.[54]

Entrepot for scores of country stores in its interior, Shawneetown shipped much salt, lumber, corn, wheat, oats, and pork. The difference in this regard between Shawneetown and other river communities was one of degree, but in other respects it had distinct advantages: a federal land office, a state-chartered bank (1816-24 and 1837-42), and relatively good road access to Golconda, Vincennes, Kaskaskia, and St. Louis. One of its earliest connections eastward was the stage route through Owensboro to West Point, Kentucky. It was located on four mail routes by 1824, a year before it was incorporated. By the early 1840s, Shawneetown also had some wholesale firms and a commission house, several attorneys, a temperance society, a Sunday school union, and a newspaper. One of its most eminent citizens was Henry Eddy, an attorney and editor who served in the Illinois General Assembly and helped to found the Illinois State Lyceum. Another was Andrew McCallen, who established a law practice in 1843 and served as registrar at the land office. He was a delegate to the 1847 constitutional convention.[55]

By 1850, Shawneetown had risen to about eighteen hundred inhabitants. The county's increase since 1820 was a respectable 72.7 percent. (It would have been even higher had not some of Gallatin's territory and population been lost in 1847 to Hardin County.) The county produced a respectable 436,000 bushels of corn. The level of manufacturing for Gallatin County, however, was quite low ($60,000 value of products). The number of inhabitants per square mile was also modest—less than twenty-five.

These characteristics both contributed to and reflected factors that led to Shawneetown losing half of its population during the 1950s and failing to achieve the goals of its founders. A local historical marker at the 1839 Bank of Illinois ironically notes that this once dominant town's bank refused to lend money to risky Chicago.[56]

That undoubtedly apocryphal explanation reflected the region's loss of stature due to population trends northward, but other communities on the lower Ohio did not suffer as Shawneetown did. Floods devastated the area four times before the Civil War. The levee built to contain the Ohio was broken in the 1870s. But other factors were at work, for floods damaged other sites. The growth of the Illinois interior, which the Shawneetown land office fed, was especially important. The statewide vote in 1824 against permitting slavery, combined with the opening of the Illinois and Michigan Canal, the building of the National Road, and the war against the Sacs and Foxes in 1832, led to a substantial expansion of central and northern Illinois. Even the growth of the interior of Gallatin County threatened Shawneetown, which in the late 1840s lost its county seat status to Equality. (In 1852, Shawneetown regained that status, but at the expense of the loss of territory to a new county, Saline, in which Equality would be seat.) Shawneetown's weak banks—the second suspended as a result of the 1837 panic—undoubtedly contributed, as did diminished production in local salines. Declining numbers of people who came through Shawneetown to purchase federal lands also hurt it. Its town trustees exhibited weak fiscal management, moreover, leading to the suspension of its charter and reincorporation in 1847. (That required town trustees to obtain voters' permission to borrow money.) Still another factor was Shawneetown residents' conservative Upper Southern political culture. One reflection of that occurred after the new state constitution was adopted in 1848. Gallatin chose to retain the county-focused form of government.[57]

Cannelton, Indiana, and Cairo, Illinois, differed from Shawneetown in two respects. They were not old communities that peaked, only to decline after midcentury. One of them would eventually grow, despite ominous beginnings, while the other was launched and crash-landed several times. More important, they were the creatures of absentee investors.

Many settlers in Perry County farmed and mined some coal. In 1837, eastern capitalists, led by James T. Hobart, purchased about 6,500 acres on the river for coal mines, which they hoped would produce brightly burning cannel coal, and named the site Coal Haven. They also obtained a legislative charter to form the American Cannel Coal Company, many of whose investors were Yankees. They built homes, some small factories and mills, and a mine; they also marketed their products to steamboats. Unfortunately, a disastrous fire in 1839, combined with the economic problems of the time, led all but five families to leave by 1840.[58]

A year later, an official of the company, Francis Carlile—who would subsequently enter the newspaper business in Evansville—leased the mine and had the site replatted as Cannelsburg. He arranged for James Boyd to become resident manager in 1843. The name Cannelton was adopted in 1844. Cannel coal was rarely found, but bituminous coal was plentiful, and Cannelton began to grow. Coal production rose to 500 million bushels in three years.

Extensive fuel shipments attracted other investors. Twelve legislative charters were granted, but only one was actually implemented—the Indiana Cotton Mill. Many of its incorporators were Kentuckians, including the governor in 1850-51. Its investors included the business and political elite of the time—Robert Dale Owen, Richard Owen, Leonidas Polk, and Salmon P. Chase, among others. A huge celebration in May 1849 praised the mill town's promise. By December 6 of that year the *Evansville Weekly Journal,* having obtained the Cannelton newspaper by steamboat, reported that the huge stone mill, 287 feet long, 65 feet wide, and four stories high—one of the state's earliest and certainly its largest factory—was nearly completed. The operation would produce five million yards of brown sheeting annually, requiring two million pounds of raw cotton. About three hundred people lived in the town.

Company promoters envisioned what one historian called "Lowell on the Ohio": the textile industry's seat would be transferred there from Massachusetts. Hamilton Smith, a highly successful Louisville attorney, was an investor in the American Cannel Coal Company and brother-in-law of an Indiana judge who owned much land around Cannelton. Smith moved the company's offices to Louisville and became its director in 1846. He also became the cotton mill's major investor and chief promoter. Smith wrote an effusive piece on the project, "Indiana—Her Resources and Prospects," for the September 1849 issue of the influential *De Bow's Review*. He argued that the use of steam rather than water power, combined with the area's vast mineral resources, would revolutionize the textile industry. Equipment made in Massachusetts was shipped downriver, and experienced workmen were brought from New England and the British Isles. Carding began in December 1850, and the first cloth was woven in January 1851. By spring three hundred employees were operating 10,500 spindles. Smith moved to Cannelton later that year.

Before the end of the summer, though, investors' hopes were dashed. Severe financial pressures were a factor. The price of raw cotton was high, and eastern mills flooded the market with inexpensive cloth. Since the coal and textile companies were one and the same, corporate inflexibility contributed to financial difficulties, as did the inability to obtain large-scale financing. Technical difficulties with steam power constituted a second problem. A third was labor: inability to attract skilled labor, problems with protracted strikes, and lengthy layoffs in the summer due to drought and low water levels. New operators took over in September 1851 and leased the mill until 1853, when wealthy cotton planters aided in selling the plant. The mostly absentee investors' dream of a planned community, with company housing, cultural amenities, and labor-management harmony, had failed.

Fortunately for the estimated 1,600 residents of 1851, though, Cannelton's subsequent textile production would be reasonably successful, and the town grew, capturing the county seat by the end of the decade. Although Smith lost much money in the mill project, he remained there twenty years as the coal company's president and was one of the town's leading citizens.[59]

Cairo was not so fortunate, although travel accounts continued to note the site's potential. Likening the place to New Orleans, George Conclin insisted that the "same kind of labor, bestowed here [good levees], will protect it against overflows, and equally as well." No one doubted "the eligibility of the position; but the failures, which have heretofore been made, seem to have inspired every one with the idea, that all attempts to build a city here, will end in failure." Conclin attributed that to the poor decisions of absentee English investors. However, the place was "tenanted by a somewhat enterprising set of inhabitants."[60]

The company to which Conclin referred was the primary backer of Cairo's second absentee corporate developers, the Cairo City and Canal Company, incorporated in March 1837. In 1836, Sidney Breese, a prominent Illinois politician, and five others had purchased the site and secured incorporation of the Illinois Central Railroad. In February 1837, the Illinois legislature created a massive internal improvements program that included the Illinois Central as a state-supported line beginning on the Ohio at Cairo—then merely a lumberyard and informal storage place for passing boats—and connecting to the north with Galena and with the Illinois and Michigan Canal. Because of the conflict between private investors and the state regarding the railroad, in June 1837 the investors relinquished their right to build the line unless the state did not proceed with it, but they also secured Cairo's position as Ohio River terminus. Construction began in 1838, and twenty-five miles or so were built northward from Cairo during the darkening days of the Panic, years in which a post office was established and Irish laborers built Cairo's first church. Neighboring towns, like Caledonia, attempted to have the terminus switched, and Democrats in the legislature encouraged this, asking why such an important line would begin and end on the Mississippi and have a southern terminus that existed in name only.[61]

Darius B. Holbrook, who had led the efforts to incorporate the railroad and the Cairo company from his office in New York City, continued to champion Cairo's future development, even after the legislature repealed the entire internal improvements program in 1840. (It did not, however, revoke the Illinois Central's charter.) Southern Illinois's Democratic leader, John A. Logan, remained Holbrook's chief legislative supporter, scorning those who portrayed Caledonia as a better site for the railroad's terminus. Logan argued that Cairo could link southern Illinois with a projected line from Memphis to Charleston and thence by water to the West Indies. To obtain capital, Holbrook promoted the vision of a grand metropolis in the center of America via a prospectus of 1838. Promising to build levees, warehouses, stores, canals, and turnpikes, Holbrook obtained $500,000, much of it in London. The New York Life Insurance and Trust Company gained a major interest. As a result, the population of the town grew perhaps to 1,000 in 1840, and by 1843 levees had been built.[62]

The bankruptcy of the London financial house, the collapse of the short-lived City Bank of Cairo at Kaskaskia (1843), the state's abandonment of its internal improvements program, and the subsequent uncertainty of the railroad project contributed to a massive decline in Cairo's fortunes. The $1.2 million borrowed from investors produced only levees of questionable value. Compounding this was the absentee owners' absolute control over the land and the future of the site, making the 113 people remaining in 1845 both sullen and lawless. Hence all concerned—residents and investors—were disconcerted with the company, and Holbrook was the company.

One of the investors, Charles Dickens, had this to say of Cairo in *Ameri-*

can Notes, published a year after his visit there in April 1841, while en route to St. Louis:

> The trees were stunted in their growth; the banks were low and flat; the settlements and log cabins fewer in number; their inhabitants were more wan and wretched than any we had encountered yet. No songs of birds were in the air, no pleasant scents, no moving lights and shadows from swift passing clouds.
>
> [On the morning of the third day of the steamboat trip to St. Louis] we arrived at a spot so much more desolate than any we had yet beheld, that the forlornest places we had passed were, in comparison with it, full of interest . . . a place without any single quality, in earth or air or water, to commend it; such is this dismal Cairo.[63]

Cairo was possibly what Dickens had in mind when he described the "City of Eden" in *Martin Chuzzlewit,* published in 1844. On paper, Eden was a flourishing city. Chuzzlewit, one of the investors, found it to be a few crude structures placed in a clearing, a place where "fetid vapours . . . rose up from the earth, and hung on everything around." Nevertheless, he displayed his sign "Chuzzlewit and Company, Architects and Surveyors" upon "the most conspicuous part of the premises, with as much gravity as if the thriving City of Eden had a real existence and they expected to be overwhelmed with business."[64]

Cairo's foul reputation would dog it thereafter. As Arthur C. Cole wrote in 1919, it had been Illinois's "great city of prophecy . . . at the most important confluence of rivers in the world and at the center of the American republic, becoming a great inland emporium, the largest city in the world. In 1850, however, it was an embryonic city of 242 inhabitants, living largely in wharf boats and small temporary shanties."[65]

When survival of the Cairo City and Canal Company was doubtful, interested parties sold the property to the Cairo City Property Trust in June 1846. Holbrook took the lead in the reorganization. No lots were sold for seven years, however, because the eastern trustees wanted to make sure that a railroad would be built there. In 1843 Sidney Breese had been elected to the U.S. Senate. In the same year the Great Western Railway Company was incorporated, with essentially the same officers and directors as the failing Cairo company, and it did some work on the abandoned Illinois Central line. Breese failed to obtain a federal land grant for the project, however, because of his ties to Holbrook, the promise of rapidly growing Chicago, and the tenuous situation at Cairo. As a consequence the railroad company's charter was repealed in 1845.

The connection between the new Cairo trust and the Illinois Central was especially close thereafter. In 1849, Breese and Holbrook obtained a recharter of the Great Western, and additional work was undertaken on the project. Backers remained hopeful that a federal land grant could be obtained, but Senator Stephen Douglas, backed by Chicago interests, obtained generous congressional land grants to states, not companies, to build railroads from northern Illinois to the Ohio and from the Ohio to the Gulf of Mexico. (Breese had since been replaced in the Senate.) Illinois's land grants of almost 1.6 million acres would permit the railroad it chartered to finance construction and to entice homesteaders. In the ensuing legislative battle, a new Illinois Central, backed by eastern capital and Douglas and his supporters, won the charter, and the Great Western's hopes were dashed. The ultimate decision was a compromise, though, as Holbrook feared that otherwise the southern terminus might be located at Metropolis. Hence he accepted a thousand shares of the new company's stock and obtained in return a Cairo terminus and company promises to build levees and other improvements. Work on the new line began in December 1851.

In the same year, Samuel Staats Taylor of New Brunswick, New Jersey, who had been sent to Illinois in 1850 as the agent of Holbrook and the other trustees, settled in Cairo, the first and only trustee ever to reside there. The other Illinois city of the future, Chicago, had already exceeded its founders' dreams. Whether Cairo's backers would also have such fortunes remained problematic.[66]

At least Cairo was alive. America, Illinois, had been problematic from the outset. Located on high ground, it had become county seat in March 1819 and several handsome brick buildings had been erected. Unfortunately, America experienced a series of epidemics, especially yellow fever in 1820, and was devastated by a fire in 1831 that destroyed Henry Webb's huge warehouse. Locals, moreover, did nothing to stop the accumulation of a large sandbar in front of the town, which made boat landings increasingly difficult. In 1833 the county seat was moved inland, to Unity, and Webb and others created a new town upriver, Caledonia. America was abandoned shortly thereafter. Conclin's 1848 guidebook described America as a dilapidated collection of a few small houses.

Alexander County seemed to be a haven for marginal sites. The grandly named Napoleon had been described as a small place in *Illinois in 1837*. A wealthy southerner named Eli Clemson built a substantial home there, but nothing came of his plans for a town, and no vestige of the place was found by the 1860s. Trinity, an unplatted and unincorporated settlement surrounding a tavern, gained a post office in 1827 that would be abandoned in 1840. Flooding was a perennial problem, and settlers also failed to improve the landing. Residents soon abandoned the place.[67]

Flooding would also contribute to the demise of other would-be river metropolises, such as Boston in Harrison County, Indiana. Some would be abandoned, and others would be, like Boston, relocated inland. This process would continue into the twentieth century, especially after the major floods of 1913 and 1937.

But floods alone did not explain communities' disintegration or disappearance. A site's reputation for unhealthful conditions, for instance, could condemn it. It could be sited on the wrong bank of the river or suffer from sandbars and shallow harbors. Sometimes entrepreneurs gave up and moved on, either selling or abandoning their sites, like Morvin's Landing in Harrison County in 1838, and nothing replaced them. A place's perennial rowdiness and anarchy, like North Hampton, Harrison County, could also contribute to its demise. And competition from nearby communities hurt a number of settlements—from Williamsville, opposite Salt Creek and West Point, to Smithland, near rapidly growing Paducah. Losing county seat status, a major problem, was both symptom and cause of declension.[68]

The vast, seemingly inexorable sorting-out process on the lower Ohio continued, as it did along other rivers of the West.

5 ∾

Change and Continuity

Community variations were not easily explained. Growth and stagnation re-flected many elements—social and cultural, economic and geographical, ideo-logical and material, and regional and national. Development was altogether another matter. This process, synonymous with modernization, featured ori-entation toward a national market economy, increased productivity, and capi-tal-intensive production, as well as rapid expansion of industry and urbaniza-tion. These were in part the result of greater agricultural productivity, improved education, literacy, and mass communications, and the formation of a society valuing change that was fluid, cosmopolitan, impersonal, and pluralistic.[1]

Support for modernization was uneven. The Indiana General Assembly in the early 1820s created publicly funded roads with revenue derived from a fraction of federal land sales. Roads leading from Indianapolis to a number of Ohio River sites, including Evansville and Mauck's Ferry, were soon under con-struction. Whig pilots of state government in mid-1830s Illinois and Indiana were eager to channel their financial resources into banking and transporta-tion projects that advanced the interests of entrepreneurs and the well-being of their citizens.

After 1815, Americans were changing the ways they made their livings. The burgeoning of market capitalism created a national market in which debt and dependency were central. In the Ohio valley, canals and the application of steam to riverboats reversed Transappalachian counterclockwise trading pat-terns and encouraged industrialization. In the rapidly expanding cities of the North and West, a working class of men and women dependent on the whims of the wage-labor market grew rapidly.[2]

One effect of this transformation was the escalation of external factors shap-ing life along the lower Ohio River. Panics had enormous consequences for an economy dependent on banks, insurance companies, commission merchants, and other components of modernization. The Panic of 1819 slowed land sales at Shawneetown, for instance, and contributed to the town's stagnation. It also delayed settlement of the Jackson Purchase. The Panic of 1837 left the governments of Illinois and Indiana deeply in debt, forcing both to abandon transportation projects. In each state, only a single canal project survived. Indiana's second state banking system, including the branch at Evansville, weathered the storm and helped to build a foundation for expansion. By contrast, Illinois's state banking system collapsed, taking Shawneetown's bank with it. Cairo lost its bank and the Illinois Central.[3]

Another external factor was reputation. Places were settled, augmented, promoted, or avoided on the basis of their agricultural and natural resources, their healthfulness, their susceptibility to floods, and their perceived promise. *The Navigator's* warnings about treacherous currents, for instance, undoubtedly retarded Paducah's growth. Evansville's expansion was amplified by favorable accounts of town growth and potential, whereas Cairo's future remained cloudy. Edmund Dana's highly regarded *Geographical Sketches on the Western Country* (1819) assessed regions of the Ohio and Mississippi valleys in several categories, including drainage and topography. No lower Ohio lands appealed to him, although he liked the prairies around the English settlement in Illinois and Vincennes in Indiana. Similarly, Karl Postel's comments about the absence of a navigable waterway into Indiana's interior undoubtedly impeded settlement below the Falls.[4]

Local promoters, of course, relied on broadsides, advertisements, and newspapers to shape the ways in which outsiders perceived their communities. Promoters' efforts to induce settlement in idyllic but nonexistent places such as Cairo, of course, forged long-term public relations nightmares. Civic promotion was fundamental, but it was effective only to the extent that it realistically portrayed a community's assets. Chicago was the winner in this regard, having built upon its advantageous location and the virtually unlimited opportunities it offered white male newcomers.[5]

A third factor was the many transportation projects that emerged in the late 1820s, mostly in response to the lucrative Erie Canal. Probably the most important was the Louisville and Portland Canal, completed in 1830 with federal as well as private funds. The canal permitted bypassing the Falls of the Ohio, a natural break in trade that had generated many services, such as warehouses. Far from weakening Louisville, the canal made it the leading city in the Commonwealth before 1840. The canal expanded Louisville's river markets and, combined with the blossoming steamboat trade, was the crucial link between eastern markets and western farmers. The creation of the Henderson-Louisville packet service in 1843 vividly illustrated that. By midcentury, through a haphazard matrix of turnpikes, canals, and railroads, an urban network had begun to emerge in Kentucky, mostly between the Bluegrass region and Louisville.[6]

The extent to which settlers were aware of the region's potential in distant markets and promoted often distant improvements was another reason for community expansion. Evansville leaders' promotion of the Wabash and Erie Canal was an obvious example, as was Henderson's merchants persuading the Kentucky legislature in 1830 to incorporate the Green River Navigation Company in order to dredge and dam that estuary. Seven years later they obtained legislative permission to build a private dirt turnpike to Hopkinsville, later extended to Nashville. Evansville, Henderson, Mount Vernon, and Rockport also launched plank toll road projects to improve access to the interior. Evansville's toll road progressed only a few miles before it was closed, as did Henderson's proposed link with Owensboro. Mount Vernon's toll road extended to New Harmony and Rockport's to Gentryville; neither lasted more than a few years. These projects were financed by the business and civic leaders of their communities.[7]

Undoubtedly the most dangerous and visionary were railroad projects. In October 1848, Willard Carpenter, John Ingle Jr., John Shanklin, and W.H. Chandler sought to bring the proposed Cincinnati–St. Louis line through Evansville and Mount Carmel, Illinois. Unsuccessful, they incorporated their new railroad in January 1849. Evansville joined county commissioners in issuing $200,000 in bonds to purchase stock in the newly chartered Evansville and Illinois Railroad. In 1853, the new line intersected the Cincinnati–St. Louis railroad at Vincennes, fifty miles north. In less than two years, it reached Terre Haute and another major connection between St. Louis and Indianapolis. Hoping to be the northern terminus of the congressionally subsidized railroad connecting the Ohio to the Gulf, Paducah leaders persuaded the state legislature of 1851 to permit the town to invest $200,000 of public funds in the New Orleans and Ohio Railroad.[8]

Similarly, some civic leaders were more active than others in seeking federal improvement of the Ohio, a task given to the U.S. Army Corps of Engineers in the Rivers and Harbors Act of 1824. One of the Corps's first projects was a wing dam built near Henderson in 1824-25 to improve channel conditions. In the 1850s, the *Evansville Daily Journal* praised a proposal to build dams that would guarantee a six-foot-deep channel year-round, stating that no federal expenditure "could be more national in its character" and benefit "so large a number of the population."[9]

Such visions reflected the dependence of these towns on legislative and business decisions made many miles away. "River Intelligence" columns in the area's larger newspapers offered information not only about river conditions and steamboat arrivals and departures but also about labor conditions and prices in distant markets.[10]

Technological innovation was also promoted in these columns, as it was another largely external influence which had vast regional import. Cannelton was a pioneering example of the importance of steam in industrial production. The most widespread application before 1850, however, was the steamboat. By then, many places along the lower Ohio had boatyards and foundries that produced, outfitted, or repaired such craft. Steamboats could navigate in only a few feet of water and their engines could operate in muddy water. Their capacity and their speed upstream cut freight and passenger rates dramatically—for example, upstream freight from Cincinnati per hundred pounds dropped from ten dollars to two or three dollars in the 1830s. Steamboats were also relatively easy to build and to purchase. More than half between 1830 and 1860 were owned by a single person or by partnerships. Without such craft, declared Louis Hunter, modernization would have been greatly retarded. The steamboat spurred population growth and dispersal and accelerated demand for river improvements and access. Packet service also provided communication, newcomers, and entertainment.[11]

External causes of local prosperity were vividly illustrated when the mercantile communities of towns began to specialize and when commission and forwarding agents opened offices. As Timothy Mahoney has shown in *River Towns in the Great West*, towns, roads, and steamboat routes combined to create a regional system of settlement and trade. River routes emerged with regular stops by steamboats, but boats' limitations stimulated a demand for better land transportation. Emerging was a shipment strategy based on price levels in the target market less the cost of transport and product. Because profit margins were low, it was essential to respond quickly to changing conditions.

Initially, the economy had been based on bartering. Then peddlers moved between river towns and the interior. Permanent merchants signified a reciprocal relationship between agriculture and urban development, as merchants purchased goods on credit from eastern wholesalers or at the nearest entrepot and sold them, also on credit, to farmers, storekeepers, and manufacturers. At some point river towns that transshipped goods to and from the interior became more specialized wholesale centers between the hinterland and the regional entrepot. Forwarding and commissioning services emerged, and a flood of specialized merchants followed. An integrated urban mercantile system, with Cincinnati the dominant force and St. Louis its shadow, appeared by the 1840s. As the scale of operations to maintain a role in this system increased, so did the demand for people, capital, and transportation. Great metropolitan centers began to control hundreds of small places, once centers of small worlds, and transformed them into provincial centers.

Instead of becoming more alike, each settlement evolved differently, as did relationships with communities inside and outside the region. If sites were to progress, adjustment and innovation were required. Some, like Galena and Davenport, were run by closed cohorts that controlled community power. Others, like Indianapolis, were open to the ambitions of newcomers. Success depended on leaders' ability to read trends and to respond creatively--by copying the plans of other places, by developing distinctive local products and services, or by fitting some local specialization into the region's needs.[12]

By 1850 much of the lower Ohio remained outside the hinterlands of St. Louis, Chicago, and Cincinnati. Evansville enjoyed a virtually unchallenged position that extended almost to the Kentucky-Tennessee border to the south, beyond Vincennes to the north, and west almost to Cairo. Commission merchants also established businesses in Newburgh, Henderson, Owensboro, and Paducah.

A more rational process was emerging from a generally disordered beginning. River improvements and expanded packet service, for example, promoted interior transportation projects. Such initiatives, combined with the National Road and the Erie Canal, accelerated the inhabitation and modernization, ironically, of the Upper Midwest. This may have been the most important factor contributing to the relative decline of the lower Ohio.

Much of the story of the lower Ohio between 1820 and 1850, in short, was the result of things often unseen and mysterious that lay beyond the decision-making power of people in the region. No place was as fortunate as Indianapolis, located on both the National Road and several major rail lines connecting larger urban places. Minimal local capital was required for these projects, and the town did not have to rest its hopes, as most on the lower Ohio did, on one or two panaceas. Rarely did a community receive such a boon as designation as the Wabash and Erie Canal or Illinois Central terminus.[13]

Local considerations also contributed heavily to communities' advancement or decline. Edmund Dana's *Geographical Sketches on the Western Country* (1819) ranked places according to eight physical criteria: quality of soil, topography, availability of timber, quality of water supply, drainage, climate or healthfulness, market access, and security of land claims. Inhabitants and investors gave greater weight to some factors than to others. Most of these settlements, for instance, had ample timber, and bottomlands were highly productive. Healthfulness in summer was very important, as the fates of America and Cairo attested. Smithland and West Point, by contrast, were places where the well-to-do went in summers to escape the heat and foul water of the interior. Similarly, the availability of a safe and reliable water supply greatly mattered. Flooding and drainage considerations were certainly important, but most of the settlements experienced flooding, and not all languished. Low elevation did not guarantee failure, just as high elevation did not produce prosperity. Chicago's drainage problems were at least as daunting as Cairo's, for instance, but investors in Chicago found means of coping with them, whereas Cairo was plagued with seepage well into the twentieth century.

Similarly, advantageous location was a necessary but not sufficient condition for success. Smithland and West Point, near the mouths of important tributaries, appeared to possess superior advantages, but dominance by Paducah and Louisville, respectively, offset those assets. Newburgh's elevation and its proximity to the mouth of the Green River did not prevent Evansville from overwhelming its economy.

But location did matter. The absence of a substantial population on the Kentucky side of the river as a rule led to minimal growth on the other side, as Golconda, Rome, and Fredonia show. The quality of land and resources on the northern shore also influenced the way in which settlement developed to the south. Lewisport's slow growth reflected the unappealing terrain in Perry County to the north. By contrast, Hawesville benefited from having Cannelton on the other side of the river, as did Henderson with Evansville and Owensboro with Rockport. Security of land claims, an obstacle to Kentucky's progress, also helped to shape the way Americans looked at the lay of the land north of the Ohio. That was a major reason for the large number of Kentuckians crossing over to Mauckport, Troy, Shawneetown, and Golconda. The absence of slavery was closely related.[14]

But much more than location was involved. Political skill mattered—as, for instance, in obtaining and retaining county seat status. Some communities declined after losing that: America, Caledonia, Fredonia, Troy, and (for a time) Shawneetown. Such an occurrence undoubtedly reflected larger problems. To be sure, some places—Cannelton, Newburgh, Cloverport, and Uniontown—progressed despite not being county seats, and some which obtained it—Rome, Smithland, Golconda, and Elizabethtown, Illinois—remained fairly small. But being a county seat was certainly not a liability.

The politics of county creation as well as county seat selection revealed a related truth. County formulation ultimately guaranteed nothing, but counties were to their creators "little engines of improvement": among other things, they could transform paths into dirt roads and turnpikes or award subsidies for canals and railroads.[15]

The ideal county would appear to have been about twenty miles square, allowing travel ten miles each way to the county seat, a distance that could be managed in one day. Making counties smaller involved the risk of lowered tax revenues. Creation of new counties, though, seemed to offer great economic and political benefit, and Illinois and Kentucky were still forming Ohio River counties in the 1840s: Hardin, Massac, and Pulaski in the former and Ballard and Crittenden in the latter. By 1843, the twenty-four counties on the lower Ohio had been formed. Only seven, however, were four hundred or more square miles in size—Harrison, Posey, and Spencer Counties in Indiana, and Breckinridge, Daviess, Hardin, and Henderson in Kentucky. Illinois's Hardin and Kentucky's Hancock, recently organized, were less than one hundred. Generally the small expanse of counties, especially in Illinois, meant low tax revenues and a small pool of qualified officeholders. Over the long haul, moreover, these counties had less political clout at the state and national capitals. What had seemed advantageous in the short run was a long-term liability, unless these places could—like McCracken and Vanderburgh, each about 230 square miles—attract innovative newcomers. Thomas Clark's observation that Kentucky has too many counties could be applied to Illinois and Indiana.[16]

County-centeredness was, especially in Kentucky, also an aspect of culture: localistic, individualistic, rural, and agrarian. Counties produced power for petty officials who ruled like medieval bureaucrats and carried on traditions inherited from Virginia. County "judges" in Kentucky, also powerful along the Ohio in Illinois, were not required to be attorneys and served as virtual sovereigns in county finances, contracts, and liquor licensing in addition to civil and some criminal cases. Justices of the peace, also men of wealth and leisure, had less power and were generally inept. Fights over appointments and rewards were frequent and vicious. Court days were community focal points.[17]

Settlements' prosperity depended in part on their electing residents to state and national office and securing influence and favors through them and their allies. Early Henderson was probably the most successful in this regard, having had extraordinary ability to see local men become members of the U.S. House of Representatives and Senate as well as governor of the Commonwealth. At the other end was Cairo, whose early leadership was absentee.[18]

Local and state political culture on either side of the river generally reflected Upper South disdain for authority and taxes, which perpetuated localism and denigrated government and especially cities. Upper southerners also resisted temperance and efforts to control settlement and landholding.[19] Internal improvement plans had strongest support among Whigs on the lower Ohio, especially in the counties that were the most urban—Henderson, Daviess, McCracken, and Vanderburgh. In the solidly Democratic Purchase region, for instance, Whigs captured all presidential races in McCracken County before 1852, as they did in Rockport, situated in a heavily Democratic area. Most inhabitants, however, perceived such projects as threats to their traditions. In varying degrees, each of the new midcentury constitutions in Illinois (1848), Kentucky (1850), and Indiana (1851) reflected provincial, agrarian values and reluctantly granted towns authority to tax and govern. Kentucky's constitution was the least progressive. Local powers were granted begrudgingly, although coping with cholera produced greater town regulatory activity up and down the Ohio.[20]

Communities also needed financial and communications resources to cope with the emerging market economy. Banking institutions, however modest, provided capital and currency, an especially important resource for local economies after the cessation of the Second Bank of the United States in 1837. Banks were, however, few and far between. As of 1850 there were just four south of the Falls: two in Evansville and one each in Henderson and Paducah, the latter created by town government in 1837.[21]

Newspapers fostered literacy and education, promoted communities, and provided information about business and civic affairs elsewhere. These were predictably most prevalent in the larger towns. Evansville, with a Whig daily, a Democratic weekly, and a German-language weekly, had the most at midcentury. Evansville, Henderson, Owensboro, and Paducah were also connected by telegraph to the larger world.

Leadership in these settlements was not necessarily cut from the same cloth. The presence of a tobacco-slave culture in Kentucky was a major reason. Openness of communities to newcomers and to their rising in class and status was a related factor. Differences in newcomers' backgrounds mattered enormously. Individuals also varied greatly in the quality of their vision and in their levels of energy and skill.

Despite their support for civic projects, such as riverfront and Green River improvements, the elite of Henderson, for example, remained a coterie of wealthy tobacco producers with Tidewater pretensions. Similar elites dominated most other river settlements along the Kentucky bank. Paducah was an anomaly, as many business and civic leaders were natives of Germany or states other than Kentucky. To be sure, communities with closely knit elites having Upper South roots were present across the river, as Elizabethtown, Illinois, and Rockport, Indiana, attested. Generally, though, newcomers avoided Kentucky's river towns and villages.[22]

The most vivid contrast was Evansville, especially after 1834. As in Indianapolis, the opportunity to rise in class and status not only validated their hopes but also served as a powerful incentive for others to settle there. In the process the composition of the community became more diverse.[23]

Newcomers' visions were inextricably linked to the cultures in which they had been reared. The ability to think in terms that transcended the local and the present was most abundant in those places that were expanding—a reason for, as well as a symptom of, local successes. Lack of enterprise, most vividly demonstrated by America and Trinity, guaranteed failure or insignificance.

The ability to achieve town incorporation was one such element which regardless of state boundaries allowed places to provide a modicum of law and order, fire protection, public water, public health, and riverfront improvement. Shortly after its second incorporation in 1846, for instance, Mount Vernon's town board spent $20,000 to improve its wharf, using the receipts from the newly created post of wharfmaster to retire the debt. Paducah's leaders in 1833 gained a board of health that was empowered to examine riverboats and riverfront conditions and to restrict dangerous activities. Taxes on and regulations for traveling shows on steamboat were also imposed. Before 1840, they had begun to sell space on their riverfront to wood vendors, granted a franchise to operate a town wharfboat, created a public well, purchased equipment for a volunteer fire department, organized a public market, graded streets, and built sidewalks. In 1842, town government constructed a public wharf. By then, the boundaries of Paducah had also been enlarged.[24]

Evansville's government services were also expansive. Town ordinances in Evansville between 1841 and 1847 reveal efforts to regulate markets, groceries, shows, and amusements, to appoint fire wardens, to organize a town watch, and to construct sidewalks.[25] These powers were enlarged on January 27, 1847, when the legislature granted it a city charter—the only community on the lower Ohio with that status before the 1850s. The charter provided for a mayor, elected every three years, and six councilmen, elected annually. One of the new city government's most important decisions, before offering support to a railroad in 1849, was to issue $35,000 in bonds to grade about two thousand feet of the nearly perpendicular river embankment. When that was completed in 1848, a wharfboat was anchored there to enhance the flow of freight and passengers. This improvement reinforced the city's importance as the major landing site between Louisville and the Mississippi. The city's first wharfmaster, P.G. O'Riley, reported that 4,282 boats arrived at Evansville between November 1848 and May 1850 and that only 187 passed without stopping. Landing fees also helped to retire city bonds.[26]

Such diversity in public regulation and subsidy reflected the close connections between business and public elites. In Evansville, for example, merchant John Shanklin served as town board president in 1829 and 1830. Between 1831 and 1847, merchant Alanson Warner was president three terms. Shanklin's onetime partner Nathan Rowley held the post twice, as did entrepreneur William H. Walker. Samuel Orr was president one term, as were businessmen John Lockwood, John Mitchell, James Laughlin, and Robert M. Evans. Conrad Baker was town attorney in 1842. Attorney James G. Jones, son of one of the three who platted the town, was the first mayor. Newspaperman John J. Chandler was the first city clerk, and Orr was its first treasurer. John Stuart Hopkins was the city's third mayor. Early city council members included John A. Reitz, Conrad Baker, and Willard Carpenter. Attorney and railroad enthusiast John Ingle Jr. was one of the few who did not hold public office.[27]

Similar tales were told up and down the Ohio. The chief differences were cultural and ideological: the desire and the ability of elites to persuade citizens to pay higher taxes to support civic improvements, especially railroad subsidies that extended the community's reach. Of the $65,000 paid by Evansville taxpayers in 1860, for instance, $18,000 was allocated to retire railroad bonds![28] Settlements that invested public monies in such endeavors generally expanded and diversified. These projects were costly and risky and sometimes disastrous. They spawned vigorous debates in those places which were prospering by regional standards: Evansville, Henderson, Owensboro, and Paducah.

The society and the culture of these settlements also explained their similarities and differences. In the simple clearings and hamlets, such as Ford's Ferry and New Amsterdam, social arrangements were fairly homogeneous and egalitarian. Residents had similar backgrounds, and most lived on the edge in a barter economy. In the larger places, however, social stratification was emerging. In the 1850 federal census, for example, Pope County, Illinois, an overwhelmingly rural and agricultural county, boasted a physician, an attorney, four teachers, seven merchants, a number of artisans, and a host of laborers.[29]

This was, of course, much more pronounced in the larger settlements. Towns and cities were loci in which occupation and wealth created class and status distinctions. The most influential were merchants, who were also often the bankers and pioneer industrialists. Close to them in rank were professionals. Below them were small shopkeepers, artisans, wage earners, and transients. At the bottom were African Americans. Although lines were not as rigid as in the East, they were important points of reference in towns. Due to their later start, however, none of these communities by 1850 had formed businessmen's clubs or boards of trade, whose purpose in cities like Cincinnati was not only business expansion but also control over the increasingly fragmented community.[30]

One symptom of stratification was the erection of what in the region would be considered palatial homes, which all of the larger settlements had by midcentury. James Young's fine brick dwelling, erected in West Point in 1805, was perhaps the first. Henderson and Owensboro witnessed the erection of spacious Greek Revival residences. Abraham M. Phelps and Union Bethell, prosperous Newburgh merchants, built grand homes. Willard Carpenter's splendid Greek Revival mansion, a block from the river in Lamasco (1849), served as a landmark for boatmen and a symbol of the city's emergence as the commercial center. Most of the Evansville elite, though, built grand homes upriver from Main Street.[31]

In the larger places, other evidence of residential stratification appeared. Row houses for workers, for instance, were constructed by businessmen in Paducah and Evansville. Workers in Evansville's mills, foundries, and shops resided downriver from Main Street, along the canal, near upper Main, and in Lamasco. Small businessmen and craftsmen dwelled on or near Main Street. Laborers in Lamasco spoke German, whereas most Evansville residents spoke English. Division Street separated them.[32]

One caveat needs to be offered: Kentucky towns were, as Thomas Clark has observed, "tinged sharply with the coloration of the rural mind." Towns also encapsulated the great contrasts between rich and poor. At midcentury, for instance, A.B. Barret of Henderson, worth $1.9 million, accounted for about a seventh of the county's wealth. In 1850, just twenty-one heads of household, of the nearly 150 residing in Owensboro, had real estate valued at over $5,000. The wealthiest, Robert Triplett, possessed property worth $167,000; the next wealthiest was his son Philip, whose real estate amounted to $22,000. Total valuation of property in the town in 1860 was about $560,000. Whether as small as Caseyville or as large as Henderson, the Kentucky town was an extension of the plantation society in which it was situated.[33]

Concentration of wealth, to be sure, was not limited to settlements in slave society. The oldest surviving tax assessment records of Evansville demonstrate that. In 1860, just eighty-seven people paid more than $150 in taxes on lots and improvements, and their assessments constituted 38 percent of the total tax bill. Eleven taxpayers paid more than $400 and accounted for 12 percent of all taxes.

Lower Ohio River towns and cities also made important cultural contributions to their environs as well as to their residents.[34] Almost invariably, the first institutions established in the counties along the river were churches, and most of these were initially organized in the villages and towns of the area.

A few examples will suffice. Cairo's first cultural organization appears to have been a Roman Catholic congregation, whereas Cannelton's was Unitarian. In almost all cases, however, the first congregations were Baptist, Methodist, or Presbyterian.[35] Mount Vernon's first preacher (1815) was apparently a Baptist; a Methodist and a Cumberland Presbyterian followed. As elsewhere, Methodists first met in a private home—in this case, town leader Jesse Welborn's. A Union Church erected in 1828 was used by several groups for several years before they constructed their own houses of worship. By the 1850s, the town had eight churches.[36]

Similar patterns could be found in practically every other settlement.

Shawneetown's first congregation, organized in 1826, was Presbyterian. Five years later the Methodists formed a Shawneetown circuit, and in 1842 the first Roman Catholic christening occurred. By midcentury, Newburgh's churches were Cumberland Presbyterian (organized by A.M. Phelps, a leading merchant) and Methodist. Rockport had Baptist, Methodist, Disciples, Presbyterian, Catholic, and German Evangelical congregations. Owensboro had a number of Baptist, Methodist, and Presbyterian congregations. Its first resident Catholic priest arrived in 1833.[37]

These churches were places in which citizens of all social stations could mix, and denominations shared common Protestant evangelical values about progress and national mission. Division was rising, however, along Protestant-Catholic as well as ethnic and racial lines. German congregations sprang up in the mid-1830s around Jasper and Evansville. A second wave arrived in many of the larger towns in the late 1840s. Evansville, Mount Vernon, and Rockport also possessed small African Methodist Episcopal churches, organized earlier in the decade. For reasons of social control, most Kentucky blacks worshipped in white congregations in which separate sections had been established for them. There were no Jewish synagogues in the lower Ohio region until the 1850s.[38]

Residents of villages and towns also established a wide array of voluntary associations. Early on, places as small as Elizabethtown, Illinois, had secret societies, usually Masonic lodges. Mount Vernon's lodge was formed in the mid-1820s by town promoter Jesse Welborn. Agricultural societies were also common by the late 1840s. Even tiny Fredonia, in Crawford County, gained one in 1840. Communities of all sizes had societies that fostered appreciation for literature, painting, theater, and music. Subscription libraries were also established by 1850 in Evansville, Mount Vernon, Rockport, Golconda, and Shawneetown.[39]

Societies to improve the habits and the health of citizens flourished. Shawneetown had local associations promoting Sunday schools, distributing copies of the Bible, and advocating temperance. After the state legislature passed a bill permitting townships to ban alcohol, Evansville's temperance union was established in September 1849. Over 140 signed its organizing document. As elsewhere, many of the town's elite were involved. Such reformers, probably because of their association with public education and antislavery, were less common across the river.[40]

The establishment of the Evansville Medical College in 1846 revealed a fairly advanced level of cultural development. This was a direct product of the formation of a county medical society the year before. Local physicians served as faculty, and the facility included a dispensary. George B. Walker was most instrumental in its advancement. The Medical College, which graduated fifty students before closing in 1887, following Walker's death, provided the only professional medical training downriver of the Falls.[41]

The Medical College was a microcosm of most cultural developments in the region. Persons associated with it were also involved in other civic better-ment projects and business enterprises. Such institutions attracted newcomers to the towns and cities of the lower Ohio and served to enhance the quality of life in rural environs.

Nowhere was this as clearly demonstrated as in public education. Gener-ally, the states of Illinois, Indiana, and Kentucky exhibited varying degrees of what Thomas Clark has said of the Bluegrass State: "a thread of casualness about educational values and objectives." Illinois and Indiana, despite constitutional promises, had no statewide public school system before the early 1850s. Local sentiments and resources determined whether there would be a school build-ing, how long the school term would be, and what would be taught. No state or local tax levies supported schools until the early 1850s, and even afterwards debate and litigation blocked development of tax-supported education. Most were subscription schools, such as those created in early Golconda and Mount Vernon. Such schools were probably better than their rural counterparts, but terms were short (no more than three months), attendance was voluntary, in-struction was generally wretched, and books were scarce and expensive.[42]

The results were not surprising. In 1840, about 20 percent of Indiana chil-dren between ages five and fifteen attended school. Relatively few of these were enrolled in academies and grammar schools, and only a handful attended the state's university at Bloomington. Slightly over 14 percent of adults could not read or write. Reflecting Upper South roots, this placed Hoosiers lowest among all northern states in literacy. Illinois and Indiana led the North in the per-centages of illiteracy and of children not attending school. Ten years later, In-diana remained the least literate northern state. One consolation, perhaps, was that the two states had better rates than Kentucky's. These differences, how-ever, were relatively slight. In Ohio, by contrast, almost 40 percent of the chil-dren attended school, and the illiteracy rate was 5 percent.[43]

Lower Ohio counties' share of their state's illiterate population in 1840 ranged from 7.3 percent in Illinois to 7.9 in Indiana and 9.5 in Kentucky—well above their proportion of the total population. The number of illiterates ranged from a low of 111 in Hardin County, Illinois, to 1,468 in Gallatin County, Illinois. Over the next ten years, the number of illiterates in some Illinois and Indiana counties declined, notably in Gallatin, Harrison, and Vanderburgh, but increased in others, most strikingly in Crawford and Perry.[44]

Schooling in Illinois's river counties was especially shaped by Upper South culture. The number of public schools was generally much lower than in Indiana: only in Gallatin County were the number of schools and the level of expenditure respectable. Only Alexander and Pulaski Counties provided local tax monies, and these were small.

Kentucky's schools were even worse. This revealed in part Tidewater reinforcement of power through private education of the elite. Public education remained a rare and pauper-related institution. The values of the backwoods South reinforced suspicions of formal education and taxation. Neither of the state's first two constitutions provided for public education, leaving the matter in the legislature's hands. Some advancement occurred in the wake of the new constitution of 1850, which made education a state commitment, and of a school funding law adopted by the legislature in 1850.[45]

Nonetheless, the number of illiterates in Kentucky's river counties remained high and even increased in the 1840s. Although Kentucky had more grammar schools and academies than Illinois and Indiana, these were private schools. The counties with the largest towns—Daviess, Henderson, and McCracken—had at most four common schools each, and Hancock, where Hawesville was county seat, had none at all. As a rule, there were also fewer pupils in common schools. No local tax monies were used in any county.

That public schools, pupils, teachers, and tax support were most prevalent in several Indiana counties testified in large part to the leadership of Yankees who associated public education with modernization. Caleb Mills of Wabash College began a campaign for common schools in 1846 with the first of six newspaper articles on the causes and cures of Hoosier backwardness. Supported by such Evansville Yankees as H.Q. Wheeler, his premise was simple: "There is only one way to secure good schools, and that is to pay for them." An 1849 law following a state referendum allowed tax-supported education, but only if a majority in each county approved it. Most counties subsequently adopted some form of public education. But only with the constitution of 1851 and the School Law of 1852 did "a permanent and true common school system" emerge.[46]

As in Illinois, opposition to public education was strongest in those areas in which settlers from the Upper South predominated. Two-thirds of Indiana counties opposing free schools in the 1848 referendum were southern, and public funding for education was quite low along the Ohio River. Strong support came from Protestant evangelical Whigs, such as Wheeler and industrialist William Heilman, who equated education with moral uplift and developmental values. Schools, like churches, were potent unifying tools. Wheeler, "father of Evansville schools," had powerful foes, especially among the growing German Catholic population in Evansville that perceived common schools as instruments of Protestant hegemony. Others argued that such schools weakened family management of children, centralized power, and produced exorbitant tax rates.[47]

In a larger sense, the cultural life of these communities mirrored those values and folkways which inhabitants brought with them and which were shaped by the climate, resources, and economy of the lower valley. Educational institutions, or the lack thereof, were only one of many means by which that inheritance was expressed. Architectural styles, place-names, recreational patterns, methods of cooking, and forms of dress were some of the manifestations.[48]

Despite evidences of commonality, one is struck by the tremendous variety of forms and styles of the places sharing a common river. Many things contributed. As in the upper Ohio valley, a system was emerging in which most settlements remained localized in focus whereas some had varying degrees of economic, social, cultural, and political influence beyond their boundaries. To be sure, growth was more dramatic in the northern Midwest, especially in Chicago, but the same process was under way along the lower Ohio. And the river remained the lifeblood of all of these places.

The next question would be how civil war, steam-powered riverboats and railroads, and manufacturing would shape the region. Some powerful clues had already surfaced.

PART 3 ∽

Communities in the Civil War Era, 1850-1880

6 ⚬

The Sifting Process Quickens

By midcentury, unprecedented challenges profoundly altered the ways many Americans lived. Some of these were technological and economic: the golden age of the steamboat, the application of steam to rails and factories, and the increasing severity of downturns following economic panics. More pervasive and disruptive was the Civil War and its aftermath. All contributed to the reshaping of the lower Ohio River community. Although most accounts associate this era with regional stagnation and decline, they fail to uncover the true richness and complexity of the story.

Between 1850 and 1880, many settlements remained superficially unchanged. The spots extending from Bridgeport in Harrison County past Ford's Ferry near Cave-in-Rock to Olmsted and the river's mouth remained places where steamboats stopped occasionally or travelers sought a ferry crossing. Many sites such as Skillman's Landing in Hancock County and Clementsburg in Crittenden County were no more than boat landings. A few, including Bay City, Illinois, Enterprise, Indiana, and Wolf Creek and East Cairo, Kentucky, were large enough to gain at least momentary notice in the federal census, but none had more than one hundred residents. Taken together, these places did not account for much of the demographic change that was occurring, but their resilience was striking.

On the other hand, all three states experienced impressive growth during this period. Significantly, the rate of regional growth of Ohio River counties exceeded state increase—even in Illinois, where the six river counties' expansion was five percentage points above the state's.[1] Illinois rose from about 850,000 to 3,100,000, Indiana from 988,000 to slightly under two million, and Kentucky from 982,000 to 1,600,000. These were hardly years in which the river counties languished. To be sure, the increases were not uniform. Alexander, McCracken, and Vanderburgh Counties' growth significantly surpassed that of their neighbors. In Illinois, Indiana, and Kentucky, the number of counties exceeding their state's rates were, in order, three, four, and seven—in short, fourteen of the total twenty-four. But none of the counties along the lower Ohio lost population between 1850 and 1880.

The primary reason for this pattern was urbanization. Population per square mile expanded in all counties, especially in Vanderburgh, which had 181 people per square mile by 1880. McCracken's 68 per square mile made it a distant second. The region remained mostly rural, but settlements listed in the federal censuses of 1850 and 1880 accounted for a growing share of the region's people—up to almost 28 percent in Illinois, 31 percent in Indiana, and 14 percent in Kentucky. The third most densely populated county was Daviess, with 58; the least heavily populated was Livingston, with 23. Eight had thirty or fewer people per square mile.[2]

The change in the size as well as the rank of river communities was striking. In 1850, Evansville and Paducah were the largest, with 4,776 and 2,428 denizens, respectively. In 1800, though, only six counties on the lower Ohio had towns of twenty-five hundred or more. Vanderburgh and Alexander, with 69 and 61 percent, respectively, were the most urbanized. No other places had more than 2,000 inhabitants. Thirty years later, ten communities did. Evansville had grown to more than six times its antebellum size, was second largest in Indiana, behind Indianapolis, and was much larger than former rivals New Albany and Madison. No other southern Indiana city had a similar experience. Evansville alone accounted for about 20 percent of the people residing in Indiana's Ohio River settlements. By 1890 it was the twelfth largest city in the Midwest and the fifty-sixth in the nation. Paducah's rise to the fifth largest city in the Commonwealth was also impressive. Its rate of growth was not as great as Cairo's, which had become second largest on the lower Ohio. Although not among Illinois's most populous cities, Cairo accounted for about 14 percent of Illinois's Ohio River denizens. During this time, Owensboro overtook Henderson and rose to fourth in the region. The other five with 2,000 or more were Mount Vernon, Metropolis, Rockport, Mound City, and Tell City. Eighty percent of the people enumerated in the settlements listed in the federal census of 1880 dwelled in these ten places; total population of these ten communities was 71,307, less than the population of Indianapolis. Evansville accounted for one-third of the 91,984 people residing in all of the river settlements south of the Falls.

A number of once-promising river locales, by contrast, declined or stagnated. Shawneetown and Uniontown experienced decline, then rebounded modestly. Cannelton enjoyed modest growth in the 1860s, only to tumble in the 1870s. Hawesville declined sharply in the 1860s. Smithland declined steadily, as did Caledonia, Brandenburg, and Caseyville. Leavenworth, Stephensport, West Point, Lewisport, Mauckport, and Troy—all with once lofty ambitions— seemed to have marginal futures. A few smaller places—Cloverport, Golconda, Metropolis, Mount Vernon, Newburgh, Rockford, and Tell City—did experience, however, modest rates of growth.[3]

The most remarkable story of this period was Cairo's. Devastated by its second corporate debacle in the 1840s, the settlement had dwindled to about two hundred residents in 1850. The commencement of railroad construction and town lot sales in the early 1850s produced a boom. Over eight hundred lots were sold in 1854, and steamboat arrivals reached almost 3,800, a figure which rivaled that of St. Louis. All this anticipated the Illinois Central's opening on January 1, 1855—the completion of the world's longest rail line. One English traveler who arrived by train in early June observed that everything had a raw, unfinished quality, including the hotel, Taylor House. But, he asserted, Cairo was a substantial shipping point, given its proximity to St. Louis and the ice-free waters to the south and its northerly rail connections for steamboat passengers. By 1860, its population was 2,188, and twenty years later it was slightly over 9,000.[4]

Many signs suggested achievement of a long-vaunted promise. Cairo completed its wharf and received a town charter from the legislature in 1857, was named Alexander County seat in 1859, and gained Illinois Central packet service to New Orleans in 1860. In the process, the IC hoped to control north-south trade which the newly opened Mobile and Ohio Railroad, stretching from nearby Columbus, Kentucky, to New Orleans, threatened. As a break in transport, Cairo in 1859 shipped 350,000 bushels of wheat and 27,000 barrels of flour southward by water and 6,900 barrels of molasses, 15,100 hogsheads of sugar, and 6 million pounds of cotton to the north. In addition to 2,000 passengers in January 1859 alone, the Illinois Central hauled tons of oranges, coffee, salt, sugar, and molasses to eager northern markets. By 1860, Cairo also boasted churches, physicians, stores, and three hotels. The Ohio Building, its first brick commercial structure, was completed in 1858. The grandest structure was the Halliday House (1859). Cairo also became known as a town that attracted minstrel and variety troupes, circuses, and theatrical companies.

Hints of the problems that would plague Cairo for decades, however, remained evident. Residents held their first election in the year the railroad reached Cairo. Absentee trustees, fearful of residents' independence in that contest, obtained the town's incorporation and thus secured greater control over Cairo's boisterous newcomers. Residents continually complained about the small sizes and high prices of town lots as well as the trustees' refusal to invest in projects that improved the town's infrastructure. A flood in 1859 broke part of the Ohio River levee, arming upriver rivals with the image of the settlement as a quagmire. But the town repaired its levee and continued to grow.[5]

The middle decades also witnessed the establishment of new communities, as investors continued to see towns on the lower river as a means of making money. Most achieved at best slim success—about fifty residents. Joppa in Massac County, for example, had been a ferry crossing since 1821. In 1871, two men who owned much of the land in the vicinity laid out a town named for a site in the eastern Mediterranean whence cedars of Lebanon were exported. One of them built a sawmill and a gristmill. Incorporation and post office were secured three years later.[6]

At roughly the same time, Rosiclare and Shetlerville were formed in Illinois's Hardin County. About 1866, German Catholic farmer and entrepreneur Joseph Shetler purchased land at what was once known as Parkinson's Landing and platted the town of Shetlerville. The community, which reached its peak of prosperity in the early 1880s, was noted for the potatoes that it shipped—35,000 bushels in 1881 alone. It also sent hogs and cattle to market, mostly in Evansville. "Tater Joe" Shetler's town also exported rock from nearby quarries. Much of Paducah's cobblestone apparently came from there. Shetler's death in 1895 and the depletion of the soil that resulted from poor farming methods led to the demise of his settlement. Four miles upriver, Rosiclare was more successful. Named for Rose and Clare, daughters of its founder, it was incorporated in the early 1870s. Rosiclare exported timber, especially railroad ties, as well as livestock, grain, and potatoes. Later it exported fluorspar, mined nearby. In 1880, 368 people lived there.[7]

One of the more intriguing new settlements was Brooklyn, adjoining Metropolis and across from Paducah. Evoking the relationship of New York City's East River neighbor, its founders obtained a legislative charter in the 1850s. The creators laid out the town, placed a value on the land, deposited a plat with the auditor of state, and established private financing through a wildcat bank, which issued notes based on the declared value of the lots. Not surprisingly, the plat showed a nonexistent railroad line under construction, and the owners valued the lots at four hundred dollars. Offices of the bank were opened in Brooklyn and Metropolis. Problems with creditors dogged the founders, and Brooklyn's "boom" was brief. Only in the late 1880s, with the coming of the Illinois Central, did it recover.[8]

Near the mouth of the Ohio, railroad building led to the formation of two other communities. East Cairo, Kentucky, was formed in 1873 as a result of the Illinois Central's securing control of two southern lines and its building track thence to the Ohio, just upriver from Cairo. Packet boats connected the two sites until 1889, when a railroad bridge was completed between Cairo and the Kentucky shore, thus benefiting Wickliffe, just below the mouth of the Ohio on the Mississippi. Consequently, the rough little village, so often plagued by floods, went into decline. Nearby Holloway, merely a place-name on today's maps, marks East Cairo's approximate site.[9]

Just upriver was Mound City, in Pulaski County. Site of a steamboat landing for a number of years, it was laid out as a town in 1854 by Moses Rawlings, one of the state's internal improvements commissioners. Despite protests from the Cairo City Property interests, Rawlings secured a charter for a three-mile spur connecting with the Illinois Central that was completed in 1856. Cincinnati entrepreneurs formed the Emporium Real Estate and Manufacturing Company, which laid out "Emporium City" adjoining Rawlings's plat. Investors paid several hundred thousand dollars for town lots before the Panic of 1857 quashed their dreams. "Emporium City" was renamed "Stump City." In that same year, Mound City was incorporated. The company's chief legacy was a marine railway and steamboat way that when reopened in 1859 formed the basis for Mound City's early growth. In 1861, the county seat was moved there, thus guaranteeing Caledonia's demise. The Civil War helped the local economy even more, as Mound City became a major ship construction center. Wood products—shingles, hubs and spokes, and staves for barrels—became Mound City's chief products after the war. Unfortunately, few companies had staying power. The termination of the federal lease of the boat facility in 1869 was especially damaging. In 1880, Mound City was less than a quarter the size of Cairo.[10]

The most successful and distinctive of the communities created at midcentury was Tell City, in Perry County, Indiana. Tell City was the work of the Swiss Colonization Society, organized at Cincinnati in November 1856 to locate a site for homesteads for German-Swiss citizens that would permit the formation of a diverse economy where there was no slavery. Location was another consideration: founders wanted it to be at least one hundred miles below the Falls and to have easy summer access to the southern market. For each share of twenty dollars the investor was to receive two plots of land. About eight thousand people purchased shares. The Society also assisted colonists in establishing homes and businesses. The Hawesville area was rejected because of slavery. The Society selected instead 4,154 acres of hills and forests just downriver and across the Ohio from the Hancock County seat. Nearly 400 town blocks and 7,600 residential lots were laid out. Planners anticipated that they could accommodate a population of 90,000 in the place named for the Swiss hero. The first payment for land—$20,000 in gold—was made at Cannelton in April 1858.

The first settlers arrived in March 1858. By the end of June there were 986 residents and 120 houses. Each stockholder was to build a brick or frame dwelling worth at least $125, and each settler was provided enough building material for a one-story, two-room home, to be paid for in three yearly installments. The Colonization Society held its second annual convention there in September and voted to lend money to those proposing worthy business or manufacturing enterprises. The Society also arranged for a wharfboat. Most of the early economy, not surprisingly, was based on wood. The first shingle factory received a subsidy to begin operations, as did the Tell City Furniture Company. By the Civil War, Tell City also had a flour mill, a steam sawmill, a plow and wagon factory, a distillery, and a newspaper—established in 1859, the year that the town was incorporated. The Society shared with the town board the cost of erecting a public school and paying its teachers. Despite its rapid growth (2,112 by 1880), Tell City's homogeneous, enterprising, and thrifty citizens did not need to build a jail until the 1870s.

By 1860, Tell City, like other larger communities, was served by three types of steamboats—for example, long-range craft connecting Cincinnati and New Orleans, shorter-range packet lines between Evansville and Louisville, and local boats that ran between, say, Owensboro and Evansville. Wharfmasters were agents of the Adams Express Company who could send money and valuables and serve as commission agents dealing in foodstuffs and other local products. Within two weeks in 1866, Tell City shipped 300,000 pounds of castings from its foundry, 4,800 chairs, 200 barrels of flour, 20,000 feet of flooring and doors, 240 cotton presses, hundreds of pieces of furniture, 60 half-barrels of beer, and other local products. By 1880, Tell City possessed a national bank (1872), a number of businesses, five hotels, and nineteen factories, eleven of which processed wood. The most distinctive was the Tell City Chair Company, formed in 1865 by the Chair Makers Union of Tell City. For over thirty years its most popular product was Pattern #1, a double-cane split bottom chair. About 12,000 were made annually. After the frames were completed at the factory, they were taken into town, where women and children attached the cane seats they had woven in their homes. This practice continued into the 1930s.[11]

Tell City's early history demonstrated the persistence of considerable variety in the formation, growth, and development of settlements. By the late 1870s, about thirty had been incorporated as towns. Led by Evansville in 1847, some gained even greater prestige and local control by securing city charters—Paducah (1856), Shawneetown (1861), Mount Vernon (1865), Owensboro (1866), and Henderson (1867). Cairo also secured a city charter in the 1860s. That Cannelton (1859), Cairo (1859), and Mound City (1861) became county seats was another sign of expansion.

Demography offered additional testimony to communities' varied textures and shapes. Race, ethnicity, and state of birth were both symptom and cause, as they reflected economic, social, cultural, and political elements in community development and also contributed to that process. To be sure, upper southerners continued to be predominant on both sides of the river. But patterns were changing.

Emancipation was the most dramatic change. The Ohio was no longer a dividing line between Kentucky and free soil. By March 1865, federal government officials estimated that 71 percent of Kentucky's slaves, valued at $107.5 million in 1860, had been freed. The Thirteenth Amendment, ratified in December 1865 despite Kentucky's opposition, ended the peculiar institution altogether. A new era began in which Kentucky blacks experienced freedom and second-class citizenship, harassment and violence, exclusion from many publicly supported institutions, and *de jure* separation. But they could achieve a modicum of the American dream in the Bluegrass State.[12]

Slavery had been an especially important element in Daviess, Henderson, and Union Counties, major producers of tobacco. By 1860, slave populations had grown to 40 percent in Henderson and exceeded 20 percent, the state average, in four other counties. Among towns for which federal census data was provided, the *number* of slaves in Owensboro and Paducah increased.

Slave population in Kentucky, however, declined steadily before 1860, the result of its exporting an ever-increasing number to the labor-hungry Deep South. River towns, especially Henderson and Paducah, were important shipping points for that human cargo, estimated at 3,400 annually in the 1850s. Kentucky's manumission laws were also somewhat less restrictive than those of other southern states. And the Commonwealth's long border with free soil territory contributed to a steady flow of runaway slaves, despite stringent federal legislation passed in 1850. The Ohio crossing remained especially appealing downriver from Owensboro, where the distance between the river and areas with high proportions of slaves in southern Kentucky and western Tennessee grew progressively shorter.[13]

Slavery, nonetheless, contributed heavily to the character of Kentucky's river settlements. One indirect effect was to drive potential newcomers to other settlements north of the river, where free labor prevailed. Slaves stemmed and packed tobacco, worked on the docks and riverboats, and provided many other forms of menial labor. Wealthy slave owners exerted a disproportionate influence in local affairs. The 1860 slave schedules of Kentucky disclosed that A.B. Barret of Henderson owned 140 slaves in Henderson County and 74 in Daviess. Senator Archibald Dixon had 124 in Henderson County and another 20 in Union. Nearly 80 planters in Henderson County and 24 planters in Union County owned 20 or more slaves. Hawesville's most powerful citizen, R.C. Beauchamp, employed 25 slaves. These numbers conceal even greater concentrations of power through ownership via other family members and associates. For example, Henderson County's Henry and Robert Dixon owned 56 slaves, and John and Henry Dixon owned 33. Jackson McClain owned 73 and was guardian of another 26. Slaves were merely numbered and categorized by age and gender. Only those reaching the age of 100—e.g., John Holloway's Lety Mumford—were named in the records.[14]

The ending of slavery beginning in 1862 not only produced a dramatic shift in the legal status of blacks in Kentucky but also led to important changes in their movements in the river counties. In the 1860s and the 1870s, blacks poured out of all Kentucky counties except McCracken, and by 1880 the black population exceeded 20 percent only in Henderson and McCracken Counties. Six counties had less than 14 percent (see table 2 in Appendix 1).

Where did the former slaves go? Many moved across the river. The black populations of all but one of Illinois's Ohio counties increased, especially in Alexander and Pulaski. In Indiana, six of the seven river counties gained black residents, especially Spencer, Vanderburgh, and Posey.

Former slaves usually could not afford to buy farmland and equipment. So they settled in the towns and cities, where jobs in domestic and public service and unskilled labor were plentiful. In Evansville, the proportion of blacks rose to 6.5 percent in 1870 and to 9 percent in 1880, or nearly 3,000 residents. Cairo's black population by 1880 was 37.2 percent, about 3,350 people.

Blacks remaining in Kentucky were drawn to its river towns, where employment awaited. The black populations of Henderson, Owensboro, and Paducah increased by 1880 to 37.7, 25.1, and 32.2 percent, respectively.[15] River towns also offered safety for freedmen. Paducah was the regional headquarters of the Union army, which in the spring and summer of 1865 served as a magnet for freedmen seeking food, clothing, and protection. Paducah was also designated one of three centers for the Freedmen's Bureau in the state. During its brief existence (to 1868), the Bureau assisted in a number of ways, including financing a brick school building and underwriting teachers' salaries. Bureau agents helped ex-slaves to locate family members and to legalize their marriages. They also provided modest coal rations and a dispensary. Hundreds flocked to Paducah in 1867-68 when roving gangs threatened the lives of rural blacks and of white farmers who attempted to rent or lease land to blacks. Henderson and Owensboro attracted rural blacks for similar reasons. Henderson, for instance, was headquarters in 1867 for a Freedmen's Bureau sub-district, and Owensboro had a Bureau dispensary for five months in 1868.

Kentucky was now a free state, and opportunities for blacks—however proscribed—were greater than ever. Although increasingly dominated by de jure segregation, Kentucky's villages and towns were separated from those across the river, where racially separate school systems and residential areas existed by custom and regulation. Yankees and Middle Staters in Indiana and Illinois, however, did help to mitigate the virulent racism of the region, and economic opportunity was relatively greater on the north shore. That attracted black newcomers especially to Evansville, Rockport, Cairo, Mound City, and Metropolis.[16]

Most European immigrants settled on the northern shore of the river and in rural as well as urban settings. In 1850, foreigners were especially evident in Vanderburgh County, where 35.6 percent of the populace had been born abroad, primarily in what would become Germany and to a lesser extent in England and Ireland. Spencer County was a distant second with 11.2 percent. Foreign-born residents accounted for more than 5 percent in three other Indiana counties and in McCracken County in 1850. None of Illinois's counties exceeded that level (see table 3 in Appendix 1).

By 1860, Vanderburgh County's foreign-born population rose to 40.7 percent. The creation of Tell City and the growth of the Cannelton Cotton Mill brought many European immigrants to Perry County. Four Illinois counties experienced modest increases, and Alexander and Pulaski grew even faster.

The flow of European newcomers accelerated after the Civil War. Urbanization and industrialization forced millions to seek a new start elsewhere. Otto von Bismarck's *Kulturkampf* against German Catholics and Socialists, along with the effects of industrialization on artisans and farmers, made the postwar an especially active period of German emigration. By 1880, Germany was the birthplace of most immigrants in five of Illinois's river counties, all of Indiana's, and eight of Kentucky's. Immigrants found employment in American distilleries, breweries, foundries, flour and gristmills, planing and sawmills, and furniture factories. They also developed religious, benevolent, fraternal, and cultural organizations in the villages and towns.[17]

Kentucky had proportionately the least number of inhabitants born outside its borders. In 1880, more than three-quarters of the people in all but one lower Ohio River county were native Kentuckians. In half of these counties, the ratio was about nine in ten. The lowest percentage was to be found, not surprisingly, in McCracken County. By contrast, in Illinois, the county with the highest percentage of native Illinoisans was Pope, with about 71 percent. Only about half of the residents of Alexander, Massac, and Pulaski Counties, the most urbanized, were natives. In Indiana, the proportion of state-born inhabitants was close to Kentucky's only in Crawford and Harrison. Vanderburgh was lowest, with about 57 percent. In all but one of the river counties in Illinois and Indiana, Kentucky was the second most frequently listed state of birth, but in no case did the ratio exceed one in ten.[18]

In addition to demographic continuity, most places experienced little change in appearance. The Ohio was their main street, and businesses and residences were intermingled on or near the riverfront. In the larger places, however, the urban landscape was being transfigured. Race, ethnicity, and economic growth contributed to that.

Blacks, for example, found themselves in sections of the larger communities variously labeled "Baptisttown" or "Smoketown." Germans in Evansville were concentrated on the West Side, largely in what had been Lamasco and Independence, as well as places farther west with such colorful labels as "Babytown" (presumably because of the fecundity of German women).

Evansville achieved "radial center" status—that is, economic development made activities specialized and reach extensive. Jon Teaford's study of midwestern cities has shown that over the years they tended to become manufacturing hubs rather than entrepots for their hinterlands. Land was increasingly segmented into commercial, industrial, and residential use. In Evansville, factories in 1880 were concentrated on Main Street and along Pigeon Creek. Commercial activities were focused on the "original Evansville" plat of 1817. Workers' residences were erected near factories. Residential neighborhoods for the well-to-do were increasingly beyond walking distance to work, thanks to the development of mass transit—the first being mule- and horse-drawn railcars in Evansville in 1867. This layout reflected ethnic influences: while well-to-do English-speaking inhabitants resided upriver of Main Street along the Ohio, their German counterparts clustered on First and Wabash Avenues to the west. German workers also resided outside of the original Evansville plat and its additions. John A. Reitz was a notable exception, as his grand "second empire" dwelling at First and Chestnut Streets, completed in 1871, was located in the enclave of English Protestant Evansville.[19]

Towns and cities north of the Ohio differed in one significant way from those to the south. As David Goldfield has shown, southern urban communities may have grown, but they remained extensions of their staple-crop, biracial contexts and thus little different in form and function from before 1850.[20]

7 ～

People and Products

The Ohio peaked as a force in regional and national development in the 1850s, when the steamboat was in its golden age and new railroads complemented river trade. Steamboats accelerated population flow, town development, commerce, manufacturing, and river improvements. Because of speed, direction of travel, and lower passenger and freight costs, farmers and merchants benefited enormously.

Lower Ohio valley railroads, as elsewhere, owed their growth to the river. The Evansville and Illinois, the New Orleans and Ohio, and the Illinois Central extended the trading regions of river communities. Railroads offered reliable year-round travel and freed merchants from the need to build up stocks for the one or two times a year that navigation was possible and freight rates were low. They accelerated trade to the early railheads and contributed to the increase in riverborne coal traffic, as the demand for that fuel for locomotives increased. Railroads threatened river transport by opening up interior markets, cutting off river towns from their trading hinterlands, encouraging bridge building, and carrying passengers and freight rapidly and cheaply year-round. Such challenges, however, were not apparent to most immediately before the Civil War. The first bridge on the lower Ohio came only in 1885, and only three were in place by 1917.[1]

The 1860s were a time of transition for the Ohio River valley. "River intelligence" sections in the newspapers remained a vital source of information for local merchants. Railroads were constructed after regional specialization and westward migration were under way, and they accelerated the rate of change. Because of the large scale of rail operations, regular service was required. Unlike the highly competitive steamboat lines owned and operated by a few people, railroads were governed by corporations. They also offered through service over long distances and sought to enhance that via connections with other lines or even steam packets. Steamboats retained an advantage in capacity and cost of service.[2]

Another important reason for economic transformation was manufacturing, much of it reliant on steam power. Processing regional resources, factories introduced early forms of mass production based on semiskilled wage labor and governed by an emerging managerial class assisted by clerical workers. Their growth accelerated the exploitation of local coal and timber, encouraged the expansion and improvement of transportation services, attracted newcomers, and sharply expanded the size and the reach of river towns. The divergent tendencies in the economies on either side of the river were generally strengthened during the Civil War. By the late 1860s the pace of industrialization had quickened. With that came a more coherent regional system in which some communities, especially Cairo, Evansville, and Paducah, were dominant, and local activities were part of a growing national market. With that also came increased sensitivity to the national business cycle, as events following the Panic of 1873 disclosed.[3]

Despite an ample supply of raw materials, a break in north-south transportation for its settlements, a central location, and an absence of external competition, the lower Ohio failed in the 1850s to produce a city like Chicago. Several of its towns, however, experienced striking rates of growth and development.[4]

Most places were so small and unorganized that they were not listed in the 1850 census or in subsequent enumerations. They offered good landings for steamboats, some basic mercantile services for area residents and travelers, and ferry crossings. A few milled grain, packed pork, or sawed timber for river trade. Even with plats and name changes, most remained quiet, unhurried clusters of buildings in clearings along an increasingly busy river. As late as the 1920s, many lacked access to the interior by good roads, let alone railroads. Local boats and some packets offered river connections to the larger world.[5]

Despite its fuel yard, small boat-building facility, lumber processing and shipping, and hotel services, for example, West Point at the mouth of the Salt River continued to be a little entrepot overshadowed by powerful Louisville. In addition to its landing, Leavenworth had a skiff shop, a chair factory, a pork packer, and a wagon works. Its modest growth, however, may have explained its founder's departure in 1850. These locales were more fortunate than some, which suffered from flooding (Shawneetown), fire (Lewisport), or competition from neighboring settlements (Smithland and Shawneetown). None of these small places had rail connections by 1860, and only Shawneetown and West Point secured them before 1880.[6]

The services offered by one Union County settlement, Caseyville, were typical. A prosperous decade allowed Caseyville to grow to 623 residents in 1860, about the same size as Brandenburg (618) and smaller than Shawneetown (914) and Uniontown (1,046). Caseyville possessed a hotel, three general stores, two dry goods stores, two grain dealers, an agricultural implements dealer, a hardware store, two blacksmith shops, two livery stables, a grocery, three shoe stores, a flour mill, a cooperage, a tobacco stemmery, a bank, and a newspaper. Merchants' records from September 1854 to February 1855 show the varied commodities that merchants imported. On Saturday, January 27, 1855, for instance, Dr. J. Collins purchased thirty-nine gallons of molasses; William Tutor bought ninety-three pounds of one-inch-round iron, twenty-two pounds of square iron, and thirty-two pounds of steel; and William Ryle spent $16.10 on forty-six yards of carpeting.

Similar transactions undoubtedly occurred in the valley's general stores for decades thereafter. They were part of the life cycle of nearby Uniontown, which with about 1,000 residents on the eve of the Civil War was experiencing unprecedented prosperity. With a newly created bank and two hotels, it was clearly a serious rival of Caseyville and other smaller river towns.[7]

These smaller communities remained vital elements in the daily lives of nearby residents, but they were increasingly caught up in regional and national commerce. In an age of ever more sophisticated technology, however, they continued to use flatboats to transport goods to market. On January 7 and 16, 1873, the *Evansville Daily Journal* offered reports from Memphis newspapers about the vast amounts of potatoes, onions, cabbage, apples, corn, and other produce sent by such places as Tobinsport, Rockport, Elizabethtown, Grandview, Leavenworth, and Cave-in-Rock. Grandview's exports for 1872 amounted to 3,134 hogsheads of tobacco, 2,800 tons of hay, 11,300 bushels of potatoes, 16,900 bushels of corn, 40,000 pounds of pork, and 100,000 pounds of bacon and lard. All of that was shipped by flatboat.

Daily rhythms were punctuated by the bells and whistles of steamboats that also signified settlements' links with distant places. Business careers often began in villages and were advanced in the region's larger towns, as was so well illustrated by the case of John Gilbert, Golconda entrepreneur and mayor, developer of the Evansville, Cairo, and Paducah packet, and prominent Evansville banker. Developing trade and communications patterns made communities on the eastern and western fringes of the lower Ohio increasingly dependent on markets in Louisville, Cincinnati, St. Louis, Chicago, and Memphis. Most of the interior, dominated by Evansville, was developed with little economic threat from those cities. The entire region was part of a national urban market, however, whether it acknowledged that or not.[8]

Urban rivalries emerged as the larger communities sought to weaken Evansville's influence. As Owensboro grew, its leaders portrayed Evansville as its chief rival, and because of proposed railroad ventures they saw Henderson as Evansville's partner in crime. Adding to the frustration, no long-distance Owensboro-owned packet service existed, and the Louisville and Evansville

Packet Company was Owensboro's chief river carrier. (Probably a major consequence was the city's failure to develop wholesale trade.) Hence a rare
Owensboro "first"—such as arc lighting in the early 1880s—prompted great
celebration. Similarly, Paducah merchants saw Evansville's commercial forays
up the Cumberland River as threats.[9]

Evansville's elite, by contrast, set their sights elsewhere. In the 1850s they
focused on upriver New Albany, the largest Indiana city, which possessed rail
connections and a seemingly solid industrial base. By the mid-1860s, however,
attention shifted to Louisville, as Evansville's reach waxed and New Albany's
waned. Louisville's new railroad bridge was a special cause of concern. By the
early 1870s, the *Evansville Daily Journal* articulated this growing sense of regional predominance, speaking of the city as the center of a "Tri-State" region
and aggressively seeking to ward off threats to it. In early 1873, for instance, it
showed that rail freight rates were no higher through Evansville to Nashville
than they were through St. Louis—a clear challenge to the Mississippi River
city's claims that it was a gateway to the South.[10]

Advancements in manufacturing contributed heavily to these changes, although patterns of growth were uneven. On the eve of the Civil War, fifteen
counties had manufacturing establishments, but only six had more than fifty.
Posey and Vanderburgh led all counties. Capitalization exceeded $700,000 in
just four counties—Vanderburgh, Breckinridge, Henderson, and Union. The
number of workers was over four hundred in only five counties: Gallatin, Perry,
Henderson, Union, and Vanderburgh. Wages surpassed $245,000 in only
Vanderburgh and Union. In value of products, only Vanderburgh, Henderson,
and Union exceeded a million dollars.

In 1880, however, agriculture remained the basis of much of the region's
economy. Corn was generally king, although tobacco was more important to
farmers in five Kentucky counties and second in significance in the others. The
value of agricultural products exceeded that of manufactured goods in 1880 in
all but seven counties. The relationship was most unbalanced in Kentucky. Even
Posey County, which experienced a substantial amount of manufacturing
growth between 1860 and 1880, still produced $400,000 more in farm prod-
ucts than in manufactured goods.

Although growth was uneven and agriculture central to most countries,
manufacturing in a number of counties grew sharply by 1880. With 357 establishments, Vanderburgh led the other coutries by far, but the others—Posey,
Spencer, and Daviess—had more than 100. Vanderburgh was the first in capitalization (14.8 million), workers (3,778), wages ($1.4 million). In other coun-
ties, capitalization exceeded a million dollars only in Daviess. The number of
manufacturing workers stood at over 500 in Massac, Perry, Daviess, and

McCracken Counties. Wages exceeded $250,000 in Daviess and McCracken, and value of products was above $1 million in Alexander, Perry, Daviess, and McCracken.[11]

Manufacturing in these communities mirrored the resources of the region and the importance of the river. Riverboat repair and construction were central to the industrial base of Metropolis, Mound City, West Point, and Paducah. Many of the early foundries and machine shops in Evansville and Paducah manufactured parts, including steam engines, for rivercraft. The growing demand for coal as a fuel in industries, steamboats, locomotives, and homes encouraged commercial mining near Cloverport, Hawesville, Cannelton, Newburgh, Evansville, Uniontown, and Caseyville, and all of these places shipped coal by 1860. One of the most distinctive features of Cloverport's antebellum economy was a distillery that produced illuminating oil from cannel coal. Local demand for coal led William Kersteman to construct Bodiam Mine, a deep-shaft facility on the west side that eventually extended under Evansville streets and the Ohio. It was opened in April 1855.[12]

The centrality of farm, mineral, and forest resources in the manufacturing sector was evident, for example, in Metropolis, which had several cooperages and sawmills. Cannelton, Indiana, manufactured not only cheap cotton cloth but also pottery, tile, and bricks. Troy was noted for its pottery and pork packing, and upriver rival Rome had a distillery as well as a pork facility. Leavenworth also packed pork. Across the river, a number of communities had tobacco stemmeries.[13]

Manufacturing was concentrated in Henderson, Owensboro, Paducah, and Evansville. Henderson's six tobacco stemmeries packed and shipped dark tobacco to distant markets. Owensboro packed tobacco, distilled whiskey, and made wood products. Although dark tobacco was also its leading product, Paducah had a more diverse economy: flour milling, lumber, and leather. Its shipyard was its leading employer.[14]

Evansville's manufacturing on the eve of the Civil War was in a class by itself. The Wabash and Erie Canal had been completed in 1853; rail connections to Vincennes and Terre Haute had been opened in 1853-54; Evansville had been established as a port of entry in 1856; and the city had annexed Lamasco the following year. Despite the national financial crisis of 1857, Evansville survived with relatively few businesses failing.

Locals also aggressively sought to protect Evansville's interests. The creation of the Evansville Board of Trade in 1857 was a milestone. Thereafter wholesale and commission houses proliferated, and annual reports from the board documented progress and challenged businesses to even greater achievements. By value, dry goods, mostly shipped south, topped the list of exports.

Liquor and hardware and iron came in second and third. Evansville was also an important market for New Orleans sugar, coffee, and molasses.[15]

Vigorous commercial expansion spurred local manufacturing. As elsewhere, in 1860, the manufacture of goods from farm and forest accounted for half of the city's manufacturing establishments. Green River tobacco, for instance, was both processed and shipped. The Fendrich brothers opened a cigar factory in 1856, and tobacco production nearly doubled by 1860. The manufacture of new wood products, such as furniture, carriages, and cigar boxes, commenced in the 1850s, as did the manufacturing of agricultural implements, boilers, edge tools, stoves, tobacco and cotton presses, and sheet iron. In value and number of workers, metals and alloys led Evansville manufacturing in 1859, followed by wood and food products.

All of this had a synergistic quality. Local factories were located near Pigeon Creek, the canal, and the new railroad. Some industries created others: pork processing led to Decker and Kramer's manufacture of soap, lard, and candles. The Kratz and Heilman Foundry began building steam engines early in 1854. These changes were also reflected in the workforce, which included about 1,000 wage earners in 1860. An enterprising German immigrant, Jeremiah Behm, established Evansville Business College in 1853 to meet the city's clerical needs, and manufacturing stimulated local mining and coal imports from upriver.[16]

In the larger towns, the interrelationship of manufacturing, commercial reach, and transportation improvements was increasingly evident. By 1858, rail connections to Cairo had encouraged the expansion of packet service to St. Louis and New Orleans. Paducah had mail packet service up the Cumberland and Tennessee Rivers. Henderson had had packet connections with Louisville since 1843.

Lacking a serious rival, Evansville gained substantial southern trade, especially after the Evansville and Crawfordsville Railroad was completed. This line offered unequaled access to northern and eastern markets for products of the Wabash, White, and Green River valleys.

By the early 1850s, Evansville merchants were taking increasing advantage of up- and downriver connections afforded by the Louisville and Henderson packet. They also had five daily steamers making round trips to Bowling Green, on the Green, two hundred river miles away. Daily service to Paducah and Cairo was established in 1857, and in 1858 lines connected Evansville with Louisville and New Orleans. By the 1860s, daily or at least weekly service was provided as far away as the upper Cumberland and Tennessee and the Wabash north of Terre Haute. The editor of the *Journal* sought, with limited success, to convince merchants in Cairo and Paducah, as well as those up the Tennessee and Cumberland, that shipping to Evansville by water, and thence by rail to eastern markets, would save at least a day and considerable cost over using Louisville as a shipping point.

Although the manufactures of the smaller communities along the lower Ohio—for example, the pottery of Troy—were purchased locally or perhaps as far away as Louisville, the goods of larger places were sent to more distant markets. Tobacco packed in Henderson, for instance, was shipped to British and European markets. Reflecting these shifts, the *Evansville Daily Journal* by the time of the Civil War included market news about New York and New Orleans as well as Cincinnati and St. Louis (but none for Chicago, whence substantial trade connections did not exist until about 1900).[17]

As rising manufacturing centers such as Tell City sought to enhance their markets, their business and civic leaders increasingly emphasized transportation improvements. Some were more successful than others, as their leaders' breadth of vision, level of political skill, and financial resources allowed them to outstrip their competitors. The Wabash and Erie Canal, the initial panacea for Evansville and its hinterlands, was revitalized after financial restructuring in 1847, but it offered only a short-term economic stimulus, and by 1860 it was widely recognized as a failure. Poor construction, unreliable water supplies, and rail competition contributed to that. Stockholders consistently lost money because tolls and water rents did not cover operating expenses. Although it was a valuable local channel of trade for coal, coffee, and flour as far north as Covington, the canal was seen as an inefficient thoroughfare. Residents of Evansville demanded that the great ditch through the city, a source of odor and disease, be filled up. Along stretches of the canal northeast of Terre Haute, however, the waterway continued to be of commercial benefit for years. It had stimulated agriculture, given rise to towns, and encouraged population growth.[18]

Steamboat connections on the Ohio in the 1850s offered a much more promising future, but here, too, experiences varied. Most communities were not directly served by large, long-range craft. Their size was an obstacle to that. But their passing by—like the *Rockport Democrat's* notice on February 16, 1861, of the new *Louisville*—was nevertheless an important event for these locales.[19]

Evansville, by contrast, was third only to Pittsburgh and Cincinnati in the number of steamboats registered in 1860—sixty-four—but it was still a secondary river town compared to these cities. Completion of its wharf dramatically expanded service in the 1850s. That, in turn, led to the construction of a new wharfboat in 1857 that had an engine for lowering and hoisting freight and an office for the telegraph company. The city wharfmaster reported in August that 199 steamboats had landed in the previous month, whereas 11 had passed by or only briefly docked.[20]

Other towns and villages were likely stops for such large packets as John

Gilbert's, as well as smaller craft connecting places such as Owensboro and
Cannelton. Typical was Golconda, Illinois—roughly midway between Cairo
and Evansville. Served by Gilbert's Tennessee and Ohio River Transportation
Company, which ran the Evansville, Paducah, and Cairo service, the town enjoyed daily connections except on Sunday. Boats left Evansville at 4:30 P.M. and
reached Cairo at noon the next day. The 200-mile journey upriver from Cairo
began at 6 P.M. and stopped for the night at Paducah, fifty miles distant, and
resumed at 9:30 A.M., arriving in Evansville at 6 A.M. the next day. Along the
way, the packet stopped at most villages and towns. Travelers from Golconda
could connect for rail or distant packet service at Evansville, Paducah, and Cairo.
In addition, Golconda residents enjoyed twice-weekly stops, each way, by the
Memphis-Cincinnati packet, as well as frequent service by the *J.S. Hopkins* and
other craft of the Evansville-Paducah line. Most of this service continued into
the 1880s. Beginning at the turn of the century, smaller gasoline-powered boats
connected Golconda and Shawneetown, fifty miles upriver.[21]

These rivercraft, like the "Grey Eagle Line" of the Louisville and Henderson
Packet Company, furnished other benefits. They brought news, entertainment,
and travelers. The *Evansville Daily Journal* of December 7, 1860, reported that
the *Floating Palace* would dock at the city wharf later that day. On board were
alleged warriors, braves, and squaws of four nations who would perform dances
and ceremonies. Steamboats also offered firsthand examples of the latest innovations, whether steam engines or electric lighting. Data for cities such as
Cairo and Evansville reinforce the notion that the "palmy days" of the steamboat extended into the early 1880s, and in smaller settlements local craft provided essential links to market and communications many years beyond that.
Charles Ambler has described the river as a "poor man's highway" because subsequent rail and road connections often bypassed rich bottomlands and hinterlands. Riverboats also held government mail contracts through the turn of
the century.[22]

River improvements on the Ohio and its tributaries had been sought since
the 1820s, but the niggardliness of Congress in appropriating funds for that
and other western projects led to the creation of a convention at Evansville in
1850 which passed a series of resolutions requesting federal aid for the West.
Chaired by entrepreneur John Law, a founder of Lamasco, the gathering called
for land grants to promote all legitimate aspects of internal improvement—
for instance, a geological survey, a national school of mines, metallurgy, agriculture, and experimentation on the capacity and safety of steamboat boilers.
Evansville took the lead again in 1857 in promoting a study by a civil engineer
who proposed a series of reservoirs on the Ohio that would guarantee a year-
round six-foot channel. No federal expenditure "could be more national in

character—none whose benefit would be diffused over so broad a surface of the Union or in which so large a number of the population would participate."[23]

As markets and manufactures expanded, leaders in Evansville intensified their calls for river improvements. Increased connections to the Cumberland and Tennessee River valleys after the Civil War underscored the importance of better river conditions. On September 21, 1868, the Evansville City Council appointed one of its members as delegate to a Cincinnati meeting on the 23rd with a congressional delegation concerned with the Ohio and Mississippi Rivers. Possibly the first of its kind after the war, the meeting apparently helped lay the foundation for a convention in late February 1872, planned by the Cincinnati Chamber of Commerce, to which each city over 25,000 could send five delegates. Insisting that the development of coal and iron was about to propel the river to an even greater level of activity, the planning committee envisioned the convention as a means of securing congressional aid. Similar meetings, often held in Cincinnati, occurred thereafter. Evansville always participated; until 1895, in fact, it was the only lower Ohio city large enough to do so.[24]

The most dramatic transportation improvement was the railroad. The earliest and most extensive system in this region was the Illinois Central, which tied Cairo to Chicago by rail and to Memphis and New Orleans by water. Cairo's rapid growth was directly attributable to this, although it underscored the river town's dependence on the Chicago market. At about the same time, Evansville's rail ties extended almost 110 miles north of the Ohio. Aided by county and city stock subscriptions, the Evansville and Illinois, originally chartered to connect with the Ohio and Mississippi line at Olney, Illinois, was rechartered in 1850 and renamed the Evansville and Crawfordsville in 1853 to take advantages of new east-west trunk lines. Hence the line connected Evansville with northern and eastern markets, resulting in spectacular commercial growth.[25]

The Evansville and Crawfordsville's success helped seal the Wabash and Erie Canal's denouement. Led by president John Ingle Jr.'s vision, drive, and political clout, the line also opened through packet service to Paducah and Cairo in September 1857, and its officers began planning a Henderson to Nashville railroad. The town of Henderson subscribed $100,000 in railroad stock in 1859, and by 1861 five miles of track had been laid. The war delayed further construction until 1866. By 1869 the line extended to Madisonville.

The Evansville and Crawfordsville also spawned efforts by former director Willard Carpenter and others to construct the Evansville, Indianapolis, and Cleveland, to be known as the "Straight Line." Carpenter, who owned a substantial amount of land along the proposed route, near the canal, declared that Ingle and others had violated their original charge by constructing the E&C

through Vincennes rather than to the northeast. A brighter future lay with a road to the capital city. The Straight Line was chartered in April 1853. Carpenter became vice president and general manager. By 1856, grading was completed to Washington, Indiana, about fifty-five miles away. Opposition was strong (for example, civic leaders in Vincennes and Terre Haute sought to derail it, and a venomous article in the *American Railway Journal* was probably written by Ingle), but Carpenter secured $100,000 in bonds from the Evansville City Council. Although not yet delivered, this represented almost half of the funding that he offered English investors in early 1857 when he traveled there to secure iron rails. Ingle's campaign against him prompted the new city council in July 1857 to renege on delivery of the bonds. Wrote Edmund Starling: "Carpenter's credit was shattered; he was unable to gain public confidence, and the principal result . . . was the loss of money that had been subscribed, much of it by small property owners."[26]

Paducah's business and civic leaders also obtained rail connections in the 1850s. Unable to secure the northern terminus of the Mobile and Ohio, Paducah leaders obtained legislative permission to subscribe public funds to build a railroad to the southwest that would connect with that line. In July 1853, citizens approved a stock subscription. (Eventually Paducah would subscribe $200,000 and the county $100,000.) West Point graduate and civil engineer Lloyd "Dick" Tilghman was hired to supervise construction. The first rail service commenced in July 1854. By 1860 the New Orleans and Ohio Railroad extended to Troy, Tennessee, on the Mobile and Ohio.[27]

The only other line of consequence for the lower Ohio River lay on its eastern boundary. The Louisville and Nashville Railroad, begun in 1851 and operational by 1854, allowed Louisville to extend its domination of north-south trade, ending whatever dreams West Point might have had of regional hegemony. Ironically, a West Pointer—Samuel Beale Thomas, who married founder James Young's daughter—contributed to that. Thomas moved to county seat Elizabethtown in 1844 to expand his stage line. One of the first subscribers to L&N stock, he secured a clause in its charter requiring all north-south trains to stop in Elizabethtown. After the Civil War, Thomas expanded his fortune by investing in the Elizabethtown and Paducah Railroad.[28]

Civil conflict effectively ended all railroad construction in the region, but between 1865 and 1880 new lines were constructed, all oriented to the Ohio and many with public stock subscriptions. Most construction occurred just before the Panic of 1873.

Cairo enjoyed considerable railroad expansion in this period. The most significant was the Illinois Central's acquisition of a terminus on the Kentucky shore at East Cairo in 1873. By acquiring several lines thence to New Orleans and standardizing the track gauge to the south, the company secured fast service between Chicago and the Crescent City through Cairo. The local elite, led by S.S. Taylor and William Halliday, invested heavily in two additional lines—the Cairo and St. Louis and the Cairo and Vincennes. Aided by a city stock subscription of $200,000, the former was begun in 1865. Completed ten years later, it went bankrupt and was sold in 1881 to a new line, which also had financial difficulties and was forced to lease it to the Mobile and Ohio. The latter, begun in 1867, was completed in late 1872, also with assistance of public funds. Like the Cairo and St. Louis, it suffered from the effects of the Panic of 1873 and eventually became part of the "Big Four" Railroad. The Cairo Short Line and two lines on the Missouri shore to St. Louis were also built. In short, Cairo was the nexus of an extensive north-south rail network, but its city treasury would be in poor shape for decades because of the failures of several of its railroad investments.[29]

The only other Illinois community on the Ohio to obtain rail connections before the mid-1880s was Shawneetown, which doubled in size between 1860 and 1880. In 1869, Gallatin County subscribed $100,000 to the St. Louis and South Eastern Railway, and track was laid to the northwest through Equality and Eldorado, connecting with the main line between Evansville and St. Louis. In the early 1880s, the road became part of the L&N. The city also invested $200,000 in the stock of the Ohio and Mississippi, gaining access to the major east-west trunk line about fifty miles to the north.[30]

Having the only north-south antebellum railroad between Cairo and Louisville, Evansville businessmen had the opportunity to substantially extend their rail ties. Public subscriptions were usually obtained. As elsewhere, some projects suffered from the Panic of 1873. The most important was the Evansville, Henderson, and Nashville Railroad, for which new ground was broken in 1866. Encouraged by Ingle, Reitz, and Heilman, the city granted $20,000 in bonds in 1867. The city of Henderson also subscribed $300,000 (but county government, unsurprisingly, refused). By March 1871, the line extended about ninety miles to the south and connected with the L&N trunk between Louisville and Memphis. Through service to Nashville was initiated. A packet line also linked this line to the Evansville and Crawfordsville. Cars could be placed on the boats, and their loads did not have to be broken up. Combined with the standard gauge on both roads, the new service seriously threatened the trading interests of Louisville merchants in western Kentucky, prompting them to build a new railroad between Elizabethtown and Paducah, later part of the Illinois Central, which was completed in 1874.

In 1869, Evansville and Vanderburgh County also purchased stock in the Evansville, Carmi, and Paducah, which gave the city rail ties to the northwest.

Two years later, this line was consolidated with the St. Louis and South Eastern, which also obtained control of the EH&N in 1872. The St. Louis and South Eastern, in turn, lost its Kentucky, Tennessee, and Indiana-Illinois divisions to the L&N in 1881, which only four years later completed a railroad bridge between the western environs of Evansville and Henderson. This was the first bridge constructed downriver from Louisville. The L&N, which changed all of its track to standard gauge, also built a rail yard in Howell, on Evansville's southwest side. In the process, Evansville and Henderson obtained reliable and efficient rail links to the west and south and became a vital part of one of the nation's strongest rail carriers. In the process, Evansville and Henderson became river crossings—no longer just river towns.[31]

The Evansville and Crawfordsville continued to extend north, reaching Danville, Illinois, in July 1869. Nearly 150 additional miles had been constructed by 1873. Four years later, the company was renamed the Evansville and Terre Haute, and in 1882 it opened a spacious new terminal in Evansville. Of all the lines in the region—excluding the Illinois Central and L&N—it was the most financially sound.[32]

In 1869, the Lake Erie, Evansville, and Southwestern was organized, which by 1873 connected Evansville to Boonville, seventeen miles to the east. Bypassed in the process, Newburgh suffered a major blow to its hopes for urban greatness because the company chose not to construct the road along the Ohio. That contributed heavily to Newburgh's subsequent economic stagnation.[33]

The "Straight Line" continued to be a subject of public debate. Arguments for public subscription to the road resumed in 1866. Backers declared New Albany saw the line as a great threat to its hinterlands and the Louisville, New Albany, and St. Louis Railroad they were building, but they failed to sway local leadership. Ingle's public attacks in the summer of 1869 helped prevent it from obtaining crucial county bonds. Portions of the road were built to the northeast, but a direct route to Indianapolis never materialized.[34]

Some of Indiana's other Ohio communities also secured rail lines. In 1868-69, for instance, the city of Mount Vernon and Posey County pledged $300,000 to purchase stock in the Mount Vernon and Grayville. The road was only partly completed, however, and city and county debts had to be settled at about a sixth of that amount and new bonds issued. In 1870, the city also invested $110,000 in the Evansville, Carmi, and Paducah. Several townships in Posey County also purchased stock in the Peoria, Decatur, and Evansville and in the Evansville and Terre Haute. As of the early 1880s, as a consequence, Posey County had fifty miles of rails. Mount Vernon had connections to the Wabash on the west and northwest and to Evansville on the east.[35]

Relatively little rail construction occurred elsewhere. In 1869, Rockport subscribed public monies in the Rockport and North Central, the aim of which was a connection with the Ohio and Mississippi to the north. That goal was not realized by 1880, as it extended only to the Dubois County seat of Jasper. An extension of the line, later known as the Cincinnati, Rockport, and Southwestern, was laid to French Lick in Orange County. Rivalries between Cannelton and Tell City contributed to Perry County's refusal to approve public funding of railroad construction until the 1880s. Rail links to the Ohio did not come until 1887, when a line between Lincoln City (Spencer County) and Cannelton, through Tell City, commenced service.[36]

In Crawford and Harrison Counties, Ohio River settlements were bypassed by an east-west railroad in their northern tier. In late 1869, Crawford County voted, by a narrow margin, to purchase stock in the Louisville, Albany, and St. Louis—but only when the road was completed! Ohio River townships consistently voted against the measure. Eventually this road, after reorganization, stretched east to west across northern Crawford County, connecting it with Corydon, New Albany, and Louisville. No rail links were ever constructed to the south in either county. With the exception of Fredonia and Ohio Township, river townships in Crawford County approved a measure in 1884 pledging public subscription to a road uniting New Albany, Corydon, Leavenworth, and Cannelton (bypassing Fredonia, as Leavenworth was wont to do). The line was not built.[37]

On the Kentucky shore, important initiatives occurred. In 1874, Paducah became the terminus of two lines—the approximately 112-mile-long Memphis, Paducah, and Northern, which extended the antebellum New Orleans and Ohio road to Memphis, and the 185-mile-long Elizabethtown and Paducah. Later known as the Louisville, Paducah, and Southwestern, eventually part of the Illinois Central, this gave Paducah a direct link with Louisville, 225 miles to the east. Owensboro's achievements were modest: the Owensboro and Russellville, which by 1880 extended thirty-five miles south, connecting with the Elizabethtown and Paducah line, but not to Russellville, on the L&N trunk.

Public revenues supported many of these initiatives. Public subscription for the Elizabethtown and Paducah as of 1871, when the state's auditor made his first report on public indebtedness for railroads, amounted to $400,000, most of which came, however, from Louisville. The New Orleans and Ohio had received $300,000—a third from McCracken County and the rest from Paducah. The Owensboro and Russellville's public commitments totaled nearly $950,000, of which Daviess County contributed $307,000 and Owensboro $75,000. Caseyville subscribed $60,000 to the ill-fated Shawneetown and Madisonville Railroad, which was supposed to connect it with the coal mines at De Koven and the southeast. The experiences of Owensboro and Paducah

were somewhat unusual, as Kentucky counties, dominated by frugal rural interests, tended to vote against railroad subscriptions.[38]

The securing of public funds manifested the vision, the tenacity, and the
political skill of local business and civic elites. Louisville's merchants after the
Civil War identified their customers as the many county storekeepers to the
south and west, not the large planters who had once visited the city annually
for supplies and credit. Drummers—many of them veterans of the Confederate army—were hired to develop and maintain ties to these local merchants.
Warding off threats to these hinterlands from Cincinnati and Evansville required public funding for improved rail connections that cut, for instance, into
the latter's inroads via the Evansville, Henderson, and Nashville. Hence the
E&P was built. Owensboro businessmen were led by Thomas S. Pettit, editor
of the *Owensboro Monitor,* who asserted in March 1866 that a rail line would
make their community "the first city in point of population and wealth between Louisville and Memphis. . . . Every advantage of location and general
adaptedness is in our favor."[39]

Despite the dynamic leadership of Pettit, who had been an active Unionist
but also an opponent of President Lincoln who had been deported behind
Confederate lines, the railroad met strong opposition from some steamboat
operators, who feared competition to their freight, passenger, and mail business. Pettit and his supporters secured a legislative charter for the Owensboro
and Russellville in early 1867 and raised a county subscription shortly thereafter. A scarcity of capital forced it to stop at the E&P crossing in 1872. A new
corporation, the Owensboro and Nashville, emerged from the bankrupt O&R
in 1877 and offered improved passenger service and extended trackage to the
riverfront. Despite additional funding through city bonds, the road was not
extended south. Only in late 1883, several years after the L&N gained control,
did the line reach the L&N trunk line. The O&N terminated at Adairville, Kentucky, near the Tennessee line. Pressure from Owensboro leaders, especially
Pettit, helped complete the road. Probably more important was the L&N's new
president, Milton H. Smith, who thought that the O&N, combined with the
building of a bridge at Henderson, would give his company control of north-
south commerce on the lower Ohio.[40]

North-south rail connections to the interior had enormous implications,
enhancing commercial and communications ties and accelerating postwar exploitation of agricultural and natural resources in the hinterlands. Coal was
an increasingly important commodity, and developers of rail lines were not
infrequently associated with the expansion of the commercial mining in the
Illinois Basin after the war. Especially important was John Ingle and Company,
formed in 1866, which gained control of Evansville's Bodiam Mine as well as

fields extending to Terre Haute and Clay County. Evansville benefited especially from this rail expansion, as its hinterland steadily grew. The experience of Vickery Brothers, a wholesale grocery firm in Evansville, illustrated that: in 1867 and 1873 the firm established branches in Vincennes and Rockport.[41]

The enhancement of Evansville's position brought it into rivalry especially with Louisville for southern trade, and accordingly its newspapers brimmed with stories of potential threats, information on distant markets, and lengthy columns on river and railroad "intelligence." The promotion of speedy, reliable transportation was essential for readers up and down the river who were part of the city's expanding reach. In August 1868, the *Daily Journal* began to list, in one table, the schedules of local rail, steamboat, and stage lines. By the spring of 1870, local merchants boasted of the city's ability to reach Terre Haute in a little over five hours and thence to Indianapolis in another two and a half hours. Going south, the rail packet left for Henderson at 3 P.M. and the EH&N train could be in Madisonville by 7:10.[42]

Over time, railroads would contribute to the relative decline of the rivers as channels of trade. They dispersed commerce and population from the Ohio outward, giving rise to cities such as Indianapolis, which enjoyed superb rail connections and a central site. They also contributed to economic specialization and urbanization in the interior. An anonymous writer in the *Evansville Daily Journal*—probably John Ingle—insisted in 1867 that the future lay with improved rail ties, as the Ohio offered limited opportunities for future expansion. River communities that became rail crossings, such as Cincinnati and Evansville, grew after 1865.[43]

As of 1880, however, the Ohio remained integral to its settlements. All of the railroads were oriented to it, and bridges lay in the future. Since most villages and towns, moreover, had not even a rail link, the river remained the primary tie to the larger world. The argument that the growth of the railroads explains everything that happened after 1850 remains simplistic.

An overlooked but obvious influence on the lower Ohio was the Civil War. In some cases, after initial disruptions, war enhanced banking, commerce, and some industry. This was especially evident in Evansville. In others, particularly on the Kentucky side, it retarded growth, and in some places war accelerated long-term decline. In Cairo and Mound City, it created illusory progress. In general, it strengthened economic divergence.[44]

The strategic importance of the region made it the scene of a number of wartime skirmishes—such as the "Battle" of Uniontown of October 1864. Union forces occupied several Kentucky communities and established bases at Cairo and Mound City. Confederate troops also laid claim to river communities, even briefly occupying Newburgh and several Harrison County villages. Strategically vital were the Cumberland and the Tennessee, which extended deeply into the South, and north-south rail connections at Cairo, Paducah, and Evansville. The Mobile and Ohio ended at Columbus, Kentucky, just south of the river's mouth, and the Louisville and Nashville dominated the eastern edge of the area. The region was also rich in livestock as well as grain, tobacco, lumber, and coal. Some of its cities were emerging manufacturing and commercial centers. At the midriff of the Transappalachian West, it not only separated two labor systems but also encompassed hundreds of thousands of citizens whose loyalties to the Union were strong and thousands more whose ties were qualified by support or sympathy for the newly formed Confederacy. President Lincoln, a son of the three states that constituted the lower Ohio, understood its strategic importance. Significantly, the river did not divide the Union.[45]

Kentucky's villages, towns, and cities experienced the greatest amount of short-term disruption, but long-term effects varied. Confederate sympathies were potent in slave-rich Pennyroyal and Purchase counties, even after the legislature declared Unionist ties late in the summer of 1861. Although more young men served in the Union army than in the Confederate, and prominent conservatives such as Senator Archibald Dixon of Henderson supported the Union, the mandate of loyalty oaths, the suspension of civil liberties, the removal of elected officials, the Union troops' depredation of property, and most of all the emancipation of slaves and the use of black troops encouraged activities against Lincoln's administration. Nevertheless, beginning with initial Union occupation of Paducah in September 1861, as a base for General Ulysses S. Grant to launch assaults up the Cumberland and the Tennessee, Kentucky's lower Ohio border was a Union stronghold.

In an economic sense, on the one hand, the war initially devastated some river communities, as Union forces gained control of the river and occupied such towns as Smithland, Henderson, Owensboro, and Hawesville. Beginning in April 1862, for instance, vessels were prevented from stopping at any settlement between Paducah and Memphis. Ferries were closed except at Henderson and Smithland, where federals controlled both sides of the river. In the process, normal business activities were disrupted. In addition, labor shortages, especially after emancipation, led to a decline in the value of land and livestock, and the freeing of thousands of slaves represented a major financial blow. The war also retarded reforms in the state's educational system. On the other hand, after initial trade embargoes, federal authorities turned to licensing of trade, provided that loyalty oaths had been taken, and by early 1864 they had rescinded trade restrictions. Demands for foodstuffs, livestock, and other supplies by Union forces and communities in the North and East more than made up for losses in southern markets. Contraband trade with the Confederacy also persisted.[46]

A cursory examination of several towns and cities below Louisville vividly illustrates this. The war interrupted work on a private twelve-mile turnpike connecting Cloverport and Hardinsburg commenced in May 1861. Construction resumed in 1868. The turnpike operated for forty-three years before being turned over to the county. (U.S. 60 generally follows this.) Plundering of public and private property by troops of both sides was common. In West Point, Confederate guerrillas wrecked and stole property of alleged Unionists in June 1864, and the Crittenden County courthouse was burned by Confederate soldiers in January 1865. Union soldiers severely damaged the Meade County courthouse in Brandenburg. Although some West Point businesses enjoyed prosperous trade after the summer of 1863, most were robbed by men from both sides. The old St. Felix Hotel in Smithland was used by Union troops as a headquarters and hostelry. Pro-rebel locals recall that livestock and grain were looted and that fine homes and churches stabled horses. Federal troops apparently destroyed two coal mines in Union County and took many citizens into custody, releasing them only after they had sworn oaths of loyalty at Henderson or Paducah. All of Caseyville's residents were taken as hostages to Evansville in late July 1862, to ensure that the United States government would be compensated for extensive damages to federal property by rebel raiders. In the summer of 1864 Hoosier "Home Guards, rough and general riff-raff and scum" from Mount Vernon, helped themselves to whiskey, salt, and other necessities in Uniontown and surrounding settlements.[47]

The experiences of larger settlements were similar. Hawesville in Hancock County was occupied by federal troops during most of the war. That some of the last occupiers were blacks aroused considerable ire there, as elsewhere. Despite initial efforts pledging cooperation with sister community Cannelton, gradually the half-mile gap, ordinarily served by a ferry, became a virtual Berlin Wall of separation. Prominent merchants and planters, led by Robert C. Beauchamp, openly expressed pro-Confederate sympathies; in June 1864, Beauchamp was accused of conspiring to obstruct the recruitment of black troops. About a month later, a Union gunboat bombarded the town in retaliation for a guerilla raid on mines south of town that supplied fuel for Union gunboats. The mines did not reopen until the 1880s.[48]

The threat of war led the Henderson City Council in December 1860 to suspend work on the Henderson-Nashville Railroad and on all city improvements not under contract. The first history of Henderson, written by Edmund L. Starling, son of a prominent planter, described the time as a scourge: intermittent occupation by federal troops, beginning in October 1861; raids and fire damage by rebel guerrillas; the loss of horses and slaves and the enlistment of about two hundred black men from the county in the Union army in August 1864; damage to the courthouse, occupied by black troops; and removal of most dry goods establishments to Evansville or Louisville. An easy-going, cultured society, Starling declared, gave way to hard relations in which friendships were strained and destroyed. One Henderson resident, visiting Evansville in May 1864 in search of a runaway slave, bitterly noted the contrast. Entering a recruiting office for black troops, he declared it was "established upon our borders for the purpose of stealing from us our property." Evansville, he added, "seems to be in a prosperous condition and one would hardly think [war was] devastating the country."[49]

In Owensboro, which supported the Constitution Union Party in 1860, such leaders as Tom Pettit gravitated to the Democratic Party, if not to outright support of the Confederacy. Confederate guerilla raids, however, disrupted business and destroyed property on three occasions. In January 1865, for instance, the courthouse was burned in retaliation for the billeting of black troops there.[50]

Paducah was the first Kentucky city below Louisville to receive federal troops. Locals generally viewed them as occupiers, not defenders, despite General Grant's prescient and courageous act, which historians generally credit with keeping the Cumberland, the Tennessee, and the lower Ohio in federal hands. The city was subjected to Confederate raids throughout the war, notably in 1864, when General Nathan Bedford Forrest twice attempted to capture the city. Trade regulations by Union and Confederate governments severely disrupted prewar business practices. The latter, for instance, prevented cotton, tobacco, rice, molasses, and other goods from being shipped through Paducah to the north. Union gunboats blocked trade south of Evansville unless federal forces were in control of the territory, and hence hay, corn, pork, salt, and whiskey were not supposed to reach Confederate areas. Despite the lifting of controls in 1864, anti-Union sentiment grew with the enlistment of black troops and the disenchantment most felt with the caliber of Union occupation, especially during the summer of 1864.[51]

The presence of Union troops, the vicissitudes of war, the recruitment of black troops, and eventually universal emancipation disrupted the staple-crop economy, freed thousands of workers to make a new start, and altered forever the relationship between whites and blacks in the Kentucky economy. Thousands of displaced refugees flooded towns and cities on both sides of the river, crowding into sordid, makeshift "colored sections" and finding employment at the lowest end of the job spectrum. Service in the Union army was an option, and the larger communities were recruiting centers for black regiments beginning in early 1863. As episodes in Hawesville and Owensboro in 1864 illustrated, these men faced harassment from hostile whites. Their families and other black newcomers braved a marginal existence. The Freedmen's Bureau, created in March 1865, offered limited and short-lived support. Ultimately these were free people, not slave laborers, and they showed their commitment to basic American values by legalizing their marriages, by seeking to purchase property, and by establishing churches, mutual aid societies, and schools.

Emancipation laid the groundwork for perhaps the most basic long-term economic change: the replacement of slave labor with sharecropping and renting of farm land by freed people and, in a region low in cash and credit, by the introduction of the crop lien system. Regulators, however, threatened the lives and meager property of rural Kentucky blacks, especially in 1865 and 1866. And a form of slavery persisted into the early twentieth century with county courts' defining orphans as bound apprentices until age twenty-one.[52]

If population is an index, the Civil War appears to have enhanced the economies of several Kentucky settlements—especially Owensboro and Paducah, and to a lesser extent Henderson (see tables 4 and 5)—while contributing to short-term decline in Hawesville, Brandenburg, Cloverport, and Stephensport and doing nothing to retard the prewar slippage of Caseyville and Smithland. Agriculture and manufacturing records also suggest uneven impact. By 1880, value of farms and products was higher than even in Daviess, Henderson, and Union Counties. Farms were worth two to three times as much there as in the other counties, as were the value of products. (These counties also compared favorably to Harrison, Posey, Vanderburgh, Spencer, and Warrick Counties, the most profitable farming counties on the north shore.) McCracken and Daviess Counties witnessed steady expansion of the number of manufacturing establishments, capital, and value of products. This occurred after the war, however. Substantial declines, by contrast, occurred in Crittenden, Hancock, Henderson, and Union Counties. Wartime damage and disruption contributed to that. Manufacturing remained focused on tobacco, whiskey, flour, and cornmeal.[53]

Disrupting channels of trade, the war generally jeopardized the commercial position of Kentucky's river towns and cities. Long-term effects, though, were mixed. Beginning with the war-induced commercial and industrial vacuum in the Tennessee and Cumberland valleys, for example, Evansville merchants moved aggressively up the Cumberland and the Tennessee, where Evansville manufactured goods found an open market. Postwar Paducah merchants and manufacturers saw their hinterlands seriously threatened, as did merchants in Louisville. Cooperation with Nashville merchants in attempting to ward off Evansville commerce was one Paducah strategy, and another for both Paducah and Louisville was the construction of an east-west rail connection.

Kentucky's government, which was low-tax and laissez-faire before the war, became dominated by "Brigadiers"—former Confederate generals and their legislative allies who blocked school reform, highway and railroad construction, and other modernizing projects. Whether a symptom or a cause of the state's economic directions before 1880, this undoubtedly persuaded immigrants to seek their fortunes elsewhere.[54]

But some river communities had aggressive business and civic leaders, such as Tom Pettit of Owensboro, who dreamed of a "New South" of industry and urban growth. By 1880, his city boasted seventeen tobacco factories, three flour mills, three planing mills, a tobacco exchange warehouse, two planing mills, a hub and spoke factory, six cooperages, a tannery, a brewery, a foundry, four banks, five hotels—and seventeen distilleries, most formed in about 1880. In the meantime, Henderson obtained a national bank in the fall of 1865. Two years later, its leaders received a new city charter, which allowed them to improve the wharf and streets as well as to subscribe public funds for the railroad to Nashville. The charter became a model for similar revisions in Newport, Owensboro, and Paducah. Henderson's growing ties to Evansville gave it a north-shore ally, which none of the other lower river towns in Kentucky possessed. The mainstay of the economy, though, remained tobacco. Under postwar mayors, especially Meyer Weil, Paducah reduced its city debt, improved its infrastructure, and improved rail links. The city's manufactures remained sawed lumber, flour and cornmeal, riverboats, and tobacco.[55]

The war also had short- and long-term effects on Illinois and Indiana communities. The disruption of river trade seemed ominous—illustrated by the capture and impounding of the Evansville packet *Samuel Orr* at Paducah in the summer of 1861 and by the closing of Kentucky and Mississippi River ports. Cannelton's coal mines and its cotton mill were operating at a greatly reduced level by September 1861, and by the summer of 1863 the mill—dependent on southern cotton—was silent. The closing of the river was a blessing for railroads to the north, especially those connecting Chicago with Indianapolis. Carrying troops and freight proved to be quite lucrative for these lines. Another important change occurred in the previously seasonal pork business. The loss of the New Orleans market accelerated pork packing in Chicago and Indianapolis. Instead of being slaughtered in river settlements, hogs were sent north by rail, as the use of ice permitted summer packing. Chicago replaced Cincinnati as the nation's leading pork packer, and Indianapolis became the state leader. Pork and other meat products were sent by rail to the Union army as well as to customers to the north and east.[56]

The war was, however, an economic boon for some communities. The absolute control that Union gunboats gained over the lower Ohio, combined with the reopening of the Mississippi River, led to not only a resumption but an expansion of commerce. Access to cotton and demand for cloth for the army revived Cannelton's mill, and the demand for grain and meat by the army and markets to the north and east kept mills and packing establishments operating in places as small as Derby and Rome in Perry County. Wartime demands for fuel and manufactured goods also benefited a number of river communities. The growing need for petroleum, for instance, led to the opening of wells in Perry, Harrison, and Crawford Counties in the winter of 1864-65.[57]

Evansville, Cairo, and Mound City enjoyed especially good economic times after initial discomfort. Evansville's prosperity resulted from the demand for grain, meat, timber, and fuel, the enlargement of its wholesale market to the south, and the expansion of manufacturing. Before the war Evansville was a major corn market for shipment south. Although the war disrupted this pattern in 1861 and 1862, its long-term impact was beneficial, and the level of southern commerce rose. The government established a quartermaster's department in the city, demand for food from the north and east increased, and river trade rose sharply as Confederate threats to the region were removed. Evansville's corn exports became the greatest of any city on the Ohio—a ninefold increase by 1867, and four times the total of second-place Louisville. Exports of wheat, hay, and salt grew substantially. Coal was also in great demand for use by gunboats and locomotives, and production at the Bodiam Mine rose sharply. Steamboat arrivals documented the expansion of commerce: from 1,493 in 1861 to 2,572 in 1865, leveling off at about 2,100 in 1866 and 1867. Boats in government service accounted for 60 percent in 1863 but only 13 percent in 1865.[58]

Southern markets were the primary destination of most goods. That was not new, but the scope was. Beginning about 1863, wholesale trade in hardware, groceries, dry goods, and drugs expanded well into the upper Cumberland and Tennessee valleys. The formation in that year of the wholesale hardware firm Boetticher and Kellogg, which did business until 1995, vividly illustrated this. The most successful of these merchants was Charles Viele, a wholesale grocer from 1840 until his retirement in 1870. Wartime disruptions to the south also expanded Evansville's tobacco market and created a cotton market. The number of hogsheads of tobacco exported more than doubled by 1873, when the level began to decline. The market for this tobacco shifted from New Orleans to New York City and the Northeast. Cotton—also shipped by rail to New York and the Northeast—was a new export, rising from nothing in 1861 to 41,000 bales in 1867. Only a fraction was used locally in manufacturing, mostly by the Evansville Cotton Manufacturing Company, organized in October 1866.[59]

In the heyday of steamboat travel, freight was piled up along four blocks of the riverfront—bales of cotton, hogsheads of tobacco, coops of chickens, as well as furniture, boxes of groceries and dry goods, and other commodities, mostly destined for the South. So heavy was traffic that many boats took on barges, one on either side, to carry additional freight.

Evansville's manufactured goods were also in great demand. In 1859, the city had about ninety manufacturing firms. The leaders were foundries, producing hardware, stoves, steam engines, and plows. One of the most successful was William Heilman's City Foundry on Pine Street. Of the newer firms, one of the most significant was the Henry F. Blount Plow Works, successor to firms created by James Urie and John H. Roelker. Processors of wood—planing and sawmills, cooperages, agricultural implements, furniture, and the like—were second. Third was food processing, especially flour. According to Evansville's most astute economic historian, Bernard Schockel, the city's takeoff from economic adolescence to maturity occurred near the end of the war. Between 1859 and 1869, the number of manufacturers rose to 281, and wage earners tripled in number. In value of products in 1867, flour led city manufactures, followed by beer, machinery, lumber, and furniture. The city's total production was valued at $3.2 million. Furniture makers led the city in number of workers, with 231. Ranked by a variety of criteria, metals and alloys, top-ranked in 1859, slipped to second behind wood products in 1869, and food products came in third. Those ranks remained unchanged until the 1930s.[60]

The experiences of Cairo and Mound City, both wartime boom towns, were different. In each, appearances were misleading. In the spring of 1861, Cairo had a population of about 2,200, five or six hotels, a bank, a modest array of retail and wholesale stores and business agents, and a few small mills. A strategic site, it was also only one of four places in the nation (the others being Louisville, Cincinnati, and Alexandria) where rail service from the north connected with rail service in the slave states. Not surprisingly, General Grant made Cairo his command headquarters and staging area for assaults up the Cumberland and Tennessee Rivers. Within four years, Cairo's population reached almost 8,600. The "ragged, straggling town sunk in a basin" had become an armed camp: the site of Fort Defiance; a training area for Union troops; a haven for refugees from the Confederacy; a vast supply depot and a fitting-out site for warships; and the base for Flag Officer Andrew Foote's western flotilla. Cairo in 1865 flaunted a number of new factories, five newspapers, and ten churches. The war, declared one editor in early 1862, "has given to Cairo the notoriety that must ever serve to continue the condition in business affairs now firmly inaugurated."[61]

Cairo's importance was reinforced by federal activity eight miles upriver, at Mound City. The federal government leased Hambleton's marine ways there, using them to manufacture and repair gunboats and to convert commercial craft into instruments of war. About 1,500 men—many rivermen whose jobs had been lost due to the suspension of trade—were hired to work at Mound City, and they produced over one hundred gunboats, twenty-two transports, thirty-two mortar boats, and eight tugs. Notable among these were three of the "pook turtle" gunboats built by James B. Eads. The place eventually sheltered the country's largest fresh-water fleet, the Mississippi Squadron, and a marine hospital. Nearby, the government also constructed a national cemetery, where 5,555 men were buried.[62]

According to Philip Paludan, the Union "won the Civil War because in the largest sense it had the economic, institutional, intellectual, and social resources for victory." But it also "had the knowledge to organize those resources and employ them in the war." Congress created long-term economic strength through a national currency, a national banking system, and a national tax structure, railroad subsidies, higher tariffs, and land grant schools.[63] According to Allan Nevins, this created "heady new impulses of vast extent and irresistible force." The expansion of the rail and telegraph networks, the development of mineral resources, the growing confidence in the nation's political system, the expansion of capital, the demand for labor, and the "irresistible process of urbanization [were] creating a new America."[64]

As in Kentucky, some north bank places were less affected by these changes than others, as many remained fairly isolated and were increasingly dependent on market forces that were created well beyond their borders. Much of the area remained heavily rural and agricultural, as the pace of urbanization and industrialization was not as marked as in the upper portions of the Old Northwest. The Panic of 1873 and the six-year depression that followed, which was unprecedented in its severity, also shaped the course of community life.

As indicated by population patterns described in the preceding chapter, the Civil War produced or accelerated unevenness—growth, stagnation, or decline. It did not fundamentally alter the economies of most communities. Agriculture remained essential to most counties. Posey County produced $1.9 million worth of commodities in 1880, and its farms were valued at almost $6.9 million. Vanderburgh was second in the region in farm valuation and fourth overall in value of products. Gallatin, Harrison, Spencer, and Warrick Counties also had impressive totals. The poorest counties were Hardin, Massac, Crawford, and Perry.

Levels and types of manufacturing were also disparate. Between 1860 and 1880 Vanderburgh County's industrial expansion was unparalleled. By 1880 the number of establishments and workers was approximately four times that of 1860, and capitalization was seven times greater. Value of manufactured goods rose to more than five times 1860's level. Alexander County finished a distant second. In the amount of capital, the number of workers, and the amount of wages, Vanderburgh County's totals for 1880 exceeded the other twelve Illinois and Indiana counties combined. Impressive rates of growth in the amount of manufacturing capital and number of workers were also registered in Alexander, Massac, and Pulaski Counties in Illinois and Perry and Posey Counties in Indiana. By contrast, manufacturing was an insignificant aspect of the economies of Gallatin, Hardin, and Pope Counties in Illinois and of Crawford in Indiana.[65]

For example, Rockport, Spencer County seat, had ten manufacturers, according to the 1879 *Illustrated Historical Atlas of Spencer County.* Four were wagon makers, and three ran flour and grist mills. The others made harnesses and saddles, tiles, and furniture. Most of the businessmen, however, were engaged in commerce. Rockport also had ten teachers, seven attorneys, and two banks. Cannelton's mill, by contrast, experienced a decline in production during the 1870s depression, but production of cotton sheeting and "Hoosier Jeans" brought employment up to 330 by 1886.[66]

Evansville produced a much greater variety and higher quality of goods than Cairo, which was limited to flour and gristmill products, sawed lumber, and barrels. Foundry and machine shop products as well as furniture were important Evansville manufactures, along with flour and sawed lumber. By contrast, Owensboro's top manufactures were stemmed tobacco, liquor, bricks and tile, and sawed lumber. Paducah's leading industries were lumber mills, ship building and repair, and foundries and machine shops.[67]

Despite the hopes of Cairo's promoters that its dreams of becoming a metropolis were about to be realized, its postwar development was stunted. Population continued to grow steadily, reaching its peak of about 15,000 by 1920. Its size and its rate of growth, however, were much lower than most cities in the Midwest. Many of the newcomers were former slaves, whose living conditions and occupational opportunities were abysmal. Residential persistence was brief, as people moved north to start over. Judging from the low number of immigrants, moreover, Cairo was not perceived as a place with substantial opportunity.

The loss of wartime spending, it was hoped, would not damage Cairo's continued development. Prosperity seemed guaranteed by steady population growth and other indices of maturation—an association of commerce in 1867, a customs house in 1867, a philharmonic society in 1868, a tobacco market in 1869, a railroad to Vincennes in 1872 and one to St. Louis in 1875, a women's club and library association in 1877, and visits by Ulysses S. Grant and Jefferson Davis in 1881. The *Chicago Tribune* reported in 1870 that local leaders were actively recruiting business at home and abroad. On the other hand, rapid growth during the war, failure to build sewers until 1866, continued flooding and seepage, and the reputation as an unhealthful, lewd, and bloody town damaged the community's image, despite the favorable impressions conveyed by Mark Twain in *Life on the Mississippi* (1883). The city's earliest historian in 1883, William Henry Perrin, attributed these ills, in fact, to the Civil War, which allegedly disrupted the city's development, created temporary wealth, and diverted trade and riches to Chicago while Cairo enjoyed its superficial prosperity. According to Arthur C. Cole, Cairo became a "city of blasted hopes."[68]

Cairo's problems had many causes. Cairo began to grow, belatedly, as the steamboat trade was beginning to decline. Even before the war, east-west rail traffic to the north was feeding Chicago while starving Cairo. The northerly flow of passengers and freight on the Illinois Central reinforced Chicago's dynamic development. Between 1869 and 1886, the value of Cairo's commerce dropped by about two-thirds. Cairo's industrial base, moreover, was limited, and its hinterland was small and sparsely populated. The city enjoyed central location, was a break in trade, and became a rail center after the Civil War. However, freight was transferred through, and not originated in, Cairo. The building of a river bridge in the late 1880s, making Cairo a river crossing, weakened an already fragile economy. And Cairo's image problem did not help.[69]

Perrin noted another problem. No city, he declared, had such natural favors and so much suffering, a fate rooted in a "South Sea Bubble, [created] by a visionary, impracticable, bankrupt corporation," which had allowed thousands of thrifty citizens to become shiftless and unreliable. Absentee trustees showed little or no interest in Cairo's development, and title disputes with city government persisted into the 1890s. The Illinois Central was also an absentee owner, concerned mainly that levees protect its property. Cairo's "remarkable natural wealth of advantages" was "among its misfortunes," as it tempted the schemer and the unscrupulous. Great cities, Perrin asserted, should not be constructed by corporations, backed by stringent, powerful legislation. Slander about its healthfulness did not help, either.

Why wasn't Cairo a great industrial center? Some of that, Perrin insisted, could be remedied by good advertising. But the town had other problems— flooding and inadequate levees, cheap wooden housing, and frequent fires. City authorities' failure to grade and fill major pieces of land retarded construction. Perrin returned to a theme many had offered before: that the city's worst times were behind it. Increased wholesale trade, a stable population, a library, several bookstores, a customs house, and other facilities would anchor Cairo's future development. "Think of it!" Perrin exulted. "Here are over thirty thousand tributary shores upon our navigable rivers and already eight railroads, with Cairo as the terminus of a majority of them."[70]

Cairo's arrested development was more dramatic than the experiences of other settlements. Nonetheless, no place along Illinois's Ohio banks approached its level of achievement.

Shawneetown secured rail connections before the 1870s, but little else. It published its first city directory in 1872, which disclosed an extremely small manufacturing base. Mound City's growth ended in the late 1860s when the federal government stopped leasing the marine ways, and the hospital was taken over by the Daughters of Charity. Although experiencing modest growth and securing its first bank in 1869, Metropolis—like other communities—depended on the exports of agricultural goods and wood products, notably barrel staves, spokes, and hubs. Hardin and Pope Counties' settlements became known for shipping livestock, timber products, and potatoes to customers elsewhere. Most of these places continued to be plagued by seasonal flooding. All remained heavily dependent on river commerce. Many were increasingly tied to markets in Evansville. So were most of Indiana's river towns. Mount Vernon's first business directory and history, published in 1882, was crowded with advertisements for business and professional services in Evansville.[71]

Evansville's postwar economic development was, by regional and state measurements, remarkable. By 1880 the city was well on its way to becoming a "radial center" for a region extending seventy-five to one hundred miles in all directions.[72] In their first postwar report to the Internal Revenue Assessor, Evansville wholesale dealers with at least $50,000 in annual sales indicated that they did a combined $10,852,000 in business for the year ending in July 1866. Mackey and Company's dry goods, with slightly over $1 million in sales, led all of them. In 1869, the *Daily Journal* observed that Evansville stoves and castings were being sold all over the South and Southwest, its horse collars in Cincinnati, St. Louis, and other urban centers, its portable engines, sawmills, boilers, and steam engines in the entire South and as far west as Kansas and Nebraska, its cooperage products in Louisiana sugar plantations and in packing plants in Arkansas and Texas, and its cotton sheetings all over the South and West. Location, abundant coal, inexpensive and reliable labor, and rail and river connections, boasted the editor, made the city the best place for a profitable investment of capital.[73]

Such promotional efforts were neither idle nor naive. By regional standards, the scale of postwar expansion was staggering. Two of the most important figures in this process were immigrants. William Heilman, the city's leading iron manufacturer, was a major investor in railroads and banks, the city gas works, the new city street railway, and—with Charles Viele and others—the Evansville Cotton Mill. His income for the year ending July 1865 was nearly $50,000—second highest in the city behind Viele's $50,441. Heilman's wealth was demonstrated by his palatial new home, built on First Avenue in 1868-69. John A. Reitz built one of the largest hardwood lumber manufacturers in the nation, established a foundry, organized several banks, and invested heavily in railroads. He also built a grand new home—in 1871, unlike Heilman, on the edge of the wealthy English-speaking residential district.[74]

Such fortunes testified to the commercial opportunities and cheap, ample coal that had changed the city's economy by the early 1880s. Over three hundred manufacturing firms produced goods worth over $8 million. Only Kratz and Heilman's foundry had exceeded $100,000 in 1860; in 1880, sixteen firms did. This increased productivity reflected greater mechanization. Capital investment grew 600 percent, to $4.7 million. Only seven firms had more than $25,000 capital in 1860; in 1880, forty-seven did. The workforce also expanded to over 3,600. An increasing number, moreover, were employed by the largest firms. By 1880, more than 40 percent worked for the fourteen firms that employed at least fifty workers, and 64.8 percent worked in shops employing twenty-five or more.

Many things explained this transformation, often encouraged by the union of merchant and manufacturer to create new firms. The most striking example was the formation of the Evansville Cotton Manufacturing Company in October 1866 by Heilman, Viele, David J. Mackey, and others. In 1875, the firm's expansion led to the opening of a new structure at the base of the hill in which Ingle's mine operated. The factory had four hundred looms and 14,000 spindles and employed three hundred—mostly women and children—making it the largest factory below the Falls.[75]

Fortunes were made—and sometimes lost—in the process. Although some, including furniture maker Cyrus Armstrong, grew wealthy in one venture, others did so by a combination of profit seeking and vision in several. John Ingle's investments in coal as well as banking and rails offered one example, as did Samuel Orr's in iron making, banking, and railroads.

Near the top was David Mackey, born in Evansville in 1833, who made a fortune in wholesale dry goods before branching out into coal mines, manufacturing, and railroads. He was a director of the city's largest bank, the Evansville (later Old) National (as were Bayard, Orr, and Heilman). Mackey became president of the Evansville and Terre Haute Railroad after Ingle's death in 1875. He purchased the Straight Line's roadway and right-of-way in 1881 and extended the line to Worthington. He was heavily involved in constructing a belt railway around the city and a branch line to Mount Vernon. He also gained control of the Terre Haute and Southern. The new line was named the Evansville, Indianapolis, and Terre Haute. The dream of extending it to Indianapolis via Spencer and Martinsville was ended by Mackey's bankruptcy in the Panic of 1893, after which the line became part of the New York Central system. Mackey spent the rest of his days in humble obscurity, dying at the Vendome Hotel in 1915 at the age of eighty-one. He was always something of an outsider. His sole interest was in business, and he was never involved in cultural, social, or political causes. He is credited with founding the Evansville Business Men's Association.[76]

Manufacturing and rail expansion were only part of the story. Charles E. Robert, author of the city's first postwar promotional book, *Evansville: Her Commerce and Manufactures* (1874), insisted that his publication was belated in appearing because its business community was too busy attending to making money to engage in the sort of puffery associated with Chicago and Indianapolis. Its citizens also worked too hard "to allow attention to what is not visibly practical."[77]

Evidence of progress was sufficient to lend some credibility to this argument. In addition to many factories, the city had three daily papers—the *Journal,* the *Courier,* and the German-language *Täglicher Demokrat.* By 1880, Evansville had five national banks—the newest two (both 1873) serving the growing German population of the region—as well as twenty-seven wholesale firms, ten commission merchants, and a board of trade. Mackey's new St. George Hotel (1874), largest and most luxurious between Louisville and St. Louis, symbolized its rise to regional dominance. That Evansville's banks and major employers weathered the economic troubles of the decade also attested to the city's vitality. Its attaining a lengthy entry in the *Report on the Social Statistics of Cities*—part of the 1880 census—was another a source of great local pride, partly because Evansville was the only lower Ohio city included.[78]

Accompanying these thirty years of economic growth were a number of other changes. More workers, for instance, were earned wages in ever-larger factories. The contest for control of the workplace and the desire for a living wage prompted the formation of an array of workers' organizations after the war. Molders and machinists, highly skilled workers, were able to defy mechanization and retain high levels of compensation, whereas wages for most skilled workers dropped. In addition, an increasing number of workers were "white collar," as a result of the expansion of wholesale and retail businesses and factories. The number of clerks, bookkeepers, salesmen, commercial travelers, and similar workers rose above one thousand.[79]

Growth and prosperity also widened gaps in income. According to federal census reports in 1860 and 1870, the number owning at least $20,000 of real estate had more than doubled during the 1860s. Internal revenue reports (before repeal of the tax in 1872) showed substantial increases in the wealth of the business elite. Although the number of prominent German merchants and industrialists grew, most of the wealthy were neither German nor manufacturers. Of the top ten income recipients in 1865, only one merchant was German, as were six of the thirty-four owning property worth $100,000 or more in federal census records of 1870. In 1868-69, the businesses of non-Germans—Charles Viele, Samuel Orr, David Mackey, and Peter Semonin—had the highest value, and Mackey's was at the top. Some German merchants and industrialists, however, also had substantial holdings. Reitz's company properties led these.[80]

Although the commercial and industrial leadership of Evansville converged on such matters as the successful pursuit of the Union war effort, it was sometimes divided, as the case of the Straight Line Railroad illustrated. This reflected a combination of factors: personalities, mercantile versus industrial interests, politics, and culture. In the case of Ingle's interests versus Carpenter's, competition for rail revenues seemed to be the chief issue. Religion and political culture were also important. Whig/Republican Heilman and Democrat Reitz chaired their respective parties. Each was a prominent layman in his church (St. John's Evangelical and Holy Trinity Roman Catholic, respectively). But ethnicity did not necessarily separate entrepreneurs. Reitz engaged in ventures with English-speaking Protestants, notably with the Episcopalian Charles Viele. Heilman was involved in projects with Mackey and Orr. Membership on Evansville's bank boards, moreover, was not determined by ethnicity or source of income. Evansville National's leadership in the early 1880s included Heilman, Bayard, Mackey, Blount, Dunkerson, and others—a mix of merchants and industrialists, Germans and non-Germans. Similar patterns existed at First National, where the board included Ingle, Hopkins, Thomas Garvin, Viele, and Reitz.[81]

Several conclusions are apt. Most places did not encounter growth or development in midcentury; in fact, some continued to decline. The places experiencing the most substantial change did so for various reasons: federal spending, wartime stimuli, expanded rail and river connections, increased availability of capital, new market opportunities, local agricultural and mineral resources, and local and state subsidies. The quality of leadership also mattered. The diversity of that mix and the vision and skill of local elites determined which of these settlements would emerge the strongest and the most capable of encountering further challenges in the evolving urban-industrial era. Railroads in 1880 were still at right angles to the Ohio, and interior trade for river export was a vital part of those places with rail connections. Most locales on the Ohio in 1880, however, lacked rail and good road connections, and they remained important entrepots for the people in their vicinities. Freight traffic—carried by barge and packet—remained strong as passenger traffic declined.[82]

The expansion of the rail network, and the urban connections that followed, may have given Evansville, and to a lesser extent the other cities on the lower Ohio, the tools with which to continue developing. But the river continued to be significant for most of the people in the region, and railroads and factories only partly determined how things were going to turn out.

8 ∾

Government,
Society, and Culture

Politics and government, social relations, and culture shaped communities during the Civil War. Their expressions continued to vary—across the river and state lines, as well as within state boundaries.

State and regional political cultures contributed heavily to the ways in which river communities approached the challenges of industrializing America. How settlements approached taxation and indebtedness, for instance, revealed much about their priorities. In 1870 and 1880 low taxes—state, county, and town or city—were the rule on either side of the river. Combined tax revenues exceeded $100,000 in only three counties—Posey, Vanderburgh, and Warrick in Indiana. At $565,000, Vanderburgh's was by far the highest. In ten counties, by contrast, taxes declined within the decade. Town or city taxes were generally low, especially in Kentucky. McCracken's $23,000 (out of $87,000 total taxes paid) was a notable exception, as was Daviess's $16,000 (of $88,000 in toto). These two counties, however, paid much lower town or city taxes than Alexander, Gallatin, Posey, Spencer, and Vanderburgh Counties. Most lower Ohio counties—except for Pulaski, Vanderburgh, Warrick, Daviess, and McCracken—fell below even their state's per capita averages. In six Kentucky counties, the per capita rate was about half the state's, which in turn was half that of Illinois's.

Local tax indebtedness in 1880 also revealed striking differences. Vanderburgh's nearly $2.1 million, most of which was owed by residents of Evansville, topped the list. A distant second was McCracken County, with $638,000. Alexander, Gallatin, and Daviess Counties were also in the top five. By contrast, total net debt was *below* $11,000 in seven counties, all but one in Kentucky, and exceeded $50,000 in only ten counties.

Figured on a per capita basis, the contrasts were even more striking. Only Alexander, Gallatin, McCracken, and Vanderburgh exceeded their states' average. The obligations of McCracken and Vanderburgh residents—$39.23 and

$40.53 per person, respectively—were highest. By contrast, in thirteen counties, per capita obligations were $2.50 or less; in nine (seven in Kentucky), they were less than a dollar.[1]

Taxation and indebtedness reflected the strong influence of agrarian, rural interests. Indiana's Constitution of 1851, which prohibited the state from incurring debt, was one manifestation. The differences among counties in these states were generally by degree. A few places, though, did not fit the molds of their environs. The level of debt was an index of local leaders' commitments to infrastructure improvements, railroads, and schools. Some debts, as in Cairo's case, proved onerous as rail ventures failed. Unwillingness to take risks, however, consigned communities to oblivion.

Each state's political environment also differed. Until the 1890s, former Confederate generals, Bourbon Democrats who were fiscal conservatives, dominated Kentucky's state house. Kentuckians' loyalties, fiercely provincial, lay with their county. That Republicans tended to cluster in towns made Democrats especially eager to limit the powers of urban governments. In railroad finance, for instance, county residents were much more reluctant to subscribe to railroad stock than were townspeople. Legislatures authorized county subscriptions if elections were held, whereas towns had to receive legislative approval for such financing and then hold separate elections to approve subscriptions.

County governments in the Commonwealth remained small fiefdoms, and not surprisingly the number of counties in the state continued to grow, reaching 120 in the twentieth century. Even the smallest, poorest counties managed to erect grand courthouses. In November 1868, for example, the people of Hancock County celebrated the completion of their new courthouse, a tall, handsome brick edifice with white trim and a slate roof that could be seen by packet boat passengers coming upriver from the "Troy Reach." Despite the ravages of war, citizens had managed to scrape up $20,000 for the structure, which Lee Dew describes as "the first stop for rural families coming to town with a wagon full of kids and produce." Court Day remained the central event of the month, when justices of the peace assembled to act as a court of claims. "This nineteenth-century folk tradition was part flea market, part carnival, part political rally, and part gigantic block party," writes Dew. It was a time for "the entire county to gather together as an extended family—to celebrate who they were and what they held dear."[2]

Local public services were generally abysmal. Roads in Kentucky remained local and private: counties subscribed funds for turnpikes, but tolls went to the toll companies. Only in 1896 were these roads sold to the counties, which operated them without tolls. State funds could not be used for highway construction before 1909. Like the South generally, Kentucky towns continued to be cultural and social extensions of their rural settings. Only a few gained city status.[3]

Across the river, political cultures were somewhat different, reflecting the intermingling of New England, Middle States, and Upper South, of native and immigrant, of Protestant and Catholic, and of rural and urban. Tightly structured two-party systems prevailed, and party loyalties determined issues and set the boundaries of political debate and government policy. Bitter partisanship, intensified by such wartime issues as the draft, the use of black soldiers, and the printing of paper currency, perpetuated two-party balance. Class and status, race and ethnicity, region, and religion all contributed to this. Party loyalty was sustained by highly competitive and intense campaigns and by substantial popular interest and participation. Democrats tended to be strongest in southern parts of these two states, among most immigrants and voters with lower status occupations, and among Roman Catholics, Lutherans, and Regular Baptists. Republicans attracted merchants and native-born artisans and members of pietistic groups that favored government's promoting Sabbath legislation, temperance, and public education.[4]

Each county and settlement had a distinctive political climate and was part of state politics and government because, as James H. Madison puts it, "the county party chairman and his associates were the workhorses of party politics." Some were strongly Democratic, whereas others were strongly Republican. However, some were "so closely contested that the leading party averaged less than 51 percent of the two-party vote."[5]

Republicans gained considerable power in many river communities, in part because of growing numbers of former slaves. That was especially evident in Cairo and Mound City, where some blacks even held minor public offices. As in Paducah—a Republican stronghold in a heavily Democratic region—the party of Lincoln also drew strength from persons whose roots lay in the Northeast. German Evangelicals and Methodists added to Republicans' strength, especially in Evansville and Mount Vernon. German Catholics in northern Spencer County made that section reliably Democratic, but along the river, Rockport and Ohio Township voted heavily for Republican presidential candidates between 1860 and 1884. Similar patterns prevailed in Perry County, where German-Swiss Tell City consistently voted Republican, while Cannelton and most of the county supported Democrats. Evansville's first German-born mayor (1876-80), John J. Kleiner, was a Democrat, but Alsatian John Dannettell, a Republican, was elected mayor in 1887. Evansville's municipal elections shifted back and forth between the two parties before the Great War.[6]

The quality of urban services offered by river towns thus mirrored regional and local political cultures and institutions. They also varied according to the demands of citizens, the character of local leadership, and the authority granted by state legislatures. Like subsidies for railroads, services were seen by some as instruments of economic development. The amount of local taxation and indebtedness was symptomatic of this.

Control and improvement of the streets and the guarantee of public safety were closely related to urban promotional efforts. The most prevalent services by 1880 were limited fire and police protection and paving of thoroughfares. The threat of epidemics, especially after cholera devastated towns in 1866, stimulated civic leaders and their respective legislatures to secure unprecedented authority to regulate citizens' behavior in matters relating to public health. In many respects, this laid the groundwork for other regulatory acts.[7]

Several examples document the varied responses to the challenges of crowded living conditions, polluted wells, muddy streets, crime, fire, and epidemics. Services in Indiana towns and cities were little different from those of Illinois and Kentucky: slow, erratic, and "always facing resistance from Hoosiers fearful of higher taxes and jealous of their individual freedoms."[8]

In 1852, the Indiana General Assembly replaced special charters with a comprehensive law providing for the incorporation of communities of more than three thousand into cities. A number of its features have remained essentially unchanged. At its core were an elected mayor and common council with the authority to regulate public safety, sanitation, and fire protection. The law, revised in 1867, also provided for a marshal as the chief law enforcement official, a street commissioner, a chief engineer of a fire department, and a board of health. Many of these powers were slowly and unevenly applied because the public was unwilling to pay taxes for public services. Often, limited municipal services were provided by private firms and organizations.[9]

In Evansville, a "city watch" comprising the city marshal, city wharfmaster, and six paid watchmen operated from 1847 to 1866, when day and night forces were created—a few years after Fort Wayne and Indianapolis. In 1874, the council authorized up to thirty policemen, although there were rarely more than twenty. The force, as elsewhere in Indiana, was highly politicized. The legislature in 1883 abolished marshals in cities over 29,000 and created metropolitan police boards appointed by the governor. Evansville's first metropolitan police force was created in 1884. The city charter in 1893, however, returned the police to mayoral control.[10]

The increasing hazard of fire, due to the prevalence of wooden structures and furniture factories, led Evansville to purchase fire engines and to build hose houses for volunteer fire companies, but not until 1888 did it have a professional fire department. The need for an adequate water supply to fight fires, rather than concern about potable drinking water, prompted the common council to build a municipal waterworks, the first in Indiana, which opened in the summer of 1871. The city had begun to pave its streets—nine of the approximately one hundred miles of thoroughfares in 1880. The city employed ten to fifteen men in street maintenance.[11]

Most Indiana communities lacked lighted as well as paved streets. State law allowed cities to create their own gasworks or to regulate those which were privately owned, but municipal ownership was rare in Indiana. In the late 1860s, Evansville's Common Council chartered the Evansville City Gas Works to supply street and residential lighting via coal gas. The company had 1,600 customers by the 1880s, when it expanded its services to include electric lighting. The utility's directors included the city's elite: William Heilman, Robert K. Dunkerson, Thomas A. Garvin, Samuel Bayard, John A. Reitz, and his son, Francis Joseph. John J. Chandler was president for many years.[12]

State law also permitted Indiana cities to protect public health. Even before its city charter, the town had instituted health ordinances, which included empowering officials to quarantine smallpox-infested residences. Prompted especially by cholera, early city councils regulated the disposal of offal, dead animals, and rubbish and required homeowners to maintain a modicum of cleanliness in their residences. Collection of garbage, a relatively rare practice in the state, began in Evansville after the Civil War. Ash elimination was the homeowner's responsibility. Garbage disposal, however, was infrequent and irregular. Judging from editorial commentaries in the newspapers, ordinances preventing the free rein of hogs were also loosely enforced. Some of this was the result of hogs (and other livestock) being driven via city streets into the new stockyard from villages such as New Harmony.[13]

Like most Indiana cities, Evansville had a fairly extensive sewer system in place by 1880, much of which was installed during Republican William Baker's lengthy tenure as mayor (1860-69, 1872-73). These lines were intended primarily for rain drainage. Most liquid and human waste ended up in porous cesspools or privy vaults, which were supposed to conform to city ordinances and to be subject to inspection by the city health officer. Few homes had indoor plumbing, and if they did, waste was channeled to storm sewers and thence to the Ohio. Packinghouses and other manufacturing establishments also dumped their refuse into Pigeon Creek and the Ohio.[14]

Public health concerns mounted over time. Evansville created a board of health about 1855 that was given broader authority during the Baker administration. Annual printed reports of health and mortality first appeared in the daily newspapers about 1865. The board had the authority to institute compulsory smallpox vaccination. The board also sought to educate citizens in matters of public health. For example, it warned citizens in August 1866 of the outbreak of cholera up and down the Ohio and advised how to avoid the dread disease. Annual reports from the board of four physicians listed monthly totals of deaths and their causes. The report of November 1867 provided the first historical statistics. Children under age five were the most likely to die. Respiratory problems and dysentery were the leading causes of death, and most deaths occurred between July and October. The board declared that two-thirds of the deaths represented a "slaughter of the innocents." The following summer it sought to extend vaccinations to the poor and to examine all tenements in order to identify needed improvements. It also ordered that the canal be completely filled in.[15]

Mayor Baker's Democratic successor abolished the board of health in September 1869, but Baker reinstated it and gave it more authority when he returned to office in 1872. *Social Statistics of Cities* (1880) reported the board included the mayor and five physicians appointed by the city council. The council also appointed a health officer and two sanitary policeman and was required to fund a city dispensary. The board was empowered to inspect dwellings, maintain sanitary conditions, and remove nuisances. In the case of epidemics, it could expend whatever funds it deemed necessary and establish a quarantine or take any measures to arrest the spread of disease. The board could order vaccinations at public expense, but only for children enrolled in the public schools.[16]

The expansion of Evansville created the need for other public services. Shortly after Indianapolis chartered a street railway, the Evansville City Council in May 1866 approved an ordinance permitting construction of a privately chartered line in which many of the city's business and civic elite had invested, led by John J. Chandler. The horse-drawn cars began service in December 1867 on track laid along Main Street from Water Street to the Evansville and Crawfordsville depot at Eighth Street. By 1880, six miles of tracks had been laid, including into Lamasco.[17]

Hospital care was rare in Indiana cities, usually offered through private auspices. One of the state's earliest was the Evansville Marine Hospital on Ohio Street, near the river, which was operated by the federal government from 1856 until 1872, when it was sold to the Daughters of Charity. Marine patients were treated under contract with the Catholic sisters until a new building was opened in the late 1880s. The Evansville Medical College also maintained a public dispensary during its brief existence, and several physicians had clinics.[18]

Burial of the city's dead was an increasing challenge. The first burial ground near Fourth and Vine Streets was publicly maintained. The city opened Oak Hill, a large cemetery on the north side, in 1860, and Locust Hill, on the northwest side, in 1874. The city's Catholics, Lutherans, and Jews had their own cemeteries.[19]

Care of the poor was primarily a private matter. Vanderburgh County had instituted a county poor asylum in the late 1830s, a place to which the most wretchedly indigent were sent and forgotten. Others—the "deserving poor" who were down on their luck—received short-term assistance from the township trustees. Private organizations, mostly churches, offered the most assistance. Four mission schools for workers' children were created by the city's most respectable churches between 1857 and 1868. The Vanderburgh Home for the Friendless, commonly known as the Christian Home for unwed or abandoned mothers, opened in May 1870. Willard Carpenter was its leading benefactor.[20]

Public parks, halls, and "pleasure grounds" were also created, some by city government. As of 1880, Evansville possessed only four public parks with a total area of about nine acres. All were donations from wealthy citizens. Sunset Park, located on the river and adjoining the wealthy upper portion of the town, was the smallest. Four other parks, groves, and salt wells were privately run. There were five private halls or theaters and one opera house. The largest was Evans Hall, at Fifth and Locust, which could seat nearly three thousand for lectures and other public programs. Constructed in 1878-79, it was a shrine to the temperance cause by the widow of Robert M. Evans, whose sons had killed one another in a drunken brawl. The Opera House was opened in the fall of 1868; its president was John J. Chandler.[21]

However limited, these services were the most comprehensive on the lower Ohio. In the smaller places, "government" was the post office, and law and order was mostly ad hoc and voluntary. The first Harrison County atlas (1882) divulged the typical: the sole public facilities in Mauckport, its largest river community, were the public square, where the town pump was located, and the town cemetery. The larger communities offered a degree of organized public safety and public health protection. During an especially devastating outbreak of cholera in Mount Vernon in 1873, for instance, one hundred died. Town authorities, who had had a health board since 1866, ordered coal to be burned on street corners and lime and other disinfectants to be run in the gutters. The town purchased a fire engine in 1880, the same year a volunteer fire department was organized. Such features as coal gas and lighted streets were in the distant future. Grandview, for example, installed streetlights in 1910, two years after the Grandview Gas Company was organized. Obtaining a city charter was an important though rare step. Cannelton and Tell City received theirs in 1886-87 in order to issue bonds for the support of a railroad.[22]

Cairo exhibited many of the same challenges and responses. Timing and format reflected distinctive local conditions—for example, the town's relatively late start and its rapid growth between 1855 and 1865. A police patrol was organized, for example, in 1856, but a full-time paid force came much later.

Similarly, volunteer fire departments were formed in 1865, but a municipal fire department was organized only in 1893. Cairo's municipal waterworks was opened in 1885. Some city sewers were laid, beginning in 1866-67, and the newly formed board of public works also did some "sheet filling" to control flooding and seepage. Elevated wooden sidewalks were constructed, and a street railway was initiated in 1892. A private infirmary was inaugurated in 1872, and a decade later a new federal marine hospital was constructed. The quality of public health service improved somewhat, but apparently no formal structure was created before 1880. Severe epidemics hit Cairo as late as 1878, when fifty residents died of yellow fever.[23]

What distinguished Cairo was the combined effects of location and corporate control. Each of the rivers skirting the city tested it during flood season, but the Ohio was especially daunting, as it flowed much faster, brought huge quantities of sand and silt, and rose and fell fifty feet. In 1884, the Cairo City Property trustees learned that almost one hundred feet of the levees had washed away since 1851. There was also seepage. Likening the city to a cup submerged to its rim in a basin of water, historian John Lansden vividly described the problem of preventing water from penetrating the city via the sandy substratum beneath it. Through its resident agent, Samuel Staats Taylor, the Cairo Trust Property blocked local government efforts to construct adequate levees because of the higher taxes this would require. Only after the devastating flood of 1884 was a compromise worked out and a strong levee system begun, but seepage persisted.

Complicating this was absentee ownership by the trustees and the perennial question of what property the trustees owned. Only in the late 1860s, for instance, did courts rule that the wharf belonged to the trustees. A consequence was city government's uncertainty about tax collection, which many residents flouted. The trustees' limited capital, moreover, was tied up in Cairo land. The Illinois Central Railroad was another powerful interest that controlled Cairo affairs from afar. The city's huge debt—nearly three-quarters of a million dollars by the middle of the depression-racked 1870s—was also a challenge. It was the result of unsuccessful investments in railroads, the costs of building levees, and the price of caring for the large number of poor newcomers from the rural South. Even after the issue of new city bonds beginning in 1878, which paid debts at fifty cents on the dollar, continued problems with creditors and a high tax burden on residents limited spending on civic improvements.[24]

Upriver town and city services also revealed uneven development. Metropolis, for instance, constructed its first wharfboat in 1866 and its second in 1880. Other amenities came much later. Street lights were installed in 1929. A professional fire department was created about the same time. Water was supplied via deep wells, not a waterworks. Civic leaders of neighboring Brooklyn, spurred by Civil War veteran and physician J.D. Young, obtained a special legislative charter in the late 1880s to allow them, via a mayor and city council, to control bootleggers and ruffians, an unplanned consequence of the arrival of the Illinois Central. Young, a Republican, became Brooklyn's first mayor. Elizabethtown obtained its water from wells until 1980 and did not have a sewer system until 1927. In settlements that were flood-prone, especially Shawneetown, much of the limited village or town income was allocated to construction and improvement of levees.[25]

Across the Ohio, town services were even more limited. Most improvements had to await special legislative approval. The charters of small towns such as Caseyville granted only basic powers to town boards—appointing a town marshal and treasurer, establishing streets and alleys, regulating public conduct, and licensing coffee houses, inns, and taverns. The town also incurred a substantial railroad debt. In 1883, the debt, with interest, was over $100,000, and taxpayers refused to pay for it. No sheriff would undertake collection of the unpopular debt.[26]

Yet important strides occurred in the cities, perhaps because of the relative lack of antebellum infrastructure and the needs imposed by the war and postwar growth. Probably the most progressive was Henderson. Aided by the city charter of 1867, Henderson's leaders implemented several major projects. After a decade of leaky and dangerous gas service, city government took over the gasworks in 1869. Soon Henderson's streets were also lighted. (Electricity came in 1896.) The city thus became the first in western Kentucky and on the lower Ohio to own a gas company. A municipally owned waterworks was initiated three years later, when a group of incorporators—wealthy tobacco men L.C. Dallam, J.H. Barret, and E.L. Starling—obtained special legislation for an election to approve it. A public parks system was also launched. As of the 1880s, fire protection was provided by volunteers, but the city purchased firehouses and equipment. The city's government also encouraged railroad construction to the south and promoted economic development in other ways, such as permitting the construction of a coal tipple on the city wharf in 1870. By the 1890s, telephones were one of the few services not owned by city government.[27]

In addition to supporting railroad construction, Owensboro's leaders, many of whom were Confederate veterans, used the new city charter of 1866 to license hotels, restaurants, riverboats, tobacco stemmeries, and distilleries, introducing some regulation while also raising revenues. City fathers also imposed strict rules regarding behavior on the Sabbath and, among other things, forbade swimming in the river. In 1868, as an attempt to cope with epidemics of cholera and smallpox, they created the position of city physician. The city council chartered an electric arc lighting company, which in 1882 introduced the first such street illumination on the lower Ohio. Two years later, another private company received a charter to operate a horse-drawn street railway. Graveling of city streets was initiated in the 1870s. In 1880, citizens voted overwhelmingly in favor of issuing bonds for street and wharf improvements. Full-time paid fire and police protection came gradually. As in Evansville, drives of livestock into town—in this case, down the old buffalo road (Frederica Street) to the river—continued until the end of the century.[28]

A similar pattern prevailed in Paducah. One of the earliest communities in the region to purchase fire equipment and construct a firehouse, Paducah continuously expanded public expenditures in these two sectors, but the city did not begin paying its firemen until Charles Reed became mayor in 1882. A paid police force, by contrast, was implemented shortly after the 1856 city charter. A new city hospital was constructed in 1872. Much of the city's postwar advancement was due to the leadership of the area's first (and only) Jewish mayor, German-born merchant Meyer Weil, who in his two terms (1871-75 and 1877-81) was also responsible for restoring the city's credit and halving its debt. During Reed's tenure (1881-89), a waterworks was constructed which carried water over twelve miles of pipes, the gas plant was completed, city streets were illuminated, and a number of thoroughfares were graveled.[29]

Support for such expanded local government powers and services came from the business and civic elites. In Henderson, prominent merchants, manufacturers, and attorneys were active in politics. Lists of city and county officeholders reveal the perennial prominence of planters and tobacco dealers. Virtually all of Henderson's political leadership was homegrown. Undoubtedly the fact that four Hendersonians served in the U.S. Senate between 1851 and 1939, and that four also were governors during the same years, gave the city extraordinary political clout in Frankfort and Washington. John Young Brown (1835-1904) was perhaps the most famous. A grandson of Senator Archibald Dixon and son of a state legislator and member of the Constitutional Convention of 1849-50, Brown moved to Henderson in 1863 and was elected to Congress in 1868. Denied his seat because he had been a colonel in the Confederate cavalry, he ran again, served two terms, and became governor in 1890. Brown also practiced law in Henderson for forty years.[30]

A somewhat similar pattern prevailed in Owensboro, except that the number of locals who achieved prominence at the state and national levels was smaller. The most renowned was Democratic senator Thomas McCreery. The 1870 federal census reported real and personal property worth $28,000, which made McCreery one of the city's ten wealthiest. First president of the Deposit Bank, the city's leading financial institution, he was a partner in that venture with James Weir, spoke manufacturer and first president of the Owensboro and Russellville Railroad. Distillers, tobacco dealers, merchants, and attorneys found places of prominence in local government. The surnames Triplett, Weir, Monarch, Taylor, and Moorman were not uncommon in lists of officeholders. Quite a few were former Confederate officers.[31]

Paducah's three mayors between 1859 and 1881 were Germans. Charles Reed, the first native Paducahan elected mayor, in 1881, was a Democrat and a Confederate veteran. Local attorneys Charles Wheeler and Alben Barkley, both Democrats, subsequently achieved prominence in state and national government, thus promoting local interests in a way that nearby Cairo never secured.[32]

In Evansville, merchants and manufacturers continued to occupy a prominent place in local politics. Even more than in Paducah, German-born business leadership came to dominate city and county government, as almost half of the city's residents in 1880 were first- and second-generation Germans. Between 1875 and 1925, all but three mayors were Germans, and Germans were prominent in county, state, and national races.[33]

Increasingly, the descendants of the city's English-speaking elite pursued various business interests and withdrew from public life. Notable exceptions occurred—the longtime service of Union veteran and attorney John W. Foster, who edited the *Journal,* chaired the local Republican Committee, served as minister to Mexico, and became Benjamin Harrison's secretary of state. Whether this was chiefly an acknowledgment of the pervasive power of the city's Germans remains to be seen. City elections between 1863 and 1888 were bitterly fought and decided by slim margins, with Republicans taking Pigeon Township in all presidential elections between 1872 and 1888. Democratic voters in other townships swung the county to their candidate in 1876 and 1884. Democrats captured city government in 1869 and 1875 with the help of black voters.[34]

Like politics and government, community leadership was an index of change. Generally hamlets and villages offered little if any opportunity to their youth or newcomers. Especially attractive were those places with rapid postwar growth where antebellum elites were unable or unwilling to block the rise of newcomers.[35]

In many towns, continuity with prewar patterns prevailed. Mount Vernon's elite, according to Goodspeed's 1886 history of Posey County, remained homogeneous. Of the 106 leaders listed, 33 were natives of Posey County, 18 were southern, 12 were born in the Mid-Atlantic states, and 2 hailed from New England. Twenty-six were of German descent. All but a handful had arrived before the Civil War.[36]

In Hawesville and Metropolis, Upper South and antebellum roots also persisted. Hawesville's most powerful man continued to be planter and Confederate sympathizer Robert C. Beauchamp, who served two terms in the Kentucky legislature after 1865. His three sons were among the county's largest landholders. Other young men who came into prominence in the late 1860s and 1870s were natives of Hancock County who had served in the Confederate army or guerilla forces.[37]

The successful men of Metropolis generally shared an Upper South heritage. Given the newness of the community, though, opportunity to rise was more widespread. One of the leaders was Samuel W. Lester, a Kentucky-born merchant whose father had settled in the county in 1853. After a variety of jobs and service in the Union army, he moved into town after the war. There he achieved prominence in commerce and Republican politics. A.C. May, son of Tennesseans who settled in the county before the war, purchased his first lot in Metropolis in 1879. Turning from farming to commerce, he became proprietor of the May House, the town's leading hotel.[38]

Configurations in the larger settlements varied. In Cairo, the successes of the five Ohio-born Halliday brothers suggested some opportunities despite absentee ownership. Samuel and William, along with trustee Taylor, formed what would become the First Bank and Trust Company in 1865. Fifteen years later the brothers purchased the town's leading hotel and named the remodeled structure after themselves. William's successes as a merchant brought him a seat on the Illinois Central board. Many Cairo leaders had Old Northwest roots. Of the one hundred or so identified in the city's first history (1883), forty-three had been born in Illinois, Indiana, or Ohio. Attorney John M. Lansden, born in Sangamon County in 1836, was typical. He settled in Cairo in 1866, and five years later he became mayor. The 1883 list also included twenty-one natives of the Northeast and twenty of German birth. Only eight were Upper South natives. At least in the immediate postwar era, the power of the property trustees and the Illinois Central did not prevent many newcomers from seeking their fortunes in Cairo.[39]

Henderson's elite was much more uniform and exclusive. An 1880 listing of its 130 leading citizens revealed, for example, that all but 23 had taken up residence there before the Civil War; 76 were Henderson County natives, another 25 had been born elsewhere in Kentucky, and 8 came from free states. Perhaps the most prominent was John H. Barret, a Virginia-born tobacco dealer, who had settled in 1835. Untypical were men such as James McLaughlin, a New York–born grocer who had come to Henderson in 1869, or S. Oberdorfer, a Bavarian hotelier who had arrived in 1873. Among the dozen who were foreign-born, nine were Germans. Henderson's elite was united as well by source of wealth, as most earned their incomes from tobacco. And relatively few persons controlled a substantial share of the county's wealth. In 1870, for instance, eighty-five people had real property worth $10,000 or more. Five owned land worth a combined $1.3 million, and their personal property totaled $905,000. The entire county's real estate was worth slightly over $4 million, and its personal property was slightly under $2 million.[40]

Owensboro was somewhat more inclusive. Wealth was more diffuse than in Henderson, and its sources were more varied. Distillers and other manufacturers were, by 1880, as prominent as tobacco growers and dealers. Of the approximately 175 in the first county atlas, only 50 were not born in Kentucky or the South. Twenty-five were German-born. Just sixty-three had arrived since 1865. Generally the same configuration appeared in the city's first history (1883). The vast majority of the nearly 140 listed were southern in birth, although only 32 were natives of Daviess County. Of those not born in the county, most had arrived since the end of the Civil War. Eleven, including the Monarch distilling family, were Roman Catholic, and seven were Jewish. Those with antebellum Upper South roots—Thomas McCreery, James Weir, John Thixton, R.H. Taylor, Richard and M.V. Monarch, among others—were prominent in postwar commerce and industry, occupying as well the directorships of the city's four bank boards and other important institutions, such as the gas company. Some were relative newcomers. Probably typical of these was John R. Osborne, a Scot, who came in 1869 from Cincinnati. For six years he was the master mechanic for the Owensboro and Russellville Railroad. Then he opened a planing mill.[41]

A somewhat more fluid environment existed in Paducah. Many of its postwar business and civic leaders were German Americans. Commerce, industry, and railroads offered many opportunities. The strength of the Republican Party in this community, located in the Democratic sea of the Purchase region, also suggests a diversity and an openness that exceeded Owensboro's.[42]

The composition of Evansville's elite was even more elastic. The city's first history, printed in 1873, listed eighty-three men of prominence, sixty of whom had arrived before 1865. Thirty-two, however, had settled since 1850. Only nineteen were natives of the Upper South. Thirty came from New England or the Middle Atlantic states, and eighteen came from England, Ireland, or Germany. About a fifth were native Hoosiers.[43]

Several aspects of postwar gentry are striking. For one thing, industrialists were increasingly a force, although merchants remained dominant. Second, almost half of the city's elite in the early 1880s were German, including Catholics and Jews. Third, although most were born in Evansville or arrived before the Civil War, a number had worked their way up the ladder (notably merchant and railroad magnate David J. Mackey).

Until the early twentieth century, Evansville's dominant families tended not to cross ethnic or religious lines in marriage. The sons and daughters of English-speaking pioneers wed each other, as did those of German Protestants, Catholics, and Jews. Ironmaker Samuel Orr, for example, married a daughter of financier William J. Lowry. Banker Samuel Bayard wed Orr's daughter Martha, and his son, James, married Kate Howes, daughter of a wholesale grocer, Lewis Howes. Another daughter wed banker Robert L. Dunkerson. Orr's niece married a son of John Shanklin. One of James Orr's daughters married the son of Charles Denby, Evansville attorney and diplomat. Rising attorney George A. Cunningham, who arrived in 1877 at age twenty-two, married a daughter of his law partner, Thomas Garvin, one of the city's most eminent attorneys and civic leaders, in 1881. Marriage connected Ingles and Igleharts, Garvins and Hopkins, and Morgans and Vieles. Among German Protestants, a notable union was Albert C. Rosencranz, German-born watchmaker and Union cavalry officer, with a daughter of Heilman. After the war, Major Rosencranz managed Heilman Plow Works (later Vulcan) and was active in Republican Party affairs. Among German Catholics, the most significant marriage was that of cigar maker Herman Fendrich to a daughter of John A. Reitz in 1864.[44]

From these unions and the passage of power from father to son came much of Evansville's leadership. Directorships of the city's banks were barometers. Reitz founded the Canal Bank, later City National. John S. Hopkins, pioneer merchant, was president of that bank from 1867 to 1880. Francis Joseph Reitz followed his father on the board, and Charles Viele succeeded Hopkins, his uncle. The board of Evansville National, later Old National, included Samuel Orr, Bayard, and Dunkerson. Orr, Reitz, and Dunkerson were also founding directors of the German National Bank.

Enterprising newcomers found places among the city's elite. David Mackey, for instance, gained a seat on the Old National board. By the early 1880s, that board also included plowmaker Henry F. Blount, a New Yorker who came to work for John H. Roelker. Eventually he bought that firm and another one, forming Blount Plow Works. By the 1880s, Blount sold 8,000 to 10,000 "Extra Point Steel Plows" annually, mostly in the South. The board of Citizens National Bank, organized in 1873, included wealthy German Jewish merchant Leopold Lowenthal and German Evangelical F.W. Cook, proprietor of the City (later Cook's) Brewery.[45]

In the larger communities, economic progress also brought a higher degree of social stratification. Town histories, usually written and published locally, began with Edward White's *Evansville and Its Men of Mark* in 1873. These signified urban progress and praised the achievements of the city's elite. Similar works appeared in Newburgh in 1881, Mount Vernon in 1882, Paducah in

1885, Uniontown in 1886, and Henderson in 1887. City directories, beginning with Evansville's in 1858 and Paducah's a year later, performed a similar role.[46]

Grand homes connoted financial success and social distance. Evansville's finest was Charles Viele's home at Water and Cherry streets, enlarged and remodeled according to French Second Empire standards in the 1870s. By contrast, Evansville's growing industrial force resided in homes often built by employers near their factories on the north and west sides. Typically these were long, narrow wooden "shotgun houses" or small brick houses with six to eight hundred square feet of living space. Little furniture or ornamentation could be found. In between, in size and features, were residences of skilled workers, clerks, and managers.[47]

To editors and other civic boosters, income differentials were not only indices of status and class but also sources of civic pride. In the 1860s and 1870s, editors used the information gained from Civil War income taxation to measure their progress against that of other communities. On July 28, 1865, for instance, the *Evansville Daily Journal* concluded that Evansville compared favorably with Indianapolis. Merchant David Mackey's $62,000 income exceeded any Indianapolis counterpart, and bankers G.W. Rathbone, Samuel Bayard, and W.J. Lowry and industrialists Samuel Orr and William Heilman held their own against Indianapolis counterparts.

Over time, the city's elite received more income and a greater share of the total. In 1866, five businessmen, including Mackey, Heilman, and Viele, reported income ranging from $43,000 to $51,000. Twelve earned at least $12,000 that year, when the typical worker spent about $100 annually on rent. Income reports for 1867 revealed that only 178 residents had incomes of $500 or more, after deductions. Charles Viele remained the wealthiest, with almost $51,000. Although New Albany could boast one industrialist, W.C. DePauw, who earned $64,000, Evansville had 116 persons earning between $1,000 and $10,000— well above New Albany, Terre Haute, and Lafayette.[48]

Payment of taxes also revealed social inequality. In a city of about 25,000, only 425 paid two-thirds of the city's property taxes for 1868—and just 72 paid a third. David Mackey's firms accounted for the highest amount of property reported in 1869, about $153,000. Entrepreneur and city council member Peter Semonin's totaled almost $70,000. Third in rank was Samuel Orr and Company's $56,000. John A. Reitz's and Charles Viele's firms rounded out the top five.[49]

Growing residential and social separation was increasingly evident in the larger communities. In Evansville, for instance, English and Scots-Irish bankers, merchants, and some industrialists clustered on Upper Water and First Streets. German American owners and managers resided on First and Wabash

Avenues in Lamasco and Independence. Because the street railway was relatively new, population dispersal was modest, for a number of retail businessmen, clerks, and skilled workers resided on or near the city's commercial core. German artisans and white-collar workers tended to converge in Lamasco, whereas their less skilled fellow countrymen who worked as laborers in the sawmills, the planing mills, the cotton mill, and the coal mines were more common in Independence, a section west of Lamasco incorporated into the city in the early 1870s. In the 1880s, the erection of large and ornate St. Boniface Catholic Church on Wabash Avenue and St. Paul's Evangelical Church on West Michigan Street attested to the growing presence of Germans. To the west were tenements and simple residences of the workers in the city's largest employer, the cotton mill. Many of these workers before 1870 were widows or single young women, who were Civil War refugees from Tennessee, Georgia, and Alabama. Gradually second-generation Germans replaced southerners at the cotton mill. In the hills west of Independence, in a German American neighborhood known as Babytown, resided merchants, factory owners, and skilled workers.[50]

Evansville's African Americans, prominent in day labor and service occupations, were concentrated in a region east of Main Street on and near the filled-in canal; much of it was owned by Willard Carpenter and Thomas Garvin. Known as Baptisttown by 1890, this neighborhood, located in the least healthful section of the city, was close to the Evansville and Terre Haute Railroad depot, the wharf, and Main Street, where menial work was available in transport, hotels, and restaurants. Industrial jobs, however, were off-limits. Another distinction was that in 1880 about four hundred black workers were women, many married. Quite a few took in washing. A few tiny black enclaves were situated on the north side of Independence and southeast of the commercial district. In each census, however, Baptisttown accounted for a growing proportion of the city's black population—80 percent by the 1880s—and many of its streets had few if any white residents.

However lowly, job opportunities north of the river were more substantial than those on the south. One historian has described Cairo as an Ellis Island for freedmen, some of whom arrived with nothing but the clothes on their backs. Poor and unskilled, they were viewed by whites as genetically unsuited for anything but day labor and service. Limited opportunity and white hostility drove many north, but the establishment of black congregations and the erection of modest edifices—African Methodist Episcopal, First Missionary Baptist, and St. Michael's Episcopal—attested to the formation of black organizations and neighborhoods.[51]

Residential separation by occupation, nationality, and race was apparent in smaller towns as well. In Henderson, for instance, eight of the tobacco stemmeries that dominated the city's economy were situated on Water or Main Streets, near the Ohio. Relatively few residences were located near them. Six of the remaining eight were situated within a block or two of the railroad depot, on the southern edge of the town center. Several coal yards and factories were also located there. Considerable subdivision of city blocks into long, narrow lots with small residences had occurred by 1880, when the first city atlas was published. The location of the German Methodist Church testified to the clustering of German Americans. By contrast, the Colored Baptist Church was stationed on the public square, on the same block as the white elite's St. Paul's Episcopal Church. On Main and Green streets, close to the town square, resided most of the city's elite, including William Soaper, Thomas Soaper, John H. Barret, and Charles Starling.[52]

Social division was also evident on the map of 1881 Owensboro. The "old river road" contained, for instance, many of the city's grandest residences. The Lutheran church, located near the city's southern border and the planing mill, the furniture factory, the hub and spoke factory, and a host of modest homes, marked a heavily German working-class region. Paducah's boundaries doubled with an 1871 annexation and would nearly double again in 1894. In the process, the residences of the city's wage earners, managers and professionals, and merchants and industrialists were far less entangled than they had been before the Civil War. There, as in Owensboro, blacks, though residing in a larger portion of the city than in Evansville, tended to be concentrated in low-lying, marginal neighborhoods near the Ohio.[53]

The passage of time also complicated and sometimes transformed social relations in the larger communities. In Evansville and Paducah, for instance, German Catholics, Jews, and Protestants constructed a number of associations and institutions of their own to advance distinctive cultural interests, of which preservation of religious values was central. Sometimes these organizations were German-speaking replicas of English-dominated ones, such as Masonic lodges. The degree to which Germans were acculturated, accepting the practices of a capitalistic, evangelical Protestant republic and learning to converse in English, depended on a number of considerations: residential and occupational proximity, encouragement by leaders, and openness of their religious organizations to change. Members of the Evangelical Synod of North America and German pietistic denominations tended to be more "Americanized" than the liturgical Catholics and Lutherans, who maintained stricter separation, especially through their schools. Sheer numbers, especially in Evansville, permitted German Americans to take a growing share of leadership positions in local government as well as in business and financial affairs. Assimilation, in the sense that descendants of immigrants blended into mainstream culture and were accepted by the earlier elite's clubs, organizations, and families, came slowly and often painfully. It was not until 1971, for example, that Evansville would elect a Roman Catholic mayor.[54]

Relations between blacks and whites were another matter. Residential racial separation, initially by custom, grew steadily more rigid toward the end of the nineteenth century. A major difference between Evansville and many Indiana and Illinois river towns, on the one hand, and Kentucky cities, as well as Cairo and Mound City, on the other, was that the much larger proportion of blacks in the latter made residential separation more difficult. Nevertheless, portions of those communities—Boxtown in Uniontown and Bucktown and Brownsville in Smithland, for instance—were distinctly black.

Legalized racial separation was not fully entrenched by the 1880s. White and black Kentuckians, like southerners generally, treated one another with "various shades of deference, condescension, affection, and respect." Some aspects of race relations were fixed from the outset: separate schools, orphanages, churches, cemeteries, parks, and seating in public halls. The most contested arena in Kentucky and the rest of the South would be railroad service, but lines would not be more sharply drawn until the early 1890s. The more closely associated a social space was to gender—to whites' worries about possible sexual relations—the more it was likely to be segregated. Private homes and exclusive hotels and restaurants were not targets. Neither were places "where people of only one gender [such as boxing rings] associated with one another." Railcars thus became targets, especially first-class cars where respectable women traveled, and not the grimy, smoke-filled second-class cars ridden by men. "Educated and assertive blacks, especially those of the younger generation, chafed at every restriction against them," declares Edward Ayers, "and [they] looked for opportunities to exercise their legal rights to attack the very assumptions and presumptions of segregation."

Terrorism and lynching also characterized relations between the races, especially in Kentucky. Concerns about black mobility and immorality provoked a series of laws and ordinances, especially after the 1880s, aimed at checking vagrancy, contract evasion, and other petty crimes. At the pinnacle was lynching, which Kentucky, "outside the maelstrom of Populism and disfranchisement, near the border of the North, and with a relatively diversified economy," permitted at "a remarkably high rate." Why this occurred frequently in the Bluegrass State is traced to several factors common to subregions in the South: "few towns, weak law enforcement, poor communication with the outside, and high levels of transiency among both races." The setting, says Ayers, "fostered the fear and insecurity that fed lynching at the same time it removed the few checks that helped dissuade would-be lynchers elsewhere." [55]

Wanton violence perpetrated by "regulators" in Kentucky, the only state outside the old Confederacy in which Ku Klux Klan activities were significant, was so common that it was treated almost matter-of-factly in the first major history of the state published after 1865. One of the most notorious cases occurred in Daviess County in October 1866, when a white man murdered a freedman in the presence of two black witnesses. The murderer was sentenced to death in federal court.[56]

Such occurrences swelled black populations in the lower Ohio's largest settlements, where newcomers formed many religious, fraternal, and mutual aid societies. As in Lexington and Louisville, these successfully protected African Americans against some of the excesses of the era. Although Freedmen's Bureau assistance was increasingly weak, other forms of federal support prevented Kentucky blacks from experiencing the degree of shameful treatment associated with the South since the end of the Civil War. With Kentucky in mind, Congress in 1871 passed a force bill aimed at controlling the activities of the Klan. Federal court rulings prompted the Kentucky legislature in 1872 to legalize the admissibility of blacks' testimony in court. Federal courts in the 1880s, however, weakened postwar constitutional and legislative protection. "New Departure Democrats" created a new constitution in 1891 that formally abolished slavery, adopted the secret ballot, prohibited convict labor, and stated that all men were by nature free and equal. On the other hand, they also formalized segregated and theoretically equal schools.

Schooling was initially private and haphazard, usually offered in churches and aided for a time by the Freedmen's Bureau, which also recruited black teachers. Large classes—typically fifty per room—prevailed. Average attendance at Smithland's school may have been typical. Fifty students were enrolled, but only thirty-five attended regularly. A Paducah school with 125 pupils reported only 75 attending daily. With the aid of the National Freedmen's Aid Association and the Freedmen's Bureau, Paducah had three schools by 1866 and completed a new schoolhouse for 250 pupils two years later. Paducah Baptists also opened a tuition school for 125.[57]

In theory, urban schools offered more opportunity and a longer school year than their rural counterparts. Hancock County's school law was more detailed than most. It delineated district lines, appointed school trustees (at least one of whom was to be black), and authorized paying teachers' salaries with tax monies. Black schools, though, existed only on paper. Henderson received special legislative permission for black public schools in 1871, two years before Covington. (Statewide authorization was granted in 1874.) At first, Henderson provided no funds for black education. As elsewhere, the scope and the quality improved slowly. Whites hired two blacks as teachers and added a second room to the school in 1878. By 1882, Henderson's black school had four teachers, 386 pupils, and offered schooling for ten months. Within ten years, Henderson had two school buildings.

Owensboro's black residents were especially active in the development of education for their youth. With contributions from blacks and help from a sympathetic white, a freedmen's school committee acquired land and opened a school in 1866 for 150 pupils. A year later, with the aid of the Freedmen's Bureau, they built a brick schoolhouse and offered two grades, charging modest tuition. The Bureau contributed forty dollars monthly toward its operating costs. Because of the limited quality of that education, black leaders demanded public education, but the legislature expressly excluded blacks when it passed a law in 1871 allowing public schools in Owensboro. Several years later, public schooling for blacks was instituted. White commissioners appointed three black trustees with nominal administrative powers. The school term was to last three months. Funding came from the state via property taxes on blacks, poll taxes on black males, and fees, fines, and forfeitures assessed on blacks. By the end of the decade, about two hundred blacks were being educated in a new brick building in which three teachers were employed.

The inadequacies of this system prompted black leaders to pressure the legislature for change. A challenge to the special poll tax on blacks, brought by Paducah blacks in federal court, led to a ruling that the state's funding system was unconstitutional. The legislature's response was a law in April 1882 that equalized funding for segregated schools, repealed the school poll tax for blacks, and increased the school property tax modestly. The bill was subjected to a referendum, which created a dilemma for black voters, as support seemingly favored segregation and opposition favored unequal funding. The passage of the referendum, moreover, guaranteed equalization of funding only in Louisville and Paducah. Accordingly, Owensboro black leaders sought to enroll their children in white schools. When denied admission, they took their case to federal court, which in April 1883 voided the legislation because the collection and distribution of funds in this manner created substandard schools, thus violating the Fourteenth Amendment "declared that state laws which allowed municipal corporations to discriminate in the collection and distribution of funds in a manner that resulted in substandard schools for blacks were in violation of the Fourteenth Amendment." Changes as a result of this ruling were significant—the addition of two more school buildings, the improvement of interior furnishings, and the near doubling of eligible blacks in schools by 1891. But acceptance of this ruling by Owensboro civic leaders was grudging, and discrimination and parsimony continued well into the twentieth century. The persistence of wanton violence—lynchings in Owensboro in 1884, and in

Henderson and Paducah in 1915 and 1916—helped to sustain that ethos.[58]

Discrimination and violence were not limited to the Kentucky side of the Ohio, however. The differences reflected, among other things, the number of African Americans, the quality of their leadership, the perceived threats that they posed, the opportunities for employment, and the support given by sympathetic whites. Postwar legislation permitted the formation of separate schools for blacks in Illinois and Indiana, and as a consequence the towns and the cities on the north shore created segregated education in the late 1860s. Black communities created a variety of religious, fraternal, and mutual aid organizations in each settlement. Uneasiness with the failure of the Republican Party to guarantee postwar covenants was much in evidence in all of them by the 1890s.[59]

Social structures and social relations mirrored many common cultural tendencies, such as Upper South patterns of worship, on both sides of the river. On the eve of the Civil War, Baptist and Methodist churches overwhelmed all others in numbers in most of the twenty-four counties. Presbyterians, especially the Cumberland variety, and Disciples of Christ, or Christians, were also numerous. Roman Catholic churches were present in most counties but were concentrated in Harrison, Posey, and Vanderburgh in Indiana and Breckinridge and Hardin in Kentucky. Similarly, German Lutherans were clustered in four Indiana counties.[60]

Voluntary associations, especially churches, and public schools attempted to unite these communities with a set of shared beliefs about human potential and progress.[61] Economic change, transportation and technological advancements, immigration, state and federal government decisions, and Civil War consequences combined, however, to diversify local customs and folkways. Accordingly, institutions and organizations arose which contested and reshaped the turf on which community building occurred.

In the largest places, divergence threatened the harmony that many thought had characterized their earlier years. It also altered public rituals and community priorities. Religious practice was one of the chief manifestations of this phenomenon. Nowhere was it as evident as in the largest city, Evansville, which by 1880 had a wealth of denominations, churches, and synagogues, and within each there was considerable variety: four different Presbyterian congregations, ten Methodist (three black and two German), three Baptist (one black and one German), four German Lutheran, Evangelical, or Reformed, four Roman Catholic (two German, one English, and one Irish), and two Jewish (one German and one Eastern European). The Disciples and the Unitarians each had one church.

Evansville's places of worship revealed the social divisions that characterized the rapidly growing community. The Sunday school superintendent of Walnut Street Presbyterian (New School) was James L. Orr. Charles Viele was the most prominent vestryman of St. Paul's Episcopal Church. Matthew W. Foster, a prominent Republican businessman and father of John, Republican editor and district leader and later secretary of state, was a longtime trustee of First Baptist Church. Eminent Republican merchants and industrialists such as William Heilman attended St. John's Evangelical, while their Democratic counterparts worshipped at Trinity Lutheran or, like John A. Reitz, at Holy Trinity. Affluent Jewish businessmen Abe Strouse, Jacob Loewenthal, and August Brentano were mainstays at B'Nai Israel, the Reform synagogue.[62]

Members of these institutions mirrored cultures that both enriched and diversified their communities. German newcomers greatly enhanced the city's social, intellectual, literary, and musical life, forming between 1853 and 1860 an athletic club, a choral society, a philharmonic society, Schiller and Mozart festivals, several newspapers, and a vine growers' association. The development of B'Nai Israel attracted the attention of the city's elite. Prominent Evansvillians attended the dedication of the new temple in 1866 at which the eminent American Jewish leader, Isaac M. Wise, spoke. With great pride the *Daily Journal* reprinted Wise's comments about his visit, published in *The Israelite* of Cincinnati.[63]

Cultural divisions, on the other hand, created zones of conflict. Many Germans, for instance, battled the evangelical Protestant elite on the issue of temperance. With support from native-born Democrats, they blocked efforts to prohibit local sale of spirituous beverages in 1853 and subsequently to prevent liquor sales and other alleged violations on the Sabbath. German Lutherans and Catholics were firmly opposed to what they perceived to be the Methodist- and Presbyterian-dominated Sunday school movement. German artisans in 1860 organized the most spectacular Independence Day celebration in the city's history, but were criticized by English-speaking merchants and industrialists for using the occasion as an instrument of class and nationality. The city's major postwar response to the needs of youth, the Young Men's Christian Association (1870), was perceived by German Catholics and Lutherans as an instrument of the English-speaking evangelicals.[64]

No issue proved as divisive as public education. Evansville's public school system came into being shortly after the passage of enabling legislation in 1852. Yankee-born leaders such as Horatio Q. Wheeler, strongly supported by German Evangelicals Christian Decker and William Heilman, touted tax-supported schools as the foundation on which the city's progress would be erected. The common school's doors opened a year later, and in 1854 the Evansville High School was established. Native Democrats, supported by Lutherans and Catholics who perceived the schools as instruments of evangelical Protestantism as well as unnecessary, unfair drains on public funds, strongly opposed their establishment. Local elections well into the 1860s turned on this question. Thereafter Democrats' criticism focused on schools' costs.

One extremely divisive issue was instruction in German, begun in 1867. Supporters defended this as a means of Americanizing children of German parents, who might otherwise keep them out of school or send them to parochial schools. It was also argued that this enabled native Americans to expand their intellectual horizons by learning another language. Germans were so numerous that by 1865 a German American was elected school board president, and Germans generally headed the board thereafter. School attendance rose steadily—from 750 in 1853 to 5,404 in 1880. In the meantime, Lutherans, Catholics, and some Evangelicals established their own schools.[65]

Everywhere along the lower Ohio, public education disclosed cultural consensus and conflict. Where it was weakest, illiteracy was greatest. In eight of the eleven Kentucky counties in 1870, the number of persons who could not read far exceeded the number of those who had attended school that year. In the other three counties, the number in school was only slightly above the number who could not read. A similar situation existed in Alexander and Pulaski Counties in Illinois. This probably revealed the number of freedmen enumerated that year as well as the low level of public support for education. In no Indiana county, by contrast, was the number of illiterates as high, even though the state's illiteracy rate in 1880 continued to be highest in the North (but only one-fifth of Kentucky's rate).

Significant intraregional differences also persisted. By 1900, only 33 percent of Kentucky's youth had six months or more of schooling, as compared with nearly 90 percent in Indiana and Illinois. In Evansville, 98 percent of the pupils were in school at least six months. The number of illiterates ages ten or older decreased in three of Illinois's river counties but rose in Alexander, Pope, and Pulaski; decreased in all of Indiana's except three (Perry, Posey, and Vanderburgh, all with high German-born populations); and increased in five of Kentucky's eleven (Crittenden, Daviess, Henderson, McCracken, and Meade). Despite some local strengths, Kentucky's weak schools were fundamentally to blame not only for the state's illiteracy rates but also, in many respects, for those across the river. Thomas D. Clark has portrayed Kentucky's culture of 1865-1910 as shabby and backwoods, reflecting the intensely rural, agrarian society of the state. Schools were the most vivid symbols of that.[66]

Cultural change or continuity varied enormously. Despite its rail links to the north and south, its postwar economic advances, and its attraction of Germans, Henderson in many respects remained rooted in the antebellum past.

On the one hand, voluntary associations flowered—twenty-nine fraternal societies, most established after the war, as well as a county medical society, a choral society, a YMCA, twenty churches, and one synagogue. On the other, the community was tied by family and income to the paternalistic plantation era. Henderson's easy-going, quiet manners, its spacious streets, and its grand homes reflected a Tidewater inheritance. With two exceptions, its religious organizations revealed and confirmed Upper South values.[67]

Owensboro and Paducah, with weaker patriarchies and a higher level of manufacturing, experienced a greater influx of newcomers and their folkways than any lower Ohio towns in Kentucky. For example, Owensboro's first history included two Catholic parishes, one German (1870), a German Evangelical church (1871), and a German Jewish synagogue, organized a few years before the Civil War. (Paducah's was formed in 1868.) Nine of the remaining ten congregations were Baptist, Methodist, Presbyterian, or Episcopal. The number of fraternal and benevolent societies was substantially greater than in Henderson. At least five of them, including the Hebrew Benevolent Society, had been organized by immigrants, and two were African American. A clear sign of cultural diversity was the presence of several temperance societies and some hotly contested temperance revival meetings. Several labor organizations had also been formed there. Paducah had a smaller Catholic population than Owensboro, but it also had German Evangelical and Lutheran congregations.[68]

In smaller settlements, cultural patterns remained relatively unchanged. Kentucky's river villages and towns were provincial English and/or Scots-Irish, evangelical Protestant outposts along a river whose travelers symbolized cultural, economic, and technological change. In Hawesville, for example, community leadership remained in the hands of the coterie which had been in control before the war. In part because of the effects of wartime damage to the economy, public schools were generally unfit, teachers were poorly prepared, and funding was low. Not surprisingly, only 28 percent of the eligible children attended school in 1880. Hawesville remained the trading center of an overwhelmingly rural, agrarian county with isolated homesteads connected by primitive roads, a place with scattered post offices, general stores, and churches tied by commercial and governmental needs to the small county seat on the Ohio. Similar observations could be made about Brandenburg, Smithland, Uniontown, and West Point, although the coming of the railroad to West Point in 1874 made it less isolated. Smaller places such as Birdsville (organized 1860) were even more homogeneous. Life revolved around a ferry, a general store, a post office, a Baptist church, and a one-room school.[69]

Somewhat similar models prevailed across the river. The cases of Metropolis, Golconda, Elizabethtown, Mount Vernon, Newburgh, and Tell City are typical. By 1880, each boasted benevolent and fraternal societies, churches (mostly Baptist and Methodist), at least one school, and a newspaper, such as the predecessor of Metropolis's *Republican Herald* (1865). As a Massac County historian aptly described Metropolis, these places were tied to the Upper South by blood, climate, and interests. Lifestyles were unhurried and manners friendly, although river towns were less relaxed and orderly than their interior counterparts. In manufacturing towns such as Cannelton, Tell City, and Mount Vernon, European immigrants and Yankees altered that somewhat. Tell City was least typical, given its Swiss-German roots, as it had no Sabbath blue laws and exulted its heritage through a strong public school system and a wealth of societies promoting physical culture, literature, and music. Hamlets and villages such as Shetlerville, Rome, Leavenworth, and Mauckport most resembled their Kentucky counterparts in customs and folkways.[70]

Whatever their size or origin, these settlements offered residents and visitors many forms of entertainment and recreation, beginning with social life sustained by churches, stores, post offices, and voluntary associations. In Hancock County, Kentucky, for instance, probably the most defining moments each week in Hawesville and Lewisport were the arrivals of packet boats, especially those of the "Gray Eagle" Louisville and Henderson line. The *Tarascon* departed downriver Tuesday and Friday mornings and returned those evenings; the *Gray Eagle* operated on Wednesdays and Saturdays, and the *Morning Star* on Thursdays and Sundays. By tradition, a mule on the Scuffletown side of the river learned the whistle of a stern-wheeler operating between Owensboro and Evansville. Passing Scuffletown at 11:30, en route to Evansville, the boat would signal for a hail or a landing. If the mule was halfway up a row, he threw up his head, responded in "regular mule fashion" to the boat, and refused to move further, demanding to be unhitched and taken to the barn for his noon meal of oats or corn.[71]

Aside from freight and passengers, these ships brought the news, the latest technology, such as the first demonstration of electric lights, and the services of drummers, gamblers, and entertainers. Many of these rivercraft also captivated crewmen, passengers, and townspeople with their speed and grace. The *John Gilbert*, built in Pittsburgh in 1881 and a mainstay of the Ohio and Tennessee Packet Company's run from Cincinnati to Florence, was the subject of one of the most famous folk songs, which began with the lines

> You see that boat a-comin
> She's comin' roun' the ben'
> And when she gets in
> She'll be loaded down again.[72]

Transient theatrical companies, ventriloquists, and showmen with wax figures were an important element in Paducah popular culture, as evidenced by the fact that one of the earliest acts of Paducah's town board had been to set fees on them. Summer brought floating pavilions, showboats, traveling dramatic troupes, vaudevillians, circuses, and medicine shows. Artists often offered their services in exchange for food. Packet boats and smaller craft also offered residents Sunday excursions. For black residents of Evansville and Henderson, who visited each other on summer Sabbaths, this was one of the few forms of recreation in their highly segregated communities. An especially important time for such outings was Emancipation Day on September 22. Later, railroads offered faster, cheaper service.[73]

In the heyday of the steamboat, the riverfront itself offered high drama and entertainment. Theodore Dreiser recalled Evansville, his hometown, as "paved with great gray cobblestones and stocked with enormous piles of cotton in bales, groceries and hardware in boxes, and watermelons and other fruits and vegetables in piles or crated, boxed, bagged, or barreled. . . . Floating docks [were] anchored lengthwise of the shore and lashed to those [were] a number of the old-time, stern wheel river steamers, with their black double stacks, double and treble decks, gilt and red or blue or green decorations, and piles of freight being taken on or unloaded."[74]

In addition to the bustle of black draymen and steamboat hands and the beckonings of entertainers and drummers, the riverfront brought the most popular form of participatory sports, baseball. Imported downriver from Cincinnati, home of the first professional team, "Town Ball" was first publicized before the Civil War. On July 14, 1860, the *Evansville Daily Journal* reported that some of the city's young men, single and married, had formed a "Base Ball" club. The editor praised the sport for its healthfulness and simplicity. That it attracted men of all social strata was also appealing. German, English, and Scots-Irish surnames appeared on the rosters, and sons of prominent merchants and factory owners mingled with artisans. Baseball also provided relaxation for spectators and served as a form of community boosterism, as towns took great pride in the exploits of their local teams. These factors helped to explain the national popularity of this game.[75]

With peace came a greatly accelerated pace of growth and popularity of the game, perhaps because of its appeal to Union and Confederate soldiers. Baseball came to be regarded as the "national game" because of the formation of the National Association and a number of regional organizations, such as the Northwestern Association of Base Ball Players (1865), which included sixteen clubs in midwestern states. The Washington Nationals' great tour of the Midwest in 1867 aroused much interest.[76]

By the summer of 1865, Cairo had two clubs, the Egyptians and the Magenta. Evansville's baseball enthusiasts erected a ballfield on the southeast side near the city limits, where they played on Saturday afternoons. The city's first sports column, an extended account of a four-inning game between the city's two teams, appeared on July 17. An amateur "Evansville Base Ball Club" was formed the following year to take on intercity competition, which in 1867 extended to a club recently formed in Paducah. The Resolutes, organized in the summer of 1867, when Evansville boasted seven teams, became the Evansville club's chief rival. The Resolutes' contest with an Owensboro team warranted a lengthy newspaper account. After the Resolutes won 59-21, team members served their opponents champagne. In late October, an Evansville club known as the Actives tied a visiting team from Henderson, the Pee Wees.[77]

The Nationals' tour accelerated the formation of teams in Cairo, Evansville, Henderson, Owensboro, Paducah, and such interior towns as Vincennes, Patoka, Princeton, and Fort Branch, all north of Evansville. Riverboats connected them. On September 19, 1867, for example, Cairo's Eclipse team, one of several in the city, took on the visiting Paducah Quicksteps in an afternoon match. Perhaps due to little advance warning or to work schedules, only two of the local team members showed up. The remainder of the squad was pulled from the crowd. Not surprisingly, the locals lost, 65-30, but even so the story secured four headlines and twenty-one paragraphs in the *Cairo Democrat*.[78]

A few months earlier, the Cairo Independents led the call for a convention in Chicago, which in July 1867 recognized Illinois members of the National Association and established a state tourney. The first was played with fifty-four teams. Intercity rivalry rose everywhere. Evansville's top two teams traveled to Indianapolis in October 1867 to take on that city's best. The following year, the larger communities gained even more clubs, such as the Olympics and the Richmonds of Henderson, which played Evansville teams several times. Regular intercity play was well established by 1868. Mount Vernon and Shawneetown clubs were soon involved in regional competition. By 1870, teams from Evansville and Louisville had begun to play one another.

Each city's elite boasted it had the best team in the region. The Evansville Base Ball Club, like others, perceived Cincinnati's professional team as "our club"—arranging a rail excursion to witness a contest with Brooklyn in late August 1869, for example. (The Evansville Club was also known as the Red Stockings.) An Evansville team's victory over a Louisville team in 1870 raised local morale sharply, since the team had challenged and lost badly to a club from Memphis that was returning home after a game in Cincinnati the previous July.[79]

In the cities, towns, and villages along the lower Ohio, team names mimicked those of larger places—Actives, Atlantics, Excelsiors, Red Stockings—or reflected local circumstances—the Riversides, for instance, or the Quicksteps, named after the fast Gilbert packet boat. Each year brought a proliferation of clubs organized by school, place of employment, political affiliation, nationality, and race.

Each city had clubs that were organized annually, solicited stock subscriptions, had constitutions and directors, and played extensive inter- as well as intracity schedules. By 1872, the Riverside club was the Crescent City's elite team. Membership included the sons of wealthy as well as middle-class families. In 1871, the team played sixteen games, winning twelve, between late April and mid-September which included teams from Jeffersonville and Louisville. All of these lower Ohio players, like the Riversides, however, were amateur, and vicissitudes of finance and occupational and business obligations made for discontinuity. The Riversides disbanded in August 1872, just before a crucial match in St. Louis. And just about every settlement, including tiny Carrsville in Livingston County, Kentucky, had a squad. In larger towns, some players—on the Riversides and on the main Owensboro team, for example, were paid to play, and they sold their services to the highest bidders. Apparently the first completely professional team that played an entire summer season was organized in Evansville in 1882. It competed with teams from Louisville, Cincinnati, and St. Louis.[80]

After the Civil War, participatory sports became very popular— croquet, bicycling, skating, lawn tennis, and archery—as did spectator sports—horse racing, prizefighting, and baseball. The growing emphasis on physical fitness contributed to that, and even in the smallest villages and towns forms of these new sports could be found. In larger places, where there was a YMCA or a Turnverein, gymnastics were promoted, and by the 1890s basketball also began to appeal to city people. Court days in Kentucky continued to offer many forms of athletic competition, from fighting to horse races.[81]

Residents of even the smallest settlements also enjoyed voluntary associations: Masonic lodges, chapters of the Grand Army of the Republic, and the "granges" of the Patrons of Husbandry (1867). These groups offered games, parties, and other attractions. Tiny Carrsville, for instance, had four churches, a band, a young ladies' social club, a Masonic lodge, and a baseball team. Medicine shows and celebrations, especially Independence Day and county fairs, offered diversions, and inns and taverns also offered recreational outlets. The pace of life, however, was slow. Commenting on Smithland's being "all torn up over a sensational elopement" of local teenagers who had gone across to Golconda to marry, an editor in another Kentucky county declared "a runaway or dog fight in that sleepy old town usually causes as much excitement as if one of the most prominent citizens had dropped dead."[82]

For those preferring more refined entertainment, larger communities offered theatrical and musical fare—lectures, drama, melodrama, comedy, burlesque, vaudeville, opera, orchestras, music halls, and minstrel shows. Some also exulted in their literary and historical societies and libraries. For the urban masses, vaudeville was by far the most popular by 1880, even more so than riverboat entertainment and circuses, because each was seasonal and railroads eroded the strength of passenger service on the Ohio. Vaudeville "combined elements of legitimate theater, variety acts, and burlesque, but with the burlesque element elevated to a high plane of respectability and moral cleanliness."[83]

For most residents of the lower Ohio valley, "cultivated" literature, music, and fine arts were only mildly appealing. Some communities built opera houses and other public halls to accommodate the tastes of their residents as well as to document their progress. Evansville's Grand Opera House of 1889 was the city's finest. Smaller cities also built them: for instance, Owensboro's Mendelssohn Hall and Hall's Opera House of the late 1870s, and four more theaters for minstrel and vaudeville shows by 1910. Opera houses were also erected in some small towns, such as Uniontown.[84]

Such facilities had their roots in traveling dramatic shows offered by riverboats, which in the 1850s offered melodrama and musical revues and established a theatrical tradition in small places such as Elizabethtown, Shawneetown, and Cairo. This, in turn, laid the basis for theatrical halls, such as Cairo's Athenaeum, built in the 1860s to supplant the declining number of showboats. By the early 1880s, when an elegant opera house was opened in Cairo that cost $35,000 and seated 1,300, a new level of entertainment had been attained which attracted such varied performances as *Ten Nights in a Barroom*, *Quo Vadis*, and the operettas of Gilbert and Sullivan. Nearby cities such as Paducah also established opera houses, which became dramatic centers—often via vaudeville—for decades to come. Paducah's St. Clair Hall was its chief center for entertainment until Morton's Opera House was opened in 1885. Another opera house was erected in 1900. Regional needs and interests produced distinctive regional dramatic forms that are often overlooked by those focusing on Chicago or New York.[85]

In some communities, men and women produced a wide assortment of literary and artistic achievements. Despite its tawdry reputation, for instance, Cairo gained one of the earliest public libraries in the state through the efforts of the Women's Club and Library Association, formed in 1877. Like many women's organizations of the late nineteenth century, this group extended to the public sphere the influence that women were supposed to exert in the private realm of home and family. Raising money to purchase over 1,200 books and a building, the association's efforts led to the opening of the Cairo Public Library in 1883. Willard Carpenter's philanthropy built the grand Willard Library in Evansville two years later. A trust he created supported its operations.[86]

Germans in Tell City, Evansville, Mount Vernon, Owensboro, Paducah, and other locales contributed heavily to the refinement of community life. The Evansville Philharmonic Society, for instance, was reorganized after the Civil War. The Central Turnverein was formed in the 1850s to promote physical education and cultural refinement of Evansville Germans. In Owensboro, Germans led efforts after 1863 for the public education of their children. Neither was it coincidental that the public hall was named for Felix Mendelssohn, the great German composer. By the 1880s, German-Swiss citizens of Tell City boasted bands, a glee club, an athletic club, a shooting society, and a women's club.[87]

The river continued to be a central aspect of residents' lives. It provided a new start for immigrants. Riverboats, whether floating by or docking in even the smallest places, offered a sense of a larger world outside. River settlements were vital places in which inhabitants' behavior was less easily regulated than in most places in the interior, but there, too, the region's first public schools, temperance societies, and other instruments of social control had emerged.

The patterns that had been in place for forty years continued to unfold, with some places advancing rapidly and others declining. As before, these reflected numerous influences, not the least of which was the quality of community leadership. And that would be amply illustrated in the heady days of rapid industrialization and the formation of metropolitan regions in the forty years to come.

PART 4 ∾

The Lower Ohio and the Industrial-Metropolitan Age, 1880-1920

9 ∽

Patterns of Communities' Growth and Development

Innovations in corporate organization were responses to the challenges of a rapidly expanding national urban market, and applications of electricity and internal combustion engines produced even faster growth. All of this, along with the emergent mass culture, fed by consumerism, and the upheavals associated with domestic reforms and foreign affairs in the progressive era would appear—according to the meager historical record of the lower Ohio in this era—to have bypassed this region.

Instead, history focuses on Chicago, the wunderkind of the emerging radial centers that dominated their hinterlands via diversified manufacturing, commerce, insurance, and finance. Spatial expansion and residential and economic segregation occurred in these places, which also offered their residents an enormous array of cultural and recreational opportunities. Large urban markets, moreover, spurred the consumer revolution through department, chain, and catalog stores and national advertising for brand-name goods. Smaller cities fell under the hegemony of these centers.[1]

Perhaps best described as a "backwater thesis," the sketchy histories of this part of the nation stress the oblivion brought on by railroads. An overview of lower Ohio River locales in this period, however, yields an assortment of stories—stagnation and decline, to be sure, but even more so growth and creation. Evansville strengthens its position as the hub of trade, manufacturing, and service for a region radiating seventy-five to one hundred miles and the urban center of a metropolis including Henderson. Cairo becomes an appendage of the economies of Chicago, St. Louis, and Memphis, and communities such as West Point and others in Meade and eastern Harrison Counties begin to blend into metropolitan Louisville. Continuity and change are also evident.

In the spring of 1894, Reuben Gold Thwaites, executive secretary of the State Historical Society of Wisconsin, floated down the Ohio by skiff armed with a primitive Kodak and seeking local color. "I wanted to see with my own eyes what the borders saw; in imagination, to redress the pioneer stage, and

Major Settlements on the Lower Ohio, 1880

2,500 or more residents	1,000 - 2,499 residents	
1. Cairo	8. Mound City	12. Newburgh
2. Metropolis	9. Golconda	13. Rockport
3. Paducah	10. Shawneetown	14. Tell City
4. Mt. Vernon	11. Uniontown	15. Cannelton
5. Henderson		
6. Evansville		
7. Owensboro		

Major Settlements on the Lower Ohio, 1880, based on *Atlas of the State of Illinois* . . . (Chicago, 1876, reprinted as *Maps of Illinois Counties in 1876* by Mayhill Publications, Knightstown, Indiana, 1972); *Illustrated Historical Atlas of The State of Indiana* (Chicago, 1876, reprinted by the Indiana Historical Society, Indianapolis, 1968); and Collins, *History of Kentucky* (1874), I:635-38 repeople it." His diary, published in 1897 as *Afloat on the Ohio,* was dedicated to his colleague at Wisconsin, Frederick Jackson Turner, whose recent thesis claimed that the "converting of the wilderness into a garden [was] the formative impulse behind the distinctly American characteristics of independence and self-reliance." John Jakle argues that Thwaites's diary "clearly reflected the maturity that the Ohio Valley had achieved by the nineteenth century's closing."[2]

By the time Thwaites and his small party passed Cincinnati, the monotony of the landscape had dulled his enthusiasm for the trip. Leaving Louisville on May 30, 1894, he found that towns downriver were few and small. West Point was a lazy-looking little village, and Brandenburg, the largest in that vicinity, was a "sleepy, ill-paved, shambling place where apparently nobody is engaged in any serious calling." New Amsterdam was a "little white hamlet" that was "trim and bright." Leavenworth was small and "characterless." Here and there were deserted cabins, whose "cracker" (a term he used for all poor whites) families had moved on or been killed by malaria. A few houseboats were to be found, as were some "whitewashed cabins of small tillers" nestled in "this world of shade." No humans were visible at Alton—"a dry unpainted place."

For the next few days, Thwaites recorded similarity: rustic landscape, small farms on bottomlands, "wretched cabins" on the slopes, shabby villages, frequent oxbow windings of the river, and lovely vistas. Rono, Indiana, impressed him as a pretty study in gray, green, and white with a Masonic hall that resembled a schoolhouse. Derby, ravaged by fire a few months earlier, was principally a timber port. Stephensport, "a straggling hamlet," was typical of the "far away, sidetracked villages" where "the world lies in the basin of the hills which there people see from their doors." Residents of such "a dead little hamlet" were "wretched." By contrast, Cloverport had a bustling riverfront where black roustabouts loaded freight onto a steamboat while "singing in a low pitch an old-time plantation melody." Like other Kentucky towns, its streets were unkempt, but its shops were well stocked, and many farmers came to town on Saturdays. Cannelton and Hawesville, with their coal mines and tipples, resembled towns he had seen on the Monongehela. Tell City was "another flourishing factory town." However, Troy was a "sleepy" place that had "profited nothing from having lively neighbors."

From Derby westward the river's banks flattened, and bottomlands growing huge quantities of corn and tobacco stretched toward the river's mouth. This region was subject to annual flooding, which required residents to take the high ground. Thwaites noted that Rockport was "romantically perched upon a grand rock." Owensboro drew little commentary other than that it possessed a pretty courthouse in a green park and had well-paved streets and clean, bright

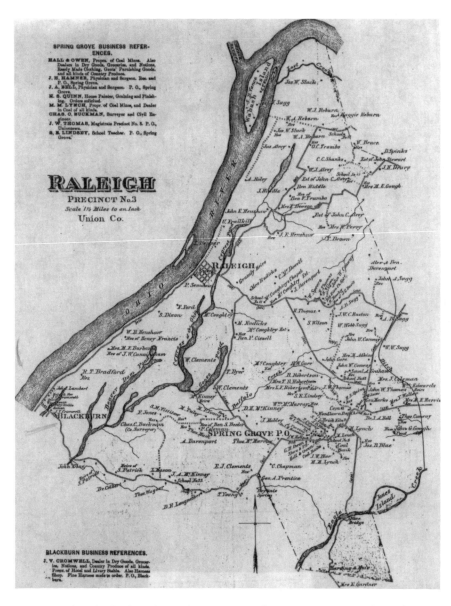

The town plan of Raleigh, in the southwest portion of Union County, Kentucky, as shown in the *Atlas of Henderson and Union Counties, Kentucky* in 1880 (author's collection)

shops. Enterprise was "an unpainted village with a dismal view," Scuffletown was uninviting, and Newburgh was a "ragged little place that has seen better days." Evansville, by contrast, was "a charming [Joseph] Turneresque study, as her steeples and factory chimneys developed through the mist." A fine, well-built town with a beautiful post office, which refuted the view that small cities had no notable government buildings, Evansville also boasted a new railway bridge and a level of business activity that Thwaites had not seen since leaving Louisville.

Thwaites found little to impress him thence to Cairo. Henderson had large tobacco interests. Mount Vernon and Uniontown were flourishing, bright and neat, set in green hills. Shawneetown, walled in by a thirty-foot levee, was a town whose lively days were long past. Elizabethtown was picturesque and dry, Rosiclare was a string of shanties with half of its residents idle, Carrsville was a dry hamlet on a hillside, and Bird's Landing, Kentucky, was "shabby but picturesquely situated." Smithland was a woebegone place. Paducah was a "stirring little city with the usual large proportion of negroes, and the out-door business life met everywhere in the South." The city had many sawmills, iron foundries, a shipyards, and an active ferry business with Brooklyn (Bridgeport), Illinois. Downriver, he recorded Joppa's unpainted, dilapidated buildings, Caledonia's nondescript businesses, and Mound City's timeworn appearance. At the mouth was Cairo, the nation's "brave little Holland."[3]

Thwaites's diary, the last travel journal of the entire Ohio, documented the emerging conflict between "industry's heavy hand" and "residual nature and the new garden that farmers had created." The Ohio Valley "represented something of an economic backwater, at least away from the cities." By bringing parallel lines to the river and bridges across it, the railroads, he argued, had diminished the Ohio as a regional system, and "a river-oriented era was clearly ending."[4]

Stagnation and decline, however, had existed before the railroads. Like growth and development, they would persist well into the twentieth century. The drama, the color, the energy, and the hopes of entrepreneurs and ordinary people continued. Visited by former presidents Ulysses S. Grant and Jefferson Davis in 1881, for example, Cairo still seemed poised to capture its oft-promised but elusive greatness. Golconda, thriving in the 1880s and obtaining a railroad connection in 1902, enjoyed unprecedented prosperity. Tell City's popular chairs seemed to guarantee limitless expansion, and its growth—compared with neighboring Cannelton—prompted it to seek the county seat in the mid-1890s. It failed (but prevailed a century later). The revival of coal mining in the 1880s seemed to offer Hawesville a second chance. Brooklyn,

Illinois, enjoyed a thriving ferry trade with Paducah and, during World War I, obtained a railroad bridge.

Even some new places were established. Howell, Indiana, was organized in the mid-1880s by L&N officials at their new rail yard southwest of Evansville. Howell prospered, although annexed by the larger city in 1916. Most new places, such as Alzey in Henderson County, would amount to little because of floods. And the decline or demise of once-promising places persisted—Caseyville, Raleigh, Smithland, Shetlerville, Maxville, Lewisport, Alton, and Fredonia, among others. Some tried on new, loftier names—Hamletsville became Hamletsburg, for instance, and Hurricane Landing in Crittenden County was renamed Tolu, after a popular hair tonic—yet they remained hamlets. Leavenworth was not as fortunate as Cannelton, losing out one night in 1894 to vigilantes, who stole the county's records and made inland English the new seat of government. Flooding in 1937 decimated the village.[5]

Most places remained what they had always been. Skillman's Landing and Emmick's Landing in Hancock County, Ford's Ferry in Crittenden County, and Berry's Ferry in Livingston County were typical. A War Department survey of the Ohio in 1916 identified just 50 organized communities beyond the Falls, but another 135—over half in Kentucky—were unplatted ferries or landings. It also identified fifteen ferry services, the first at Brandenburg and the last at Metropolis, and only three railroad bridges.[6]

Many small market centers persisted. In 1920, one found nine villages, three more than in 1880—Rosiclare, Shawneetown, Golconda, Brookport, and Elizabethtown, Illinois; Cannelton and Newburgh, Indiana; and Cloverport and Uniontown, Kentucky—with between 1,000 and 2,500 residents. Another seventeen—from Stephensport, with 214, to Hawesville, with 829—had less than 1,000 inhabitants, but they were large enough to be listed in the 1920 census.

Nine other communities were considered urban, having more than 2,500 residents. Most were small. They ranged in size from Rockport, with 2,581, to Evansville, with 85,264. Four had less than 10,000 residents, and the second largest, Paducah, had slightly less than 25,000. The timing of their crossing the "urban threshold" of 2,500 varied. Evansville was the earliest, in the 1840s, and Paducah the next, in the 1850s. Four attained that in the 1860s, and four more before 1900. None crossed over after 1900. Moreover, none of these places was large enough, before 1920, to be considered the center of the Census Bureau's new "metropolitan districts," although Evansville attained that in 1930—the only lower Ohio city to gain that distinction in the century. Its population density—12,000 inhabitants per square mile in the central city—was well above Cincinnati, Indianapolis, and Louisville, but half the total of New York and somewhat less than Chicago and St. Louis.[7]

Evansville boosters on the *John Stewart Hopkins* at Cairo, 1907 (University of Southern Indiana Special Collections)

Evansville's public landing in 1904. To the right of the wharf boat are the packets *Sunshine* and *Park City*, and the *Grand Floating Palace*, towed by the *Cricket* (Inland Rivers Collection, Cincinnati-Hamilton County Public Library).

The bluff overlooking the Ohio at Rockport, circa 1920, with a gasoline-powered boat in the foreground. Rockport's first settlers erected homes and businesses at the base of the bluff (Willard Library).

The main north-south street in Newburgh, 1907, looking toward the Ohio, with the new Citizens Bank building on the left (Willard)

The ferry at Uniontown, Kentucky, circa 1920, which linked Uniontown with Posey County, Indiana (Willard)

Lock and Dam 48, one of the earliest improvements of the Corps of Engineers, near Henderson, under construction, circa 1921 (USI)

Before canalization in 1929, the Ohio regularly froze over, providing citizens a unique opportunity to walk on water. The winter of 1918 was especially cold, producing this view at the Owensboro riverfront (Daviess County Public Library)

The Ohio afforded people many forms of recreation and economic opportunity. This bucolic scene of turn-of-the-century Hawesville reveals one of them (Wade Hall, *Greetings from Kentucky*).

An 1869 print of Evansville, shown from the perspective of the southwest (tracks from the Bodiam Mine are in the foreground), seems to show river commerce, industrial smoke, church steeples, and fishing in harmony (USI).

Above: During the 1913 flood—one of the worst—a packetboat, barges, and gas boats are tied up at Lower Water Street, hundreds of feet inland from normal anchorage in Evansville (USI). As shown on the set of markers (*left*) at one of Tell City's oldest wood-working establishments, the flood of 1913, like that of 1884, paled by comparison with the monster flood of 1937 (author's collection). *Below:* A "bird's eye" view of Evansville in 1888 (USI)

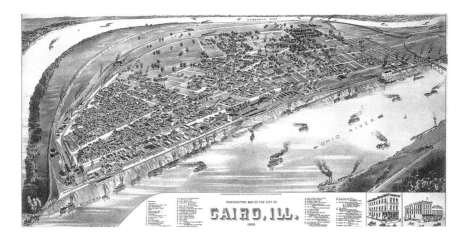

"Perspective Map of the City of Cairo" prepared by Henry Wellge of Milwaukee, 1888 (Library of Congress, Geography and Map Division)

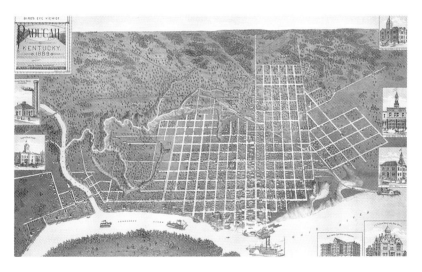

A "bird's eye" view of Paducah in 1889 by J. Blanton, artist (Library of Congress, Geography and Map Division)

A postcard vividly illustrates the aesthetic effects of telephone and electric lines, as well as the trolley tracks and automobiles, on the business district in turn-of-the-century Henderson. The street, though, is unpaved (Wade Hall, *Greetings from Kentucky*).

Designed by Henry Wolters of Louisville, the baroque Vanderburgh County courthouse opened in 1891—a testament to local prosperity and the presence of a skilled work force. Photograph circa 1915 (USI)

The landing at Old Leavenworth (Crawford County, Indiana), looking west toward the ridge on which rival Fredonia, second county seat, was located (author's collection)

Despite the decay of its small business district, Mauckport has preserved its town pump, a focal point of community life since the Civil War era (author's collection).

Top: One of the oldest inns in Rockport, this antebellum Federal structure was, by local legend, a place where Abraham Lincoln stayed on his political tour of southern Indiana in 1844 (Willard). *Middle:* Once the grandest hotel on the lower Ohio, the St. George of Evansville was situated on First between Locust and Walnut streets. The Ohio (background) was a block away. Built in 1874, it was replaced in 1917 by the even grander McCurdy (USI). *Bottom:* The graceful Gothic Grace Episcopal Church, begun in 1873 in Paducah (author's collection)

Above left: St. Boniface Roman Catholic Church, on Wabash Avenue in Evansville. This view, taken from a stereopticon slide, dates from the early 1880s. The edifice, one of the largest and grandest on the lower Ohio, was completed in 1881 (USI). *Right:* The First Presbyterian Church of Golconda, Illinois, built in 1869. The congregation is the state's oldest Presbyterian communion (author's collection).

Below: In the near downtown neighborhoods of the turn of the century, housing stock was quite varied, and services like groceries and saloons were widespread. This Evansville neighborhood, in the process of gaining bricked streets, contained several modest "shotgun" houses (USI).

The horse-car lines, replaced in the early 1890s by trolleys, facilitated the construction of affluent residential neighborhoods away from the center of town. This is Washington Avenue on Evansville's southeast side, circa 1890 (USI).

The Rosencranz Apartments, opened in 1915 at Sixth and Chandler in Evansville, were designed by local architect Clifford Shopbell (USI).

The first on the lower Ohio, the L&N bridge between Henderson and Vanderburgh County, Indiana, was opened in 1885 (USI).

One of the major catalysts in the transformation of river towns in the late 1920s, this vehicular bridge between Brookport, Illinois, and Paducah was opened in 1929 (Willard).

The Henderson-Vanderburgh County vehicular bridge was opened in 1932. Thence until the 1960s, only three highway bridges operated south of the Falls. Cairo's was the third (Willard).

L&N engine 309, with crew, at the Howell yards near Evansville, circa 1910 (USI)

The Evansville and Terre Haute Station on Seventh Street in Evansville, circa 1890. Note the horse-car, which connected the station to the riverfront and water-borne transport at the largest passenger facility on the lower Ohio at the time (USI).

The Igleheart Brothers flour mill on the canal (present-day Fifth and Locust streets in Evansville), pictured in the late nineteenth century (USI)

The 1876 Atlas of Daviess County included lithographs of several industries, among which Richard Monarch's distillery was one of the most prominent. Whiskey was the city's leading product by the early 1880s (Daviess County Public Library).

The Evansville Cotton Mill, shown circa 1890 (USI)

The skyline of Tell City, early in the twentieth century. Wood products were a mainstay of the Swiss German community (Willard).

Women at work stemming tobacco at Fendich Tobacco Company of Evansville, circa 1915 (USI)

The employees of the Evansville Brewing Association, formed in the early 1890s out of several breweries. Pride in craft was amply evident in this turn-of-the-century photograph (USI).

Assembling Graham Brothers Trucks on Evansville's north side, circa 1920 (USI)

As noted in the WPA guide to Cairo, published before World War II, this levee control floodgate of the Illinois Central Railroad resembled the portcullis of a medieval city (WPA, Cairo).

Baseball teams flourished in the late nineteenth century. Many companies had their own teams (USI).

Recreational opportunities for youth were mostly provided by private groups early in this century. Many of those were sponsored by Germans. These boys participated in Central Turverein (Evansville) Youth Athletics, circa 1915 (USI).

For working-class men, the corner saloon (in this case, Joe Folz's, on Evansville's north side) was the chief recreational outlet in the early industrial era (USI).

Because of a geographical quirk, the territory between Evansville's southeast side and the Ohio was part of Henderson County, Kentucky. A horse-racing park, named Dade, was opened there in 1922, and residents of Evansville and Henderson flocked to it. The region soon was notorious for gambling

Few lower river towns had high schools before the early twentieth century, and few youth in towns that did attended them. These are graduates of the region's first high school, Evansville High School (now Central), in the late 1870s (USI).

The band from Frederick Douglass, the black high school in Evansville, circa 1922 (USI)

The Evansville, Suburban, and Newburgh station in Newburgh, Indiana, in 1907, with a group waiting to board a car (Willard)

The truck—in this case, one employed by R. Pennington of Evansville—contributed to the urbanization of the region because of its capacity, durability, and speed (Willard).

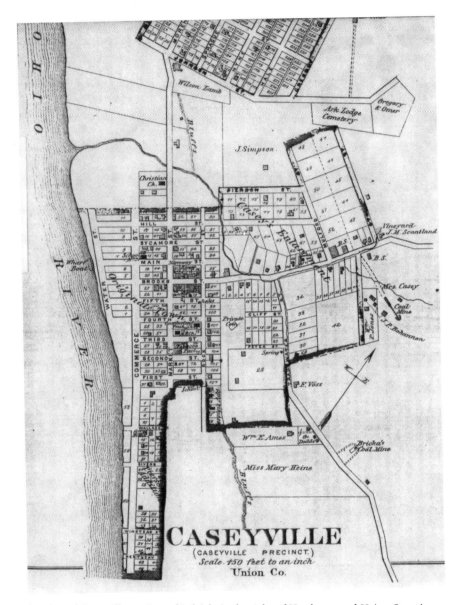

The plan of Caseyville, upriver of Raleigh, in the *Atlas of Henderson and Union Counties, Kentucky* in 1880 (author's collection)

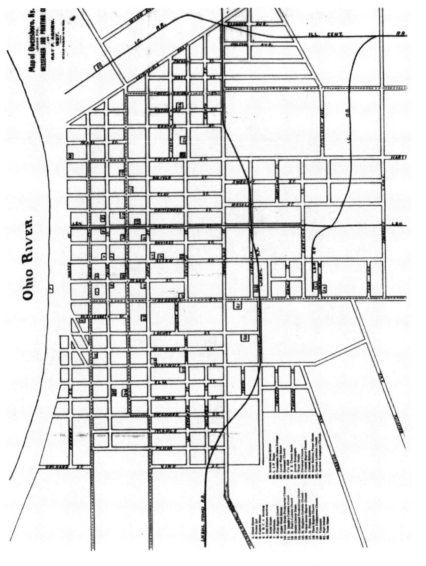

A map of Owensboro (1897), drawn for the *Messenger*, showing the community's growing prosperity (Daviess County Public Library)

Generally, the population of the lower river communities rose, but not as rapidly as the rates of the three states. Illinois's population more than doubled between 1880 and 1920, while Indiana's and Kentucky's expanded by about 50 percent. Ohio River counties in these states grew, respectively, by 23, 12, and 25 percent. Their overall share of their state's population also declined. Illinois's river counties, their proportion miniscule to begin with, dropped to 1.3 percent in 1920. Indiana's declined from 7.9 to 6.7 percent, and Kentucky's dropped from 11 to 9.1. (Having many more river counties and a much longer river border, Kentucky's proportion was always higher than that of Illinois's and Indiana's.)

These statistics shrouded significant internal changes in each state. Predominantly urban counties increased, but rural areas declined or stagnated. All but one of Indiana's Ohio River counties lost population, as did four of Kentucky's eleven and two of Illinois's six. Sixteen of twenty-four declined in size by 1920. That process began as early as 1890 for three and between 1900 and 1910 for nine more. With 394.1 persons per square mile, Vanderburgh was by far the most densely populated county. Next highest were McCracken, with 155.8, and Alexander, with 106.1. Fifteen counties, by contrast, had fewer than fifty persons per square mile. Of the counties with urban places, Vanderburgh was most urbanized—92.4 percent of its population. McCracken, with 66.4, and Alexander, with 63.4, were next highest. Eight of these counties were less than 40 percent urban. Eleven had no urban places; all but one of these had been stagnant or in decline since 1880. By contrast, the two most urbanized counties, McCracken and Vanderburgh, exceeded their state's rate of growth, and three others—Alexander, Daviess, and Pulaski—grew by at least 50 percent.

The larger towns accounted for most of the region's growth. Cairo's increase represented roughly 40 percent of the rise in Illinois's river counties. Increases in urban river communities in Illinois and Indiana were 60 and 73 percent, respectively, of the expansion of Ohio counties. Taking out the growth of Paducah, Owensboro, and Henderson would have meant a *loss* of population for the eleven Kentucky counties on the lower river. The five largest cities claimed well over 80 percent of regional growth. Cairo, for instance, expanded by 6,100 between 1880 and 1920, accounting for roughly two-fifths of the growth in Illinois's river counties. Evansville's 56,000 additional residents by 1920 represented two-thirds of the population increase for all twenty-four counties.

Fourteen settlements listed in federal census reports of 1920 experienced at least modest expansion between 1880 and 1920. Of these, however, Cloverport, Rockport, Cannelton, Newburgh, Leavenworth, Grandview, Troy,

Mauckport, Hamletsburg, and New Grand Chain began losing population after 1900. Shawneetown, Hawesville, Brandenburg, Smithland, Caseyville, and Stephensport were smaller in 1920 than they had been in 1880.

All of this revealed a broader pattern: largely rural counties in the southern Midwest lost population or stagnated after 1880, and river settlements, if they grew, expanded more slowly than many of those in the interior. Cairo was the only southern Illinois city in the state's ten largest, and its growth rate after 1880 lagged perceptibly behind that of the state. In southern Indiana, only Vanderburgh and Monroe Counties showed appreciable growth. Among cities of the southern Midwest, only Cincinnati and Evansville experienced significant development. Louisville nearly doubled in size. These cities did not grow as quickly as Indianapolis, Cleveland, Detroit, and Chicago, however. A notable Ohio River exception was Pittsburgh, which grew from 235,000 to nearly 590,000. Although Evansville swelled from 29,280 in 1880 to 85,264 in 1920, Indianapolis expanded from 75,056 to 314,194. By 1920, moreover, Evansville had dropped to third place in the state, behind Fort Wayne. No other river city ranked in Indiana's largest ten.[8]

Lower Ohio towns continued to vary demographically. In 1920, Illinois's foreign-born population was 18.6 percent, whereas Indiana's was only 5.1 percent and Kentucky's was 1.3. The proportions of foreigners in the river counties were well below their states' averages. Only Vanderburgh's came close to Indiana's. A similar pattern prevailed in the towns and cities. Only Henderson exceeded its state's average. Evansville, Cairo, and Tell City led the corridor in foreign-born population. The proportion of foreign-born was much lower in 1920 than in 1870 and 1900. Combined with the fact that the vast majority were German, that underscored the settlement of "new immigrants" from southern and eastern Europe elsewhere. And first-, second-, and third-generation German Americans were clustered in a few communities, mostly in southwestern Indiana. In most places by 1920, few residents could not ultimately trace their roots to Kentucky and the Upper South.[9]

Another pronounced difference lay in racial composition. The ratio of blacks to whites in Illinois and Indiana rose modestly between 1880 and 1920. This disguised dramatic increases after 1915 in Chicago and Indianapolis. Kentucky's black population declined steadily, reaching 9.8 percent in 1920. The proportion of blacks in lower Ohio River counties of Illinois, Indiana, and Kentucky also decreased. This was not caused by overall population increases alone but rather by declines in the *number* of blacks as well. In Illinois and Indiana counties, that decline generally occurred after 1900.[10]

In Kentucky, a significant decrease in the proportion of black residents began after 1880. By 1920, only Henderson County was more than 20 percent black, and only four counties exceeded the state average. The *number* of black residents in counties with the largest towns rose steadily between 1880 and 1900, but whites' growth rates were greater. McCracken's black population rose steadily, to 7,283 in 1900. Similar augmentations occurred in Henderson and Owensboro. After 1900, however, the number as well as the ratio of blacks fell in all of these places. By 1920, Henderson and Paducah blacks were 20 to 25 percent of the total. Numerical decline of blacks in rural counties began in the 1890s.[11]

A similar pattern can be found across the river. After 1900, the ratio of blacks to the general population declined sharply in Cairo and Mound City. By 1920, Mound City continued to lead the region, with slightly over 33 percent, followed closely by Cairo, and 20 to 25 percent of Henderson and Paducah were black. Metropolis, with one in seven, also had a significant nonwhite populace. Evansville, Mount Vernon, and Rockport were well below this, with less than one in twelve or thirteen. Evansville's black community had risen to about 7,500 in 1900, or 13 percent of the population, but fallen to approximately 6,300 by 1910. The number would remain at that level until the 1940s. The proportions of African Americans in these towns, however, continued by far to exceed those of their respective states.

A steady depopulation of blacks along the lower Ohio began in Kentucky in the 1890s and in Illinois and Indiana in the early 1900s. This was not a simple case of blacks leaving for better occupational opportunities to the north. The "great migration" to employment in northern cities, especially Chicago, did not begin until 1915. More significant was the worsening racial climate (see chapter 11).[12]

In addition to demographic changes, the industrial age altered urban landscapes. On the one hand, most communities remained compact places focused on riverfront activities and the few public buildings, churches, hotels, and shops that were clustered nearby. Business establishments and homes of prominent residents were interspersed throughout the community. Central streets, usually unpaved, were used by wagons, carriages, horses, and mules, but mostly by pedestrians, whose walking times determined locations of businesses, work, and social activities. Land use was mixed, and social relations were relatively integrated by race, class, and ethnicity.

In the cities, on the other hand, several forces were shaping a process that was simultaneously centripetal and centrifugal. One was the arrival of newcomers from rural surroundings and from Europe. "Push" and "pull" factors were involved in both cases. Thousands left farms because of "the impact of mechanization, the consolidation of landholdings, and the rise in farm tenantry." Although rural free delivery (1896) and parcel post (1913) brought better

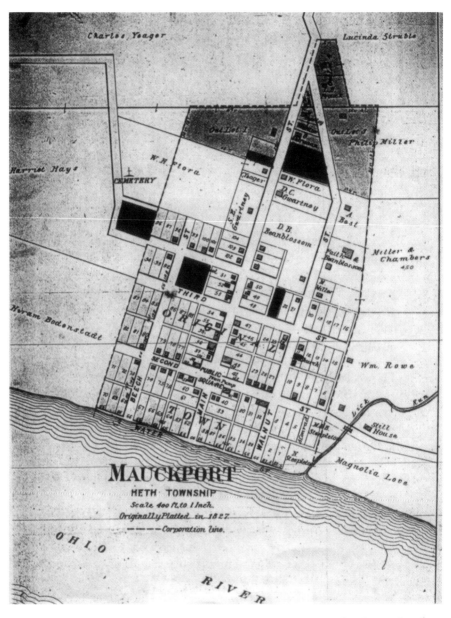

The town plan of Mauckport, from a 1906 *Atlas of Harrison County*, evokes the continued hopes, but small scale of development, in most lower Ohio villages (author's collection).

roads and hence catalogs from mail-order department stores such as Sears, Roebuck and narrowed the distance between rural markets and urban centers, rural areas continued to lose people to cities. Foreigners were also attracted by the economic opportunities in cities.[13]

European newcomers in Evansville, Henderson, Owensboro, Paducah, and Cairo were a long way from home—mostly southern Germany—and likely to settle with others having similar roots. In Evansville, Germans continued to move into Lamasco and Independence, German neighborhoods since the midcentury. They also concentrated according to region of origin—Alsace, Baden, Bavaria, and Saxony, for instance. The 1880s appear to have been the most active decade, when many Germans left their homelands because of economic conditions as well as antisocialist and anti-Catholic practices in Bismarck's Germany. Many moved directly into the cities, especially Evansville, instead of settling first in rural enclaves. Such German American neighborhoods included residents of differing classes and status, although on the eve of World War I industrialists Benjamin Bosse and John Fendrich built grand homes in the English-speaking Riverside neighborhood. Eastern and southern Europeans, few in number, clustered on the edge of the downtown, opening shops on Southeast Fourth Street and residing above them.

One of the most distinctive enclaves was Howell, southwest of Evansville, annexed by the city in 1916. Unlike the rest of the west side of Evansville, this town was occupied from the outset by Kentuckians and Tennesseeans. The railroad provided these residents a livelihood and offered them a sheltered community, and over time people of diverse economic levels came to reside there. Not surprisingly, Eugene V. Debs's brand of unionism made Howell a bastion of the Socialist Party.

In all of these cities, residential segregation by race accompanied urban dispersal. As whites moved away from the urban core, black enclaves were consolidated into larger, black-only residential areas. Moving from them to outlying neighborhoods was virtually impossible due to law, custom, and violence. Black communities such as Baptisttown in Evansville were, by the 1920s, essentially isolated from the larger community. Three-quarters of the city's blacks resided north and east of Canal and Eighth streets, beyond the C&EI rail station. Blacks dwelled on only 10 percent of the city's streets, and nine in ten blacks lived on streets which were at least 50 percent black. The index of dissimilarity—the measure of the degree to which blacks dwelled in racially segregated settings—rose to 72 in 1950.[14]

Mass transit also altered the urban landscape. The horse- or mule-drawn railway was succeeded by electric streetcars in Henderson (1889), Paducah

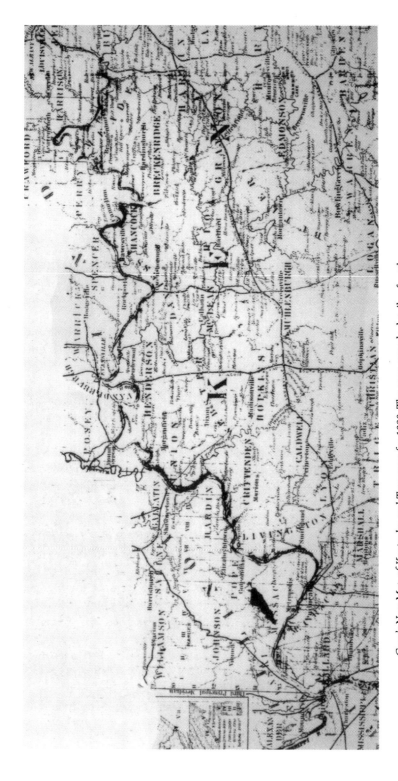

Gray's New Map of Kentucky and Tennessee for 1880. The map reveals details of settlements and transportation on both sides of the Ohio. (Daviess County Public Library)

(1890), Evansville (1891), Cairo (1892), and Owensboro (1893). This form of transportation accelerated the physical expansion of the city, encouraging the construction of homes for the rising middle and upper classes far from the noisy, congested, and often crime-ridden urban core. Evansville's Washington Avenue in the 1890s and Outer Lincoln Avenue in the 1920s became prime targets for upscale housing. These areas, in turn, were gradually annexed by city governments. Mass transit also catalyzed the specialization of land use, as the "downtown" assumed primarily mercantile, financial, and cultural activities, and lower-income workers settled in the new industrial districts adjoining older areas of the city. The opening of the lower Ohio's only interurbans, beginning with the Evansville, Suburban, and Newburgh (1889) and later the Evansville and Ohio Valley, which connected Mount Vernon, Newburgh, Rockport, Grandview, and Henderson between 1907 and 1912, also dispersed people.

The improvement of city streets and county roads, of which the automobile and the truck took advantage, quickened this process immeasurably. Some of these vehicles, in fact, were manufactured in the region. Two automobiles were produced in Evansville in the early 1900s: Willis Copeland's Simplicity and the Sears, Roebuck car made by the Hercules Buggy Company. The Graham Brothers Truck Company was acquired by Dodge Brothers in 1924.[15]

The urban landscape also reflected the changes in manufacturing and transportation. The establishment of an "industrial satellite" such as Howell on the fringes of Evansville vividly illustrated that, as the formation of Gary, Indiana, would two decades later. By the 1890s, large sections of Evansville's north side were set aside for large factories, around which modest housing for workers was erected. In 1902, the Evansville Business Men's Association lured buggy manufacturer William McCurdy to town. McCurdy soon opened a huge factory on a three-block site on the northeast side, adjoining city limits, where a new buggy rolled off the line every five minutes. By 1920, the company also manufactured gasoline engines and truck and wagon bodies.[16]

In 1910, Igleheart Brothers relocated their flour mill on outer First Avenue, on the north side adjoining the new railroad beltway, to manufacture nationally marketed Swans Down cake flour and other products. Two years later, John Fendrich opened a factory on the north side that employed hundreds of women in the manufacture of the popular Charles Denby cigar. At about the same time, Benjamin Bosse, a second-generation German American, consolidated a number of furniture companies on the city's west side into the Globe-Bosse-World Company, purportedly the world's largest manufacturer of popular furniture. Transportation changes also altered the city's landscape. The Evansville and Terre Haute Railroad station at Eighth and Main Streets, constructed in 1882 and replaced by a larger, more ornate structure in 1905, helped to shift the axis of the city away from the river. So did the building of the L&N passenger-freight station, a block from the Ohio in old Lamasco, in 1902.

Many influences, in short, shaped the size, interior landscape, and reach of some lower Ohio communities. However vast, these paled by comparison with the awesome power of the Ohio to alter settlements along its banks. Although floodwaters were never a threat to such places as Rockport, Henderson, Newburgh, and Mount Vernon, they annually challenged other settlements, including Evansville and Paducah. The floods of 1884 were especially daunting, as they poured over levees at Cairo and Shawneetown. To smaller places, such as Caseyville, Lewisport, and Mauckport, they precipitated massive decline. An even more devastating flood in 1913 brought heavy damages to Evansville, Paducah, and most other communities. After the January-February 1937 flood, the worst of all, a more effective system of levees would be introduced. Most of Evansville, Shawneetown, and Paducah were flooded. The destruction of Leavenworth and Shawneetown led to their relocation on higher ground inland. Other places, such as Smithland, never recovered.[17]

But acts of God alone did not explain the profound changes occurring along the lower Ohio. An understanding of economic, political, social, and cultural factors is also required.

10 ∽

Making a Living

In the four decades following the end of Reconstruction, most lower Ohio settlements continued to be overwhelmingly agrarian and rural. In all but a few, the value of crops far exceeded manufactures—a gap made even larger if livestock are included. Only in Alexander County, Illinois, and Vanderburgh County, Indiana, did manufactures significantly exceed crops. Here, too, economies more closely resembled those of northern cities. In Massac and Pulaski (Illinois), Spencer (Indiana), and Daviess and McCracken (Kentucky) Counties, products of factories edged out those of farms. Years of poor farming techniques, combined with thin topsoil and hilly ground in many places, also meant that in many nonmanufacturing counties, such as Hardin and Pope (Illinois), Perry (Indiana), and Crittenden (Kentucky), the value of agricultural goods was quite low.

Some changes were occurring on the land, however. In Kentucky, for instance, a different strain of tobacco was introduced and popularized before World War I, and the raising of livestock spread. By 1914, farmers in all three states were exposed to new and more efficient means of working the land. In much of southwestern Indiana and northwestern Kentucky, moreover, bituminous coal emerged as a major source of income and employment.[1]

Most settlements lacked diversified economies. They had few, if any, semiskilled or white-collar workers. They were not centers of technological innovation or places where steam and electricity powered huge industrial facilities. Neither were they regional marketing and financial centers.[2]

The Ohio remained essential to these counties. Charles Ambler has described it as a "poor man's highway," even after railroads, beginning in 1885, crossed the lower river at right angles and usurped much of its role in regional development. Rich bottomlands and hinterlands not served by rail remained open to steamboat traffic. Riverboats continued to receive government mail contracts into the early twentieth century. The river was a vital artery for wholesalers and manufacturers in larger places who supplied settlements with goods obtainable only by water and who also secured raw materials such as tobacco and timber from these places. Shipbuilding and repair continued, especially at

Paducah. Although passenger traffic was declining, barge traffic was growing, taking coal, iron ore, iron, petroleum, and bauxite to the mills and communities along the Ohio and beyond. Immigrants also used riverboats well into the 1880s because they offered good service at low cost. By the late 1880s, however, the river's importance was diminishing.

Smaller communities were not inactive or unimportant. A vivid illustration of that is found in the *Kentucky State Gazeteer and Business Directory for 1895-1896*. Whether as boat landings, ferries, or small market centers, they were indispensable. Livingston County's river communities were typical. Smithland had a post office, general stores, groceries, blacksmith shops, a hotel, several sawmills, a gristmill—and two judges and thirteen attorneys. Upriver, Birdsville, Bayou, and Berry Ferry, each with fewer than one hundred inhabitants, had general stores, post offices, and services such as blacksmithing and livestock sales. Carrsville, twenty miles from Smithland, had a post office, three general stores, a combined general store and flour mill, two drug stores, a grocery, and a carpenter's shop.[3]

These settlements were economic and social links for their inhabitants, nearby residents, and river travelers. Well into the twentieth century, ferry service was essential to the local economy. Shawneetown had probably the oldest service—150 years—before a bridge was built in 1956. The general store was the core of these settlements, and whatever their size, such establishments were cogs in an ever-widening network of trade. Inexpensive flour and stoves, made in cities such as Evansville, helped to change diets, as biscuits replaced cornmeal products as a daily staple. General stores were also sources of credit and news. Competition from mail-order catalogs gradually weakened such enterprises, as did specialty and department stores in larger communities. But the absence of rail service and good roads made these small places essential.[4]

Kentucky continued to be heavily dependent on staple-crop agriculture. Although some of the new urban centers such as Nashville, Durham, Birmingham, and Tampa possessed a more complex industrial base, most were involved in processing tobacco, cotton, and timber. Such activities took place within an increasingly interdependent national economy. Whatever their size and character, though, these places were biracial, and their economies, which in the case of Kentucky were based on tobacco, depended on northern manufactured goods and credit.[5]

Most towns—places that ranged between 1,000 and 5,000 in 1920—did not achieve the degree of development or influence enjoyed by Evansville or Paducah. However, they benefited from and participated in the broader changes creating a national urban market. The largest, Mount Vernon and Metropolis, enjoyed enhanced rail connections and expanded manufacturing.

Mount Vernon, sixth largest city on the lower Ohio, had grown steadily since 1870, almost doubling its population. Its chief employer by 1913 was the Keck-Gonnerman Company, which produced steam engines, threshers, portable sawmills, and coal mining equipment. Rail and river ties allowed the firm to ship its products to many parts of the nation. The company employed two hundred men, almost all skilled workers, and paid annual wages averaging $750 per capita, a substantial amount at that time. The town had at least another dozen smaller factories, all locally owned, that processed farm and timber products. Some were creations of Keck or Gonnerman. A number (notably Sunlight and the Fuhrer-Ford milling companies) sold brand-name products in distant markets, primarily in the Southeast. These manufacturers also formed three national banks, and in 1907, Keck-Gonnerman established the town's first auto dealership. The coming of the interurbans, which provided connections to Grandview on the east, to Henderson on the south, and to Princeton on the north, tied citizens more closely to the Evansville hinterland, which was a factor in the small city's prosperity. Mount Vernon's development was also manifest in its two newspapers and a number of impressive residences as well as public and commercial buildings. Most striking was the IOOF edifice on the town square (1898), which later became People's Bank. A major liability was the absence of bridges over the Ohio and the Wabash, just to the west. A vehicular toll bridge on the Wabash, opened in the 1930s, would only partially lessen the city's isolation.[6]

Downriver, Metropolis nearly doubled in size between 1880 and 1920. Its many wood-working factories depended on logs shipped in by river. Its other factories produced flour and tiles. Travel and trade were mostly by steamboat, notably the *George H. Cowling,* which connected residents twice daily with nearby Paducah, and the *Dick Fowler,* the last of the three Fowler boats that plied the river between Cairo and Evansville. The river's importance was evident in late October 1907, when two hundred residents joined another eighty-five from adjacent Brookport (which was, until 1901, known as Brooklyn) to travel to Cairo. President Theodore Roosevelt spoke there at the conclusion of a weeklong series of events that had begun in Pittsburgh to promote river improvements. Metropolis's major newspapers merged to become the *Republican and Herald* in 1918.

Railroads were a major catalyst for the growth of Metropolis and nearby Brookport. Residents of Metropolis subscribed in the late 1880s to the St. Louis and Cairo Railroad, soon part of the Illinois Central, which also built a spur to Bridgeport. Bridgeport thrived because it was an important transfer point for passengers and for river-borne freight, primarily railroad ties. Beginning in 1898, the town boasted a newspaper, the *Eagle.* Downriver, Joppa, which ob-

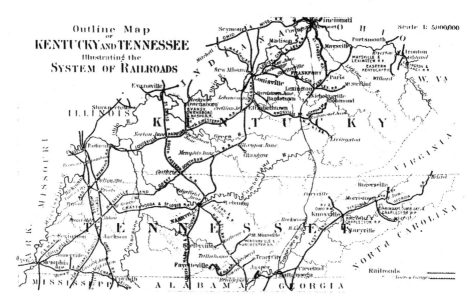

A portion of Gray's New Map of Kentucky and Tennessee showing all of the rail lines constructed as of 1880 in the lower Ohio region (Daviess County Public Library).

tained a Chicago and Eastern Illinois Railroad connection in 1900, also grew rapidly by 1910 due to its export of lumber and railroad ties. Its short-lived success encouraged Metropolitans to seek a railroad bridge. In 1910, the Chicago, Burlington, and Quincy brought a rail line into the city from the northwest, and in 1917 completed only the third railroad bridge south of Louisville, connecting Metropolis and Paducah. In 1918, the Illinois Central, one of the bridge owners, also opened service.

Ten years later, the IC completed the Edgewood Cutoff, which speeded up north-south connections to Metropolis and permitted longer trains because of improvements in road construction. This enhanced Metropolis and Paducah at Cairo and Bridgeport's expense. As elsewhere, the combined effects of ice and low water, railroads, bridges, automobiles, and good roads led to the gradual demise of passenger boats—the last of which stopped in Metropolis about 1920. The opening of a vehicular bridge from Massac County to McCracken County in 1929 further altered the river's role. By the early 1920s, though, Metropolis and Bridgeport continued to benefit from growing barge traffic, accelerated by the construction of Lock and Dam 52, begun in 1924 and completed in 1929. Joppa's peak was 1912, when its population was 734. Its rapid decline resulted from decreased river traffic, dwindling wood supplies, and isolation of its railroad spur by developments at Metropolis. In 1930, it had 462 residents.[7]

Upriver, the eighth largest settlement, Tell City, was so prosperous that in 1896 its leaders built a grand structure, which was intended to be the new county seat. The fortunes of this wood-manufacturing community were boosted by the *Tell City Journal,* a rival of the *Perry County Tribune.* Cannelton and its county allies, however, blocked that initiative. In the process, Tell City gained a brand-new city hall. Perry County's Troy, Rome, Derby, and Rono (renamed Magnet in 1899) were not nearly so fortunate. Troy was the most prosperous of the four. In 1880, it had several tobacco warehouses, a flour mill, a sawmill, a brewery, a distillery, and a blind and sash factory, and exported a significant amount of grain and hay. Its fortunes sagged because of declining river trade, several major fires, and failure to obtain rail service. By 1890, its wharf boat was closed; its hotel ceased operations in 1920. In all four towns, the marginality of Perry County agriculture thwarted their development.[8]

Cannelton's uneven development was in many respects the result of competition from low-cost southern mills. Its chief employer manufactured inexpensive cotton sheeting and, beginning in 1899, "Hoosier jeans." Of the other twenty-five manufacturers, probably the most promising was the Cannelton Sewer Pipe Company, which commenced operations in 1908. Funded by Louisville capital, powered by local coal, and supplied by ample amounts of local clay, it produced vitrified clay sewer pipes. Over 1,000 carloads were shipped via the twenty-three-mile segment of the Louisville, Evansville, and St. Louis "Air Line" (later part of the Southern), which had been built to Lincoln City in the late 1880s. Other factories in Cannelton's "industrial quarter" suffered from floods, fires, poor leadership, and limited capital. The pottery, the brewery, the flour mill, the spoke factory, and the shingle mill all closed before 1890.[9]

Floods plagued Tell City as well as Cannelton, but the Swiss town continued to prosper. The Tell City Furniture Company and the Tell City Chair Company were its mainstays. The Ohio supplied timber and carried goods to market. Some new industries arrived—notably the United States Hame Company in 1903, purportedly the largest factory of its type in the world. Railroad connections increasingly offered local industries more reliable transportation than the Ohio. The fiftieth-anniversary homecoming celebration of July 4, 1908, symbolized Tell City's solidarity and pride. Tell City's level of manufacturing was low, however—not a good sign for long-term prosperity—and it depended heavily on furniture. Competition from southern manufacturers beginning in the 1920s would threaten its economic base.[10]

Tell City was also much better off than Rockport, which despite its age, its being a county seat, and its high elevation experienced decline between 1910 and 1920 after three decades of modest growth. One reason for this was transportation. The construction of a rail line from Owensboro to Louisville, the ferry service from Rockport to Owensboro, and the opening of interurban ser-

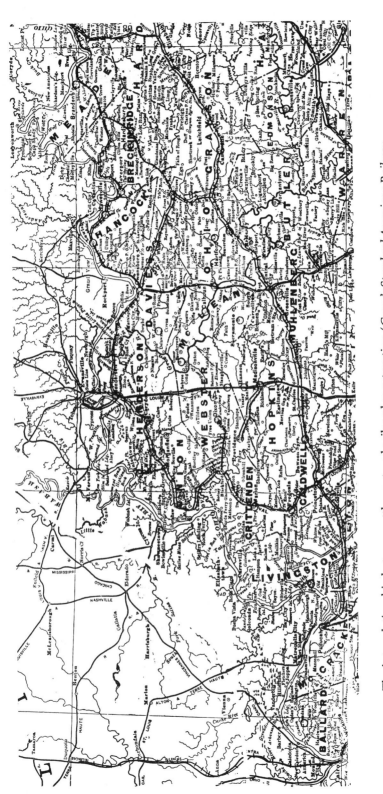

The interrelationship between settlement and railroad construction (*Cram's Standard American Railway System Atlas, 1902* [New York: George F. Cram, 1902], Willard Library)

vice to Evansville in 1906 facilitated east-west travel. It did not, however, appreciably improve Rockport's fortunes and may have speeded up population outflow and enabled residents to commute to work in Evansville or Owensboro. Rockport's rail connections were limited to a short northerly line to Jasper. Another factor was change in the marketing and manufacturing of tobacco, a major product of Spencer County agriculture. The city's chief liability was clearly its failure to develop a manufacturing base. Spencer County remained overwhelmingly agricultural. The value of crops in 1919-20 was more than twice that of manufacturing. The decline in river passenger traffic and the transformation of river commerce accelerated their descent.[11]

Similar problems existed for Mound City, which with a population of 2,756 was slightly larger than Rockport in 1920. Its overall population had risen by almost a quarter since 1880, but its economy was weak. The ending of the Emporium Company charter in 1882 was symptomatic. Although levees were built, flooding remained a challenge, as did the place's reputation for unhealthfulness. Failure to develop manufacturing was fatal. The number of manufacturing firms in Pulaski County in 1919 was the same as in Pope County, although these firms employed more workers than most of the lower Ohio counties. The value of its manufactures was close to Spencer's. Pulaski's agricultural products were not as lucrative as Spencer's, however. Its lawyers, physicians, groceries, and general stores served its immediate vicinity. Large numbers of transient African Americans performed menial jobs associated with river trade.[12]

Seven other places with populations of 1,000 or more in 1920 failed to move across the urban threshold and to secure a stable, diverse economy. In general, these places lost population, primarily after 1910. A notable exception was Cloverport, which grew 43 percent after 1880. It benefited from the construction of a railroad line connecting Henderson and Louisville in the late 1880s; by 1920 the railroad was the town's leading employer. By the early twentieth century tobacco's importance had dwindled. The value of crops in 1920 ($5.1 million) far exceeded that of manufacturing ($690,000) in Breckinridge County, though, and only 228 persons worked in factories.[13]

Uniontown, which shrank after 1910, was slightly larger in 1920 than it had been in 1880. The exploitation of vast coal reserves and the building of rail connections to the interior helped this town. The latter was mostly the work of entrepreneur Percival G. Kelsey, whose Ohio Valley Railroad to Madisonville, completed in 1886, eventually became part of the Illinois Central. With the aid of L&N agent Lee Howell, another line tapped coal resources from Morganfield to the southeast. By 1920 coal was second in value only to agriculture in Union County. On the other hand, this remained predominantly a farming area. Value of crops exceeded most counties in the region. Tobacco was king, but some diversification was evident. Farmers raised more cattle, hogs, and horses by 1910, devoted more land to hay, and produced dairy, poultry, and orchard goods, much of which was sold in Evansville. Manufacturing was minuscule by 1919. The town lost its tobacco stemmery in 1912, because new tariff rates discriminated against stemmed tobacco, and Union County farmers shifted to the Henderson market. Fires and floods devastated businesses and residences.[14]

Nearby Shawneetown, despite some periods of growth, had been steadily losing population and economic clout. Rail connections offered little apparent benefit, as its vicinity remained overwhelmingly rural and agricultural. Declining river trade also hurt the community, and flooding remained a major threat. Despite levees, high waters periodically ravaged Shawneetown.[15]

Newburgh was virtually unchanged. The town secured interurban connections to Evansville in 1889 and Rockport by 1907. In addition to passenger service, the former carried freight, including coal from the area's burgeoning mines. In this sense Newburgh and Uniontown had much in common. The two communities were also similar because agriculture remained essential in their regions and manufacturing relative unimportant. The disappearance of the local tobacco market before 1920 diminished what little commerce and manufacturing the town provided. Like Elizabethtown, Illinois, Newburgh also failed to obtain rail service.

Newburgh's river heritage remained integral, though, as some river commerce connected it with other places nearby. The town's elevation allowed it to escape the ravages of flooding, thus keeping intact its small business district overlooking the Ohio. And beginning in 1923, federal monies brought some life to the local economy, when construction of Lock and Dam 47 commenced. The project, completed five years later, accelerated Warrick County coal production.[16]

In three instances—Golconda, in Pope County, and Rosiclare and Elizabethtown, in Hardin County, Illinois—patterns of growth seemed to defy the regional paradigm.

Golconda grew steadily, reaching about 1,250 in 1920, a 24 percent increase over 1880. Its peak period of prosperity was 1870-1900; its dependence on the Ohio was substantial. Packet boat service was vital to the community. Golconda supplied cattle, grain, and timber to Evansville. Cattle and other commodities were also shipped northward by rail to Chicago. As the packets declined, gasoline-powered craft filled in some of the gaps. The county's economy remained predominantly agricultural in 1920, and the level of manufacturing was about as low as Gallatin County's. The construction of Lock and Dam 51 between 1924 and 1929 brought short-term economic stimulus. The decline of river traffic, the lack of a manufacturing base, the relatively simple form of local commerce, and the competition from towns in the Illinois and Kentucky interiors that rose with the building of good roads after World War I contributed to a reversal of fortune after 1920. Flooding also plagued the settlement. Golcondans were prosperous enough, however, to establish a bank in 1911, to have a newspaper, and to support a Rotary Club. Rail lines first reached Golconda about 1902, when an Illinois Central spur skirted it and connected with the Ohio northeast of the village. About 1921 another line traversed the northwest corner of the county.[17]

Rosiclare and Elizabethtown experienced rapid growth in the early twentieth century. Especially dramatic was Rosiclare's rise to 1,522 by 1920, an increase of 314 percent. Elizabethtown grew 118 percent, to 1,055. Although in each instance this enlargement was short-lived, it did not produce "ghost town" status, as in the case of Shetlerville after "Potato Joe" Shetler's death. Timber and grain had always been important to the economies of these places, but erosion of land and depletion of forests diminished their significance. Fluorspar, an abundant mineral important to the burgeoning iron and steel industry, replaced them. The building of a rail line in 1911 to Rosiclare and demands for fluorspar during the war stimulated its rise, which continued into the 1940s. Elizabethtown, the county seat, also boasted jobs in mines and quarries as well as river trade. Between the late 1880s and about 1908 it also had a newspaper. Both places had banking institutions. But Hardin County, the state's second smallest in territory, had perhaps the weakest overall economy among lower Ohio counties. Changes in river trade and the fragility of fluorspar mining created long-term financial uncertainty.[18]

The experiences of the five largest cities were exponentially different. All five grew considerably, although at different rates. In 1900, Owensboro climbed into third place in 1900 and Paducah, which trebled in size, rose to second. Evansville continued to be the largest in 1920, with a population of 85,264 in 1920—a 191 percent increase since 1880. The population of Paducah rose 208 percent in that period, to 24,735, and Owensboro experienced a 180 percent increase, to 17,424. Cairo, with 15,203, had a population about 69 percent higher than it was in 1880, and Henderson, with 12,169, had a population 116 percent greater than it had in 1880.

The influence and the character of these places differed enormously. An 1888 federal report on the internal commerce of the United States included this description of Evansville:

> This city transacts a more diversified business upon Western river highways than any other along the whole course of the Ohio. It occupies a commanding position over the Green and Barren, the Cumberland, Tennessee, and Wabash rivers, and

holds the reins for their commerce. . . . The commerce of the city is still and for years must continue to be chiefly conducted over the rivers named, although there are excellent railway facilities here. . . . The city transacts . . . business with an immense area of country contiguous and adjacent to the navigable streams mentioned, whose only outlet is afforded by water, and the annual aggregate of trade between Evansville and these vast regions, where the whistle of locomotives is never heard, reaches into a sum far greater comparatively than is netted by rail carriage.[19]

Trade, location, manufacturing, resources, and such factors as external decision making, government, and leadership produced these divergences. The state environment also mattered. The Kentucky of this period, as Thomas Clark has observed, was one of blood feuds, crippling political demagoguery, and stagnant economic development due to poor rural roads, limited railroad construction, low agricultural prices, and discriminatory railroad freight rates. Agrarian, rural values prevailed, although some important advancements occurred just before World War I as a result of school reforms and road improvements.[20]

Illinois, by contrast, was a rapidly industrializing and urbanizing state. Even before 1900, more than half of its citizens resided in urban settlements, especially Chicago. Much of the state's economy depended on iron and steel, although Illinois was also noted for the manufacture of farm implements and the packing of meat. Coal production in the south central counties fueled the state's industrial take-off. The revised state constitution of 1870, reflecting the influence of migrants from New York and New England who resided in the northern part of Illinois, encouraged such enterprise, which by the 1920s had brought Illinois conclusively into a structured society dominated by huge industrial combinations and bureaucracies. Accelerating economic development were an expanded public education system and, after 1914, a state plan for highway development. Little of this massive change, however, was evident in the far south.[21]

Indiana also experienced substantial advancement, especially in its central and northern counties. Some of its Ohio River counties also shared that development. Coal production in the region extending up the Wabash Valley from Vanderburgh and Warrick Counties expanded greatly. Main track railroad mileage expanded steadily to 7,426 in 1920, although most lines were dominated by eastern investors and syndicates. Manufacturing products rose from $337 million in 1899 to $1.9 billion in 1919, and the number of wage earners doubled. Indiana manufacturing ranged from flour and gristmill products to automobiles and iron and steel. Traffic at Lake Michigan ports, not surprisingly, rivaled that of the Ohio. Agriculture, though more diverse, depended on livestock and grain production. The General Assembly abetted these changes. It responded to the stimulus of the federal highway legislation of 1916 by creating a highway commission, which adopted a state plan of highways in 1920. And it also gradually strengthened public schools.[22]

Against this backdrop, river trade remained important to lower Ohio cities. "River News" in newspapers continued to be essential. The *Evansville Daily Journal* of September 5, 1892—Labor Day—reported five boats were departing that day to Henderson, Louisville and Cincinnati, Owensboro, Bowling Green, and Paducah. On the same day, the *Evansville Courier*'s "News of the River" occupied two-thirds of a column with such information as dredge work, arrivals and departures, and river levels. The scale of river commerce mirrored the population and resources of the hinterland, the site's advantages as a break in transportation, and the quality of community leadership.

River-related commerce was generally of a different character by the end of the Great War. In Cairo, for instance, the number of steamboat arrivals and the tonnage of steamboats and barges steadily declined between 1872 and 1886, and the value of Ohio River commerce passing through the city fell from $20 million to $7 million. The chief reason was the strong railroad network in the upper Midwest. Consequently, no major common carrier operated on the Mississippi by 1900.

Cairo, though, gained an advantage as an intersection of seven railroad lines by the mid-1880s and continued to be an important break in transportation between north and south. These nodal activities did not contribute much to the city's growth, however, except for jobs related to the ferries, since Cairo was a connection point, not a critical source of or destination for freight or passengers. Unlike Evansville or Paducah, wrote Conrod, the city "never became a classification center for railroad freight, a wholesaling center, a manufacturing point, or any other activities stimulated by the ferrying operation." Bridge building ended the city's being a transportation break: the Illinois Central bridge on the Ohio in 1889, the Missouri Pacific bridge over the Mississippi in 1905, and the CB&Q bridge at Metropolis in 1917. In addition to the adverse impact of the Edgewood cutoff (1928), the closing of the Illinois Central's classification yard at Mounds, north of town, also hurt it.[23]

Cairo's location, in short, remained an insufficient factor in its development. The railroads, the Civil War, and the direction of settlement worked for east-west growth to the north, and even the Illinois Central diminished Cairo's importance, making it a source of agricultural goods for Chicago and a mere way station on the trip to the Gulf. Other factors were also at work—flooding and seepage; perception of a poor climate; isolation from potential tributary areas in Kentucky and Missouri due to extreme seasonal rise and fall of the rivers, frequent floods, and inadequate ferry service because of the lack of firm soil or rocks on opposing river banks; and Cairo's dependence on a small trade area, a narrow peninsula of southern Illinois that was hilly and forested, had poor soil, lacked mineral resources, and had few people. Cairo's merchants failed to exploit even this limited advantage. The erection of vehicular bridges over the Ohio (1929) and Mississippi (1938) broke down some of the city's isolation, but by then it was too late. The rivers offered advantages and challenges: they made Cairo "what it is, but they have been as walls encompassing the city and shutting out local trade, which would otherwise have been a constant source of growth and prosperity."[24]

The perhaps unfair portrait persisted, wrote Harry Bennett Abdy, of "the flat and uninteresting little Cairo that squats on the cold, damp soil behind the high, protecting levee." Despite its gaining four national banks and five savings and loans organizations, several vigorous newspapers, and an impressive array of religious, cultural, and fraternal organizations by 1910, Cairo's unflattering image survived. After 1920, long-term population decline began. Many factors were involved, including the weakening of its wood-related industries. More important was the legacy of absentee owners, much of whose land was unsold in 1912. These men had blocked local initiative and infrastructure improvements for years. City ownership of the wharf was unsettled until 1919. Construction of adequate levees and pumping stations did not begin until the 1920s, but by then history had passed Cairo by.[25]

Paducah, however, had a more favorable location. The city was a trading center for surrounding farms and for the cargoes shipped between the Ohio and the Tennessee, because larger steamboats on the Ohio preferred to transship goods to and from tributaries at such places. Over time, economies of scale permitted Paducah merchants to gain control over service on the nearby Cumberland as well, thus cementing Smithland's fate. In 1919 Abdy pictured Smithland as an "Arcadia that our first impressions led us to expect." Smithland's picturesque old houses and gentle, trusting residents made it "a delightful anachronism."[26]

Paducah's trade was primarily on the Cumberland and the Tennessee, not through traffic on the Ohio. The economic center of the Purchase, it depended heavily on tobacco, collected chiefly for transport, although some was processed locally into cigars and plugs. The city was the state's third largest tobacco market. Timber from the interior made sawed lumber its second leading product. Coal was an increasingly lucrative commodity. Much was shipped downriver from Uniontown and assembled into larger loads for markets up and down the Ohio.[27]

Railroad lines changed that somewhat, extending Paducah's connections to the south, east, and north, especially after the line to Louisville in 1872 tied the city into the eastern railway grid. By the mid-1890s, construction and financial restructuring put most of its lines in the Illinois Central system. City financial support for the Paducah, Tennessee, and Alabama (1889), later part of the Burlington system, extended connections to the southeast. The CB&Q bridge, the Edgewood Cutoff, and the opening of a major railroad repair center for the Illinois Central at Paducah in 1928 made the city a major nodal point for the nation's railways. Its economy became heavily dependent on external capital and leadership. Paducah, nonetheless, struck Abdy as having "a charm, for she gives the stranger a certain 'comfy' feeling that she is 'homey' and prosperous. . . . She is just a well-to-do, pleasant mannered Southern matron."[28]

River and railroad connections allowed Paducah to serve "a moderately high central place function for western Kentucky and southern Illinois." Cairo's decline and the absence of serious competitors on the Illinois side meant that Paducah probably drew more of the trade of southern Illinois. A distinct disadvantage, though, was the poor quality of the soil and the paucity of mineral resources there.[29]

Evansville, by contrast, had long enjoyed a thriving river trade which was only enhanced by other transportation improvements. Location had made her an excellent transshipment point between through traffic on the Ohio and Mississippi Rivers and interior points. Promoters of Green River commerce in the 1890s, for instance, portrayed Evansville as the federal report of 1888 had— as the "natural terminus" for their corridor rather than Henderson. Evansville had an excellent harbor and ample water and rail connections to markets all over the world via seven railroad and seven packet lines. The latter included the Evansville, Ohio, and Green River Transportation Company, formed in 1889 by a group that included Lee Howell, the general freight agent of the L&N in Evansville. After the opening of the Henderson-Evansville railroad bridge, tapping the coal deposits south of Henderson was increasingly attractive to investors. Regional timber and coal were in great demand in Evansville factories. Second in importance to manufacturing was the city's jobbing and supply trade.[30]

Evansville was neither as large as Cincinnati or Louisville nor as important commercially, but it remained second in rank in Indiana and largest west of the Falls. In 1886, forty-three steam vessels were registered on the city's port list. Trade on regular packet lines was estimated as 170,000 tons, worth $10.6 million. Unrecorded trade on the Wabash and long-distance trade not originating in Evansville, but entering into trade there, brought the total to $15 million.

Evansville was also a successful commercial center, especially in wholesale goods. As late as 1898, seven packet lines offered regular service to Bowling Green, Cairo, Louisville, and Nashville. According to the federal report on commerce in 1888, Evansville industries received about three-fifths of their raw materials—chiefly tobacco, cotton, coal, grain, and timber—from Kentucky and Tennessee and sold over three-fourths of their manufactured goods there. That reflected the accessibility of southerly communities by water as well as rail. Waterways remained important pathways even after the bridging of the Ohio at Henderson, because most communities were not served by rails or adequate roads. Evansville's commercial and retail hinterland was strengthened by the completion of the bridge—the only one between Paducah and Louisville for decades—as well as by interurban and rail lines. The city's commercial reach extended well over halfway to Louisville on the east, roughly halfway to Terre Haute on the north, well past Paducah, almost to Cairo, on the west, and nearly to the Kentucky-Tennessee border on the south. Location combined with business acumen and strong transportation ties, in short, gave Evansville a favorable position well into the twentieth century.[31]

From the perspective of nodality, Evansville's location and its being a natural break in transport had made it the major trading center below Louisville since about 1840. These also stimulated manufacturing related to the river as well as goods that served the regional market. The city continued to be a major river port and grew in importance as a rail center. River traffic was changing because of the rise of barges and towboats, which, according to Conrod, "reduced port time and capital costs of the towboats, as barges could be quickly picked up and dropped en route." Also important was the completion of a uniform nine-foot channel on the Ohio by the Army Corps of Engineers in 1929. Bulk cargoes—petroleum, coal, grain, and chemicals—dominated this trade, and other cities, notably Mount Vernon and Owensboro, would overtake Evansville in this category after the 1970s. Over time, the orientation of these lines would weaken the city's strong trading traditions along Ohio tributaries to the south and open the city to competition with Chicago and Indianapolis.

And rail transport from Evansville focused on the city's manufactures and could not compete with the major east-west lines to the north. Evansville's interurbans, moreover, ran only about thirty miles into the interior and did not connect with the large Indiana interurban system. For long-distance trade, the city was no longer a major commercial center by the 1950s. It was simply a crossing point on the Ohio.

By the early 1900s, the city's economic base had shifted to manufacturing, and because of good roads and trucks it had "developed more of a central place function in the twentieth century." Wholesale trade, always an Evansville staple, rose fivefold by the 1950s and was exceeded in volume of sales only by Indianapolis.[32]

The level of manufacturing in the five largest towns differed markedly. Whereas Evansville became a manufacturing city, Henderson remained a more traditional base onto which some manufacturing had been added. Between these extremes lay Cairo, Owensboro, and Paducah.

In Henderson County as late as 1919 crops remained far more valuable than manufactures. Expanded rail connections, though, helped contribute to modest growth in manufacturing. In addition to the L&N bridge, an important moment was the opening of the Louisville, St. Louis, and Texas in 1889 (which went to neither St. Louis nor Texas), connecting Henderson with Louisville, via a number of towns along the south shore of the Ohio. The lower Ohio's only line paralleling the river, it demonstrated the suitability of terrain only in that area for an east-west road. Rails to the south and southwest opened rich coal fields. As in Evansville, Owensboro, and Paducah, coal became an important element in the Henderson economy. Between 1884 and 1900, eight coal mines were opened in the county. The principal producer was the Henderson Coal and Manufacturing Company, incorporated in 1875. Coal production more than tripled between 1903 and 1920. Most coal was shipped out of the county.[33]

The *Kentucky Gazeteer and Business Directory of 1895-1896* and the city's first city directory, printed in 1899, revealed some manufacturing. Two textile factories, aided by New England capital, had opened in 1882 and 1883. The Henderson Woolen Mill was known for its Kentucky jeans. It employed about 190, including many women. The Henderson Cotton Mill was the city's leading employer before closing in 1931. Its 200 workers manufactured 160,000 yards of "fine sheetings" a week at the huge factory, situated on fourteen acres. Other industries included the Henderson Buggy Company and the George Delker Company, which manufactured buggies and carriages and shifted about 1920 to furniture.

But the leading product remained tobacco. The *Kentucky Gazeteer* described Henderson as "the largest tobacco exporting point in the United States. Immense quantities are shipped to Europe every season." The 100 miles of county bottomland produced 1,200 to 1,500 pounds per acre—the heavy, coarse leaf used for plug or pipe tobacco—while the uplands produced richer, smoother leaves used for wrappers in twists or cigars. The city directory of 1899 listed seventeen tobacco stemmeries, one tobacco manufacturer, one tobacco extract works, and two cigar factories. (Outside the city, the county had another thirty or so tobacco stemmeries.) Most of the tobacco was packaged for shipment and processing elsewhere, but some chewing tobacco and cigars were manufactured. The peak of local production was the early 1920s, with 40 million pounds.[34]

Several notable changes occurred, though, largely because of external developments. The entrance of the tobacco trust into the local market was perhaps the most significant. Consolidated Tobacco and American Tobacco, for instance, owned some of the stemmeries as early as 1899. The explosion of tobacco use after the introduction of cigarette manufacturing in the 1880s, moreover, changed the tobacco culture by altering the market and the type of tobacco grown. Instead of sales based on auctioning off the loads of wagons surrounding the various stemmeries, by about 1910 most tobacco was sold in tobacco houses, where leaves were arranged according to grade and sold at auction there. This had the effect of concentrating tobacco sales in Henderson and Owensboro and eliminating smaller markets in towns such as Uniontown or Hawesville. Bright leaf, burley tobacco began to replace dark leaf tobacco as the product of choice. By providing cigarettes to millions of soldiers in World War I, the federal government greatly stimulated local tobacco production (and expanded postwar markets).[35]

Despite Henderson's growth—symbolized by its four banks in 1899, which had combined assets of nearly $1 million, and its two newspapers—its industrial base was limited and also increasingly shaped by corporate decisions made outside the city. In 1919 the number of manufacturing establishments, thirty-one, was the lowest among the five largest cities on the lower Ohio, down from 107 in 1900. The number of wage earners dropped steadily after 1900, from 1,475 to 976. The value of Henderson manufactures in that period rose to about half that of Owensboro. Although only about two in five firms were owned by corporations, for example, the percentage of value of products manufactured by corporations was over 90 percent, and corporations employed 94 percent of the workers—in both cases, the highest ratios among the three Kentucky cities on the lower river.[36]

Exogenous forces were evident in many other ways. Evansville and Henderson, though only twelve miles apart, connected by rail on the L&N bridge and on the Illinois Central by a daily steam packet, and by a ferry until the completion of the vehicular bridge in 1932, diverged when it came to freight rates. The railroad bridge, the only crossing below Louisville before 1889, was thus a blessing and a curse. Businessmen could not compete effectively with Evansville merchants because of freight-rate differentials that made Evansville manufactures and trade goods easier to sell in the South. Only after a decade of litigation that produced sweeping changes in Interstate Commerce Commission rate setting in 1918 was the bridge much less of a liability for Henderson merchants.[37]

External influences were evident in other ways. The auto, the truck, and the state road system fatally injured the city's buggy and carriage manufacturers or forced them into other lines of production. Competition from textile mills farther south gravely threatened Henderson's mills. Prohibition in 1920 ended the city's beer and whiskey production. The development of other sources of tobacco production in the British Empire and its imposition of tariffs on American tobacco seriously hurt Henderson tobacco in the 1920s.[38]

Not all of Henderson's economic weaknesses, however, were exogenous. Local reliance on grain and tobacco created long-term economic difficulties. Henderson was also dependent on the coterie of families that had controlled the city since the antebellum era. Alves, Barrets, Soapers, and Starlings, for instance, figured largely in its banks, manufacturing, and mining establishments. The leading hotel in 1885 was the Barret House. Eventually Henderson also had a Soaper Hotel.[39]

Cairo eventually lost its influence in part because of the weakness of its manufacturing base. Cairo's manufactures were worth far more than its county's crops and livestock as late as 1919-20, when Cairo's manufactures were valued at $3.2 million and Alexander County's agricultural products at $1.7 million. Industrial products, though, were the lowest in value among the five lower river cities. Significantly, this amount was even lower than in 1900. As compared with their counterparts in other Illinois cities, however, Cairo's workers typically worked more hours each week. Almost 68 percent worked at least fifty-four hours weekly. Among lower Ohio cities, this was also high, and only Owensboro's wage earners came close. Externally based corporations also dominated the city. Only in Owensboro was the percentage of firms owned by corporations higher. Cairo led the region in value of manufactures produced by corporations (about 94 percent) and was near the top in the percentage of workers (92.1 percent) employed by corporations.

Manufacturing patterns of the pre-1880 period persisted in Cairo. By number of workers, wages, and value of product, the leading manufactures continued to be sawed lumber, flour and gristmill products, cooperage goods, and foundry and machine shop products. By the turn of the century, Cairo's hinterland cotton production supported two gins and a cottonseed oil plant, the city's largest employer. Lumber, by contrast, was a growth industry, due to local supplies and timber rafted downriver or carried cheaply by rail. Wood products were generally shipped by rail to northern markets, especially Chicago. The Singer Sewing Machine Company began producing hardwood sewing machine cabinets in 1881, and hardwood flooring, led by the E.L. Bruce Company, later become a major Cairo product. Before it closed in 1971, Bruce was Cairo's second largest employer. After World War I, though, wood manufactures had begun to decline here as elsewhere due to depletion of local resources and cheaper production to the south. Coal was never an essential part of the Cairo economy.[40]

Raw materials–dependent Cairo was also "too distant from large markets to attract market-oriented industry, and too small for labor-oriented industry. She [was] short of land that is free of the threat of floods." Cairo lacked "any comparative advantage that would attract industry." Its exports and services, whether steamboats or wood, had limited appeal. Railroad bridges across the Mississippi and the Ohio obviated the need for most transportation services. Riverboat construction elsewhere, especially Paducah and St. Louis, was more profitable. According to Charles Conrod, "Cairo's limited hinterland, scarcity of raw materials, isolation from Kentucky and Missouri, and small size have also contributed to her inability to generate exports." Although much traffic "passed through and by Cairo . . . little originated there."[41]

Owensboro and Paducah, by contrast, developed an impressive amount of manufacturing, although much was the materials-based production of the past. Daviess County showed signs of important changes by the end of World War I. Although the county's agricultural output grew substantially, to $8.2 million, leading the eleven Kentucky counties on the lower Ohio, its manufactures rose even faster, to $12.5 million. This was largely because of manufacturing in Owensboro, where the level came close to Paducah's but was well below Evansville's.

The completion of the Owensboro and Nashville rail line to Russellville and the opening of the Henderson to Louisville road in the late 1880s were major factors in the city's expansion. (Both lines fell under the management of the L&N by 1905.) In the late 1890s, Owensboro, according to the *Kentucky Gazeteer and Business Directory,* had twelve distilleries, twenty-five tobacco stemmeries, three flour mills, numerous foundries and carriage and wagon factories, and a host of other establishments. Business leaders organized a chamber of commerce in 1913 that succeeded the businessmen's association. Of additional value was the expansion of the coal trade by the early twentieth century, especially after the opening of rail ties to Central City. Unlike in Henderson, most coal was consumed in local factories and homes. Local production of petroleum also expanded after 1889, although it did not take off until the 1920s. As elsewhere in Kentucky, the county's purchase of its private toll roads early in the century effected a more coherent and less expensive system of roads.[42]

Most of Owensboro's industrial output, however, was dependent on three products, all of which were highly sensitive to external influences: tobacco, whiskey, and wagons. As in Henderson, changes in corporate control and the popularization of the cigarette greatly altered the Owensboro market. By World War I, all but one of its tobacco houses or floors were operated by the Owensboro Loose Leaf Company. Production of the bright leaf rose from 2.6 million pounds in 1909, when it was first sold in Owensboro, to well over 13 million pounds by 1932. The Owensboro Tobacco Board of Trade was formed in 1919 to promote this product.[43]

Whiskey production expanded greatly between 1879 and 1883, when eight distilleries were opened. At its peak, eighteen factories were in operation. The most notable was James Thompson's Glenmore Distillery, heir of the Monarch Distillery, which by 1918 produced 120 barrels, or 6,000 gallons a day, four times the rate when the facility was purchased in 1901. After 1890, though, whiskey production tumbled, due to federal tax laws, temperance movements, the curtailing of grain supplies, and the imposition of national prohibition. Before the implementation of the Eighteenth Amendment, only five distilleries operated in Owensboro. Despite its demise between 1920 and 1933, whiskey had attracted a heterogeneous, highly skilled workforce.[44]

Skilled workers, an ample hardwood supply, and the poor condition of southern roads explained the rapid expansion of the Owensboro Wagon Company, founded in 1884. The leading employer among the city's many foundries and wagon and buggy manufacturers, it built 10,000 wagons annually by 1910 and sold them in twenty-two states and in Cuba. Its highly skilled workers received $2.50 a day in 1901, as compared with $1.00 for most workers. Another major employer was the F.A. Ames Buggy Company, which claimed to be the largest company of its kind in the world. The city's links to a national market were also evident in the Owensboro Wagon Works' importing parts from Illinois and Pennsylvania. Improved county roads, a state system of highways, and the automobile and truck, however, contributed to the demise of these industries.[45]

Because Owensboro's manufacturing base was somewhat fragile, the number of wage earners declined between 1900 and 1914, but rose thereafter only because of the Great War. The value of products was essentially flat before the war, too. A notable exception was the Kentucky Electric Lamp Company, organized about 1899 to manufacture lightbulbs. In 1918, Pennsylvanian Roy Burlew purchased the company and, backed by several investors, expanded production to radio tubes. By 1929, when the company was renamed the Ken-Rad Tube and Lamp Company, the number of workers had increased tenfold, to 1,000. By 1937, the company employed over 3,000. It also opened plants in Tell City, Bowling Green, and Huntington (Indiana).[46]

Turn-of-the-century Owensboro was a growing city, with eight banks. To be sure, the city's agrarian context remained strong, and many leaders had blood ties to the antebellum elite. Attorney and civic leader James Weir was one of the most eminent, serving as president of the National Deposit Bank between 1864 and 1906 and as a partner in several major industrial ventures. Also prominent were such men as John Weir, R.H. Taylor, George Triplett, J.D. Powers,

T.S. Venable, John Thixton, and members of the Monarch family. The establishment and the expansion of Ken-Rad, like Glenmore, though, revealed that Owensboro was more open to outsiders and more likely to offer chances for advancement than many other communities. Charles Field, who established what would become a prosperous meat-packing firm in 1915, was another successful newcomer. Owensboro's relatively large proportion of Germans—notably John G. Delker, who established the city's leading furniture factory—also suggested it was not dominated by Tidewater culture.[47]

Owensboro's workers, however, were generally not as well off as those in other lower Ohio cities. Per capita income for its 1,380 wage earners in 1919 was about $725, almost the same as in Henderson, but well below wages in Evansville ($854), Cairo ($949), and Paducah ($1,001). Eighty percent worked at least fifty-four hours a week, the second highest proportion among the five cities and about twice the state's average. The percentage of firms owned by individuals (14 percent) was by far the lowest of the five. By 1920, the city had twenty labor organizations, including a Central Labor Union, four railroad unions (two white, two black), as well as plumbers, painters, miners, and the like.[48]

The Ohio remained indispensable to Owensboro's economy. As late as 1905, the city was served by packet boats—chiefly the six steamers of the Louisville and Evansville Mail Packet Company and the boats of long-distance lines connecting Memphis, New Orleans, and Cincinnati. Gasoline boats also connected the city to a number of small locales, although these eventually gave way to buses, particularly those of the Evansville and Ohio Valley line, which replaced its interurbans in the mid-1920s.[49]

River trade was also important in Paducah. By 1900 it was the lower Ohio's second largest city—a rank it would hold for many years. Paducah's experiences in manufacturing in many respects resembled Owensboro's, as did its reliance on packet and gasoline boat service into the early twentieth century. The *Kentucky Gazeteer* for 1895-96, for instance, listed Paducah's chief businesses as "several extensive tobacco commission houses (whose annual sales amount to many thousand hogsheads), leaf tobacco stemmeries, flour mills, machine shops and foundries." Lumber interests were defined as the state's largest and hardwood lumber as the nation's second largest market. In 1883, the Landstaff-Orm Manufacturing Company claimed to be the largest saw and planing mill in the West. Paducah also produced carriages, wagons, spokes, hubs, furniture, and other wood products.[50]

Although the chief manufactures, tobacco and wood were not the only elements of this city's growing and comparatively diversified economy. River-related employment—in dry docks, boat building and repair services, and river trade—remained essential. Rooted in the construction of a marine railway in the 1840s, it was greatly expanded by the incorporation of the Paducah Ship Yard Company in 1882. Perhaps a third of Paducah's workers depended on the rivers for their livelihood by the 1890s.[51] The transformation of river traffic to tows and barges gave these services a great boost during and after World War I. As of 1909, however, the city's leading industries were tobacco, lumber, and general shop construction by steam engine companies. Tobacco remained important, chiefly in a stemmed form for export, but after 1909 it was shipped elsewhere for processing, and its significance to Paducah declined. Wood also declined—for the same reasons as elsewhere.

By 1919, the number of wage earners in McCracken County was second only to Vanderburgh's. As a percentage of the workforce (88.7 percent), the proportion of wage earners in Paducah exceeded the other four cities. Paducah's manufactures, valued at $11 million, were more than three times the 1900 level and second only to Evansville's $70.2 million. As noted earlier, Paducah's workers also enjoyed a relatively high wage level. Corporations were an important part of Paducah's life, although the value of their manufactures was lower than in three of the five cities. An increasing amount of capital came from outside the city, and by the 1920s Paducah boosters were actively recruiting even more companies to relocate there.

The first and most important example of that had been the Illinois Central Railroad. Rail transportation, not manufacturing, came to dominate the city's economy. Local attorney Q.Q. Quigley is credited with persuading the Elizabethtown and Paducah, later a part of the Illinois Central, to move its repair shops to Paducah in 1884. When IC repair facilities were expanded in 1928, IC became the city's leading employer with a workforce of 1,800. The IC's hold on the city was strengthened as well by the opening of the bridge and the Edgewood Cutoff. Rail expansion also enhanced coal shipment from the interior.[52]

Evansville's experiences mirrored those of Paducah in some respects but differed sharply in others, especially in the diversification of its commerce and industry and the pace of its citizens' lifestyle. A traveler on the Ohio in 1919, Harry Bennett Abdy, captured this, noting Evansville's substantially larger size and level of business activity—the greatest amount of river traffic he had seen since leaving St. Louis. He contrasted that with towns on other shores that were "more picturesque, and decidedly richer in that quaint Southern flavor that affects the life along most of the Ohio." Evansville, nonetheless, possessed much charm, especially because of the long, graceful, boulder-paved riverfront, set in a sweeping flourish on an easy-curving bend of the river. Also impressive were Evansville's skyline, Sunset Park, old riverfront homes, and soot and aromas from its many factories and shops.[53]

One of the smallest in square miles on the lower Ohio, Vanderburgh

County's agriculture, low in output when contrasted with its manufacturing, was one of the reasons for its strength. In value of crops and livestock, it ranked above all but eight other lower Ohio counties. The county's grain, livestock, dairy products, orchards, and truck farms sustained a growing city and provided raw materials for a number of local industries.

In manufacturing Vanderburgh County in 1919 had no serious regional rival, with three and a half times the number of establishments and four times the number of wage earners as second-ranked McCracken County. The value of its manufactures was four and one-half times the level of Alexander County. In Evansville, as elsewhere, the number of establishments had declined since 1900, but unlike the other four cities, the number of its wage earners had steadily expanded to over 12,500 in 1919, and value of manufactures had risen sharply, from 14.2 million in 1900 to $70.2 million in 1919. The city's diversification was also evident in the large number of professionals and clerical workers, which together accounted for about a seventh of the workforce, a much higher share than in any of the other four cities.[54]

In 1919 in Evansville, 14,145 men and 3,893 women, or about half of the workforce of 37,811, were employed in factories. Trade ran a distant second, and domestic and personal service placed third. Transportation—now more oriented to rails and roads than to the river, which employed only 150—came in fourth. Manufacturing as a proportion of the workforce was declining, but it remained a powerful fact of life.[55]

Between 1865 and the 1920s, change as well as continuity were evident in the manufacturing profile of this urban anomaly on the lower Ohio. In 1880, the manufacturers of steam engines, plows, stoves, and other metal products led the city in numbers of workers and in wages, but ranked third in annual value of products. By 1904, these manufacturers had dropped out of the top three, reflecting the decline of steamboat transport and shifts in agriculture. Makers of stoves and ranges, sold chiefly in southern markets, broke into the top three in each category by the 1919 industrial census, only to lose that place ten years later.

Wood products were the city's primary industry. In 1880, furniture makers—who also sold most of their products in the South—were the second leading employer and were ranked third in wages. In the same year, lumber and mill products ranked third in number of workers, second in amount of wages, and second in annual value of products. By 1904, furniture makers employed the largest number of workers and paid the most wages, and the value of their products had risen to third. In 1919, furniture dropped to second in number of employees, even though the total had doubled since 1904. In wages, however, furniture remained first, as it also would in 1929, and in annual value of products it rose to first in 1929. This indicated especially the strength of Globe-Bosse-World, formed before 1910 by second-generation German American Benjamin Bosse. The firm, which occupied thirty acres on the city's west side, claimed to be the largest furniture factory in the world. Such boasts were not unusual for Bosse, who by 1913, when he was elected mayor, was one of the city's wealthiest and most enthusiastic promoters. The erection of a Furniture Exchange Building adjacent to the courthouse during the first decade of the century also attested to the growing power of Evansville's furniture makers.

The use of brand-names, introduced by such companies as Procter and Gamble in Cincinnati, revealed the rapid growth of a national urban market to which manufacturers of consumer goods responded with innovative product images. Cigars soon had brand-names, and Evansville's Fenrich Cigar Company promoted its most popular product as the Charles Denby, named after the Evansville attorney and diplomat. By 1929, cigar making ranked second only to furniture in wages and value of products. When all factors are considered, tobacco products rose to fourth in 1929.[56]

These continuities belied some fundamental changes. The Evansville Cotton Mill, for instance, once the city's chief employer, closed about 1905, defeated by the costs of labor and materials and cheaper competition from southern mills. Nearby supplies of iron ore all but disappeared, and costs of iron and steel production rose. Timber had to be shipped in from ever greater distances to the furniture factories, and furniture workers grew increasingly assertive in the face of wage cuts. In early March 1919, after a series of disputes stretching back several years, over 900 men joined the Furniture Workers Union. A six-week strike occurred a year later. During the 1920s, the number of furniture workers declined, but wages increased. Rising costs of labor and materials made Evansville companies vulnerable to rising competition from nonunion manufacturers in North Carolina and contributed to the industry's decline after 1929.[57]

Evansville's manufactures were mostly exported to a national market, chiefly southward, and not sold locally. Rising competition from southern and western manufacturers, combined with the expansion of manufacturing in Indianapolis, weakened Evansville's manufacturing position.[58]

Instead of stagnating, though, Evansville business leaders were able to diversify their base, laying the foundation for industries that would dominate the city's economy after the 1920s. Despite the "deaths" of such enterprises as steamboat construction and repairs and cotton goods, "births" occurred in the twentieth century: cake flour, bottle caps, railroad headlights, structural and building steel, cigars, automobile and truck bodies and assemblies, infant foods, and refrigerators.

Notable additions to the Evansville economy were Bucyrus, Hercules, Evansville Automobile, Graham Brothers, and Mead Johnson. Bucyrus, which arrived in 1910-11, built a large factory on the edge of Howell to manufacture steam shovels and other heavy equipment. Its parent company was located in Milwaukee. Hercules Buggy Company, formed in Cincinnati in 1894, was lured to Evansville at the turn of the century by the Evansville Business Men's Association. Its founder, William H. McCurdy, built what was then the city's largest factory on the near north side. Shortly thereafter, McCurdy began to produce a car for Sears, Roebuck. As a side product, beginning in 1914 his company made gas engines and wagon bodies. Although its auto business was short-lived, Hercules also expanded its manufactures to wooden ice boxes and gasoline-powered coolers, which in the 1920s grew to include electric and gas-powered refrigerators. McCurdy obtained the Swedish patent for gas-absorption refrigeration, and in the late 1920s the company was reorganized as Servel ("Serve Electrically"). Hercules also made truck bodies.[59]

Motorized vehicles were also manufactured, albeit briefly, by Willis Copeland and the Graham brothers. Copeland's Evansville Automobile Company manufactured the Simplicity, a chain-driven gearless vehicle. The three Graham brothers began manufacturing trucks on the north side, near Pigeon Creek, before 1920. In 1924, the company was sold to Dodge Brothers, which closed the plant. Two years later, though, the Grahams initiated plans for building the Graham-Paige automobile in a new factory nearby. The Depression unfortunately ended their second enterprise, but the Grahams left two modern plants and a number of skilled workers. In 1935, Chrysler began assembling Plymouth automobiles in the older facility. Bodies for Plymouths were built at the new car facility run by Briggs Corporation of Indiana.[60]

Motor vehicles and refrigerators—the foundation of Evansville enterprises from the 1920s to the late 1950s—evolved from existing manufactures: buggy and carriage works, and furniture and machinery fabrication. These represented external economies within industries and a great deal of luck. Having a trained workforce and a number of large manufacturing facilities also helped.[61]

Igleheart Brothers began selling their Swans Down flour nationwide in the mid-1890s. Fifteen years later, they expanded their facilities on the city's north side.

In the case of Mead Johnson, fate, location, and initiative combined to bring another new manufacturing facility in 1915. The closing of the Cotton Mill left a huge westside manufacturing facility adjoining L&N tracks. E. Mead Johnson, seeking a site to produce his new infant nutritional, Dextri-Maltose, was lured from New Jersey to Evansville because it had a factory for sale and access to an ample supply of corn. Articles of association were filed in October

1915, and production began shortly afterwards. Mead Johnson soon became one of the city's leading manufacturers, selling its popular nutritionals nationwide. Pablum was probably its most famous product.[62]

Although dependent on the Ohio for much of its enterprise and its identity, Evansville increasingly became an industrial city. Over 37 percent of its workers were employed in manufacturing by 1920. (In 1950, 40 percent were, well above the national average of 29 percent and the proportion of workers in Fort Wayne, Indianapolis, Chicago, Toledo, and Cincinnati.) Manufacturing, moreover, was increasingly the province of large corporations: almost 65 percent of the workers in 1919, for example, were employed in factories where the workforce numbered 100 or more. One-fifth worked where 500 or more were on the payroll. Over half of the firms were run by corporations, but most of these—unlike Cairo and Paducah—were locally owned and controlled. Evansville's industries contrasted sharply with Cairo's, which failed to develop manufacturing to exploit its commercial advantages or its raw materials, and with Terre Haute's, which did not recover successfully when it lost its raw materials–based industries and markets early in this century. They also differed markedly from Henderson, Owensboro, and Paducah—in the first two cases, because of their continued dependence on the processing of raw materials, and in the third because of its dependence on the IC Railroad.[63]

Not all of Evansville's workers were in manufacturing, but most were. These workers shared several distinctive traits. Between 1860 and 1929, their wages were about 11 percent lower than the national average for nonfarm workers. They also worked a relatively high number of hours each week. In 1919, almost 60 percent worked at least fifty-four hours. Such conditions explained the formation of many unions in the city and accounted for labor disturbances. Among the most restless and reform-minded were the railroaders of Howell. Eugene Debs visited the city in 1908 and 1912 and thought it one of the nation's most promising socialist communities.[64]

Evansville generally prospered and developed, though. A symptom (as well as cause) was the strength of local capital: twelve banking institutions by 1920. The largest were the Old State National Bank, formed in 1834, whose president was William McCurdy; the City National Bank, the former Canal Bank, whose president was Francis Joseph Reitz; and Citizens National Bank, established in 1873 as the successor to W.J. Lowry and Company, and whose president was William J. Gray, a real estate entrepreneur. Demonstrating the impact of American banks on the twentieth century urban landscape, Citizens led the way in erecting a new ten-story building, the city's first "skyscraper" and the second on the lower Ohio, in 1914.[65]

Expanded rail service was also an essential part of the city's manufacturing take-off. Much—including the construction of the city's belt line in the 1880s—had been strengthened under David J. Mackey's administration, when he gained control of the "Short Line," E&TH, and the Paducah, Decatur, and Evansville. The panic of 1893 and subsequent financial restructuring, however, left Mackey bankrupt and the city with rail service that was largely externally owned and controlled. Chief among these lines was the L&N, which had accelerated Evansville's development and its integration into the national market. This company collaborated with the Chicago and Eastern Illinois and the E&TH, acquired by the C&EI in 1912. The C&EI also acquired various smaller lines tapping the coal fields of southwestern and western Indiana as well as the Evansville Belt Railway. (It was in turn secured by the L&N in the 1960s.) The Cairo Division of the "Big Four" (Cleveland, Cincinnati, Chicago, and St. Louis), the New York Central's largest Indiana subsidiary, had not only an extension from southern Illinois to Vincennes but also, after 1906, a line running north from Evansville to Vincennes through Mount Carmel, Illinois. The Illinois Central gained control of the road extending from Evansville through northern Posey County into southern Illinois, and in 1900 the Southern augmented its network by securing the "Air Line"—the Louisville, Evansville, and St. Louis.[66]

Changes in commerce and manufacturing exhibited several causes. Railroads, bridges, state roads, automobiles, and trucks spurred this economic transformation. Cumulatively, these innovations represented a grave threat to river-related economic activity up and down the Ohio, from Pittsburgh through Cincinnati and Louisville to the Mississippi. Their influence, however, was uneven. The construction of an east-west rail line between Henderson and Louisville that paralleled the river, for instance, was undoubtedly a more serious threat to river commerce among Kentucky locales than rail lines across the river. On the north shore, especially in Indiana, hilly terrain minimized the construction of east-west rail lines near the Ohio. Vehicular bridges were perhaps the quintessential sign of a new era, and twenty-four of them were constructed on the Ohio between 1922 and 1933—three on the lower Ohio.

The river, nonetheless, remained a significant part of the region's economic life. In addition to local service provided by gasoline boats, the Ohio witnessed the rise of the towboat and the barge, which efficiently carried bulky, low-unit-cost commodities such as coal and corn. In 1908, the Inland Waterways Commission identified Pittsburgh, not New Orleans, as the nation's leading river port. The prospect of increased freight commerce, as passenger service declined, prompted civic leaders along the river to seek federal guarantee of a year-round minimum depth. In 1895, Cincinnati businessmen formed the Ohio Valley Improvement Association (OVIA) to lobby for the construction of locks and dams. The third annual meeting was held in Evansville in October 1897, when delegates from Wheeling to Cairo attended what an editor termed one of the city's most historic moments. Civic leaders eventually gained the support of Congress, President William Howard Taft, and the newly formed Inland Waterways Commission (1907). In 1910, Congress approved the construction of fifty-four locks and dams providing for a nine-foot channel.[67]

Appropriations lagged, however, until about 1920. The overburdened rail system during World War I led Congress to create the Federal Barge Line (reorganized in 1928 as the American Barge Company of Louisville) to attempt to break the rail logjam. The development of more powerful and efficient diesel-powered tows and modern steel barges also strengthened the river's commercial appeal, and congressional appropriations for river improvements increased substantially after 1922. Along the lower Ohio, the earliest construction began six miles below Henderson in 1912 and three miles below West Point in 1914; the latest to start was at the foot of Grand Chain, Illinois, in 1925. The earliest completed were Locks and Dams 43 and 48, near West Point and Henderson, respectively, in 1921. Eleven lower Ohio locks were built. The final dam, Number 53 at Grand Chain, was opened August 27, 1929. Shortly thereafter, members of the OVIA staged a dedication cruise from Pittsburgh to Cairo, with President Herbert Hoover participating.[68]

This dream had been neither universally shared nor promoted along the lower Ohio. At the 1896 meeting of the OVIA in Pittsburgh, for instance, the only Kentucky community sending an emissary was Paducah, and only W.H. Halliday of Cairo came from Illinois. By contrast, Cannelton and Tell City each sent representatives, and Evansville sponsored seven, including the congressman and the mayor—the largest delegation from the lower Ohio. Of the thirty-six OVIA vice presidents from Kentucky listed in the 1929 dedication program, one each came from Owensboro and Hawesville and two from Henderson, but Paducah supplied thirteen, the largest number from the Bluegrass State. Of the twenty-six from Indiana, Evansville had the most, fourteen, while Tell City, Grandview, and Rockport had one each. Among Illinois's thirty-two vice presidents, seventeen came from Cairo (one a son of W.H. Halliday). Mound City had four, Metropolis and Joppa each had three, Brookport had two, and Rosiclare, Golconda, and Shawneetown each had one.

Evansville business and government officials remained the linchpin on the lower river. They hosted OVIA meetings on at least two occasions after 1897. On one of these, an "Ohio River—Past, Present, and Future" feature appeared in the April 28, 1912, issue of the *Evansville Journal-News,* an illustration of the continued importance of newspaper editors as community and regional boosters. Evansville leaders traveled down the river to Memphis in 1907 aboard the *John Stuart Hopkins* to rally support for a year-round river channel. And beginning in the early 1920s, planning commenced for the region's first river-rail-truck terminal, which opened in January 1931.[69]

To assert, as most do, that the coming of the railroads produced decline among river communities is to overlook a number of points. To be sure, one must consider the implications of rail lines and bridges for the accelerated dispersal of population into the interior. Three places on the lower river were river crossings by 1917, and in varying degrees they participated in growing north-south trade with the aid of two huge rail systems. Markets shifted as population mushroomed in such places as Indianapolis and South Bend. Getting there was easier by rail than by water, and it could be done year-round.

The steamboat's demise had many causes, as Louis Hunter has observed. Rail lines did not single out packets for rate wars. Cutthroat competition among the "Big 7" packet lines in the 1880s may have been more devastating. Railroads operated year-round, which required a larger scale and a more sophisticated form of organizations than riverboat operators had. Railroads carried specialized cargoes in separate cars and offered local and express service. Steamboats required large crews to fuel and maintain bulky engines. Riverboats were, however, more cost-effective when they carried bulky, low-unit-cost freight. Probably the most fundamental fact, though, was that steamboats had thrived when most people west of the mountains were concentrated near the Ohio.[70]

Other causes of the steamboat's demise need to be considered. Large corporations such as U.S. Steel, for example, used their own barges for shipping but relied on rail lines they controlled or favored. The westward spread of industry meant suppliers did not have to transport raw materials over long distances to reach factories. The introduction of the more reliable and efficient diesel engine and the screw propeller in the 1920s, as well as the speedier, gas-powered motorboats, hurt packet service. The motor truck was especially damaging to steam-powered freight service. In addition, low wages paid rivermen made for a low caliber of workers, and "way charges" collected by wharves and levees were increasingly costly. The vagaries of weather also damaged river transport.[71]

The demise of the steamboat did not mean that the river or its settlements were doomed. West Point's Kosmos Portland Cement Company, established in the 1880s, expanded into the steam tow business and later into the construction of diesel and gas tows at Kosmosdale.[72] Towns and cities continued to grow. Each locale's history should be examined separately.

Well after the coming of the railroads, the Ohio was a vital economic and communications link. First, the settlements offered vital services, especially for places with little or no rail service. Second, railroads alone did not account for the lower Ohio valley losing rank to the Upper Midwest. Ironically, for ex-

ample, the Ohio and its tributaries dispersed population into the interior beginning in the early nineteenth century, and that contributed over time to its
relative demise. Also, the river was not bridged until 1885; four years later, the
Illinois Central crossed the river at Cairo. Not until 1917 did the Burlington
do the same between Brookport and Paducah. Bridges made these places river
crossings, not merely river towns. The few other places with rail service, such
as Owensboro and Rockport, were rail heads. But the record does not indicate
that river crossings became significantly less dependent on the Ohio. Being a
river crossing, moreover, did not necessarily transform communities, as the
cases of Cairo and Brookport-Metropolis demonstrate.

One must consider other factors. These include the impact of automobiles and trucks, but significantly only after the end of the Great War, when
state road systems were put in place in all three states. Vehicular bridges did
not cross the lower Ohio until the late 1920s, and by 1932 only three existed
south of the Falls—at Evansville-Henderson, Brookport-Paducah, and Cairo.
Also worth considering is the impact on river communities of school consolidation, begun simultaneously with road improvements, and the combined effect of retail services in larger interior towns and of the growing national reach
of consumer goods offered by large corporations. The short-sightedness of
many river communities' leaders, who generally sought local pork-barrel aid
and not improvements in the entire waterway must also be viewed as a factor.

The emergence of Evansville as the center of an extensive metropolitan
region and the expansion of Cairo, Henderson, Owensboro, and Paducah dis-
pel, though, the theory that the entire corridor was governed by a premodern,
barter-oriented economy and that backwater places such as Rome and Troy
were typical. By 1920, these five cities boasted not only steady and in some
cases impressive population increase but also an array of industries, businesses,
services, and amenities.[73]

The construction of concrete-surfaced state roads, beginning about 1920
in all three states, was an especially serious threat. The "Good Roads Movement" commenced in the 1890s had been the result of the coming of automobiles, bicycles, and rural free delivery (1896). The first indication of rural mail
delivery's impact on roads came in 1899, when the U.S. Post Office ruled that
rural routes would be established only where roads were usable year-round.
Rural free delivery meant not only free mail service but also cheaper access to
market, better schools and churches, and an end to isolation. An appropria-
tion in 1912 to improve rural route roads laid the basis for forcing states to
share the cost of road improvements with the federal government. That, in
turn, contributed to the landmark Highway Act of 1916, a cost-sharing program financed by a gasoline tax that required states to create plans for high-

ways in order to receive federal funds for construction of concrete-surfaced roads.[74]

Good roads, more than rail lines and even the auto, facilitated interior travel and accelerated the decline of country stores, one-room schools, and other service providers in countless small places. Golconda's decline offered a vivid example of that. Road improvement and automobile and truck usage also accelerated the demise of buggy and wagon companies, an especially important part of Owensboro's economy. Vehicular bridges added to the speed of change in the 1930s.

Decisions made by local, state, and federal officials were also important. Local political cultures in the three states remained significant, and the range and character of public services varied. The commitment of all three state governments after 1910 to improved public education and state roads enhanced the fortunes of many river communities. So did a number of federal actions—not only the Highway Act of 1916 but also the building of locks and dams, which benefited small places such as West Point and Golconda in the short run by creating construction jobs and in the long run by enhancing the river's ability to sustain year-round barge traffic. World War I demonstrated the importance of barges in providing an effective flow of freight, and federal subsidies brought benefits to such places as Paducah, whose barge construction and repair facilities expanded. The war also brought munitions and other war-related contracts to industries such as Evansville's Bucyrus, which produced shells, and offered an enormous stimulus for the region's grain production. Ironically, however, wartime grain demands and rising support for prohibition while also helping to prepare for the cessation of whiskey production in cities such as Owensboro. The demand for fluorspar in steel production stimulated the growth of Rosiclare and nearby Tolu, Kentucky, and in 1918 the Illinois settlement gained a federally funded hospital. The need for army training facilities led to the expansion of Camp Young, established in 1903 on the edge of Hardin County. In 1917 this became Camp (later Fort) Knox, expanded to 100,000 acres, and one of the West Point area's leading employers.[75]

Still another external factor shaping the character of lower Ohio communities was the metropolis. Defined by the Census Bureau as a metropolitan district between 1910 and 1950, it was described by 1930 as a central city of at least 50,000 residents and surrounding territory with a combined population of 100,000. The district featured integration of economic services and a minimum of 150 persons per square mile. The term *standard metropolitan area* was used in 1950, and *standard metropolitan statistical area* was introduced in 1960. In each case, more sophisticated criteria were used. The number of metropolises expanded from 82 in 1900 to 147 in 1950, or from about one-third to three-fifths of the nation's population. These regions grew much faster than the nation as a whole. Especially dramatic was the pace of development in the outlying rings of these areas, where villages and towns became tributaries to a larger urban center, which in turn depended on its hinterland for its labor force, its raw materials, and its markets. Smaller centers in the metropolis provided narrowly specialized functions, while the center specialized in administration and control.[76] The upriver community that first experienced this was West Point. Only Evansville, among lower Ohio cities, achieved the designation of metropolitan district by 1930, and well after mid-century it was the only metropolis between Louisville and the Mississippi. Initially including only Vanderburgh County, by World War II the metropolitan district included Henderson as well.[77]

Another external influence on the lower Ohio was the corporation that was neither owned nor controlled locally. The consolidation of railroad lines, especially the Illinois Central and the L&N, offered early and powerful examples of the ways in which corporate leadership could affect communities' well-being. Evansville and Paducah benefited especially in this regard, as did Henderson, Metropolis, and Owensboro. Cairo was the most adversely affected. Corporations subsequently had enormous impact on cities in which tobacco, automobiles and trucks, furniture, and other consumer durables were manufactured. The twentieth-century corporation was also responsible for innovations in mass communications, which were creating a mass culture through motion pictures, radio, advertising, and popular magazines.

But community development was also shaped by local decision making. When leaders offered realistic visions and pursued them aggressively and also provided opportunities for newcomers, their communities prospered. Unfortunately, these characteristics were not found in all settlements. Evansville's elite, beginning in the 1850s, saw the importance of river improvements, for instance, and consistently worked to achieve them. Active participation by business and civic leaders in the efforts of the Ohio Valley Improvement Association was uneven. Evansville and Paducah representatives were most prominent at OVIA meetings. And once the canalization of the river was completed in 1929, only a handful of places either saw the potential that the re-formed Ohio afforded or responded appropriately with such projects as Evansville's Mead Johnson Terminal.

An important aspect of urban advancement was the formation of business associations in Evansville, Henderson, Owensboro, and Paducah in the 1880s that attempted to form a coherent and progressive front. Evansville's Business Men's Association of 1887, for instance, was incorporated to promote the welfare and the advancement of the city, to diffuse information regarding its advantages, to secure laborers at home and abroad, and to promote investment in the city. Such boosterism often paid off when accompanied by adequate resources, effective leadership, and realistic expectations, as in Owensboro's securing what became the Ken-Rad firm and in Evansville's gaining the L&N shops and Hercules, Bucyrus-Erie, and Mead Johnson. In both cities the businessmen's associations evolved into chambers of commerce—Owensboro in 1913, and Evansville in 1915. And slogans followed which sought to combine realism with boosterism. Evansville portrayed itself as "Gateway to the South," and Paducah's motto was "Rails, Rivers, Roads Hub."[78]

The creation of such business and industrial leadership was neither guaranteed nor smooth. German American furniture manufacturers on Evansville's west side formed their own business association in early 1909 because their leader, Benjamin Bosse, complained that the EBMA overlooked west side interests. Within three years, however, the irrepressible Bosse secured the presidency of the EBMA, and in 1915 he helped to organize the chamber of commerce, which supplanted the EBMA. This process illustrated the accommodation of the older commercial leadership, symbolized by Charles Viele, founder of the EBMA, to the rising industrialists, as well as the emergence of prominent German Americans in the once English-dominated civic and business elite. Although family ties continued to matter in, for example, the composition of Evansville's bank boards and other symbols of power, the inclusion of newcomers underscored the city's comparatively open access to those who wanted to make it. Paducah was probably closest to Evansville in this respect, whereas Henderson remained the most tied to the leadership structures of the past.[79]

Such patterns helped explain why Evansville, Owensboro, and Paducah were most successful in securing a more diverse economic base by the early 1920s. To be sure, this also reflected a great deal of luck and timing, as well as the cultural heritage of each community. Yankees and Germans, for instance, continued to shape Evansville, and Cavalier and Upper South values were influential across the Ohio. In between, to varying degrees, were the leaders of Owensboro and Paducah. Cairo's leaders, rooted in the Upper South and in the factional and identity problems that had stymied progress for years, seemed unable to prevent their town's inexorable decline.

Whatever the size of the place, the Ohio River remained a vital, if altered, part of the residents' lives. Whether providing the mussel shells from which buttons were produced in Crawford or Hardin (Kentucky) Counties or carrying coal from modern facilities at Paducah, the river continued to shape the settlements on its shores. Not the least of these was the way in which annual high waters and periodic flooding affected the economic and residential patterns of the communities.[80]

In turn, the Ohio's shape and its functions were altered to meet the new challenges of an industrial era. In only a few places did leaders fully understand and appreciate what was happening. The degree of persistence or change in this respect revealed not only economic considerations but, as before, the qualities of political life, social arrangements, and culture in each village, town, and city.

11 ∾
Living Together: Society and Culture

After the 1870s, most people living along the lower Ohio experienced dramatic changes in the ways in which they ordered their lives. According to Chudacoff and Smith, "The agrarian way of life, with its slow pace, moral sobriety, and self-help ethic, had been waning ever since urbanization accelerated." Although present in the 1920s, and despite some nostalgic campaigns for "the simple virtues of an imagined past," everywhere "signs pointed to an urban ascendance."[1]

Even though most neither dwelled in cities nor were employed in manufacturing, they felt the influences of the metropolis within and outside the region in numerous ways—for example, in the growth of consumer-oriented industry, in the emergence of corporate and government bureaucracies, in the transformation of the workforce, and in the appeal of the city as a source of entertainment, employment, and greater personal autonomy. In the smaller places, the range of government services, social organizations, and cultural activities remained fairly simple, and residents maintained a quality of relationships that resembled that of their ancestors. Only in the largest settlements were spectacular changes occurring in the structure of local government, the organization of social relations, and the forms of cultural expression. But even in the hamlets, writes Gunther Barth, the new ways of life associated with city people that fused "utility and human kindness . . . made this urban culture the national way of life." Spread by steamboats, railroad lines, and telegraph and telephone wires, this new culture, with its apartment houses, vaudeville shows, metropolitan presses, department stores, and ball parks, created common links that enabled city people "to accept and to overcome the contrasts and divisions in their surroundings."[2] The coming of the automobile, the truck, and the bus, the flowering of the suburb, and the popularity of tabloids, movies, and radio gave rise to another form of urban culture by the 1920s. This, too, would shape the people of the lower Ohio.

The unpretentious size and level of development of most places meant that local government amenities remained fairly simple. Government was generally limited to the police powers afforded by the county sheriff. Town government, organized police and fire protection, and paved streets were at best inchoate in such settlements as Grandview, Troy, Rome, and Mauckport, whose town pump, in the center of the public square, symbolized the limits of these services. Periodic bouts with devastating fires reflected such small settlements' inability to protect themselves. (Uniontown experienced a major fire in 1918; Tolu was nearly wiped out by floods in 1884 and 1913 and was all but destroyed by a fire in 1924.) Most of these places were also unable to garner the resources to guard against high waters. Fire and flood, in turn, prevented these places from growing. Not surprisingly, Caseyville's population dropped steadily before 1900 to about two hundred and remained there until the 1930s. With sixty-seven people listed in the 1940 census, it was the smallest incorporated place in the Commonwealth.[3]

Urban services were also limited in the larger villages and towns. Cloverport, which lacked a fire department, had to call for the aid of fire brigades in Evansville and Owensboro to combat a devastating fire in 1901. Elizabethtown, Illinois, depended on well water until the 1980s. Cloverport did not have electric streetlights until 1913, two years after Breckinridge County secured control of the toll road that extended thence to Hardinsburg (later part of U.S. 60). Stephensport obtained a city hall only in 1896, but until 1915 was governed by town trustees, who appointed a marshal, levied taxes, issued licenses, and regulated behavior. City lighting came only in the 1930s. Uniontown had a similar form of town government, which bore a heavy burden of debt from railroad investments and had to cope with substantial economic stress as well as seasonal flooding and fire damages.[4]

More advanced was Hawesville, which secured electric lights, telephone service, and public water service between 1896 and 1899, installed its first sewers in 1901, and gained natural gas service in 1905. Metropolis, which drilled deep wells for its public water supply in the 1880s, proceeded at a similar pace. Governed by city trustees, Mount Vernon boasted brick sidewalks and gravel or macadamized streets in 1882, installed a public water supply and purchased a fire engine in 1886, and in 1913 claimed ninety-five blocks of macadamized streets and thirty-three blocks of asphalt streets. It was also the center for fifteen rural mail routes.[5]

Cairo continued to endure the fruits of its distinctive heritage. In 1892-93, its government created a drainage district and a fire department and franchised an electric street railway. In addition, in 1913 its residents adopted a city commission form of government, a progressive tool that replaced the mayor-council with a small group of commissioners, each elected at large and responsible for a single area of municipal administration. Such a plan weakened the powers of politicos and made city services theoretically more accountable, although it lacked the coordination provided by a single chief. On the other hand, in the early 1890s Cairo voters rejected expensive but in the long run essential sheet filling and pumping.[6]

Urban amenities reflected political leadership, economic base, political culture of the region and state, and powers of local governments. Consequently, the largest towns displayed similarities and differences. Cities in Kentucky, for instance, operated under the tight restrictions of the 1891 constitution, the product of rural, agrarian, and low-tax interests. Under the legislature's charter provisions of 1893, Owensboro became a "third-class" city. Paducah moved up to "second-class" in 1902, a distinction which gave the mayor and the council greater authority. Almost as limited were the powers of larger settlements in Illinois and Indiana. Before 1920, the legislatures of Kentucky and Illinois permitted cities to adopt the progressive city commission form of government, and in 1921 Indiana's legislature—responding to election scandals in such cities as Evansville and Terre Haute—permitted a city manager–type of government only if voters approved it in a referendum. (Evansville's reformers were resoundingly defeated in a special election in June 1921.) In 1929, the Indiana Supreme Court invalidated the enabling legislation. Between 1891 and 1909, Indiana's General Assembly did, however, create some long overdue reforms of local government: a uniform plan in which the mayor was given broad authority to appoint members of administrative boards and departments without city council approval and in which larger municipalities could elect a city judge and a city clerk.[7]

On both sides of the river, strong Democratic Party affiliation and fiscal conservatism prevailed. Some diversities existed. Blacks in Cairo, Paducah, Metropolis, Mound City, and Evansville helped to guarantee a strong Republican presence. Democratic leadership, moreover, varied enormously. Many of Kentucky's political leaders in the 1880s were Confederate army veterans, but Evansville's leaders were mostly German entrepreneurs such as Benjamin Bosse and John W. Boehne Sr.[8]

Boehne and Bosse represent another characteristic of the leadership of lower Ohio municipalities: the continued involvement of the commercial, manufacturing, and professional elite in local government, a rare occurrence in larger cities. Soapers and Starlings, for example, were Henderson city councilmen in the 1890s, and Weirs, Delkers, and Thixtons, representatives of wood and whiskey interests, played prominent roles in Owensboro government. James H. Hickman, a tobacco merchant and large landowner, served longer than any of its mayors—six terms between 1890 and 1926. Paducah's mayors included merchant Meyer Weil, wholesale grocer James P. Smith, and attorney Frank N. Burns. Attorney Charles K. Wheeler became Paducah city attorney in 1895 and was elected to a term in Congress two years later. The most eminent proved to be attorney Alben W. Barkley, who first served as county judge and was elected to the House of Representative in 1913 and the Senate in 1927.[9]

Local government by the early 1900s differed only by degree from that of the mid-1800s. If Evansville's history is instructive, it reveals the rise of German Americans to prominence in both parties. At the same time, many business leaders never ran for office and at most held occasional government appointments, choosing instead to exercise their influence through friendly interests in city and county government. The Quigley-Landstaff family union in Paducah, like that of the Orrs with Shanklins and Cliffords or of the Reitzes and Fendrichs in Evansville, exerted power primarily through hired supporters. C.B. Enlow, president of City National Bank, became president of Evansville's school board as a consequence of his support for Mayor Benjamin Bosse, and in turn his bank served as depository for school funds. After Bosse's death, Enlow managed to gain a substantial interest in Bosse's *Evansville Courier,* which for many years served as Enlow's mouthpiece.

Local government did relatively little, moreover, to control the vice associated with river city culture—gambling, abuse of liquor laws, and prostitution. Although some mayors, such as Boehne, attempted to eliminate vice, most allowed it to persist, choosing instead to trade votes and revenue for selective administration of local ordinances. Bosse's administration vividly illustrated that tendency. Reformers were eventually able to create city commissions and park boards and to pass housing ordinances.[10]

Important differences in the range and the quality of urban services also surfaced. Henderson's patriarchal culture produced what by contemporary standards was highly "progressive" government: city commission government in 1922, and municipally owned water, gas, and electric utilities. Its electric street railways were the first on the lower Ohio, operating from 1889 to 1923. Historian Edward Ayers has suggested that streetcar companies arose earlier in the New South than elsewhere because there was little infrastructure to replace or dismantle. Electric lighting arrived early and expanded quickly for similar reasons. By the mid-1890s, Henderson boasted not only paved streets and paid police and fire departments but also a board of health, a city physician, and a city park, thanks to the donation of land by Mayor John C. Atkinson Jr.[11]

Neighboring Kentucky cities also registered impressive advances. After becoming a third-class city, Owensboro experienced substantial growth, in part because of the powers granted its city government. The privately owned, publicly franchised street railways were electrified in 1893. Five years later the city organized a paid police department, followed in 1901 by a professional fire department. Citizens also agreed to spend $200,000 to obtain a water plant and a municipal electric plant. (The two were merged in 1937.) In 1902, the city and county gained control of their private toll roads; the city also expanded its acquisition of park lands, securing five (one for blacks) between 1894 and 1930. A county health department was organized in 1918. Owensboro, like Henderson, also paved its streets and expanded its boundaries through annexation. By 1920, the city adopted a city commission form of government.[12]

Paducah's urban services were somewhat less advanced than those of Henderson and Owensboro, but advances were impressive, nonetheless. Under Democrat Charles Reed (1881-89), who served with Lloyd Tilghman at Shiloh and Corinth, the city obtained a paid fire department; a city waterworks and over twelve miles of mains, 159 hydrants, and purified water; a city gas plant; and a free city mail delivery. Electrified street railway service similar to Henderson's began in 1890, and later in the decade Paducah expanded water service and opened its first public park. Under David A. Yeiser Sr., who served longer (1891-97, 1901-08) than any other Paducah mayor to that time, the city improved fire protection, electrified streetlights, constructed city sewers, extended city boundaries, paved many streets, and built a new hospital. His successors motorized city vehicles, enhanced health standards, and attempted to bring city saloons under control by increasing the price of a license to $500. War in 1917 brought municipal coal and milk departments and the closing of fifty-six saloons. By the mid-1920s, Paducah also possessed a planning and zoning commission and a health officer. Its voters agreed to return to the city commission form of government, which had been initiated in an effort to clean up the city in 1915 but suspended in 1922 because fewer patronage jobs had been available under it.[13]

All three cities operated in a political culture in which the county was the focus of public life and the county judge was the most powerful force in local government. The advances secured in these years in urban services were especially impressive, given the predilections of the legislature as well as the county political establishments.

Evansville had a number of basic services—police, fire, municipal water, sewers, among others—many years before the other cities of the region. A new state charter for the city in 1893, amended in 1895, enhanced the powers of the elected mayor and expanded the regulatory duties of the council. The rising use of electrified streetcars and automobiles accelerated the paving of city streets. The rapid growth of the city and of concern for public health produced a larger waterworks and purified water in the mid-1890s. The city's common council granted franchises to private utility companies—first for gas and in the 1880s and early 1890s for electricity, telephone service, and electric street railways. Not surprisingly, intense competition, political payoffs, and controversy were associated with these projects. Over time, in turn, these utilities, like so much of the basic business services, reflected the mergers and external controls that were part of corporate America. Cumberland Bell, which served Owensboro and other locales, eventually gained control of Evansville's lines, and it later became part of Indiana Bell. The gas and electric light companies, which merged in 1882, acquired the street railway company and the interurbans, combined with several short-lived competitors, and emerged by 1921 as the Southern Indiana Gas and Electric Company, a subsidiary of the huge Commonwealth and Southern holding company.[14]

The extension of utility and streetcar lines, the paving of city streets, the increased use of automobiles and trucks, and the construction of industrial satellites and residential subdivisions steadily expanded the city's boundaries. The most important addition was the annexation of Howell in 1916. By the early 1920s, Evansville was at least twice its 1880 size, and its residents demanded a higher quality of services. One of these was for city parks and other forms of public recreation. After 1901, the General Assembly, following its experience with Indianapolis in the late 1890s, permitted Indiana cities to establish park boards and to build playgrounds, public baths, and swimming pools for residents' use.[15]

In Evansville, as elsewhere, this spurred the expansion of publicly owned spaces, limited mostly in the 1890s to Sunset Park along the river, which were the only alternatives to popular private summer facilities, such as Cook's Park and Barnett's Grove. The city's park movement was sparked by a gift of land from ironmaker George L. Mesker, and in January 1901 the city council purchased adjoining ground to create Mesker Park on the west side. A few months later, Mrs. Martha Bayard donated a substantial plot on the east side. A decade later, the city purchased, with financial assistance from Benjamin Bosse, the private park of Thomas Garvin on the north side. In the same year that Garvin Park opened, 1915, the city also launched adjoining Bosse Field, touted as the world's only municipally owned baseball stadium. Bosse Field was home to the Evansville Evas of the "Class A" Central League. By a quirk of geography, the south side of Evansville lay in Kentucky, and after the Great War horse racing at Dade Park in that area was a major attraction to Evansvillians.[16]

Urbanization also brought demands for protection of public health and welfare, much of it via centralized control and direction. Congestion, polluted water, epidemics, coal soot and smoke, and other by-products of industrial growth made the city the catalyst for mounting concern in all three states for organized efforts to protect public health. The gradual acceptance of the germ theory of disease was the primary reason for establishment of state boards of health. Indiana's board, formed in 1881, could collect vital statistics, make sanitary inspections, and investigate causes of disease. It could also explore the impact of intoxicating beverages on citizens. The enabling legislation created local boards of health where they did not already exist. In Evansville, this had the effect of strengthening existing efforts and leading to the formation, with the 1893 charter, of a board of health and charities, one of seven executive departments of city government. (Under the terms of the 1905 legislation, public health was to be one of six city departments.) Public health officials were also in place by the late 1890s in the other lower Ohio cities. Dr. Pinckney Thompson of Henderson, instrumental in founding the Kentucky Board of Health, also helped to establish his city's three-member board. Closely related was the gradual introduction, first in Evansville and Paducah, of "purified" drinking water. On paper, Evansville also had milk and food inspectors during the Bosse administration.[17]

Such initiatives were offset by a number of liabilities. Some health boards, such as Daviess County's (1918), were formed only after the onset of a community health crisis. Public health officials' powers were generally advisory, and members were often political hacks. Local ordinances blocked serious efforts to control industrial smoke and soot, an especially daunting aspect of life in Evansville, where in 1900 one-third of all deaths were caused by respiratory problems. Effective local control over air pollution as well as germ-ridden dairies, butcher shops, and restaurants would not emerge until the late 1940s. Sewer and water service in the largest cities did not keep pace with residential and industrial expansion, and storm and sanitary sewers were synonymous. Not surprisingly, one in fifteen in 1900 Evansville died of cholera or typhoid. The leading cause of death was consumption. (In Paducah, consumption was second, following pneumonia.) In both cities, also not surprisingly, death rates per 1,000 for blacks were about 50 percent higher than for whites. In 1915, most homes still lacked running water or connection to city sewers. Not until the late 1940s and early 1950s, following federal legislation creating the Ohio River Sanitary Commission (ORSANCO), did cities begin treating waste before dumping it in the Ohio.

Public health and medical care efforts, moreover, remained primarily private. The Public Health Nursing Association opened in Evansville in 1888 to provide home health care for the indigent; in 1915 it began offering a free clinic.[18]

In the cities of the lower Ohio, hospital care was also mostly private. Federal funding supported marine hospitals for rivermen in Evansville and Cairo through the early twentieth century, and some local public funding was involved in the formation of Henderson's City Hospital, listed in its first city directory, and in Paducah's Riverside Hospital, created in 1909. Cairo's and Evansville's hospitals were more characteristic. Shortly after the Civil War ended, Roman Catholic nuns established St. Mary's Infirmary in Cairo and St. Mary's Hospital in Evansville; both moved into larger quarters in 1892-93. The German Evangelical Deaconess Hospital opened in Evansville in 1892, two years before Edwin Walker inaugurated a sanitarium that later became Welborn Baptist. Deaconess and Walker also featured nurses' training programs that expanded health care services along the lower Ohio. By the 1890s, moreover, medical associations were established in the larger cities.[19]

Public charitable assistance, generally limited in scope, was delivered by private groups. Evidence of collaboration, however, was mounting. Stimulated by the work of such clergy as Indianapolis's Oscar McCullough, community leaders on both sides of the river established not only a number of single-issue charities but also citywide initiatives to aid the poor and helpless. Statewide charity boards, such as Indiana's, gradually extended their influence to prisons, hospitals, orphanages, poor asylums, and poor relief, and local groups followed suit. By the early twentieth century, Evansville organizers had created the Babies' Milk Fund, the Young Women's Christian Association (1911), the Vanderburgh County Tuberculosis Society, and the Evansville Blind Association. Stimulated by the organizing discipline of World War I, such groups formed a coordinated community fund drive in November 1920, the forerunner of the United Fund. Social agencies were usually formed and led by the wives of prominent professionals, merchants, and industrialists. Owensboro's Welfare League, formed in 1920, was rooted in earlier efforts to coordinate community charities that oversaw relief and juvenile work. In all communities, many social welfare workers were also active supporters of temperance and prohibition causes.[20]

Business interests saw local government as an instrument of promotion and development. The powers of government usually did not extend to those activities considered detrimental to businesses.

The rise of the industrial metropolis also affected the character of social relations. Especially important was the segmentation brought by nationality, class and status, and race. In larger towns, schools and churches—institutions that provided social cohesion in an earlier time—were additional instruments whereby those divisions were extended.

Race continued to be the most powerful force. In Cairo, Mound City, Henderson, Owensboro, and Paducah, which had a high proportion of blacks, residential separation was more difficult to arrange. Nonetheless, each of these places had at least one section, always in the least desirable part of town, that was considered "colored," and blacks also occupied marginal housing in the alleys near the town's center and the homes of the well-to-do. In Kentucky, according to George C. Wright, blacks "lived close to but not in white neighborhoods ... [and] some marker—the railroad tracks or businesses and warehouses—usually separated black residential areas from white neighborhoods."[21]

Over time, though, in matters of domicile as well as occupation, education, entertainment, shopping, and religion, lines between the races became clearer and more rigid. Whites in Henderson, for instance, created deed restrictions about 1913 that were designed to limit blacks' residential mobility. Such practices were widespread in Kentucky.

By 1891, as historian Marion Lucas has observed, "declining support from white liberals and diminishing national concern over their fate" gave black leaders "few options." They "placed their hope for future equality in the false premise that full acceptance in Kentucky society only required that they build respect for their race by becoming responsible, hard-working citizens."[22]

Rail travel, especially across the Ohio, was especially problematic. Beginning in the early 1890s, black leaders protested in federal courts the practice of requiring blacks to sit in a special section of the train, usually a separate portion of a smoke-filled, poorly outfitted car just behind the engine. Although designed for travel within the state and not across state lines, the Kentucky law of 1894 that supported this received Supreme Court endorsement six years later. Travel on the Illinois Central or L&N from Cairo or Evansville southward thus required that blacks move to the blacks-only car when entering Kentucky. Sometimes—as in several instances in 1906 involving travel between Cairo and Paducah—blacks refused to comply, but violent punishment followed. Resistance by force was rare. Much more common were attempts by black leaders to force railroads to comply with the "separate but equal" ruling of 1894. In 1919, the L&N was forced to provide an entire coach for blacks on each nonstop train between Louisville and Nashville. Twenty years later, though, conditions on these and other accommodations remained inferior.[23]

The Kentucky legislature pursued ever-expanding ways of separating the races, even in state-supported institutions for the mentally insane and the blind. The pinnacle for such racism was the Day Law of 1904, which ousted black students from Berea College, a private school which had admitted blacks for more than thirty years. White Kentuckians were obsessive about separating blacks in clearly inferior schools, limiting occupational opportunity, and assigning blacks to distinctive places in public facilities. They were not nearly as successful as their Deep South comrades in disfranchisement, partly because of the liberalizing influence of political culture along the north shore of the Ohio.[24]

Local proscriptions of blacks' rights grew. Historians have not been attentive to "Jim Crow" activities at this level, probably because size and tradition enabled whites to rule through informal controls as well as extralegalism. Occupational patterns, however, were uniform: blacks worked as common laborers on farms, riverboats, and roads, bridges, and railroads, and were also found in such jobs as personal servants, garbage collectors, street cleaners, stable hands, maids, waiters, stewards, porters, cooks, nurses, washwomen, barbers, and janitors—but not in factories. In black society, the highest ranking were janitors, post office workers, teachers, clergymen, physicians, and attorneys. A small number operated businesses, some of which lasted from the 1870s until the Great Depression. Owensboro had black-owned barbershops, groceries, saloons, restaurants, and one photographic studio, perhaps the only one in the state in the 1890s. Paducah had three physicians who formed a partnership and opened a pharmacy. Henderson, though, had the most. Until the 1940s, a large number of entrepreneurs operated in the heart of the city's business district. Their success reflected their "ideal location, adequate financial backing, and the patronage of both blacks and whites."[25] A significant reason was the size of the Henderson black community.

Henderson, Owensboro, and Paducah blacks were segregated and made to feel inferior. In Paducah, by the early 1900s public facilities for blacks were separate but not equal. Train stations imposed separate rest rooms, waiting rooms, and restaurants. In addition, black women were forbidden to try on clothing in Paducah stores. Blacks attended their own churches and schools. Even the funeral parlors were racially segregated.[26] Hotels, restaurants, and theaters owned by whites excluded blacks, although some theaters had separate sections for them. The Commonwealth's new public libraries only admitted whites. Henderson's library board, which opened a facility in 1904, believed from the outset that blacks' access "'would totally destroy the usefulness of the Library to this community.'" Responding to complaints from blacks about exclusion "from yet another public institution, library officials moved a few books, which were 'suited to the needs of the colored population,' to the Eighth Street Colored School." Not surprisingly, the blacks' library received only about one-fifteenth of what was spent on the whites-only library. Wright noted that black citizens were also denied treatment at public hospitals, even in emergencies. Sometimes limited care was offered in segregated wards in hospital basements, but more frequent was service by black physicians at small clinics. Orphanages were also segregated.

Public parks in Kentucky initially were not segregated, but between 1900 and 1920 rigid lines were established. Henderson's Barret Park, for instance, was transformed in 1903 at the urging of white civic leaders and with the compliance of black spokesmen. After August 30, blacks were limited to the use of that section of the park abutting the city wharf.

As before, schools remained separate and unequal. In a state with schools that were "grossly underfinanced and ranked at the bottom when compared with white schools throughout the nation, even in the South," black schools, according to Wright, were "vastly inferior to those for whites." No elementary school in the Commonwealth and, "even worse, none of the few black high schools had libraries but rather relied primarily on concerned teachers and citizens donating a few books to be used as reference materials." School buildings were generally old and dilapidated. These few blacks who entered high school rarely went past the tenth grade. Normal school training, available for whites in most cities, existed only in Louisville.

Despite federal court rulings in the 1880s, equal funding remained an illusion. White citizens spent only the minimum required by state law because they saw blacks' education as a burden. Even in the places with the largest numbers of African Americans, equalization was "consistently violated to provide far more funding for white schools." Combined with the failure of some counties to provide any black schools, this created a high rate of black illiteracy—56 percent in 1890. Among southern and border states in 1900, the state ranked sixth highest, at 40.1 percent. Among persons ages ten and older, blacks accounted for 48.2 percent of the illiterates in Daviess County, 67.6 percent in Henderson County, and an astonishing 73.4 percent in McCracken County. In the more rural counties, rates ranged from 16 percent in Crittenden and Livingston Counties to 70 percent in Hardin. Reflecting increased overall support for the state's schools after 1910, blacks' illiteracy rate dropped to 15.4 percent in 1930.[27]

Well into the 1920s, Kentucky school districts provided a shorter school year for black students—generally three to six months. In part, this mirrored the poverty of rural black families, which needed their children to work. One resident of Henderson County in 1923 wrote the NAACP in frustration over the closing of the local school before the academic year had ended for whites.

> Superintendent N.O. Kimbler . . . has ordered the J. Boyd Colored School closed after teaching three and one-half months and the teacher has a contract for seven months. We are paying taxes on nearly nine hundred acres of land, have bought books and clothes for 19 children [and] now they must grow up in ignorance. The Patrons are compelled to pay hundreds of dollars in school taxes. If these children get to school any more they most go down in their pockets. . . . He has closed another colored school [in] Scuffletown. The teacher is still teaching although the Supt. has told her she would not get any money. We have appealed to the State Board of Education. . . . We need help, Dr. [W.E.B.] DuBois.[28]

White superintendents and school boards consistently found reasons to drag their feet on adequate funding. Often they blamed the victim—as, for instance, in their criticizing black pastors for exercising too much influence in blacks' education. Without churches, though, little opportunity would have existed. "Foot-dragging" was especially evident in the establishment of black high schools. By the 1890s, Owensboro and Paducah, as well as six other Kentucky cities, had them. The state's County School Law of 1908 requiring each county to establish a public high school did not mention blacks. Consequently, in 1916 only nine black high schools existed in the entire state—including one recently established in Henderson. The course of study in these schools emphasized vocational training.

Frederick Douglass High School in Henderson exhibited the difficulties blacks encountered in creating such schools. "Double-taxation" was involved: after paying their taxes, blacks "raised additional funds, purchased or donated land, bought the building materials, and provided the labor for the construction of schools in their communities." Henderson school officials finally acceded to blacks' petitions for a high school in 1905 by appropriating funds to hire a few teachers. After raising funds for several years, blacks purchased a lot and began building a separate facility. The school board then allocated funds to complete the project.[28]

The only black college on the lower Ohio was Dennis Henry Anderson's Western Kentucky Industrial College, established in Paducah in 1910. Modest state appropriations commenced in 1918. Anderson's tuition-free school, designed to train teachers and assist blacks in acquiring vocational skills, remained small and never realized its goals. Appropriations were cut in the 1930s, effectively closing the school. In 1938 the legislature created the West Kentucky Vocational Training School for Negroes on the WKIC site. It was closed with the coming of desegregation in the 1950s.[29]

Educational advancement revealed the vitality and the resilience of black citizens. Schools, like churches, offered meaning and support for lives. So did other activities: welfare institutions for orphans, the aged, and the infirm, annual school graduation ceremonies, and special events such as Emancipation Day. Celebrated in some communities on January 1, Emancipation Day generally occurred September 22, the date of the preliminary emancipation proclamation in 1862. Schools were closed, and all churches and fraternal orders were involved in the festivities, which included parades, picnics, and speeches by the "old soldiers"—veterans of the Union army. Steamboat and later rail excursions were often arranged.

The most distinctive celebration was in Paducah, where freedom was celebrated August 8, possibly because that was the day of emancipation for West

Indian slaves in the 1830s. In 1906, for instance, thousands of blacks came by boat and later by rail from as far away as Chicago, Louisville, St. Louis, and Memphis to attend a carnival with concession booths lining the streets and to dance at the ball park. This celebration undoubtedly reflected the common origins of African Americans in the Purchase Region and their kin across the river. Metropolis and Brookport blacks also observed the event on that day, as did citizens of Elizabethtown in Hardin County.[30]

Community life also included shady characters and illegal enterprises. Although the *Paducah News-Democrat* was hardly a disinterested observer, its portrait of the city's low life in 1918 cannot be discounted. Prostitution, gambling, and frequent homicides were part of Paducah's black community life, and efforts by local police to eliminate it were generally futile. Although much worse in Louisville and Lexington, such activities reflected in part denial of access to most avenues of employment and most residential areas. Many chose crime and vice as ways of advancing themselves. Whites' unwillingness to end illegal activities in and around black neighborhoods also displayed their belief that criminal activity was to be expected of blacks. The exclusion of black clergy, teachers, and social workers from the organizations designed to eradicate these problems reflected racial prejudice as well.[31]

Blacks in Kentucky faced an increasingly proscribed public sphere and intimidation and violence if the rules—written and unwritten—were broken. Southern states in the 1890s, for instance, intensified legalized disfranchisement and racial separation and passed laws to control black mobility—such as restrictions against vagrancy—which produced more black arrests and prison terms and encouraged inhumane treatment in convict camps. Newspapers, fed by racial theories that dehumanized blacks, publicized and exaggerated black crime and white retaliation. The New South, wrote Edward L. Ayers, was "a notoriously violent place." Kentucky, "largely outside the maelstrom of Populism and disfranchisement, near the border of the North, with a relatively diversified economy, saw a remarkably high rate of lynching." This was "a way for white people to reconcile weak governments with a demand for an impossibly high level of racial mastery, a way to terrorize blacks into acquiescence."[32]

By the turn of the century, segregation and racial violence were also evident across the river. As Evansville's black population grew and became more self-confident, for example, intimidation and wanton violence also expanded, encouraged by such literature as Thomas Dixon's book *The Clansman,* by the virtual absence of controls on liquor sales and consumption, and by widespread possession and use of firearms within city limits. The apogee occurred July 4-10, 1903, when the city experienced the worst racial disturbance in its history, after a white policeman and a black man shot each other near a notorious saloon in Baptisttown. Before the state militia restored order, scores had been killed and wounded, substantial damage had been done to black homes and businesses, and hundreds of blacks had fled Evansville, many permanently.

To be sure, the riot alone did not explain population shifts after 1900, but it was a symptom of larger matters—limited economic opportunity, combined with increased institutional racism and extralegalism—that plagued the lower Midwest. And lynching was not solely a southern matter, either. Rockport, for instance, experienced racial disturbances in the fall of 1895 and two lynchings in the fall of 1900. (A third person was taken for safekeeping to Boonville, but lynchers caught up with him there.) Cairo had a lynching November 11, 1909.

"Jim Crow" was also present. About 1910, for instance, restrictive housing covenants were implemented in Evansville. By 1915, school officials instituted vocational education as blacks' primary educational opportunity, instituted segregated seating at school concerts, created a salary structure formalizing a two-tier method of payment, and commenced planning to consolidate black schooling into one building, which would accelerate residential segregation. Limited medical care was available either in the basement of two of Evansville's hospitals or in a black clinic of the third, for instance. Nonetheless, a strong and resourceful black community offered some protection. An additional asset was that voting was not proscribed, and public accommodations and travel were not segregated by law.

In Illinois, separate schools for blacks existed in Brookport, Metropolis, Mound City, and Cairo. For high school, students in smaller communities—with the apparent exception of Joppa—generally had to travel to a black school in a larger town. In Brookport, students took their course of study at Dunbar, the elementary-secondary school in Metropolis. Distinctive residential areas continued to mature, such as the Oak Grove region of Metropolis. Custom, not law, defined that, for blacks knew they were unwelcome on the east side of town. Massac County had no black doctors or dentists. Residents needing medical care had to go to Cairo or to Paducah's Illinois Central Hospital. Contemporary historians, such as John Lansden in Cairo, took a patronizing view of black citizens, labeling them "industrious and law-abiding" and explaining racial animosity as the product of the "floating element."[33]

Segregation and violence, though, remained far more pronounced across the river. According to Wright, "The exact number of Afro-Americans lynched in Kentucky from the end of the Civil War to 1940 will never be known. At least 353 people died at the hands of lynch mobs during these years." The highest percentage (42) occurred in the Purchase Region, a sparsely populated area with a high percentage of blacks. Violence was not limited to rural areas, however, as Paducah recorded a lynching in 1892, as did Hawesville in 1897. Owensboro had two—in July 1884 and December 1896. Prodded by Governor William Bradley, the legislature passed an antilynching law in 1897, but seventy more lynchings occurred after 1900. The number dropped significantly after a stronger law was passed in 1920.[34]

Lynching remained a threat, but police brutality, Klan activities in the 1920s, and flawed criminal justice also intimidated blacks. Blacks were more likely than whites to be arrested and imprisoned for crimes, however petty. Such persistent injustice produced organized protest and efforts to elect blacks to public office. Over time, blacks became skeptical of Republicans' loyalties and more independent in their political affiliations.[35]

Ethnicity also divided lower Ohio river settlements, but along lines that were neither rigid nor as a rule enforced by law or violence. Relations were such, moreover, that practices of European newcomers often were blended into those of the previously dominant culture as families intermarried and communications at all levels improved.

Generally the "new immigrants" after 1880 bypassed the lower Ohio, settling instead in the Northeast and upper Midwest. Immigrants, in fact, tended not to settle in the region. In 1900, none of the river counties of Kentucky had more than 2 percent foreign-born inhabitants. The same was the case in Gallatin, Hardin, and Pope counties in Illinois and Crawford in Indiana. Only in Alexander County in Illinois and Perry, Posey, Spencer, and Vanderburgh Counties in Indiana did the foreign-born exceed 4 percent. Vanderburgh led all by far, with 9.5 percent.

The vast majority of the region's foreign-born were southern Germans, whose numbers peaked in southwestern Indiana in the early 1880s. Most settled immediately in urban areas and sought employment in factories. By 1900 close to 40 percent of Vanderburgh County residents were German-born or had German-born parents. Twenty years later, Evansville continued to have the highest percentage of foreign-born residents on the lower Ohio.

Germans influenced many dimensions of life in the region. In rural areas, isolation, language, religious leaders, and family traditions combined to retard acculturation. In urban regions, German inheritance was apparent in the Evangelical, Lutheran, and Roman Catholic churches, many of which had their own schools. By sheer numbers, Germans came to play a major part in city politics in Evansville and Paducah, but ethnic separation remained evident in German American mutual aid, civic, and religious associations, such as Evansville's Germania Maennerchor (1900), its Knights of Columbus chapter, and its German Masonic lodges. Perhaps the most vivid illustration was the popularity of the *Täglicher Demokrat*, a newspaper published since 1863. Before its premature demise in April 1918, its circulation rose to about 5,000.

For most of these residents, even in urban areas, language and religion created identity. Well into the 1920s, most Evansville firms, for instance, employed at least one person who could speak German if they wanted to do business with the predominantly German west side. Before 1918, classes in public elementary schools were taught in German. Most German Catholic and Lutheran and some Evangelical youth were confirmed in German before 1917, and many clergymen discouraged the use of English in church and school activities. The complexity of this was evident at Trinity Lutheran (Missouri Synod) in Evansville, where services on the eve of the Great War were conducted in German. Those who wanted to sing hymns in English sat in a separate section. For Catholics and Lutherans, parochial school instruction before 1918 included a great deal of German. Typically, such "secular" subjects as mathematics were taught in English, whereas "sacred" ones, especially religion, were discussed in German. Students desiring schooling beyond eighth grade had to attend Evansville High School, but Catholics created their own high school before World War I and opened a new facility, Reitz Memorial, in 1925.

German influence was also pronounced in the other cities. In Cairo, for instance, one of its two Catholic parishes had been organized for Germans, and its Lutheran congregation was sufficiently prosperous—and Americanized—to build a new edifice in 1896, about the same time that it hired its first English-speaking pastor. By the time Owensboro's first history was printed in 1883, Germans had organized Catholic, Evangelical, and Jewish congregations as well as several fraternal and mutual aid associations. The trustees of a school association formed in the 1860s to promote free education of German American children conveyed the property to the city in the late 1890s because adequate public schools had been established. This property became the nucleus of the Owensboro-Daviess County Hospital.[36]

In Henderson, Germans established such cultural organizations as the Mozart Society in 1886 and the Liederkranz Society in 1889. Eminent manufacturers of wood products were Germans, including Alles and Delker. By 1920, the city had a Jewish synagogue and an Evangelical church.

Paducah's Germans were somewhat more influential. As of the 1920s, three congregations—Evangelical, Lutheran, and Jewish—traced their roots to the mid-nineteenth century. Germans played a major role in Paducah politics as well as commercial and industrial activities from the Civil War onward. One of the most prominent was Joseph L. Friedman, president of the Old Commercial Club, who was instrumental in attracting new businesses and in training community leadership. Other prominent Germans were James C. Utterbach, president of the City National Bank, and Charles G. Vahlkamp, president of the City Consumers Company.[37]

The German presence in Evansville, though, meant that its influence on

that city's character was substantially greater. Aside from their impact on public and private schools, Germans dominated local politics, as Lutherans and
Catholics, responding to perceived or real Republican threats to faith and practice via public schools, temperance, and blue laws, became the bulwark of the
Democratic Party. Evangelicals, wary of Catholics and eager to promote public schools and cooperate with English-speaking Protestant pietists on various
social causes, formed the core of the Republican Party. German influence on
the town's civic ceremonies was evident in, for instance, the singing of "Die
Wacht am Rhein" at chamber of commerce gatherings before World War I,
and the annual celebration of German Day between 1890 and 1915. German
intellectuals' influence on the shape of the public schools was pronounced—
for instance, in the physical education program highlighted by an annual field
day organized by Julius Doerter. German citizens also created what would become the Evansville Philharmonic and the Evansville Museum in the 1920s
and 1930s.

Germans in Evansville, as elsewhere, were neither homogeneous nor united
in their views on acculturation and assimilation. Descendants of liberal "Forty-
Eighters," for instance, promoted appreciation for German culture through
physical education at the Evansville Central Turnverein and contributed substantially to the extension of democratic values among German Americans.
The most resistant to change were German Catholics and Missouri Synod
Lutherans, whose organizations paralleled those of the English-speaking majority and allowed them to accept American values on their own terms.

Many forces eroded Old World loyalties over time, but the most dramatic
was World War I. Led by their German American mayor, citizens sought to
prove that Evansville was totally committed to the Allied cause. Accordingly,
they changed German names: the Turnverein [athletic club] became Central
Turners, and Second German Methodist Church became Fourth Street Methodist. Preaching in German ceased, by agreement among local pastors. Ended
forever, by threat of vigilante action, was the publication of the *Täglicher
Demokrat*. German instruction in elementary schools also ceased. Prohibition,
combined with a legacy of ethnic and religious hatred that spilled over into
the 1920s, afterwards retarded the resurrection of German language and culture. The rise of the Ku Klux Klan in Evansville, site of Indiana Klavern #1
(summer of 1921) and base for the strongest state Klan organization in the
North, is directly traceable to anti-Catholic, anti-bootlegger sentiments, both
of which had strong ethnic implications in the Evansville region.[38]

Class and status shaped community life, especially in larger towns. As settlements grew, the location of rail lines and factories increasingly defined areas
of working-class residence. Aided by the street railway and later the automo-

bile, those with greater means located their homes and churches in neighborhoods that differed physically and aesthetically from those of railroad or factory workers. Between the commercial core, or business district, and the wealthy enclaves on the urban perimeter lay "zones of emergence"—places of varying economic and social standing where citizens of lesser means resided. Over time, occupational success brought residential mobility, or access to neighborhoods of higher standing farther away from the core. In the largest towns, though, a significant majority of dwellings were rented—from a high of 65.3 percent in Cairo to a low of 59.1 in Owensboro in 1900. Twenty years later, rental housing continued to prevail, with Cairo's 70.1 percent at the top and Henderson's 54.9 ranked fifth.[39]

In Evansville, class and status led to distinctive working-class neighborhoods on the north and west sides and in Howell. By World War I, affluent managers and proprietors moved east to Washington Avenue, into Bayard Park, and along the city's eastern border, Kentucky Avenue. After the war, substantial residential development occurred further east, notably along Lincoln Avenue, where the city's first college and the Catholic high school were located. Older wealthy persons continued to reside in the Riverside neighborhood adjoining the commercial district, although some began to move to Outer Lincoln Avenue. As before, ethnic loyalties perpetuated strong German neighborhoods defined by income levels on and near First Avenue, Wabash and Fulton Avenues, and West Maryland Street.[40]

Class and status, race, and nationality, in short, weakened centripetal forces in the larger communities. Although churches, voluntary associations, and schools had once created a more homogeneous community life, they reflected residents' differing loyalties. Ironically, while legislators in all three states created stronger public educational systems, and thus lowered illiteracy rates and strengthened civic culture, schools also symbolized social divisions through their location, condition, appearance, and offerings.

But long-overdue school reforms did arrive. In Kentucky, public education progressed after 1908. Especially important in this regard was John Grant Crabbe, superintendent of public instruction between 1907 and 1911, who secured the creation of the two normal schools, the regulation of child labor, the formation of a textbook commission, and the institution of compulsory school attendance. The landmark education legislation of 1908, known as the Sullivan Law, was a result of Crabbe's campaign for reform. The law, according to Clark and Birdwhistell, "marked a distinct end to the era of the one-room district school, burdened by the infamous three-trustee system." Much of the law dealt with "the election, administration, and conduct of officials and the operation of schools." One of the law's most important features was "the mandate that the counties levy a school tax at the rate of at least twenty cents ... on each $100 of assessed property value, with the proceeds to be set aside for education." The cardinal provision was this: "'All laws and parts of laws in conflict with this act are hereby repealed.'"[41]

In 1914, the Kentucky legislature mandated a public high school in each county. Six years later, it instituted the appointment of county school superintendents and reduced the number of school districts. These changes were evident in the opening of Hancock County High School, a four-year institution in Hawesville, a two-year high school in Lewisport, and a four-year facility, Livingston County High School, in Smithland. All of this occurred between 1910 and 1920.[42]

In Indiana, the "great awakening," which began in the seventies, included the formation of graded schools, a regular procedure of graduation (1884), and the publication of the first state curriculum manual (1892). A state board of schoolbook commissioners was formed in 1889. Compulsory attendance was instituted in 1897, and by 1913 the law extended to most children ages seven to sixteen. By 1907, district schools with fewer than twelve pupils were discontinued, and as in the other states, according to Clifton Phillips, "the pace of school consolidation was greatly accelerated ... and the team-drawn, and later the gasoline-engine, hack carrying farm children to school over often barely passable country roads became a familiar sight." A course of study for high schools was initiated in 1892, and graduation requirements from commissioned high schools were instituted in 1912. Practical or vocational training in secondary schools began in Indianapolis in 1895 and soon extended to Evansville. And Hoosier public education received a steadily increasing amount of revenue from state and local taxation.[43]

As of 1920, the effects of these changes in lower river counties were dramatic. The percentage of students (ages five to twenty) ranged from 89.7 to 96.2 in Illinois's six counties, 93.8 to 97.7 in Indiana's, and 83.5 to 94.7 in Kentucky. In Evansville, the 96.7 percent attendance rate in 1920 was well above that of 1900, when it was, respectively, 52, 31, and 45 percent for native white, foreign-born, and black children.[44]

Such reforms notwithstanding, schools signified and in many respects reinforced social division. Evansville's city directory of 1920 vividly illustrated that. The now thirty-one public schools included three high schools: two white and one "colored," known after 1913 as Frederick Douglass. The newer white school, opened on "Coal Mine Hill" on the west side, was named for banker Francis Joseph Reitz. Five of the schools were black. Name and location also revealed significant class and status divisions. Wheeler, named for school pioneer Horatio Q. Wheeler, was situated on Mulberry Street, in the affluent upper Riverside neighborhood. Workers' children attended Carpenter, Howell, Ingleside, and Tekoppel. Centennial and West Heights served mostly Germans. Reitz High School's students were the sons and daughters of Germans factory workers or farmers and Howell railroaders. Another eighteen schools were private, thirteen of which were Roman Catholic. Two were run by Missouri Synod Lutherans.[45]

In smaller places, of course, a much higher level of homogeneity persisted, but there, too, traditional community values were being weakened. School consolidations closed many one-room schools. In the broadest sense, the changes effected by demography, economic activity, social relationships, and other facets of industrialization concurrently altered and reflected the ways in which residents of lower Ohio communities ordered their lives. Theodore Dreiser's and Harry Abdy's images of life in river towns in the 1910s, noted earlier, captured the essence of this cultural phenomenon: that these places varied enormously, despite a great deal of common experience with an extraordinarily important waterway. Some of the variety was traceable to size, as smaller places on either side of the river shared an unhurried, season-oriented lifestyle that remained focused on the Ohio as a source of information, travel, recreation, food, and employment.

Variety also emanated from the folkways of the peoples of the three states and their subdivisions. School-age residents of Illinois and Indiana were still more likely than their Kentucky counterparts in 1920 to have attended school, although the gap had narrowed considerably. Illiteracy for men and women over age twenty-one, moreover, was twice as high in Kentucky as in Illinois or Indiana. Illiteracy in urban areas on both sides of the river was, of course, much lower than in rural regions, and school attendance was higher. For blacks in these communities, rates continued to exceed the average and were highest in Kentucky. Some 13-14 percent of Cairo and Evansville blacks ages ten and older were illiterate. Almost 20 percent in Henderson, Owensboro, and Paducah were illiterate. Only Gallatin County, with 22.3 percent, exceeded that among northshore counties. The highest percentage of illiterate blacks, 28.3, resided in Union County.[46]

Residents of Illinois, Indiana, and Kentucky villages, towns, and cities did things differently from each other because of the sizes and the functions of their settlements, the political cultures of their respective states, the continued interplay between heritage, location, and resources, and the degree of urbanization in their counties.

In a narrower sense of the word, *culture* also described the tastes and the interests of ordinary people in the region. A number of sources contributed: information about and access to shopping in larger communities, whether via mail-order catalog, improved roads, or automobiles; the impact of newspapers published in the settlements of the area; and the promotion of "modern" values through movies, radio, advertising, or mass-produced magazines and tabloids.

Before the 1920s, the most important source of information about the community, the nation, and the world was the newspaper. Aided in most cases by links to the outside by Associated Press or United Press wire services, newspapers in addition to their partisan political activities provided their readers with sensational coverage of local and national news, sports, and entertainment. In the 1920s, cartoons, photographs, and serialized stories joined with features on health and successful living to make the newspaper a major force in local popular culture.

By World War I, the largest towns had at least one daily. Evansville had the most—the Democratic *Courier,* the Republican *Journal-News,* the independent and progressive Scripps *Press* (established in 1906), and the *Demokrat.* Paducah's *News* and *Democrat,* with roots in the Civil War era, merged in 1901. Its other paper, the *Evening Sun,* purchased the *News-Democrat* and became the *Sun-Democrat* in 1929. Owensboro's *Monitor,* the leading pro-railroad voice of the post–Civil War era, went out of business in 1877, but its materials became the basis of the *Messenger,* formed in the same year and in 1880 combined with the *Examiner.* The daily's only serious rival thereafter was the *Inquirer,* begun in 1884 and consolidated with the *Messenger* in 1929. Pre–World War I Cairo had two newspapers—the *Bulletin,* formed in the late 1860s, and the strongly Republican *Citizen,* established in 1885. Henderson in the mid-1880s boasted three papers, the most lasting of which was the *Gleaner.* Originally a weekly created in 1885, the *Gleaner* became a daily in 1888. Also published daily by the end of the century was the *Henderson Journal.* The two were merged in 1914 and published daily as the *Morning Gleaner* and *Evening Journal* until 1954, when the daily *Gleaner and Journal* surfaced. Leigh Harris, longtime publisher, resembled his *Evansville Press* contemporary, Frank Romer Peters, in his tireless promotion of local business development, his advocacy of better roads, recreational facilities, and hospital care, and his opposition to political corruption.[47]

Summer riverboat excursions were augmented and then replaced by rail and especially automobile outings. Automobiles also provided a new means of spending summer vacation time and spurred, for the well-to-do, access to distant retreats. Most town governments by the First World War had created some form of public park system. Beginning in the first decade of the century, moreover, small "nickelodeons" supplemented vaudeville by offering ordinary people inexpensive access to one-reel melodramas and comedies. Changes in the composition and the location of filmmaking and the courting of middle-class audiences sealed the fate of the nickelodeon, which gave way to family-oriented theaters. According to Daniel J. Leab, independents and the movie trust "made longer, more ambitious films ... and soon one- and two-reelers became program fillers." By World War I, small and large town residents on the lower Ohio could see the film *Birth of a Nation*. They also enjoyed Mack Sennett's slapstick comedies, Douglas Fairbanks's adventures, and William S. Hart's Westerns.[48]

An important part of Hawesville's entertainment was the *Water Queen*, a floating theater, and its successor, the *Theatorium* (1889), a barge that seated 624. In the summer of 1907, Metropolitans could take the *Island Queen* to Cairo, and for shorter outings board the *George Cowling* for a picnic on the Paducah shore. They could attend a Temperance Chautauqua, replete with lectures, songs, moving pictures, and stereopticon slides. In July, the comedy drama *Honor Bound* and an electrical scenic production of the Johnstown flood were offered on the Eisenbarth-Henderson showboat, and in August Cooley and Hagan's floating "wonderland" theater played at the riverfront. Traveling stock companies performed in tents at Market Square.

Metropolis was undoubtedly characteristic in its many diversions for most of its residents. Opportunities for reading, for example, were expanded by improved literacy, public libraries, and mass-produced publications. These included popular novels such as those by Booth Tarkington and Zane Grey; pulp fiction, including the Horatio Alger series; fashionable magazines such as *Ladies Home Journal*, home magazines such as *Comfort*, and youth magazines, such as *Young Wild West Weekly*; self-help and self-improvement books; local newspapers and sometimes those from Chicago, Cincinnati, St. Louis, or Louisville; and, of course, the Bible and religious literature. Many homes had pianos and stereoscopes, and families played checkers, dominoes, and card games. In colder months, dramas were offered at McCartney's Music Hall. The locals also boasted a baseball team, the Metropolis Blues, which challenged teams in Golconda, Dixon Springs, Cairo, and Paducah, which they reached on the steamer *Dick Fowler*.[49]

Baseball, of course, remained the most popular spectator sport, and sundry levels of competition could be found in most settlements along the river. "No game," asserted *Sporting News* in 1891, "has taken so strong a hold on Americans as base ball." The "national game" benefited from improvements in the quality of play, competition aided by the press, civic pride, and personal identification with local clubs, and improvements in the settings of play. Aesthetic and sensory appeal, abetted by mounds of statistics, reinforced its year-round grip on popular imagination, and it had no serious competition from other sports. And baseball met the need for increased leisure, amusement, and higher living standards created by industrialism and the growing emphasis on health and exercise.[50]

Baseball teams were organized in the high schools beginning about 1900. Competition also developed among factory workers, such as the members of the Goldblume Athletic Club of the F.W. Cook Brewery in Evansville, who played other company teams in the region. Teams were organized by German American and African American associations. Larger towns had a group of unpaid players from all walks of life who represented the community and defended its civic pride in intercommunity competition. Some players in the largest communities were paid. The *Evansville Daily Journal* distinguished between professionals and amateurs. A story on September 6, 1892, indicated that the Cook players, apparently all of whom were brewery workers, had defeated the Owensboro team, which included five professionals. The Evansville Evas were the first team to compete in a professional league, the Central, beginning about 1910.

Other team and spectator sports joined the national game. Football, once the province of the well-to-do, was increasingly popular. High school rivalry was common after 1900, and teams were also fielded by other organizations. Before 1920, young Catholic workers in Evansville, for instance, participated in clubs that practiced three afternoons a week and played each other—no doubt to the chagrin of local evangelicals—on Sundays. Sacred Heart parish had the powerful Rowans, named after a popular priest, and the Marquette Club of St. Boniface was strong enough in the early twenties to play the Green Bay Packers. The recently invented sport of basketball soon created matches among high school teams and those formed by such groups as the YMCA, the Central Turners, and the Knights of Columbus. The opening of Dade Park about 1920 on the north side of the Ohio, on Kentucky land that abutted Evansville's southeast side, brought horse racing and gambling. Not surprisingly, illicit betting on horses became a major problem in Evansville and Henderson thereafter.

The well-to-do in Evansville and Paducah, by contrast, formed country clubs where they played golf and tennis. Discrimination against Catholics and Jews meant they had to seek other outlets for such sports. So they developed public links and courts, as well as their own clubs.

Laborers, clerical workers, and managers had other recreational outlets. For many factory workers, the saloon was, after the church, the most important—and sometimes only—social outlet. Joe Folz's Saloon at First Avenue and Columbia Street in Evansville, one of three hundred in a city with only seventy-five churches, was patronized by a largely German Catholic clientele of workers in the nearby furniture factories, the packinghouse, and the stock-yards. That was a major reason for the fairly limited success of temperance advocates before World War I in cities along the lower Ohio. In Owensboro, for instance, supporters of saloons defeated drys in two votes on local option in 1897 and 1907. Heeding the calls of early advocates of "welfare capitalism," employers formed social and recreational groups for their workers, such as the women's drum and bugle corps of the Buckskin Breeches Manufacturing Company of Evansville.

Not all cultural expression was aimed at the masses. A surprisingly large amount of "high" culture can be found. Henderson's Mozart Society formed in 1885 and gave its first concert two years later. Literary and musical societies were functioning in most communities by the 1880s. These organizations—as in the establishment of the public libraries in Cairo and Mount Vernon or of the Evansville Public Museum about 1904—often laid the groundwork for permanent institutions for cultural advancement, which backers linked to civic advancement. A vivid illustration was the formation of Evansville College. Buoyed by the enthusiasm of a booster mayor, the organizational skills of an elite band of citizens led by George Clifford, and the patriotic atmosphere of 1918, citizens raised a million dollars to bring a struggling Methodist college to Evansville from southeastern Indiana. A year later, it opened its doors. The same mayor also sought to enhance the city's image by bringing grand opera to the new Soldiers' and Sailors' Coliseum, opened in 1916.

Libraries were a favorite cause of the elite. Willard Carpenter, for instance, had built and endowed one in Evansville in 1885. Promoted by such philanthropists and aided by challenge grants from Andrew Carnegie, public libraries became common in most river settlements by 1913. Cannelton obtained Carnegie funding in 1896, and Grandview in Spencer County had a town library in 1899. Four years later, Henderson, pushed by the editor of the *Gleaner*, obtained Carnegie funding, as did Paducah and Mount Vernon in 1904-5. Relative latecomers were Evansville, which opened a public system with two buildings in 1912 (and a separate one for blacks the next year), and Owensboro in 1913.[51]

Civic associations proliferated. Well-to-do women, for instance, organized local Young Women's Christian Association branches for working girls in Evansville (1911) and Owensboro (1923). Many settlements, such as Cloverport in 1890, had active chapters of the new Women's Christian Temperance Union. Paducah women organized the state's first Business and Professional Women's Club in 1920. Business and professional men formed a host of civic clubs.

Evansville's Rotary Club, formed in 1913, was the region's first, and from the outset it was, as in other cities, located at the top of a pecking order of men's clubs, such as the Kiwanis and the Royal Order of Lions.[52]

One of the most striking features of the larger cities was the erection of grandiose city halls and courthouses beginning in the 1880s. A sign of affluence and civic aspiration, these structures also exhibited varying degrees of architectural and aesthetic appeal. The largest and most ornate was the Vanderburgh County courthouse, completed in 1891, a few years after the erection of a flamboyant city hall that would stand until 1971. Designed by Louisville architect Henry Wolters, the courthouse was constructed by German American artisans.

One of Evansville's most distinctive attributes from the 1870s onward, however, was that most of its notable public and private structures were designed by talented local architects. This reflected the city's size and its level of cultural development. Works by Wolters or Richard Montfort, designer of the L&N station (1902), were thus exceptions to the rule. In the late nineteenth and early twentieth centuries many architects with training in Europe or on the East Coast settled in Evansville, and this schooling was reflected in the quality and sophistication of their designs. The works of Boyd and Mursinna, F. Manson Gilbert, Jesse Vyrdagh, the Reid brothers, Frank J. Schlotter, Anderson and Veatch, and Clifford Shopbell made Evansville one of the most architecturally significant cities in Indiana. Paducah architects A.L. Lassiter, W.L. Brainerd, Tandy Smith, and D.A. McKinnon also left their distinctive marks on the skyline.

Whatever the origin of their design, grand public and private structures came to dominate the urban landscape by World War I. One of the most notable in Evansville was the lower river's most fashionable hostelry, the McCurdy, opened in 1917 on the site of the once grand St. George Hotel (1874). The new YMCA building, opened in 1891, was one of many downtown additions that bespoke civic progress. The completion of a lavish new movie house, the Victory Theater, and the adjacent Hotel Sonntag, in 1921 also testified to urban prosperity. Between 1914 and 1916, the three largest banks opened much larger and more impressive buildings on Main Street. By far the most striking was Citizens National Bank at Fourth and Main. (Citizens Bank, though, was not the first "skyscraper," as Paducah gained that honor four years earlier.) And private residences were also symbols of personal and civic success. Such architectural landmarks were the most visible documentation of the maturation of the largest towns.[53]

To varying degrees, the largest cities along the lower Ohio shared similar experiences: securing a broader economic base and a growing populace, they provided a number of new services for their citizens, whether via government or cultural and social organizations. They were also more likely than their nineteenth-century counterparts to bear the burdens of division by race, nationality, religion, and class and status. Amenities and services, from police forces to health departments to baseball teams, libraries, and literary and musical societies—an aspect of urban life on the lower Ohio that historians have generally overlooked—were extensive, touching many of the smaller places as well. Evansville and Paducah were also well on their way to becoming service centers for a number of counties in their vicinity.

Divergent shapes, sizes, and textures continued to characterize the communities of the lower Ohio in the early 1920s. Places as small as West Point and as large as Metropolis differed enormously in their residents' patterns of work, play, worship, and voting. Their racial, ethnic, and class relations were also varied, despite certain common strains.

Most communities were neither moribund nor deceased. The Ohio River provided a common thread that united these diverse and sometimes forgotten places.

Conclusion ༈

Continuity and Change on the Lower Ohio

This work has examined the settlement and the development of a little-known part of the United States. Beginning in the late eighteenth century, it traces the creation of communities through the heyday of the steamboat, the rise of the railroad, and the emergence of the industrial metropolis. It closes shortly after World War I.

I chose that ending for several reasons. The coming of railroads after 1850 neither stopped the growth and development of many towns and cities on the lower Ohio nor explained the area's *relative* decline. Such communities as Smithland began to lose before the rails came, and others declined in size after the late 1880s. For most, declension began in the 1920s and sped up during the Great Depression and World War II.

Between 1920 and 1930, for instance, all of Illinois's river counties except Pulaski lost population. Cairo slipped by 11 percent, Mound City by 20 percent, and Elizabethtown by over 50 percent. Villages such as Joppa and Hamletsburg also decreased, but Brookport and Metropolis grew noticeably, and Shawneetown also expanded somewhat. During the twenties all of the Ohio River counties in Indiana except Vanderburgh shrank, as did all of Indiana's villages, towns, and cities except Cannelton, Tell City, Troy, and Evansville. The latter rose 22 percent, to over 100,000, and in the process achieved metropolitan district status. In Kentucky, only Daviess and McCracken Counties grew, and Owensboro and Paducah increased by about 30 percent, because of Ken-Rad and the Illinois Central Railroad. All of Kentucky's other villages and towns dwindled in size except Uniontown.

Some of these places lost even more population in the 1930s, while others gained some. The same thing occurred during World War II. As of midcentury, the only Illinois county larger than it had been in 1920 was Massac (Metropolis). In Indiana, Posey and Warrick were slightly larger, but Vanderburgh expanded to 160,422 (almost 75 percent). In Kentucky, just four counties gained population: Daviess, Hardin, Henderson, and McCracken. Henderson's growth was slight, whereas Hardin (West Point and Fort Knox) doubled, Daviess gained about 60 percent, and McCracken grew 33 percent. Among villages and towns, Cairo was 16 percent smaller in 1950 than it had been in 1920. Slightly larger were Rosiclare, Shawneetown, Metropolis, Cave-in-Rock, and Joppa. Smaller were Brookport, Golconda, Hamletsburg, and Elizabethtown. Among Indiana communities listed in the federal census, all but five lost residents. Evansville was up to nearly 130,000—almost 50 percent larger than in 1920. Mount Vernon was 20 percent larger. Cannelton, Tell City, and Newburgh increased slightly. Among Kentucky communities, all three cities grew—especially Owensboro, which doubled in size to about 34,000, overtaking Paducah as second largest on the lower river. Among villages and towns, Hawesville, Lewisport, and Brandenburg grew slightly, and West Point doubled in size. The rest shriveled.[1]

The most important factors reshaping the region were those generally associated with the 1920s: the proliferation of the automobile, the truck, and the bus, which resulted from and stimulated the construction of state roads and, beginning in 1929, vehicular bridges over the lower river; the completion of the locks and dams in 1929, made possible with federal funding; the emergence of mass culture and consumerism, which among other things involved the spread of brand-name goods and the creation of chain stores; the consolidation of local schools, closely associated with the good roads movement; and the vagaries of modern corporate decision making. All of these processes were enhanced in later decades.

Several general conclusions can be drawn. Nothing about the unfolding of communities on the lower Ohio was inevitable. An ideal location, as Cairo learned, guaranteed nothing. Many factors—including site, resources, market economy, political culture, leadership, and luck—determined a community's future. Decisions made in state capitals and in Washington also mattered.

And throughout this, the river was a tenacious force: shaping communities, it was also shaped by them. By the early 1930s, three vehicular bridges joined three railroad spans, in theory making Cairo, Metropolis-Paducah, and Evansville-Henderson river crossings rather than mere river towns. Some of these places, however, were little changed by this advancement. By the late 1990s, ten vehicular bridges had been built. Accidents, repairs, and other closings made residents and travelers painfully aware that the Ohio remained a major barrier, as crossings were located many miles apart. Levee construction escalated, especially after the 1937 flood. Cannelton and Tell City, for example, built a gigantic concrete wall, aesthetically similar to that of cold war Berlin. Evansville's levee was almost as ugly, but it, like the others, allowed communities to turn their backs on the river and build new neighborhoods in flood plains. A few places—notably Leavenworth and Shawneetown—reconstructed themselves on

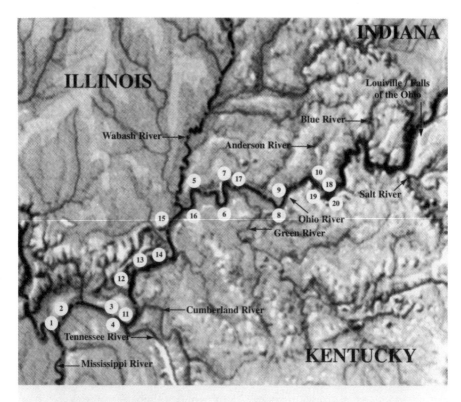

Major Settlements on the Lower Ohio, 1929

2,500 or more residents		1,000 - 2,499 residents	
1. Cairo	6. Henderson	11. Bridgeport	16. Uniontown
2. Mound City	7. Evansville	12. Golconda	17. Newburgh
3. Metropolis	8. Owensboro	13. Rosiclare	18. Cannelton
4. Paducah	9. Rockport	14. Elizabethtown	19. Hawesville
5. Mt. Vernon	10. Tell City	15. Shawneetown	20. Cloverport

Major Settlements on the Lower Ohio, 1929, based on census data of 1920 and the Army Corps of Engineers's *The Ohio River: Charts, Maps, and Description . . .* (Washington, 1929), including only places with one thousand or more residents higher ground. Spring high waters along the river, though, reminded residents of the river's persistence. That was especially evident in 1964 and 1997. And often people were forced to remember that they lived on a major waterway used by millions of people and hundreds of industries upriver. For example, a chemical spill on the Monongehela—over seven hundred miles away—could force citizens to boil their drinking water for nearly a week.

In all, by the early 1920s the lower Ohio had produced places of differing sizes, shapes, and characters, while uniting them with a common river corridor and many cultural continuities. In most respects the patterns laid well before then would persist into the late twentieth century. In size and influence, Evansville would remain the leading community on the lower river, as it had been since the 1840s. The sorting-out process, though, continued. Although rankings by size would remain about the same, Owensboro—fueled by Ken-Rad in the 1920s and postwar river commerce—would surpass Paducah in size after World War II. Grain, mainstay of the nineteenth-century economy, continued to be a major export—especially at Mount Vernon, which became the Ohio River's second largest port in the late 1970s. Grain-handling facilities and grain milling were also vital to Evansville and Owensboro. Whiskey remained a major product of Owensboro, while tobacco manufacture and export thrived in Henderson, Owensboro, Paducah, and Evansville well after the Great War. Wood manufactures continued to be important to many communities. Coal, the leading product shipped on the river, led to the creation of huge power-generating facilities, especially at Rockport, after World War II. The McCracken County seat also continued to depend on ship construction and repair. The expansion of oil production beginning in the 1920s brought additional prosperity to Evansville, Henderson, Hawesville, Owensboro, and Uniontown.

The improvement of the river channel after the turn of the century had a synergistic effect. Evansville and Paducah became major shipbuilding centers during World War II. Upriver, Fort Knox's expansion accelerated West Point's inclusion in metropolitan Louisville, while in Union County a new military installation, Camp Breckinridge, trained tens of thousands of troops. The growth of Evansville and Paducah during and after the war helped to explain the expansion of nearby communities: Henderson, Newburgh, and Mount Vernon, Joppa, and Metropolis. Aided by the Tennessee Valley Authority, the Paducah area became home of major coal-generating stations as well as recreational facilities on Kentucky Lake and nearby Barkley Lake. Cheap and abundant coal also accounted for the formation in the 1950s of large aluminum-processing facilities near Hawesville, Henderson, and Newburgh. The lock and dam system, in turn, had to be modernized in the 1970s to accommodate longer, wider tows.[2]

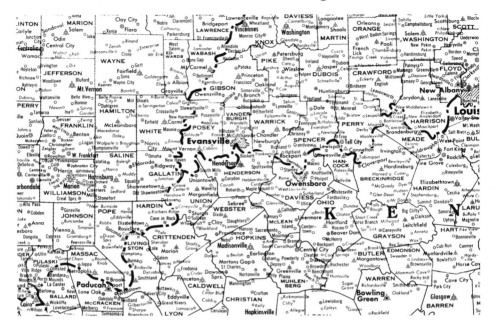

Counties and Towns of the Lower Ohio in 1997 (Smith and Butterfield Company of Evansville)

Beginning in the 1930s, with the decline of furniture making, Evansville became heavily dependent on the manufacture of refrigerators and automobiles, two consumer durables which brought only temporary prosperity, as mid-1950s crises led to major disruptions in both industries. The city's economy has since become much more diverse, with service—especially communications, education, health care, and retail business—becoming its modern base. Evansville, however, remains the dominant metropolis in approximately the same territory as a century earlier. Through commerce in grain, coal, chemicals, and metals, as well as such recreational uses as boating and riverboat casinos, the Ohio River continues to be a major factor in the city's economy.

Modern times have brought other changes: depopulation of city centers in places such as Paducah and the expansion of suburban communities such as Newburgh. The three largest Kentucky cities have community colleges, and since 1965 Evansville has had a public university, known since 1985 as the University of Southern Indiana. Private colleges have also been created in the past eighty years: the University of Evansville, and Owensboro's Brescia College and Kentucky Wesleyan College. Intellectual and aesthetical development are also promoted by impressive symphony orchestras and museums in Evansville and

Owensboro. With the arrival of such institutions, as well as the impact of corporate hiring, such places have become demographically and culturally more
diverse than in 1920.

Yet tradition persists here, too. The Upper South's mark on the tastes, values, and habits of the people of the lower Ohio remains strong, whether in
accents, fondness for barbecue, or propensity to vote Democratic. Communities tend to be jealous of their prerogatives, suspicious of change, and skeptical
of authority. Local leaders, less influential in the shaping of their communities' futures, still make a difference.

Below the surface homogeneity found in shopping malls, modern highways, and fast-food outlets, the lower Ohio's many hamlets, villages, towns,
and cities offer the visitor as much tantalizing divergence as they did in the
days of the flatboats and keelboats. Reflective of their environs and of their
people, they remain creatures of their distinctive pasts—each a special place
with different stories to tell. The river was—and is—largely responsible for
that.

APPENDIX 1 ⌇

Population Tables

Table 1. Population (in Thousands) of Lower Ohio Counties, 1800-1920

County	1800	1820	1840	1860	1880	1900	1920
(Illinois)							
Alexander	0	.7	3.3	4.7	14.8	19.4	24
Gallatin	0	3.2	10.8	8.1	12.9	15.8	12.9
Hardin	0	0	1.4	3.8	6	7.4	7.5
Massac	0	0	0	6.2	10.4	13.1	13.6
Pope	0	2.6	4.1	6.7	13.3	13.6	9.6
Pulaski	0	0	0	3.9	9.5	14.6	14.6
(Indiana)							
Crawford	0	2.6	5.3	8.2	12.4	13.5	11.2
Harrison	0	7.9	12.5	18.4	21.3	21.7	18.7
Perry	0	2.3	4.7	11.8	17	18.8	16.7
Posey	0	4	9.7	16	20.9	22.3	19.3
Spencer	0	1.9	6.3	14.6	22.1	22.4	18.4
Vanderburgh	0	1.8	6.2	20.4	42.2	71.8	92.3
Warrick	0	1.7	6.3	13.2	20.2	22.3	19.9
(Kentucky)							
Ballard	0	0	0	8.7	14.4	10.8	12
Breckinridge	.8	7.5	8.9	13.2	17.5	20.5	15.6
Crittenden	0	0	0	8.8	11.7	15.2	13.1
Daviess	0	3.9	8.3	15.5	27.7	38.7	40.7
Hancock	0	0	2.6	6.2	8.6	8.9	6.9
Hardin	3.7	10.5	16.3	15.1	22.6	22.9	24.3
Henderson	3.3	10.8	9.5	14.3	24.5	32.9	27.6
Livingston	2.9	5.8	9	7.2	9.2	11.4	9.7
McCracken	0	0	4.7	10.4	16.3	28.7	37.2
Meade	0	0	5.8	8.9	10.3	10.5	9.4
Union	0	3.5	6.7	12.8	17.8	21.3	18

SOURCES: Francis A. Walker, *Compendium of the Ninth Census (year ending June 1, 1870)* . . . (Washington, 1872), 38-43, 49-53; U.S., 10th Census, 1880, *Statistics of the Population of the United States* (Washington, 1883), 56-57, 62-63, 388-89, 392-93, and 431-34; U.S., 12th Census, 1900, *Population* (Washington, 1901), 1:499-501, 504-5, 535-36, 540-41; U.S., 14th Census, 1920, *Population* (Washington, 1922), 3:251-79, 289-311, 368-86.

Table 2. Population (in Percentages) of African Americans in Lower Ohio
Counties, 1800-1920

County	1800	1820	1840	1860	1880	1900	1920
(Illinois)							
Alexander	0	0	0	2.1	31.1	32.6	26.8
Gallatin	0	9.4	6.4	4.9	5.4	4	2
Hardin	0	0	7.1	2.6	3.3	2.6	1.1
Massac	0	0	0	1.6	16.3	16.4	15.2
Pope	0	3.1	2.4	3.0	4.5	5.1	3.5
Pulaski	0	0	0	0	34.7	40	34
(Indiana)							
Crawford	0	0	0	0	0	0	0
Harrison	0	1	1	1	1.9	1.6	1.1
Perry	0	1	0	0	1.2	1.3	1
Posey	0	0	0	1	4.8	5.5	2.7
Spencer	0	0	0	0	6.8	5.9	3.1
Vanderburgh	0	1	1.6	1	9	11.2	7.1
Warrick	0	0	0	0	3	3.2	1.8
(Kentucky)							
Ballard	0	0	0	19.5	11.8	14	11.5
Breckinridge	5.2	16.9	19.1	17.4	12.6	10.2	5.2
Crittenden	0	0	0	11.4	10.2	5.8	3.6
Daviess	0	22.2	24.1	23.2	17.7	14.4	11.1
Hancock	0	0	23.1	12.9	9.3	7.2	5.3
Hardin	9.2	14.2	15.3	17.2	14.6	9	6.4
Henderson	12	21.2	34.7	40.6	31	26.8	20.6
Livingston	16.1	18.1	18.9	18.1	10.9	6.9	5.2
McCracken	0	0	14.9	17.3	27	25.3	18.8
Meade	0	0	24.1	22.5	12.6	8.4	6
Union	0	30	26.9	24.2	18	14.6	9.8

NOTE: Percentages are rounded to the nearest tenth. None recorded for Illinois and Indiana in 1800. For 1820 and after, a zero is shown if the percentage is less than .5; a percentage of between .5 and .9 is shown as 1.

Table 3. Population (in Percentages) of Foreign-Born Residents in Lower Ohio
Counties, 1850-1920

County	1850	1860	1880	1900	1920
(Illinois)					
Alexander	3.9	21.3	8.8	4.1	1.9
Gallatin	4.2	4.9	3.1	1.2	0.5
Hardin	0.1	2.6	16.7	1.1	0.5
Massac	1.8	6.5	4.8	2.6	1.2
Pope	1.5	4.5	3	1.5	0.6
Pulaski	2.3	12..8	4.2	2.6	1
(Indiana)					
Crawford	0.8	2.4	1.6	0.9	0.4
Harrison	7.7	9.2	5.2	2.6	0.8
Perry	8.7	24.6	13.5	6.7	2.2
Posey	9.5	14.4	9.1	4.3	1.5
Spencer	11.2	13.0	8.1	4.1	1.4
Vanderburgh	35.6	40.7	20.1	9.5	3.6
Warrick	4.5	9.1	6.4	3.4	1.3
(Kentucky)					
Ballard	0.3	1.1	0.7	0.5	0.1
Breckinridge	0.6	1.5	1.0	0.5	0.1
Crittenden	1.5	2.3	0	0.1	0.1
Daviess	1.2	2.6	2.5	1.4	0.6
Hancock	2.2	8.1	2.3	1.1	0.4
Hardin	0	2.0	1.3	0.8	0.8
Henderson	1.3	2.8	2.4	1.7	0.9
Livingston	3.0	1.0	1.1	0.3	0.2
McCracken	6.3	9.6	4.9	0.2	0.9
Meade	0.8	1.1	1	0.6	0.3
Union	1.9	6.3	1.7	0.7	1.3

SOURCES: Francis A. Walker, *Compendium of the Ninth Census (year ending June 1, 1870)*
... (Washington, 1872), 38-43, 49-53; U.S., 10th Census, 1880, *Statistics of the Population of the United States* (Washington, 1883), 56-57, 62-63, 388-89, 392-93, and 431-
34; U.S., 12th Census, 1900, *Population* (Washington, 1901), 1:499-501, 504-5, 535-36,
540-41; U.S., 14th Census, 1920, *Population* (Washington, 1922), 3:251-79, 289-311,
368-86.

NOTE: Statistics for 1850 are included because that was the first year in which birthplace
was recorded in the census.

Table 4. Population of Lower Ohio Towns with 2,500 Residents by 1920, 1820-1920

Town	1820	1830	1840	1850	1860	1870	1880	1900	1920	Change (%)
Evansville	119	346	2,121	4,776	11,484	21,830	29,280	59,007	85,264	191.2
Paducah		105		2,428	4,590	6,866	8,036	19,446	24,735	207.8
Owensboro		229		1,215	2,308	3,437	6,231	13,189	17,424	179.6
Cairo			1,000	242	2,188	6,267	9,011	12,566	15,203	68.7
Henderson		483		1,775		4,171	5,635	10,272	12,169	116
Mt. Vernon				1,120	1,930	2,880	3,730	5,132	5,284	41.7
Metropolis				427	1,079	2,490	2,668	4,069	5,055	89.5
Tell City					1,030	1,660	2,112	2,680	4,086	93.6
Mound City					832	1,631	2,222	2,705	2,756	24
Rockport				412	834	1,720	2,382	2,882	2,581	8.4

SOURCES: J.D.B. De Bow, *Seventh Census of the United States: 1850, Embracing a Statistical View of Each of the States* (Washington, 1853), 612-13, 703-14, 759-78; U.S., 8th Census, 1860, *Statistics of the Population of the United States* (Washington, 1864), 88-101, 113-27, 182-83; U.S., 9th Census, 1870, *Statistics of the Population of the United States,* vol. 1 (Washington, 1872), 108-59, 189-90; U.S., 10th Census, 1880, *Statistics of the Population of the United States* (Washington, 1883), 130-59, 189-95; and U.S., 14th Census, 1920, *Population* (Washington, 1923), 1:197-204, 207-9, 222-25. (See also U.S., 4th Census, 1820, *Population Schedules of Vanderburgh County,* National Archives microfilm M33, roll 14, *Indiana,* 179-83; U.S., 5th Census, 1830, *Population Schedules of Vanderburgh County,* National Archives microfilm M19, roll 32, *Indiana,* 386-422; U.S., 6th Census, 1840, *Population Schedules of Vanderburgh County,* National Archives microfilm 704, roll 96, *Indiana,* 321-60; U.S., 7th Census, 1850, *Population Schedules of Vanderburgh County,* National Archives microfilm M432, roll 176, *Indiana,* 727-1008. See also Collins, *History of Kentucky,* 2:262-65; Conrod, "Limited Growth of Cities in the Lower Ohio Valley," 82, 185, and 244; Lansden, *History of the City of Cairo,* 209.

NOTE: Change indicates percentage of growth between 1880 and 1920. Population data prior to 1850 is limited and sketchy; often places are not listed in the printed federal census. Cairo's population in 1840 is an estimate. Only those communities listed in the printed census of 1850 are shown. Evansville's total for that year includes Lamasco, annexed in the 1850s. The 1880 census of Massac County includes Massac City, which is probably Brooklyn; the entry in Pulaski County is for Mound City Precinct, a bit larger than the town. Mound City, Mt. Vernon, and Rockport lost population between 1910 and 1920.

Table 5. Population of Lower Ohio Villages with 1,000 to 2,499 Residents by 1920, 1850-1920

Settlement	1850	1860	1870	1880	1900	1920	Change (%)
Cannelton		2,155	2,481	1,834	2,188	2,008	9.5
Rosiclare				368	278	1,522	313.6
Cloverport		920	849	1,056	1,656	1,509	42.9
Shawneetown	1,764	914	1,309	1,851	1,698	1,368	-26.1
Golconda		398	858	1,000	1,140	1,242	24.2
Newburgh	526	999	1,464	1,282	1,371	1,295	1
Brooklyn/ Brookport			104	413	865	1,098	165.9
Elizabethtown				484	668	1,055	118
Uniontown		1,046	896	1,015	1,531	1,041	2.6
Hawesville	420	1,128	855	872	1,041	829	-4.9

SOURCES: J.D.B. De Bow, *Seventh Census of the United States: 1850, Embracing a Statistical View of Each of the States* (Washington, 1853), 612-13, 703-14, 759-78; U.S., 8th Census, 1860, *Statistics of the Population of the United States* (Washington, 1864), 88-101, 113-27, 182-83; U.S., 9th Census, 1870, *Statistics of the Population of the United States*, vol. 1 (Washington, 1872), 108-59, 189-90; U.S., 10th Census, 1880, *Statistics of the Population of the United States* (Washington, 1883), 130-59, 189-95; and U.S., 14th Census, 1920, *Population* (Washington, 1923), 1:197-204, 207-9, 222-25.

NOTE: Change indicates the percentage of increase or decrease between 1880 and 1920. No totals are available before the 1850 census. Conclin, *A New River Guide*, 49-67, offers these informal totals for 1848: Cannelton, 300; Shawneetown, 1,200; Hawesville, 500. These places lost population after 1910: Shawneetown, Brookport, Cannelton, Newburgh, Uniontown, and Hawesville.

Table 6. Population of Lower Ohio Villages with Fewer Than 1,000 Residents by 1920, 1830-1920

Settlement	1830	1840	1850	1860	1870	1880	1900	1920	Change (%)
Cave-in-Rock						195		349	79
Caledonia/ Olmstead			284			132	268	318	141
New Grand Chain						88	451	397	351.1
Hamletsburg							280	219	
Joppa								651	
Leavenworth					576	716	655	611	-14.7
Grandview						686	822	689	0.4
Troy					486	495	599	454	-9.1
Mauckport						278	290	239	-14
Alton					137	259	238		
Brandenburg	331			618	427	587	218	503	-14.3
Smithland	388		882	805	690	570	579	559	-1.9
West Point					206	441	489	724	64.2
Caseyville				623	520	399	217	263	-34.1
Lewisport					308	362	328	572	58
Stephensport	316	634		181	160	218	241	214	-1.8

SOURCES: J.D.B. De Bow, *Seventh Census of the United States: 1850, Embracing a Statistical View of Each of the States* (Washington, 1853), 612-13, 703-14, 759-78; U.S., 8th Census, 1860, *Statistics of the Population of the United States* (Washington, 1864), 88-101, 113-27, 182-83; U.S., 9th Census, 1870, *Statistics of the Population of the United States,* vol. 1 (Washington, 1872), 108-59, 189-90; U.S., 10th Census, 1880, *Statistics of the Population of the United States* (Washington, 1883), 130-59, 189-95; and U.S., 14th Census, 1920, *Population* (Washington, 1922), 1:197-204, 207-9, 222-25.

NOTE: This table does not include data from fourteen settlements that were listed only once in the federal census, nearly all in 1880. That census lists only three villages with a population of more than one hundred--New Amsterdam, Ind., had 186 residents, Concordia, Ky., 138, and Derby, Ind., 103. Cave-in-Rock, New Grand Chain, and Mauckport were listed on the census as unincorporated.

APPENDIX 2 ↷
Settlements on the Lower Ohio River

State/County/Settlement	Earlier Name(s)
(Illinois)	
Alexander	
Fort Defiance*	
Cairo	
Trinity*	
Pulaski	
Mound City	Emporium
America*	
Olmsted	Caledonia
Metcalf Landing*	Wilkinsville *
Hays Landing*	Grand Chain Landing*
Coffman Landing*	Va. Bache*
Massac	
Owen's Landing*	
Fletcher's Landing*	
Joppa	Copeland's Fy
Metropolis	Massac, Massac City, Bellegard, Wilcox's Ferry, Cooper's Landing, Ft. Massac, Ft. Ascension, Ft. Assumption, Ft. Cherokee
Brookport	Baptist Town, Robinsville, Brooklyn,
Davis Landing*	
Pellonia*	Sharp's Landing*
Owen's Ferry*	
Pope	
New Liberty	
Hamletsburg	Hamletsville, Hamlet's Ferry
Bay City	Bayfield, Breckinridge
Breckinridge*	
Golconda	Lusk's Ferry, Sarahsville, Lusk's Landing?

State/County/Settlement	Earlier Names(s)
(Illinois, Pope County, cont.)	
Quarry*	
Clark*	
Grand Pier*	
Hardin	
Shetlerville*	Parkinson Landing
Mineral City*	
Rosiclare	Twitchell's Mill
Elizabethtown	Elizabeth
Cave-in-Rock	Big Cave, Ford's Ferry, Robin's Ferry
Gentry Landing*	
Battey Rock*	
Sellers Landing*	
Saline Landing*	
Gallatin	
Old Shawneetown	Shawneetown
Rheburn's Ferry*	
(Indiana)	
Posey	
Mt. Vernon	
West Franklin	
Vanderburgh	
Howell	Fairplay (?)
Evansville	
Warrick	
Newburgh	Sprinklesburg
Spencer	
Enterprise	
Rockport	Hanging Rock
Grandview	Blount's Landing
Maxville	
Perry	
Troy	
Tell City	
Cannelton	Coal Haven
Rocky Point	Rock Island*
Tobinsport	
Rome	
Derby	
Magnet	Rono, Dodson's Landing

State/County/Settlement	Earlier Name(s)
(Indiana, cont.)	
Crawford	
Alton	
Fredonia	
Old Leavenworth	Leavenworth
Harrison	
New Amsterdam	
Mauckport	
Morvin*	
Boston*	
Evans Landing	
Rosewood*	
Salina*	
Bridgeport	
(Kentucky)	
Ballard	
Holloway	
McCracken	
Paducah	
Woodlawn	
Livingston	
Ledbetter	
Smithland	
Birdsville	
Bayou	
Berry Ferry	
Carrsville	
Crittenden	
Tolu	Hurricane, Kirksville
Cookseyville*	
Ford's Ferry*	
Union	
Caseyville	
Raleigh*	
Uniontown	
Henderson	
Alzey	
Henderson	

State/County/Settlement	Earlier Name(s)
(Kentucky, cont.)	
Daviess	
Owensboro	
Hancock	
Lewisport	
Hawesville	
Skillman's Landing*	
Breckinridge	
Cloverport	Joesport, Lower Cloverport
Addison	
Holt	
Stephensport	
Ammons	
Chenaultt	
Mooleyville	
Meade	
Concordia	Wolf Creek*
Battletown	
Brandenburg	
Doe Run	
Long Branch	
Rock Haven	
Hardin	
Howard	
West Point	

SOURCES: Genealogical Society of Southern Illinois, *Maps . . . of the Saga of Southern Illinois* (Centerville, Ill., 1986), 26, 31, 33, 39, 42, and 43; *Illustrated Historical Atlas of Indiana* (Chicago, 1876; reprint, Indianapolis, 1968); Thomas Clark, *Historic Maps of Kentucky* (Lexington, 1979), 50 and 53; Rand McNally, *Commercial Atlas and Marketing Guide* (Chicago, 1984), 148; 1996 highway maps of Illinois, Indiana, and Kentucky.

NOTE: Asterisks indicate ghost towns. The list reads west to east for each state.

Notes

Abbreviations

Evansville Courier	EC
Evansville Daily Journal	EDJ
Evansville Journal-News	EJN
Evansville Press	EP
Evansville Weekly Journal	EWJ
Indiana Magazine of History	IMH
Illinois Historical Journal	IHJ
Journal of the Illinois State Historical Society	JISHS
Register of the Kentucky Historical Society	RKHS

Introduction

1. Oscar Handlin, foreword to Lantz, *Community in Search of Itself,* ix-x. A recent example of comparative history within a region that stresses place and market forces is the thorough and provocative work by Mahoney, *River Towns.*

2. See, e.g., Lippincott, *History of Manufactures,* 3-19.

3. See, e.g., Schlereth, "Regional Culture," 166-67, 171.

4. Among the many studies of American urban and regional growth, the follwoing are especially valuable in understanding the settlement and development of this region: Abbott, *Boosters and Businessmen*; Blumin, *Urban Threshold*; Chudacoff and Smith, *Evolution of American Urban Society*; Doyle, *Social Order of a Frontier Community*; Goldfield and Brownell, *Urban America*; Mahoney, *River Towns*; Mohl, *Making of Urban America*; Monkkonen, *America Becomes Urban*; Rishel, *American Cities and Towns*; Teaford, *Cities of the Heartland*; and Wade, *Urban Frontier.*

5. An exploration of the three major historical journals in these states reveals few articles in the past fifty years dealing with towns and cities on the Ohio. The otherwise comprehensive *Kentucky Encyclopedia,* ed. Kleber, has articles only on a handful of Ohio River communities and offers no sections on urban development or municipal government. Share, *Cities in the Commonwealth,* is a brief history of Lexington and Louisville with a few sentences on other places. An attractive state bicentennial publication by the *Louisville Courier-Journal, Our Towns,* includes only two river counties below the Falls, and in these (Hardin and Union), the town celebrated is not on the Ohio. There are no studies on urbanization in Illinois and Indiana and only a few reliable histories of communities along the Ohio.

6. Weisenburger, "Urbanization of the Middle West," 19-30. In the spring 1996 issue of *History News*, Patricia Mooney Melvin states that contemporary urban history focuses on six themes: the establishment and distribution of town sites; the city-building process; the interrelationship among work, residence, and social and educational institutions; the city as a whole or as a sum of its parts; the communities outside city limits; the transformation of urban concerns into national issues after 1945; and the ways in which people shape, and are shaped, by urban environments. This book deals primarily with the first, second, and sixth, and touches on the third and fourth.

7. A summary of significant recent studies of smaller places and a call for much additional study is found, e.g., in the introduction to Rishel, *American Cities and Towns*, 4-5. Significant examples are Mahoney's work on the upper Mississippi valley, Doyle's study of Jacksonville, Illinois, and Blumin's book on Newburgh, New York. Maureen Ogle's essay, "Beyond the Great City," in Rishel, *American Cities and Towns*, 48-66, examines the development of urban services in three small Iowa towns. Monkkonen, *America Becomes Urban*, 9-30, compares the strengths and the weaknesses of three approaches to urban history that might be expanded to one's study of smaller places as well: the humanist, which idealizes the village and town but also gives us a broad understanding of the city; the statistical, which suffers from discontinuities in information but takes seriously the need to use large numerical overviews; and the "new urban history," which shows in stupefying detail that it was difficult for most Americans to get ahead but also helps us understand the impact of urban structures on individuals.

8. Blumin, *Urban Threshold*, xi-xii; Cronon, *Nature's Metropolis*, 25-54; Goldfield and Brownell, *Urban America*, 15-18.

9. Mahoney, *River Towns*, 143; see also 128, 145-75. Also note Mohl, *Making of Urban America*, 300-301; Goldfield, *Cotton Fields and Skyscrapers*, 28-79; Teaford, *Cities of the Heartland*, vii-xii.

10. Doyle, *Social Order of a Frontier Community*, 4, 3.

11. Stroble, *Okaw's Western Bank*, 1-6; Abbott, *Boosters and Businessmen*, 198-208. Abbott, 8-9, identifies his work as a synthesis of analyses. Blaine A. Brownell argued that public discussion was dominated by a guiding complex of beliefs about cities, an "urban ethos," not a coherent set of ideas, that primarily helped set the terms for debating problems and secondarily explored its impact on specific choices. On the other hand, Julius Rubin, Charles Glaab, and others focused on concrete decisions to weigh the role of ideas as a determinant of development. Abbott says his approach places popular economic thought in the context of specific urban experiences and of general ideas regarding urban and economic growth.

12. Wade, *Urban Frontier*, 42. See also 30-35. Mahoney makes a similar point about the upper Mississippi. See Mahoney, *River Towns*, 16-32, 55, and 89. Abbott's study of cities in the 1840s and 1850s provides a less thorough but nonetheless important analysis of aspects of the same question.

13. Conrod, "Limited Growth," 4-79, 263-78. This study examines Evansville, Cairo, Paducah, and Terre Haute.

14. Monkkonen, *America Becomes Urban*, 2-8. See also Wade, *Urban Frontier*, 33-34, and Mahoney, *River Towns*, 273-74, for similar perspectives.

15. Wade, *Urban Frontier*, 345.

16. See, e.g., Collot, *Journey in North America*, 1:171.

17. See especially the provocative study by Jakle, "Toward a Geographical History," 177-209, which offers insights that are applicable to the entire region.

1. Hamlets and Villages

1. Braudel, *History and Environment,* 264. See also Buley, *Old Northwest,* 1:410-21, and Robinson, *Navigation in the Ohio River Basin,* 1, and Hartley, *Economic Effects of Ohio River Transportation,* 9-13.

2. Chinn, *Kentucky,* 1-4; Lee, *Brief History,* 1-5; Clark, *History of Kentucky,* 9-15.

3. Barnhart and Riker, *Indiana to 1816,* 3-4.

4. Howard, *Illinois,* 8-9; Sutton, *Colonial Years,* 18; Colby, *Southern Illinois,* 19-21; Starke, "Indigenous Iron Industry," 432-33.

5. See especially Kellar, *Prehistory of Indiana,* 23-60, 62-63, for a study of Indiana, Ohio, Kentucky, and Illinois. See also Madison, *Indiana Way,* 10-18; Chinn, *Kentucky,* 8-9; and Carrier, *Illinois,* 9.

6. Barnhart and Riker, *Indiana to 1816,* 57-130. See also Ross, "Fur Trade," 417-43; and Rawlyk, "'Rising French Empire,'" 41-59.

7. See Clark, *History of Kentucky,* 2-58; Chinn, *Kentucky,* 81-109; Barnhart and Riker, *Indiana to 1816,* 178-236.

8. See, e.g., Clark, *Kentucky,* ix-x, 16-18.

9. Rohrbough, *Land Office Business,* 3. See also Horsman, "Ohio River Barrier," 42; and Havighurst, *River to the West,* 32-104. George Washington's interests in the valley and in a new constitution are discussed in Elkins and McKitrick, *Age of Federalism,* 43.

10. Chinn, *Kentucky,* 485; Barnhart, *Valley of Democracy,* 34-44; Rohrbough, *Trans-Appalachian Frontier,* 17-36.

11. Barnhart and Riker, *Indiana to 1816,* 246-54, 374-404; Elkins and McKitrick, *Age of Federalism,* 250, 270-71, 436-40.

12. Rohrbough, *Trans-Appalachian Frontier,* 132, 138; Buley, *Old Northwest,* 1:17-20.

13. Collot, *Journey in North America,* 1:160-61, 166, 171-72, 174, 191-93. The reprint, as well as the original edition, is in the Indiana Historical Society Library. The 1797 observation is noted in Rohrbough, *Trans-Appalachian Frontier,* 138. The French government at the time—the Directory—was interested in persuading Spain to cede Louisiana to France and in preventing American expansion west. See Elkins and McKitrick, *Age of Federalism,* 503-4, as well as Kyte, "Spy on Western Waters," 427-42, and Echeverria, "Collot's Plan," 512-20.

14. Cramer, *Navigator,* 133, 140-41.

15. Ibid., 130, 133, 134-35, 139, 140-41, 142-43, 272-73.

16. Barnhart, *Valley of Democracy,* 27-33; Rohrbough, *Trans-Appalachian Frontier,* 848-49.

17. Imlay quoted in Clark, *Kentucky,* 74-75.

18. Buley, *Old Northwest,* 1:11-14; Ambler, *Transportation in the Ohio Valley,* 31-80.

19. Clark, *The Kentucky,* 61; Clark, *Historic Maps,* 40-43; Sprague, "Town Making," 337, 340. The chief reason for the formation of Paducah much later than this (as well as for Ballard County's retarded and primitive development) was Chickasaw opposition to

white intrusion into their hunting lands as well as protracted dispute over the land warrants given to George Rogers Clark in that area. See Robertson, "Paducah," 108. In a provocative essay that could apply to Illinois and Indiana, James C. Klotter declared that historians of Kentucky have paid scant attention to local public and private records and tended to focus on the Civil War, primarily its military aspects. Although he noted the need for regional studies, he did not identify town building or, surprisingly, the impact of the Ohio in Kentucky's history. See Klotter, "Clio in the Commonwealth," 65-88. The best account of the pioneer period is Rice, *Frontier Kentucky.*

20. Mary K. Bonsteel Tachau, "Early Land Claims," in Kleber, *Kentucky Encyclopedia,* 535. See also Thomas D. Clark, "Surveying," in Kleber, *Kentucky Encyclopedia,* 862-63.

21. Rohrbough, *Trans-Appalachian Frontier,* 53; Chinn, *Kentucky,* 274-86, 505; Clark, *History of Kentucky,* 174-91, and *Historic Maps,* 51-60; Share, *Cities in the Commonwealth,* 48-49.

22. Clark, *Kentucky,* 239-40, *Historic Maps,* 51-60, and *History of Kentucky,* 174-91. See also Chinn, *Kentucky,* 498-99. Fischer, *Albion's Seed,* 406-8, offers a view of Cavalier folkways in government and politics that reinforces the linkages between early Kentucky and the Tidewater. See also J. Allen Singleton, "Highway Development," in Kleber, *Kentucky Encyclopedia,* 429-30.

23. Some slaves lived in Indiana and Illinois. They were the consequence of decisions made by southern-born territorial leaders before 1820. Indiana's indentured servitude law of the pre-1810 period, which created slavery by another name, had long since been rescinded, and those remaining slaves would have their legal status changed by state court rulings in the 1830s. Illinois slaves resided largely in Gallatin County, where they labored in the federal salines of the region. See, e.g., Thornbrough, *Negro in Indiana,* 7-30.

24. Clark, *History of Kentucky,* 192-212; Livingston County Historical Society, *Livingston County, Kentucky,* 1:57-62. See especially Eslinger, "Shape of Slavery," 1-23. Also note Lucas, *Slavery to Segregation.* The 1850 Constitution made emancipation more difficult. The manumitted person had to leave the state, and the owner needed to provide funds for transporting the former slave and maintaining him or her for a year after leaving.

25. Allen, *History of Kentucky,* 18; Federal Writers Project, *Kentucky,* 57; Barnhart and Riker, *Indiana to 1816,* 219-20; Fraser, "Fort Jefferson," 1-24; Federal Writers Project, *Henderson,* 21-37; Clark, *History of Kentucky,* 42-46.

26. Upp, *Western Adventure,* 7-8, 15, 30.

27. King and Thurman, *Henderson's River Book,* 1-2.

28. Federal Writers Project, *Henderson,* 5-6, 21-37.

29. Havighurst, *River to the West,* 151. See also King and Thurman, *Henderson's River Book,* 2-4, 10-12; Federal Writers Project, *Henderson,* 21-37, 53-57; Cramer, *Navigator,* 38; and Starling, *Henderson County,* 253-374.

30. O'Malley, *Union County,* 10, 12-68, 509-65, 567-620, 681-94; Federal Writers Project, *Union County,* 1-42, 150-56, 168-71, 202-3. See also Collins, *History of Kentucky,* 2:735-36.

31. Potter, "Owensboro's Original Proprietor," 1-16; Allen, *History of Kentucky,* 251-53; [Boulware], *Daviess County,* 94-111.

32. Lee A. Dew, "Owensboro," in Kleber, *Kentucky Encyclopedia,* 700; Collins, *His-*

tory of Kentucky, 2:151-56; Potter, *Owensboro and Daviess County,* 2-3, 5-9, 15; [Boulware], *Daviess County,* 49-62, 79-93, 94-111.

33. Robertson, "Paducah," 108-9. See also Neuman, *Story of Paducah,* 17-44. (The book was first published in 1920. The 1927 printing includes an introduction by Paducahan Irvin S. Cobb.) Dyson, "Naming of Paducah," 149-74, offers persuasive evidence that Chief Paduke never existed and that the name was a version of "Padouca," a name equivalent to Slav which Europeans used to denote the more easterly Indians who regularly supplied captives to their European associates. No self-respecting Chickasaw would have used such an epithet. There is no evidence that General William Clark had a friend who was a Chickasaw chief by that name. Probably "Paducah" was created to memorialize a once mighty and respected people. This high-minded remonstrance was lost on subsequent leaders and historians of the town. Neuman, 17 ff., is one of many to perpetuate the notion that Paduke was Clark's friend. A Lorado Taft sculpture of the chief is a major feature of Paducah's landscape.

34. Waldrep, "Interloper in the Oligarchy," 115-22. In discussing the process that eventually led to the division of this county, Waldrep argues that the traditional picture of county government's being in the hands of a few wealthy gentlemen, aristocratic justices of the peace with Virginia roots who held power for generations in a closed system, is not always appropriate. The Livingston County aristocracy could not prevent the county seat from being moved from Eddyville to Centreville in 1808 and admitted to its circle a person who proved to be a swindler. In 1809 Caldwell County was created out of Livingston, and Salem became Livingston's seat of government. When Crittenden County was formed in 1842, the seat was moved to Smithland. See also Collins, *History of Kentucky,* 2:478-79.

35. Trail, "Livingston County," 239-72.

36. *Travels on an Inland Voyage,* quoted in Federal Writers Project, *Kentucky,* 412. See also Ron D. Bryant, "Smithland," in Kleber, *Kentucky Encyclopedia,* 832; Livingston County Historical Society, *Livingston County History,* 1:8-12, 36-39; Collins, *History of Kentucky,* 2:478-79. Ohio settlements upriver—Birdsville, Bayou, Berry's Ferry, Carrsville, and several in what after 1842 would be Crittenden County—did not exist before 1820. A somewhat romantic view of Smithland's early history is found in Watts, *Kentucky Settlement.*

37. Collins, *History of Kentucky,* 2:306-19; Bolin, *Ohio Valley History,* 3-7 (a source that must be used with care, given the inaccuracies of many of its dates); McClure, *Elizabethtown and Hardin County,* 10-11, 72.

38. Briggs, *Early History of West Point,* 6-28, 65-71. On Ohiopiomingo, see Allen J. Share's brief essay in Kleber, *Kentucky Encyclopedia,* 690. See also Arbuckle, "Ohiopiomingo," 318-24.

39. Briggs, *Early History of West Point,* 9-12, 16-17, 20-21, 65-71, and 94.

40. Bolin, *Ohio Valley History,* 78-84; Collins, *History of Kentucky,* 2:96-100; Federal Writers Project, *Kentucky,* 404; Thompson, *Breckinridge County,* 7-10; Ridenour, *Meade County,* 9-17; Ron D. Bryant, "Meade County," in Kleber, *Kentucky Encyclopedia,* 623.

41. Ridenour, *Meade County,* 19-25, 41-56.

42. Charles A. Clinton, "A Social and Educational History of Hancock County, Kentucky" (a report prepared by the National Institute of Educational Experimental Schools Program of Washington, D.C., contract #OEC-0-72-5745, and reproduced in typed format by Abt Associates of Cambridge, Mass., September 25, 1974), 1-15, 21-28; Jett, *Hancock County,* 6-10. See also Lee A. Dew, *Shaping Our Society,* 1-4.

43. Barnhart and Riker, *Indiana to 1816*, 345-463.

44. Griffin, *Corydon and Harrison County*, 1:51; Roose, *Indiana's Birthplace*, 7-15. Roose's work was originally published by the Tribune Company of New Albany in 1911. Arville L. Funk was responsible for the 1966 edition. See also the unpublished manuscript written in the 1970s by Harrison County teachers on file at the Indiana Historical Society, "The Influence of the Ohio River on Harrison County," 1-2.

45. See, e.g., Pleasant, *Crawford County*, 1-9.

46. De La Hunt, *Perry County*, 8-27; Taylor, *Indiana*, 219-22; Sesquicentennial Committee, *Rockport-Spencer County Sesquicentennial, 1818-1968* (*N.p., [1968?]), 4-9, 17-21.

47. Goodspeed Company, *Warrick, Spencer, and Perry Counties*, 21; Burleigh, *Look at Newburgh*, 1-21; Taylor, *Indiana*, 214.

48. Histories of Evansville and Vanderburgh County are plentiful and usually as unreliable as they are pietistic. McGary's origins were inaccurately portrayed, for instance, until Iglehart, *Vanderburgh County*, 21-24, 28-29. Among the older histories the most thorough and useful is Brant and Fuller, *Vanderburgh County*, 30-44, 94-131. Among the recent works the most reliable is McCutchan, *Bend of the River*, 10-13.

49. Leonard, *Posey County*, 54-68; Goodspeed Company, *Posey County*, 357-58.

50. Roose, *Indiana's Birthplace*, 68-71; Taylor, *Indiana*, 176; Funk, *Harrison County*, 11-29, 39. Mauckport was platted in 1827. Evans's Landing apparently was never organized and had no post office.

51. Edmund Dana, *Geographical Sketches on the Western Country Designed for Immigrants and Settlers* (1819), cited in Lindley, *Early Travelers*, 201, 208, 209-12; Taylor, *Indiana*, 229-30; Pleasant, *Crawford County*, 1-30; Samuel R. Brown, *The Western Gazeteer, or Emigrant's Directory* (1817), cited in Lindley, *Early Travelers*, 137-58.

52. De La Hunt, *Perry County*, 28-54; Goodspeed, *Warrick, Spencer, and Perry Counties*, 668-79; Kleber, "Naming of Troy," 178-80. Samuel Taylor's observations on the Anderson River are found in Lindley, *Early Travelers*, 137, as are David Baillie Warden's on 218. He was the author of *A Statistical, Political, and Historical Account of North America* (1819). Also see Taylor, *Indiana*, 228.

53. Sesquicentennial Committee, *Rockport-Spencer County Sesquicentennial*, 4-9, 17-21; Goodspeed, *Warrick, Spencer, and Perry Counties*, 326-54, 384-85; Dana, *Geographical Sketches*, 212.

54. Barnhart and Riker, *Indiana to 1816*, 415-16; Brant and Fuller, *Vanderburgh County*, 42-44; Iglehart, 26; *Vanderburgh County*, 21-24, 47-50; McCutchan, *Bend of the River*, 13. A still valuable analysis of county seat conflicts is Ernest V. Shockley, "County Seats and County Seat Wars," *IMH* 10 (March 1914): 1-46.

55. Joseph Lane's recollections of early Evansville are found in Minutes of the Vanderburgh County Historical Society, vol. 1, 1881, 29-31. This lengthy letter was sent to VCHS officers who had sought to compile the memories of pioneer settlers. Lane completed it on September 27, 1880, a few months before his death.

56. William Cobbett, *A Year's Residence in the United States of America* (1828), and Dana, *Geographical Sketches*, 212, 510. David Thomas's comments are in Lindley, *Early Travelers*, 113. Also see Iglehart, *Vanderburgh County*, 21-24; McCutchan, *Bend of the River*, 10-13; Brant and Fuller, *Vanderburgh County*, 42-44. *EDJ*, December 21, 1874, contains reminiscences of the town in 1818-1819.

57. Goodspeed, *Posey County,* 358-62; Leffel, *Posey County,* 87-121; Leonard, *Posey County,* 16-36, 54-68; Posey County Commissioners, minutes of 1817-1820, 8-11 (May 17, 1817), and minutes of 1820-1829, 196-204. Samuel Brown's and Edmund Dana's comments are found in Lindley, *Early Travelers,* 163, 201.

58. Sutton, *Colonial Years,* 1:5, 155; Howard, *Illinois,* 56-58.

59. Birkbeck, *Letters from Illinois,* xv, 33. This is a reprint of the 1818 edition, printed in Philadelphia, Boston, and London—altogether seven editions in English that year. See also Rohrbough, *Land Office Business,* 28, and Stroble, *Okaw's Western Bank,* 7-9.

60. Howard, *Illinois,* 114-18, 260-61; Jensen, *Illinois,* 3-31. It is interesting to note the virtual absence of commentary on Illinois's Ohio River region in early travel accounts, which focus instead on the promise afforded by the lush prairies inland.

61. Mahoney, *River Towns,* 16-32.

62. Lansden, *City of Cairo,* 255-60.

63. Caldwell, "Fort Massac," 265-81, and "Fort Massac since 1805," 47-72. Also see Cramer, *Navigator,* 141.

64. Federal Writers Project, *Illinois,* 432-33. Lansden, *City of Cairo,* 29, observes that Reuben Thwaites sought to locate the ruins of Wilkinsonville during his 1894 journey down the Ohio. He also says Aaron Burr passed through it in 1805 and 1806 and that Andrew Jackson stopped there for three nights in January 1813, to replenish his food supply with wild game. Probably Lansden has confused this with Fort Massac.

65. Hardin County Historical and Genealogical Society, *Hardin County,* 8-10.

66. Federal Writers Project, *Illinois,* 435-36; Buck, *Illinois in 1818,* 60; Pease, *Frontier State,* 6-9; Howard, *Illinois,* 112; Buley, *Old Northwest,* 1:40-41.

67. Goodspeed, *Gallatin, . . . Williamson Counties,* 13-77; Howard, *Illinois,* 105-14, 132-33; Rohrbough, *Trans-Appalachian Frontier,* 357-59; Federal Writers Project, *Illinois,* 28, 58; and Pease, *Frontier State,* 176-77. Most of the trade was done in bartering, with a bushel of corn being worth two gallons of whiskey. The salines were sold to private interests in 1852 and closed in 1873, the victim of the Panic of 1873 (overproduction, low prices, and strong competition from other salt works).

68. Quoted in Buley, *Old Northwest,* 1:41. See also Federal Writers Project, *Illinois,* 436; Hall, *Letters from the West,* 1:213-16. See also Pease, *Frontier State,* 19-30.

69. Allen, *Southern Illinois,* 16-17.

70. Hardin County Historical and Genealogical Society, *Hardin County,* 8-24; Pope County Historical Society, *Pope County,* 11-14; Howard, *Illinois,* 109-112; Lohmann, *Cities and Towns of Illinois,* 30; Barge and Caldwell, "Illinois Place Names," 189-311.

71. Cramer, *Navigator,* 40; Federal Writers Project, *Cairo Guide,* 16, 55; Federal Writers Project, *Illinois,* 55; Lansden, *City of Cairo,* 30-33; Lantz, *Community in Search of Itself,* 7-13; Conrod, "Limited Growth," 89-90. See also Schultz, *Constructing Urban Culture,* 12-13. Schultz confused Cairo with the town of America.

Various theories have been offered about the origins of "Egypt" as a synonym for southern Illinois. Probably the most plausible is the naming of Cairo in 1818, followed by other Egyptian names at the southern tip of the state such as Thebes and Karnak. The naming of Memphis to the south reinforces this conscious linkage of river settlements with the Nile delta. A second, imaginative theory is that during an antebellum drought in central Illinois, southern Illinoisans lent grain to their fellow countrymen, recalling the generosity of Egyptians in the time of Joseph. See Botkin, *Mississippi River Folklore,* 402-3, for instance.

72. Schultz, *Constructing American Culture,* 13. Noah Ludlow and his river-borne theatrical troupe apparently stopped at America to purchase a haunch of venison during their trip by keelboat down the Ohio in late 1817. The appearance of the place was not described. See Havighurst, *River to the West,* 262. See also Conrod, "Limited Growth," 91. According to one account, Alexander was agent for Riddle and three others, including Henry Webb, the latter of whom established a tavern and other services at the mouth of the Cache. The settlement, Trinity, grew up around it (although this author spells it Trenity). The precise relationship among these men is unclear: Riddle and Webb were subsequently associated with the formation of Caledonia after America's demise. How America and Trinity were linked is not stated. See Sneed, *Ghost Towns,* 1-9, 163-69.

73. Audubon quoted in Havighurst, *River to the West,* 162. Lansden, *City of Cairo,* 39-42, 211-19; Perrin, *Alexander, Union, and Pulaski Counties,* 459-65, 521-23. See Sneed, *Ghost Towns,* 164-65.

2. Patterns of Growth

1. Wiebe, *Opening of American Society,* 142. 152, 167.

2. Havighurst, *River to the West,* 156-61.

3. Stroble, *Okaw's Western Bank,* 9; Buley, *Old Northwest,* 1:6, 44-46. See especially Monkkonen, *America Becomes Urban,* 31-68, and Mahoney, *River Towns,* 32-55.

4. Monkkonen, *America Becomes Urban,* 2-8. See also Chudacoff and Smith, *Evolution of American Urban Society,* 37-40; Rohrbough, *Trans-Appalachian Frontier,* 53; and Wade, *Urban Frontier,* 72-73. David Hume's vision is described in Elkins and McKitrick, *Age of Federalism,* 110-11. See also Share, *Cities in the Commonwealth,* 48-49.

5. White, *Evansville,* 9-10; Brant and Fuller, *Vanderburgh County,* 94-132; Iglehart, *Vanderburgh County,* 35-47, 50; *EDJ,* December 21, 1874; McCutchan, *Bend of the River,* 9-31; Hopkins, "Hopkins," 1-3. (The latter is handwritten and was prepared for a meeting of the Vanderburgh County Historical Society. The document was in the possession of Hopkins's granddaughter, the late Susan Hopkins Ingle; a copy is in my possession.)

6. See, e.g., Federal Writers Project, *Henderson,* 21-37; Goodspeed, *Gallatin, . . . Williamson Counties,* 92-102; Briggs, *Early History of West Point,* 6-28; Brant and Fuller, *Vanderburgh County,* 94-132.

7. Trail, "Livingston County," 239-72.

8. Wiebe, *Self-Rule,* 50. The Jeffersonian image of cities is ably described in Elkins and McKitrick, *Age of Federalism,* 192-93.

9. Pease, *Frontier State,* 6-9, 23.

10. Mahoney, *River Towns,* 32-55, 89-109. Although these concepts were developed for upper Mississippi communities, they have substantial value for understanding other regions. See also Conrod, "Limited Growth," 91, which relies on Thwaites, *Early Western Travels,* 14:86-87.

11. Freehling, *Reintegrating American History,* 20-23, 83-104. Neely discusses slavery's impact on Thomas Lincoln in *Last Best Hope,* 3-7.

12. Clark, *Kentucky,* 99.

13. Goldfield, *Cotton Fields and Skyscrapers,* 28-79; Share, *Cities in the Commonwealth,* 16-25.

14. Clark, *History of Kentucky,* 92-96; Collins, *History of Kentucky,* 1:274-75; Ireland, *County in Kentucky History,* 1, 3, 12, 19-27, and 54-67. By contrast, e.g., see Madison,

Indiana Way, 80-81. Indiana received 3 percent of the proceeds of land sales for transportation projects, and that funding established the General Assembly's program in 1821 for a system of state roads. Henderson's distinctiveness is stressed, e.g., in Federal Writers Project, *Henderson,* 13-37.

15. Madison, *Indiana Way,* 127; Howard, *Illinois,* 260-61.

16. Wilhelm, "Settlement," 72-81. The reference to Birdsall and Florin, *Regional Landscapes,* is cited on 77. See also Barnhart, *Valley of Democracy,* 105.

17. See, e.g., Monkkonen, *America Becomes Urban,* 31-68.

3. The Sifting Process Begins

1. Flint, *Recollections,* 103-5; Rohrbough, *Land Office Business,* esp. 136. The Land Act of 1820 ended the selling of land by credit, but it lowered minimum acreage to eighty and the price to $1.25 per acre. In principle this helped the pioneer, but scarcity of cash proved a major obstacle, and speculators benefited more. By 1841, though, the preemption (squatter sovereignty) principle of an 1830 law was permanently adopted, thus legalizing settlement before purchase and making settlement, rather than revenue, a priority.

2. Walker, *Ninth Census,* 28-43, 48-53, and 407-15. See also Blumin, *Urban Threshold,* 101, and Rohrbough, *Trans-Appalachian Frontier,* 171, 176.

3. See Wiebe, *Self-Rule,* 67, 68, 84, and *Opening of American Society,* 152, 167.

4. The proportion of Kentuckians living on the lower Ohio may have been slightly higher in 1820, given the settlement of the area from which Ballard and McCracken Counties were taken, but upriver no similar circumstance existed, since the post-1820 counties of Crittenden, Hancock, and Meade were formed out of Livingston, Henderson, Daviess, Breckinridge, and Hardin. Livingston's modest growth may be attributed to the removal of McCracken and Crittenden Counties, but the drop-off of about 30 percent in the 1840s is striking.

5. Walker, *Ninth Census,* 38-43, 48-53, and 407-15.

6. Rudolph, *Hoosier Zion,* 96-100. For a description of the farming season following initial settlement, see Esarey, *Indiana Home,* 86-99.

7. The most thorough account of blacks in Kentucky in the antebellum era is Lucas, *Slavery to Segregation.* See also U.S., 6th Census, 1840, *Compendium,* 72-75, and U.S., 7th Census, 1850, *Statistical View,* 611-12.

8. Boggess, *Settlement of Illinois,* 5:183-85.

9. U.S., 7th Census, *Statistical,* 630, 717, and 780. For an analysis of Indiana, see Rose, "Hoosier Origins," 201-32. Torrey, "Western Lowell," 276-304, offers the best discussion of the early years of that town. Also note De La Hunt, *Perry County,* 130-33.

10. U.S., 7th Census, 1850, *Compendium,* 230-35; U.S., 7th Census, 1850, *Population Schedules of Vanderburgh County,* National Archives microfilm M432, roll 176, *Indiana,* 727-1008. The 1850 population schedules were the first to identify residents' birthplaces. See Rose, "Distribution," 224-60; U.S., 7th Census, 1850, *Population Schedules of Daviess County,* National Archives microfilm M432, roll 198, *Kentucky,* 346-55; McCracken County Genealogical Society, *History and Families,* 297.

11. Leonard, *Posey County*, 54-68; Posey County Historical Society, *Posey County*, 66-77; Burleigh, *Look at Newburgh*, 105-30; De La Hunt, *Perry County*, 85-93; Sesquicentennial Committee, *Rockport-Spencer County Sesquicentennial*, 4-9.

12. U.S., 7th Census, *Statistical View*, 632-41, 737-45; Potter, *Owensboro and Daviess County*, 52-54.

13. Collins, *History of Kentucky*, 2:151-56; Potter, *Owensboro and Daviess County*, 30-37; Dew, "Whig Party," 15-21. McCracken County Genealogical Society, *History and Families*, 172-73; Starling, *Henderson County*, 517-817, passim.

4. Perspectives on Lower Ohio River Communities

1. Jakle, *Ohio Valley*, vi-vii, 158-63.

2. Cumings, *Western Pilot*, 22-29. First published in 1822, Cumings's guide was issued in several subsequent editions. This became the basis for Conclin's *New River Guide*, and James, *River Guide*. See also Savage, "Illinois Immigrants," 39.

3. Conclin, *New River Guide*, 53-67.

4. Timothy Flint, quoted in Lindley, *Early Travelers*, 450; Thurston, *Journal*, 23.

5. Bernhard, *Travels*, cited in Lindley, *Early Travelers*, 418.

6. Karl Postel quoted in Lindley, *Early Travelers*, 523-24, 527.

7. Trollope, *Domestic Manners*, 28-29; Tocqueville, *Democracy in America*, 345-46. See also Drake, *Pioneer Life*, 180-81.

8. Genealogical Society of Southern Illinois, *Maps . . . of the Saga of Southern Illinois* (Centerville, Ill., 1986), 26-43; De La Hunt, *Perry County*, 115; Goodspeed, *Warrick, Spencer, and Perry Counties*, 680-83; Roose, *Indiana's Birthplace*, 68-71; Pope County Historical Society, *Pope County*, 30-31, 34; May, *Massac County*, 188-95; and Sneed, *Ghost Towns*, 148-62.

9. Smelser, "Material Customs," 40-41.

10. Hardin County Historical and Genealogical Society, *Hardin County*, 8-24; Fohs Hall Community Arts Foundation, *Crittenden County*, 1:12-14; Sneed, *Ghost Towns*, 61-70; Goodspeed, *Warrick, Spencer, and Perry Counties*, 354-59, 368-71.

11. De La Hunt, *Perry County*, 28-54, 113-14; Goodspeed, *Warrick, Spencer, and Perry Counties*, 668-77; Taylor, *Indiana*, 221-22; Baertich, *Troy*, 201-27; Conclin, *New River Guide*, 49-52. The founder of the Indiana Pottery Company was a Staffordshire potter, James Clews, who had heard that local clay was well suited for manufacturing chamber pottery. Backed by American capital, he formed the company in 1837, but left a year later because he deemed the clay inferior and he was unable to secure experienced English workers.

12. Pleasant, *Crawford County*, 1-138, passim; Conclin, *New River Guide*, 49-52; Griffin, *Corydon and Harrison County*, 2:200-234; Taylor, *Indiana*, 167. The Mauckport crossing and road northward into central Indiana would be a major transportation artery for decades. In Franklin, just south of Indianapolis, a major north-south road is still call Mauxferry Road.

13. Briggs, *Early History of West Point*, 6-28, 49, 65-71, 110-11; Conclin, *New River Guide*, 49-52; Thompson, *Breckinridge County*, 27-32, 72.

14. Clinton, "Hancock County," 26-29; Jett, *Hancock County,* 6; "Hancock County Tax Records," 17-21, 31-36, 42-47, 62-64; Ford, *Hancock County,* 1-50. The road map is found in Hodges, *Fearful Times,* opposite page 1. In 1846, almost 56 percent of the taxable wealth in the county was invested in land, and another 28 percent was invested in slaves.

15. Federal Writers Project, *Union County,* 56-60, 68-69, 150-56; O'Malley, *Union County,* 509-65; Conclin, *New River Guide,* 53-67. In 1860 Uniontown had 266 slaves in a population under 1,000. Caseyville had another 171. One might reasonably assume that Uniontown's slave population in 1850 was at least 30 percent.

16. Collins, *History of Kentucky,* 2:736; Federal Writers Project, *Union County,* 1-42, 168-71, 202-3; O'Malley, *Union County,* 567-620, 681-94; Conclin, *New River Guide,* 53-67. Details on imports and exports may be found in the introduction to the fascinating two-volume collection compiled by Simpson, *River Merchant Trade.*

17. In addition to the still valuable study by Shockley, "County Seats," see Schnellenberg, *Conflict.* Schnellenberg's brief and sometimes ahistorical book focuses on forty-nine cases of violent controversy (defined as involving fatalities or serious injury, forcible removal of records, or calling out the militia) in the Midwest. He records only one in Indiana—Crawford County's seat in 1894—and three in Illinois, including the Equality-Shawneetown crisis of 1849-52 (27-34).

18. Hardin County Historical and Genealogical Society, *Hardin County,* 8-24; Conclin, *New River Guide,* 62-67.

19. Pope County Historical Society, *Pope County,* 28-30; Wormer, *Pope County,* 46; Howard, *Illinois,* 153; Cole, *Civil War,* 949-83.

20. Federal Writers Project, *Illinois,* 433; Conclin, *New River Guide,* 65-67; May, *Massac County,* 182; Page, *Massac County,* 128-37. This may have been the scrawny settlement named "New Thermopolae" in Dickens's *Martin Chuzzlewit,* which he viewed en route to the City of Eden (375). Dickens said the place was located on a steep bank and that a barnlike hotel sat atop it. There were also a few scattered sheds and a wooden store building.

21. Goodspeed, *Warrick, Spencer, and Perry Counties,* 326-54; Conclin, *New River Guide,* 49-52.

22. Goodspeed, *Warrick, Spencer, and Perry Counties,* 83-84; Adams, *Warrick County,* 27, 29; Fortune, *Warrick,* 33; Burleigh, *Look at Newburgh,* 32-66; Conclin, *New River Guide,* 53-55. Many of the records of Bethell's mercantile establishment can be found in the Bethell-Warren Papers at the Indiana Historical Society Library. See, e.g., the account statements and receipts for the 1850s in box 1, folders 3 and 4. In 1859, e.g., his firm regularly paid for telegraph connections, via the Evansville and Western Telegraph Company, with New Orleans as well as for freight carried on packets connecting Louisville with Henderson, Memphis, and New Orleans.

23. Goodspeed, *Posey County,* 358-68; Leonard, *Posey County,* 54-68; *Biographical Cyclopedia,* 122-23. Posey County Commissioners minutes, 1820-1829, May 10, 1825, 196-204; Leffel, *Posey County,* 46-63, 86. In his *New River Guide,* George Conclin said little of the place, noting only that it was the county seat and small.

24. Lucas, *Slavery to Segregation,* 1-2, 5, 17, 24, 29, 46, 59-60, 61, 70, 96, and 139.

25. Collins, *History of Kentucky,* 2:598-99; Conclin, *New River Guide,* 49-50; Ron D. Bryant, "Brandenburg," in Kleber, *Kentucky Encyclopedia,* 113; Ridenour, *Meade County,* 59-82; and Sims, *Meade County,* 1-97.

26. Quoted in Whittlesey, *Fugitive Essays*, 257. See also Conclin, *New River Guide*, 50-52; Lee A. Dew, "Hawesville," in Kleber, *Kentucky Encyclopedia*, 419; Clinton, "Social and Educational History of Hancock County," 21-28; Collins, *History of Kentucky*, 2:304-6; Bolin, *Ohio Valley History*, 78-84.

27. Ford, *Hancock County*, 7, 17, and 30.

28. Conclin, *New River Guide*, 52; Lee A. Dew, "Owensboro," in Kleber, *Kentucky Encyclopedia*, 700; Potter, "Owensboro's Original Proprietor"; Potter, *Owensboro and Daviess County*, 10-27, 115-16, and 172; [Boulware,] *Daviess County*, 79-93.

29. Potter, *Owensboro and Daviess County*, 30-37; Conclin, *New River Guide*, 52; [Boulware,] *Daviess County* 79-93; *Owensboro Messenger and Inquirer*, March 30, 1992.

30. Conclin, *New River Guide*, 53-67; U.S., 9th Census, *Compendium*, 38-43, 49-53, 407-15.

31. Collins, *History of Kentucky*, 2:334-38; Starling, *Henderson County*, 253-374.

32. Starling, *Henderson County*, 294, 530-31; Federal Writers Project, *Henderson*, 21-27, 53-57, 78-87; Arnett, *Annals and Scandals*, 115-19; King and Thurman, *Henderson's River Book*, 57; *EDJ*, February 26, 1850.

33. Boynton Merrill Jr., "Henderson," in Kleber, *Kentucky Encyclopedia*, 423; "Archibald Dixon," in Kleber, *Kentucky Encyclopedia*, 267-68; Lowell H. Harrison, "Lazarus Whitehead Powell," in Kleber, *Kentucky Encyclopedia*, 731-32; Starling, *Henderson County*, 575-817; Federal Writers Project, *Henderson*, 78-87.

34. 7th Census, 1850, *Compendium*, 219, 225, 231, 237, 243, and *Statistical View*, 611—12; U.S., 8th Census, 1860, *Slave Schedules, Kentucky*, National Archives microfilm M652, roll 402, *Daviess County*, 38-80; roll 403, *Henderson County*, 139-76; roll 404, *Union County*, 420-21.

35. See John E.L. Robertson, "Paducah," in Kleber, *Kentucky Encyclopedia*, 705, as well as his *Paducah*, 6-8, 12-17, and his "Paducah," 109-15. See also Conclin, *New River Guide*, 53-67; Conrod, "Limited Growth," 246-49; Collins, *History of Kentucky*, 1:59; Neuman, *Story of Paducah*, 45-60.

36. Conrod, "Limited Growth," 246-49; McCracken County Genealogical Society, *History and Families*, 12-15.

37. U.S., 7th Census, *Statistical View*, 611-12, and *Compendium*, 219, 225, 231, 237, 243.

38. See, e.g., *EWJ*, September 23, 1847; August 30, 1848; November 8, 1849; and October 8, 1850. For a description of the economy, see Snepp, *Channels of Trade*, 325-30; Schockel, "Manufactural Evansville," esp. 125-29 and 137-39; and Conrod, "Limited Growth," 184-89, which relies heavily on Schockel and Snepp. The most reliable of the local histories remains Brant and Fuller, *Vanderburgh County*. See especially 94-132.

39. Schockel, "Manufactural Evansville," 125-30, 137; White, *Evansville*, 32-35; Brant and Fuller, *Vanderburgh County*, 94-132.

40. See especially Lipin, *Producers*, 77-84.

41. Lockwood, recollections appended to the minutes of the VCHS of February 28, 1880, 16. See also Elliott, *Evansville and Vanderburgh County*, 14-18; minutes of the Vanderburgh County Historical Society, September 1879 to January 1884, transcribed by the Society 1933, 14-15 and 29-32; Igleheart, *Vanderburgh County*, 227-34; McCutchan, *Bend of the River*, 9-31.

42. According to the *EWJ*, ground was broken November 1, 1834. Work on the canal had begun at Fort Wayne in 1832, five years after the state received a federal land grant to

support its construction. In the internal improvements act of 1836, state funding was to construct the Central Canal portion from Peru through Indianapolis and Terre Haute and thence over land to Evansville. Madison, *Indiana Way*, 82-83, 86. See Fatout, *Indiana Canals*, 39, 52, 60, and 67, and Gray, *Transportation*, 113-34.

43. See, e.g., Brant and Fuller, *Vanderburgh County*, 140-43, who note that in the late 1830s the "easy-going habits of earlier pioneers was abandoned."

44. Brant and Fuller, *Vanderburgh County*, 147-64, 311; Iglehart, *Vanderburgh County*, 234-55; White, *Evansville*, esp. 19-21, 25-29, and 203-6. Shanklin's two sons were eminent in local and regional newspaper matters, and his daughter married Justice John Marshall Harlan. Marilyn Harshbarger's research paper, "A Study of the Philanthropic Contributions of the John Augustus Reitz Family," discusses Reitz's early life (1-2). A copy may be found in special collections at the University of Southern Indiana library.

45. *Evansville Journal*, July 3, 1845, August 31, 1848, and October 3, 1850. For a discussion of the early German community, see Bigham, *Reflections*, 4-5.

46. White, *Evansville*, 328; Brant and Fuller, *Vanderburgh County*, 315-20; Iglehart, *Vanderburgh County*, 234-55.

47. Brant and Fuller, *Vanderburgh County*, 213-16.

48. Hopkins, "Hopkins," 1-8.

49. Ibid., esp. 31-36, 60-61, 75-76.

50. *Sunday Courier and Press*, January 2, 1949; Brant and Fuller, *Vanderburgh County*, 70-82.

51. Brant and Fuller, *Vanderburgh County*, 94-132; Snepp, *Channels of Trade*, 326-30.

52. Perrin, *Alexander, Union, and Pulaski Counties*, 515 (see also 585-88); *Illinois in 1837*, 73; Lansden, *City of Cairo*, 211-19, and Conclin, *New River Guide*, 67.

53. Conclin, *New River Guide*, 60-67; Ron D. Bryant, "Smithland," in Kleber, *Kentucky Encyclopedia*, 832; Watts, *Kentucky Settlement*, 481-82; Livingston County Historical Society, *Livingston County*, 1:8-12, 36-53; U.S., 7th Census, 1850, *Compendium*, 123, 235, 241, 247.

54. An example of the simple but unappealing explanation is found in Bryant, "Smithland," 832. See also Collins, *History of Kentucky*, 2:264, 478-79; U.S., 7th Census, 1850, *Compendium*, 220-23, 226-29, 238-46; U.S., 9th Census, 38-43, 49-53.

55. Hall, *Letters from the West*, cited in Sutton, *Prairie State*, 1:213-17; Peck, *A Guide for Emigrants*, inside front cover and 284-85; *Illinois in 1837*, 128; Thurston, *Journal*, 28; Conclin, *New River Guide*, 53-67.

56. Rohrbough, *Trans-Appalachian Frontier*, 357-59; Goodspeed, *History of Gallatin, . . . Williamson Counties*, 13-77, 17-102; Howard, *Illinois*, 112; Pease, *Frontier State*, 164; Cole, *Civil War*, 450; Lawler, *Gallatin County*, 17, 40, 107; Gallatin County Historical Society, *History and Families*, 1:8-22; Stroble, *Okaw's Western Bank*, 76, 84, and 113.

57. Stroble, *Okaw's Western Bank*, 99. For census data, see U.S., 7th Census, 1850, *Compendium*, 223, 235, 241, 247; U.S., 9th Census, 1870, *Compendium*, 38-43, 49-53, 407, 415.

58. Goodspeed, *History of Gallatin, . . . Williamson Counties*, 92-148, 209-21, 379; Howard, *Illinois*, 260-61; Boggess, *Settlement of Illinois*, 5:187.

59. Taylor, *Indiana*, 225-28.

60. De La Hunt, *Perry County*, 85-93, 130-44, 156-72; Torrey, "Western Lowell," 276-304.

61. Conclin, *New River Guide*, 66, 67. See also Peck, *Guide for Emigrants*, 284.

62. Pease, *Frontier State,* 212, 219-20; Lansden, *City of Cairo,* 39-56; Lantz, *Community in Search of Itself,* 7-13; Federal Writers Project, *Cairo Guide,* 55-56. An Eastern architect, William Strickland, prepared a town plan using squares and parks, not the grid plan. The influence of that was evident in the plan of Blandville, in Bland County to the south. Strickland also prepared a grand sketch that showed commercial and industrial activities and a level of development that was nonexistent. See Kentucky Heritage Commission, *Historic Sites,* 9, 10-12.

63. *Illinois in 1837,* 33; Lansden, *City of Cairo,* 19-56; Lantz, *Community in Search of Itself,* 7-13; and Pease, *Frontier State,* 219.

64. Dickens, *American Notes,* 30:186-87. See also Sutton, *Prairie State,* 1:233-40, and Lansden, *City of Cairo,* 170-76.

65. Dickens, *Martin Chuzzlewit,* 380-82.

66. Cole, *Civil War,* 1-2. See also Lansden, *City of Cairo,* 175-76.

67. Stover, *Illinois Central Railroad,* 9-28; Lansden, *City of Cairo,* 58-62, 96-110, 190-200; Lantz, *Community in Search of Itself,* 13-19; Cole, *Civil War,* 32-38, 52; Federal Writers Project, *Cairo Guide,* 27-28; Howard, *Illinois,* 243-45.

68. Peck, *Guide for Emigrants,* map inside cover; *Illinois in 1837,* 73; Lansden, *City of Cairo,* 39-56, 211-19; Perrin, *Alexander, Union, and Pulaski Counties,* 503-51, 585-88; Conclin, *New River Guide,* 67; Sneed, *Ghost Towns,* 8, 164-65. Roose, *Indiana's Birthplace,* 68-71; Funk, *Harrison County,* 26.

5. Change and Continuity

1. McPherson, *Ordeal by Fire,* 2.

2. For a review of changing trading patterns, see Bigham, "River of Opportunity," 141-53.

3. Robertson, *Paducah,* 6-8; Rohrbough, *Trans-Appalachian Frontier,* 357-59; Madison, *Indiana Way,* 84-85; Howard, *Illinois,* 198-207; Pease, *Frontier State,* 316-26.

4. Robertson, *Paducah, 1830-1980,* 6; Conclin, *New River Guide,* 49-67; Mahoney, *River Towns,* 21-46. The Postel citation is in Lindley, *Early Travelers,* 523-24.

5. Abbott, *Boosters and Businessmen,* 198-208; Wade, *Urban Frontier,* 101-57.

6. George Yater, "Louisville and Portland Canal," in Kleber, *Kentucky Encyclopedia,* 580-81; Kreipke, "Falls of the Ohio," 197; Share, *Cities in the Commonwealth,* 44.

7. For an assessment of this costly and ultimately unprofitable means of improving land transportation, see Abbott, "Plank Road Enthusiasm," 95-116. See also Brant and Fuller, *Vanderburgh County,* 70-82; Posey County Historical Society, *Posey County,* 1; Sesquicentennial Committee, *Rockport-Spencer County Sesquicentennial,* 4-9; and Arnett, *Annals and Scandals,* 115-19.

8. *EWJ,* October 5, 1848, and January 3, 1850; Snepp, *Channels of Trade,* 360-65; Robertson, "Paducah," 116-19. See also Robertson, *Paducah,* 20.

9. *EDJ,* September 21, 1857. See also Federal Writers Project, *Henderson,* 53-57; Charles E. Parrish, "Ohio River," in Kleber, *Kentucky Encyclopedia,* 691; and Fatout, *Indiana Canals,* 22-51

10. Smelser, in "Material Customs," 40, says that all the improvements in southern Illinois—including a bicameral legislature, public education, and county government—were imposed from the outside.

11. See Hunter, *Steamboats,* which is the most thorough study of this subject. Also

valuable are Taylor, *Transportation,* and Ambler, *Transportation in the Ohio Valley.*

12. Mahoney, *River Towns,* esp. 145-279. Mahoney gives each criterion numerical value and totals them, achieving as a result a sort of nineteenth-century "Top Ten" of lower Ohio River places to live. This is misleading and ahistorical, for criteria were not equally important to settlers.

13. Abbott, *Boosters and Businessmen,* 179-80.

14. See, e.g., Conrod, "Limited Growth," 52-56, and Mahoney, *River Towns,* 209-11.

15. Ireland, *County in Kentucky History,* 54-67.

16. Visher, "The Location of Indiana Cities and Towns," 345-46; Clark, *Kentucky,* 278. The Indiana Constitution of 1816 (Art. 11, Sec. 12) forbade the creation of new counties if that reduced the older county or counties to less than four hundred square miles. See Hawkins, *Indiana's Road to Statehood,* 89. Kentucky produced 120 counties—some in the early 1900s. Indiana's last was formed in 1859. Its largest in territory is Allen, with 657 square miles, and its smallest is Ohio, with 87.

17. Ireland, *County in Kentucky History,* 1, 3, 12, 28-36. See also Dew, "County Fever," 14-17.

18. Lantz, *Community in Search of Itself,* 146-69.

19. Sellers, *Market Revolution,* 384-86; Wiebe, *Opening of American Society,* 237-48 and 187-88, and *Self-Rule,* 70-71.

20. See, e.g., *EDJ,* May 8, 1850; Dew, "Whig Party"; Robertson, *Paducah,* 26; and Goodspeed, *Warrick, Spencer, and Perry Counties,* 299-306. A small but impressive body of evidence suggests that infrastructure improvement and community promotion in smaller midwestern towns were seen as inseparable. See, e.g., Ogle, "Beyond the Great City," 48-66. Kentucky's towns are discussed in Share, *Cities in the Commonwealth,* 44-65. See Etcheson, *Emerging Midwest.* She focuses on the degrees of blending of northern "cultural imperialism" and upper southern independence and democracy. Examples abound: log cabin construction, speech, food, religion, and temperament. Milking to southerners was women's work, but to Yankees it was a man's responsibility. The term *Hoosier* is generally regarded as a derisive term for backwoods southerners (4-5, 9). Upland southerners were suspicious of internal improvements and public education, supportive only if direct benefit to localities could be shown (52-54). Memories of planter elites made them fiercely jealous of independence. To them, rights were to be expanded in the face of temperance and land issues but restricted where blacks or foreigners were concerned (63, 84).

21. Robertson, "Paducah," 114-15.

22. See, e.g., Starling, *Henderson County,* 575-817, passim; Federal Writers Project, *Henderson,* 78-87; Ford, *Hancock County, Kentucky, 1850 Census,* 1-50; Robertson, *Paducah,* 12-19, 26; Taylor, *Indiana,* 219-21; and *Hardin County,* 8-24.

23. White, *Evansville,* reveals that thirty of the eighty-three "leaders" of 1873 had been born in the northeastern states. Another eighteen had immigrated from England, Ireland, or Germany. Only nineteen were natives of the Upper South. For discussion of Indianapolis, see Abbott, *Boosters and Businessmen,* 178-82, which relies heavily on Madison, "Businessmen." The *EWJ* of January 17 and 31, 1850, offers vivid illustrations of German impact on the city.

24. Goodspeed, *Posey County,* 367-68; Robertson, *Paducah,* 12-17. See also Sneed, *Ghost Towns,* 8, 164.

25. See, e.g., Vanderburgh County Commissioners record book A, May 13, 1818, 5,

and July 1825, 218, and record book E, September 1838, 115-16. In December 1980, a former student of mine, Rebecca Williams, prepared a list of town ordinances, 1841-47, and abstracted them. Copies are to be found in the city clerk's office in Evansville as well as in special collections at the University of Southern Indiana library.

26. *EWJ,* March 4, 1847, and April 6, 1848; *EDJ,* March 16, 1848, and May 8, 1850. See also Brant and Fuller, *Vanderburgh County,* 129-30. Carpenter, a Democrat, objected strenuously to the terms of the city construction contract, stating that some members of the city council were dupes of the company that was awarded the contract. Marcus Sherwood was one of the company's proprietors.

27. Elliott, *Evansville and Vanderburgh County,* 69-76.

28. City of Evansville, tax assessment book for 1860. This is found in the Vanderburgh County Archives, salvaged in July 1971 by some University of Southern Indiana students and faculty, including the author, from the old city hall, which was razed a few weeks later. The collection is housed at Willard Library.

29. Wormer, *Pope County,* 46.

30. Wade, *Urban Frontier,* 101-28, 203-30.

31. Briggs, *Early History of West Point,* 16-17; Goodspeed, *Warrick, Spencer, and Perry Counties,* 83-88; Clark, *History of Kentucky,* 260-65; Starling, *Henderson County,* 253-74; and Brant and Fuller, *Vanderburgh County,* 315-21.

32. Clark, *History of Kentucky,* 260-65; Darrel E. Bigham, *Album,* 1-14.

33. Clark, *Kentucky,* x, and *History of Kentucky,* 260-65; Starling, *Henderson County,* 195. See also U.S., 7th Census, 1850, *Population Schedules of Daviess County,* National Archives microfilm M432, roll 198, *Kentucky,* 346-55.

34. For a review of cultural development in older river cities, see Wade, *Urban Frontier,* 129-57, 231-69.

35. See especially Hatch, *Democratization,* 193-209. The federal census of 1850 (see *Statistical View,* 632-41, 737-45, and 799-807) offers a denominational count in each of these counties. In Illinois, Alexander County had two Baptist and two Methodist churches; Gallatin County had four Methodist and three Presbyterian churches; Hardin County had six Baptist churches and one Methodist; Massac had two Baptist and three Methodist churches and one Presbyterian; Pope had nine Baptist, eleven Methodist, and eight Presbyterian churches, as well as one Lutheran; and Pulaski County had two Baptist, six Methodist, and two Presbyterian churches, as well as one Catholic and one Lutheran. In Indiana and Kentucky, similar patterns existed. Roman Catholics were most likely to be found in Breckinridge, Daviess, Hardin, McCracken, Meade, and Union Counties in Kentucky as well as Perry, Spencer, and Vanderburgh Counties in Indiana. Evansville, Henderson, Smithland, and Paducah alone had Episcopal congregations.

36. Federal Writers Project, *Cairo Guide,* 55-56; *Sunday Courier and Press,* October 14, 1945; Goodspeed, *Posey County,* 257-58.

37. Goodspeed, *History of Gallatin, . . . Williamson Counties,* 103-48; Burleigh, *Look at Newburgh,* 105-30; Sesquicentennial Committee, *Rockport-Spencer County Sesquicentennial,* 8-9; Potter, *Owensboro and Daviess County,* 52. For a review of the evolution of reformed, evangelical Protestantism, see Conkin, *Uneasy Center.* A comprehensive, encyclopedia approach to religious institutions in Indiana is Rudolph, *Hoosier Faiths.*

38. Lucas, *Slavery to Segregation,* 121, says that blacks generally belonged to white churches before Emancipation. Detailed analysis of river towns would seem appropriate.

The desire for separate churches was strong among most slaves and freedmen. See Raboteau, *Slave Religion,* esp. 151-221.

39. Hardin County Historical and Genealogical Society, *Hardin County,* 8-24; Briggs, *Early History of West Point,* 6-28; Goodspeed, *Posey County,* 369-70; Pleasant, *Crawford County,* 71-138; Robertson, *Paducah,* 12-17; *EDJ,* November 2, 1850; De Bow, *Seventh Census of the United States,* 632-41, 731-37, and 797-98.

40. Pease, *Frontier State,* 30; *EWJ,* September 20, 1849; Madison, *Indiana Way,* 106.

41. Brant and Fuller, *Vanderburgh County,* 223-68; White, *Evansville,* 60-61, 196-97; Iglehart, *Vanderburgh County,* 201-7.

42. Clark, "Public Education," in Kleber, *Kentucky Encyclopedia,* 744; Madison, *Indiana Way,* 110-11; Goodspeed, *Posey County,* 269-72; Pope County Historical Society, *Pope County,* 28-30. For a survey of public education see Buley, *Old Northwest,* 2:326-416.

43. Madison, *Indiana Way,* 112-13.

44. See U.S., 6th Census, 1840, *Compendium of the Enumeration of the Inhabitants and Statistics of the United States* (Washington, 1841), 75, 83, and 87, and De Bow, *Seventh Census of the United States,* 622-23, 721-26, and 784-89.

45. Clark, "Public Education," in Kleber, *Kentucky Encyclopedia,* 745-46; Fischer, *Albion's Seed,* 344-49, 721-27.

46. Madison, *Indiana Way,* 113-14.

47. For a review of the school debate in Evansville, see *EDJ,* beginning with the announcement of August 16, 1853, that free public schools would be opened to all white persons ages five to twenty-one on August 22.

48. Fischer, *Albion's Seed,* 783-859, passim.

6. The Sifting Process Quickens

1. U.S., 10th Census, 1880, *Statistics of the Population of the United States* (Washington, 1883), 56-57, 62-63, 388-89, 392-93, 431-34. See also Thornbrough, *Civil War Era,* 555-61, and Teaford, *Cities of the Heartland,* 48-49. Regional growth rate in Illinois's river counties was 267 percent and in the state 262; Indiana's rates were 121 and 101 percent; and Kentucky's were 91 and 68 percent.

2. U.S., 10th Census, 1880, *Statistics,* 130-59, 189-95; U.S., 14th Census, 1920, *Abstract of the Fourteenth Census of the United States* (Washington, 1923), 27-32.

3. U.S., 10th Census, *Statistics,* 120-59, 189-95.

4. Stover, *Illinois Central Railroad,* 56-56, 74, and Lansden, *City of Cairo,* 162-78; Ferguson, *River and Rail,* 370-88, cited in Sutton, *Prairie State,* 1:355-57.

5. Stover, *Illinois Central Railroad,* 81-84; Lansden, *City of Cairo,* 162-87, 190-207; Federal Writers Project, *Cairo Guide,* 30-34, 47-52; Briggs, "Entertainment," 232-51.

6. May, *Massac County,* 192-95.

7. Collins, *History of Kentucky,* 2:598-600; Sneed, *Ghost Towns,* 61-70, 126-32, 150; Hall, *Hardin County,* 30-57; Hardin County Historical and Genealogical Society, *Hardin County,* 8-24.

8. Page, *Massac County,* 284-87, and May, *Massac County,* 164, 188-92.

9. Stover, *Illinois Central Railroad,* 158-66, and Ballard-Carlisle Historical-Genealogical Society, *Ballard and Carlisle Counties History* 1:371-72.

10. Perrin, *Alexander, Union, and Pulaski Counties,* 503-80; Allen, *Southern Illinois,* 306-7.

11. De La Hunt, *Perry County*, 184-203; *Tell City News*, centennial supplement, August 8, 1958; Taylor, *Indiana*, 222-23; centennial pamphlet, Tell City Chair Company (n.p., 1965[?]), 4, 6 (Indiana Historical Society Library). This proud company, the town's largest, came to an end in the fall of 1996 after labor-management disputes, among other things, led to bankruptcy earlier in the year.

12. Lucas, *Slavery to Segregation*, 160, 323-24; Howard, *Black Liberation*, 29-71.

13. Lucas, *Slavery to Segregation*, xix-xx, 5. Slave populations ranged in 1860 from 10.7 percent in Crittenden County to 40.4 in Henderson. See also U.S., 8th Census, 1860, *Statistics of the Population of the United States* (Washington, 1864), 5-8, 61, 88-101, 113-27, 182-83. Data for the town of Henderson was in 1860 was not provided in the federal census.

14. U.S., 8th Census, 1860, *Slave Schedules, Kentucky,* National Archives microfilm M652, roll 402, *Daviess County*, 383-425; roll 403, *Henderson County*, 139-76; and roll 404, *Union County*, 400-429.

15. See Bigham, *Fair Trial,* 21-36, for population trends there before 1900. Only the data for larger towns and cities was provided in the printed census. Cursory analysis of the population schedules of Mound City, Metropolis, Mount Vernon, Newburgh, and Rockport reveals that almost all of their counties' blacks resided in towns. George W. May discusses the impact of black newcomers in Metropolis in *Massac County,* 99-101, and *History Papers of Massac County,* 20-32.

16. See Lucas, *Slavery to Segregation*, esp. 181, 186, 194-95, 204, 242, and 244; and Howard, *Black Liberation*, 72-176. Data about black populations in Kentucky in the period from 1870 to 1880 are provided in U.S., 10th Census, 1880, *Statistics,* 130—59, 185-95, 417-18, 448.

17. Bodnar provides an able overview in *Transplanted.* See also U.S., 10th Census, 1880, *Statistics,* 56-57, 62-63, 388-89, 392-93, 431-34.

18. U.S., 10th Census, 1880, *Statistics of the Population of the United States* (Washington, 1883), 504-6, 509-11.

19. Goldfield and Brownell, *Urban America,* 16-18, 198-200; Chudacoff and Smith, *Evolution of American Urban Society,* 37-53; Teaford, *Cities of the Heartland,* 48-71; Schockel, "Manufactural Evansville," 62-64.

20. Goldfield, *Cotton Fields and Skyscrapers,* 80-132.

7. People and Products

1. See Thornbrough, *Civil War Era,* 318-460, for a thorough account of economic growth and development. See also Bogle, "Railroad Building in Indiana," 211-31.

2. Much of this is based on Hunter, *Steamboats,* 500-503, 660, and Snepp, *Channels of Trade,* 334-36, 364-67. The *EDJ,* January 20, 22, and 29, 1857, offers details on the volume of trade at the newly created Port of Evansville. A board of trade had recently been organized to collect such information and to promote the city's commercial outreach. One example of the "River Intelligence" column is in the *EDJ,* June 3, 1872. The piece noted that in the previous three days the river had fallen five inches and that large steamers would find navigation difficult thence to Louisville and Cairo because the channel was less than nine feet deep. It reported the arrivals and departures of vessels since the first listed boats due that day and added that the famous low-pressure *Quickstep* (of the Evansville, Cairo, and Memphis line) departed at 5 P.M. for Cairo. The column offered

news about a stabbing on an in-bound steamboat, listed well-to-do passengers departing that day, observed that one ship had attached several barges loaded with iron ore, and chided city fathers for not removing cottonwoods on the sandbar across from the wharf which, if not removed, would produce a towhead.

3. Snepp, *Channels of Trade*, 365-69; and Schockel, "Manufactural Evansville," 31-81. Conrod, "Limited Growth," 214-31, and Lipin, *Producers*, 77-111, rely heavily on Snepp and Schockel.

4. For a review of the lower Ohio's apparent advantages, see Conrod, "Limited Growth," 51-59. See Mahoney, *River Towns*, 214-72, for a discussion of the emergence of the regional system upriver from St. Louis.

5. See, e.g., Page, *Massac County*, 192-95; Goodspeed, *Warrick, Spencer, and Perry Counties*, 368-71; and Fohs Hall Community Arts Foundation, *Crittenden County, Kentucky*, 12-14.

6. See, e.g., Briggs, *Early History of West Point*, 33-44, 65-92; Goodspeed, *History of Gallatin, ... Williamson Counties*, 92-102; Watts, *Chronicles of a Kentucky Settlement*, 480-82.

7. Federal Writers Project, *Union County*, 150-56, 168-70; O'Malley, *History of Union County*, 509-620, passim; George B. Simpson, comp., *Caseyville River Merchant Trade and Sale Records for 1854 and 1855 and the Tradewater Valley Farmers, Planters, and Miners* (Sturgis, Ky., 1988), 2:515-17; and *An Illustrated Historical Atlas of Henderson and Union Counties, Kentucky* (1880; reprint, Evansville, 1969), 4, 17-21.

8. *The Biographical Review of Johnson, Massac, Pope, and Hardin Counties, Illinois* (Chicago, 1893), 199-200; Pope County Historical Society, *Pope County*, 58-59; O'Malley, *Union County*, 526-27; *Biographical Cyclopedia*, 1-49; Conrod, "Limited Growth," 70-79. The biographical sketches in the two works cited above provide numerous examples of mobility patterns among business and civic leaders. Illustrative of Mount Vernon's dependence on Evansville is Leonard, *Posey County*.

9. See, e.g., Dew and Dew, *Owensboro*, 78-79, 99-105, and Gilbert, *Evansville and Vanderburg [sic] County*.

10. See, e.g., *EDJ*, November 4, 1857, August 1, 1860, May 16, 1866, March 11, 1868, and July 17 and 22, 1868. The November 4, 1857, article noted presciently that New Albany's economy rested on boat building and jobbing in the region and that it was increasingly in the shadow of Louisville. The August 1, 1860, article illustrated the importance of long-term business connections, as "River Items" contained news of river and business conditions all the way to Pittsburgh and printed business cards from persons in Louisville, Cincinnati, and New Orleans. Thornbrough, *Civil War Era*, 555-61, discusses population changes in these years. New Albany, which was the largest city in Indiana in 1850, grew to nearly 13,000 in 1860, but Indianapolis surpassed it with about 18,000. Thereafter, due largely to Louisville's superior trade and communications, New Albany's growth was slow, and the city reached slightly more than 16,000 in 1880. By then Indianapolis had 75,056 residents and Evansville had 29,280. Fort Wayne and Terre Haute also had overtaken New Albany, and Lafayette, South Bend, and Richmond were about to do the same thing. For a comparison of the Evansville and New Albany economies, see Lipin, *Producers*, chapters 2, 4, and 7. References to lower river valley predominance and false claims in St. Louis are found in the *EDJ*, May 28, 1872, and January 7, 1873.

11. Secretary of the Interior, *Manufactures of the United States in 1860; Compiled for*

the Original Returns of the Eighth Census (Washington, 1865), 3-113, 117-40, 168-93; Census Office, Department of the Interior, *Compendium of the Tenth Census(June 1, 1880)* . . . (Washington, 1883), part 1: 696-700, 704-6, 761-62, 772-77, and part 2: 960-61, 913-65, 971-73.

12. See, e.g., Perrin, *Alexander, Pulaski, and Union Counties,* 503-51; Page, *Massac County,* 128-37; Robertson, *Paducah,* 14-28; Dew, "Hawesville," *Kentucky Encyclopedia,* 419; *EDJ,* June 14, 1854, April 9, 1855, and September 28, 1858. Bodiam Mine received tangible support from local government: permission to tunnel under city streets and a five-year exemption from taxes. The demand for coal resulted from its expanded supply following the extension of rail connections into coal fields, lowered resistance to its use by those who once considered its odor and by-products unattractive, and the dwindling supply and increased price of wood.

13. Page, *Massac County,* 128-37; De La Hunt, *Perry County,* 258-67; Holzborg and Preflatish, *Crawford County,* 56-64; Goodspeed, *Warrick, Spencer, and Perry Counties,* 668-79; Federal Writers Project, *Union County,* 67-69.

14. Starling, *Henderson County,* 276-77; Federal Writers Project, *Henderson,* 53-57; [Boulware], *Daviess County,* 358; McCracken County Genealogical Society, *History and Families,* 29-30; Conrod, "Limited Growth," 249-60; Battle, Perrin, Kniffin, *Kentucky,* 94-97.

15. Snepp, *Channels of Trade,* 327-28; Schockel, "Manufactural Evansville," 118, 234-38. Both rely heavily on Foster, *Board of Trade.*

16. Schockel, "Manufactural Evansville," 4-5, 91-92, 125-30, 207-10. See also Snepp, *Channels of Trade,* 328, and Lipin, *Producers,* 100.

17. Snepp, *Channels of Trade,* 328-33, 365-70; Schockel, "Manufactural Evansville," 118; Goodspeed, *Warrick, Spencer, and Perry Counties,* 668-76.

18. Snepp, *Channels of Trade,* 341-60. See *EDJ,* January 22, 1855, November 13, 1856, August 5-26, 1857, March 17-31, 1859, September 8, 1860, and June 18, 1863. See also Gray, *Transportation,* 113-34.

19. For the steamboat's impact on Ohio River communities before 1860, see Taylor, *Transportation,* 153-75. The Rockport notice is found in Bennett and McCord, *Progress after Statehood,* 484-85. The *Louisville* was 235 feet long and 38 feet wide. Drawing only three feet of water, it boasted five boilers, each of which was 28 feet long. One of its water wheels was 30 feet in diameter. Perhaps its being built in New Albany, like many other larger craft, contributed to the Rockport notice. No packet service originated at Owensboro. See Dew, "Owensboro's River Trade," 27-37; Huff, "Steamboat Trades," 27-36.

20. See Hunter, *Steamboats,* 333, 639. Large cities usually offered two to three boats weekly to smaller communities. The Louisville and Evansville packet was one of the most durable, lasting until ca. 1909. An extremely valuable collection of newspaper clippings is Miller, "Steamboat Clippings," This unpublished three-volume collection has been preserved by Willard Library in Evansville, and John W. Powell edited it in 1994. The January 6 and 19 and August 6, 1857 articles in the *EDJ* are found in 2:1-17.

21. Pope County Historical Society, *Pope County,* 58-59. Similar experiences are recorded in many other communities. See, e.g., May, *Massac County,* 160-62, and Dew, *Shaping Our Society,* 5-15.

22. Foster's *Annual Report of the Board of Trade for Evansville for 1867,* 59, states that the number of steamboat arrivals at Evansville between January 1, 1861, and December

31, 1867 increased from 1,493 in 1861 to 2,097 in 1867. The peak year was 1865, with 2,572 arrivals. In 1873, more than 2,500 steamboats docked at Evansville, and 60 craft were registered there. Consult Lee Burns, "The Ohio River, Its Influence on the Development of Indiana," *IMH* 19 (June 1923): 180. Cairo's steamboat arrivals were 4,274 in 1873, but dropped steadily thereafter, with the exception of 1880, when 4,280 boats arrived. In 1886 the total was 2,868. Tonnage also declined, but more modestly, from 1.5 to 1.1 million tons. See Conrod, "Limited Growth," 106.

23. *EDJ*, September 21, 1857. See also Thornbrough, *Civil War Era*, 9-10; Thomas, *Lee*, 86-112, describes Lee's four years as an army engineer at St. Louis (1836-40) and his frustrations when attempting to improve river transportation with limited and capricious funding. Mahoney, *River Towns*, 209-42, discusses the effect that improved river travel had on efforts to ameliorate travel on land.

24. *EDJ*, May 15, 1866, September 10, 1867, July 17 and September 22, 1868, and January 1, 1872. Possibly due to the politics of city government, the *Journal* editor in 1872 said that businessmen interested in the river, not city government, should fund their trip. The author has found no evidence of leaders from other lower Ohio communities forming such advocacy groups or participating in Ohio River conventions. Possibly the first was the initial meeting of the Ohio Valley Improvement Association, held October 8-9, 1895, in Pittsburgh, to which Cairo and Paducah sent one delegate each. Evansville sent seven (and Louisville eleven). No other lower Ohio community was represented. See Ohio Valley Improvement Association, *Official Program and History: Dedicatory Celebration of the Completion of the Nine Foot State from Pittsburgh to Cairo, October 19-23, 1929* (N.p., [1929]), 37, 65-66.

25. Snepp, *Channels of Trade*, 362.

26. Starling, *Henderson County*, 315-28, 363-65. The E&C was rechartered as the Evansville and Terre Haute in 1877. In 1911 the Chicago and Eastern Illinois Railroad system acquired control of it as well as the Evansville Belt Railroad. Carpenter's account of the affair is found in *Biographical History of Eminent and Self-Made Men of the State of Indiana* (Cincinnati, 1880), 1:12-15. Critical points in the Straight Line's history are found in *EDJ*, May 15, 1851, April 19 and 22, 1853, July 29 and November 18 through December 14, 1854, April 16, 1855, September 13 and October 30, 1856, February 7, April 27-29, July 9-14, and September 2-13, 1857, April 14 and 27 and May 5, 1858, January 18 and March 14-19, 1859, and May 7 and 9, 1860. Efforts to revive the project after the war were abortive. See Klein, *L&N Railroad*, 104, and in Kleber, *Kentucky Encyclopedia*, 432. See also Bogle, "Railroad Building," 221-31. Although promoters in Evansville, Jeffersonville, Madison, and other river cities visualized themselves as tapping the valuable Indiana hinterland, ultimately the larger cities on the edge of the state—Cincinnati, Toledo, Louisville, Cleveland, and especially Chicago—exerted the greatest pull.

27. Neuman, *Story of Paducah*, 144-51; Robertson, "Paducah," 116-19, and *Paducah*, 20-21; Collins, *History of Kentucky*, 1:211. Mound City, Illinois, "took off" in part because speculators assumed that the Mobile and Ohio would terminate across the river. Paducah's sandbar and flooding apparently contributed to its not being selected as the terminus.

28. *Elizabethtown [Ky.] News*, September 24, 1940; Briggs, *Early History of West Point*, 49-58.

29. Lansden, *City of Cairo*, 220-30; Perrin, *Alexander, Union, and Pulaski Counties*, 195-220; Stover, *Illinois Central Railroad*, 149; Klein, *L&N Railroad*, 201.

30. Goodspeed, *History of Gallatin, . . . Williamson Counties*, 13-77.

31. *EDJ*, July 20, 1867, and March 13, 1871; Klein, *L&N Railroad*, 101-5, 111, 138, 154-59; Starling, *Henderson County*, 315-28.

32. *EDJ*, July 14, 1869, and October 14, 1882; U.S., 10th Census, 1880, *Report on the Agencies of Transportation in the United States* (Washington, 1883), 158-63, 188-93, 194-99. The E&TH's net earnings during the 1879-1880 fiscal year were $199,000 (on gross earnings of $698,000). The related Evansville, Terre Haute, and Chicago line had net earnings of $128,000 (on gross earnings of $292,000). By contrast, the Cairo and St. Louis lost $76,000, and Memphis, Paducah, and Northern lost $1,400. The Owensboro and Nashville also lost money. The Cairo and Vincennes earned a modest $15,000 (on gross income of $343,000). Only the Elizabethtown and Paducah came close to the Evansville line, with net income of $97,000 and gross income of $395,000. Railroad development was second only to river news in importance to the editor of the *EDJ*. Illustrative of the promotion of sometimes ill-fated initiatives was the case of the Jackson (Tennessee) and Evansville. See the issues of April 27, May 7, 8, 15, 21 and June 28, 1872, for instance.

33. *EDJ*, July 30, 1867, January 13, 1869, and October 23, 1871; Fortune, *Warrick*, 22.

34. *EDJ*, April 30 and May 1, 1866, and July 9 and September 8, 1869. Another "white knight" appeared in March 1872, but nothing came of his efforts. See *EDJ*, March 30, 1872.

35. Leonard, *Posey County*, 68-69, and Goodspeed, *Posey County*, 374-78.

36. *Rockport-Spencer County Sesquicentennial*, 4-9; Baertich, *History of Troy, Indiana*, 36-41; De La Hunt, *Perry County*, 310-16. Perry County residents had first promoted a rail line to Nashville through Hawesville in the 1850s, but nothing came of that. The first election on public subscription came in 1871, when Cannelton and Tell City voted against each other and the measure was defeated. Voters approved aid for a line between Newburgh and English, via Leopold, a year later, but the road was not constructed. Lacking rail lines and fearing encirclement, Cannelton and Tell City secured new charters in 1886, and as cities they were able to offer public funds for railroads. The first train arrived in Perry County in January 1888.

37. Pleasant, *Crawford County*, 307-463; Thornbrough, *Civil War Era*, 351.

38. Collins, *History of Kentucky*, 1:211; [Boulware,] *Daviess County*, 101-5; Share, *Cities in the Commonwealth*, 68-74. In November 1871, the president of the Elizabethtown and Paducah sold $450,000 of its bonds to a financial house in Amsterdam at 87.25 cents on the dollar, plus interest. In February 1873, the legislature—reluctant to fund transportation projects—allowed Louisville to subscribe an additional $1 million in stock to that line. Paducah was permitted a month later to subscribe $200,000 to the Paducah and North Eastern Railroad, a line which was not developed, although rail connections to Brooklyn and Metropolis were secured in the 1880s. See Collins, 1:195, 220, 240, 245. Some towns and counties also aided railroad companies by loans and donations of property. The Commonwealth was prohibited from directly aiding railroads, but its legislature offered liberal charters and some tax exemptions. In return, some lines were required to offer lower rates on some commodities. See Charles B. Castner, "Railroads," in Kleber, *Kentucky Encyclopedia*, 753.

39. Cited in Dew, "Owensboro's Dream of Glory," 26-27. See also Share, *Cities in the Commonwealth*, 68-71, and Huff, "Steamboat Trades."

40. Klein, *L&N Railroad*, 153-54, 182, 191, 277, 335, 398, and 405; Dew, "Owensboro's

Dream of Glory," 42-45. The O&N was a separate line controlled by the L&N until much later, when it was absorbed into the L&N system and the company was dissolved in 1936. Pettit's dream of an east-west road connecting Henderson and Louisville, through Owensboro, was realized in the late 1880s, when the St. Louis, Louisville, and Texas—which never reached St. Louis or Texas—opened service. The L&N acquired control of it in 1905. Klein, 241 and 257, discusses the L&N's role in Paducah in the 1880s and afterwards, and Stover, *Illinois Central Railroad*, 202, 229-30, 291-92, reviews that line's activities in Paducah in the same period.

41. Schockel, "Manufactural Evansville," 10-12; Conrod, "Limited Growth," 190-210; Vanderburgh County miscellaneous papers, box 1, Indiana Historical Society.

42. *EDJ*, May 8, 1867, March 11 and August 17, 1868, and May 19, 1870. The February 26, 1872, issue listed six daily rail departures and six arrivals and seven daily to weekly packets.

43. For the relationship between river and rail transport, see Ambler, *Transportation*, 264-94, and Hunter, *Steamboats*, 602-5. See also *EDJ*, January 15, 1869.

44. Whether the war accelerated or retarded industrial growth remains a hotly debated historiographical issue. Still valuable is Barnhart, "Impact of the Civil War," 183-224.

45. A reliable introduction to the western border question is Nevins, *War for the Union*, 119-36. See also Thornbrough, *Civil War Era*, 85-123; Clark, *History of Kentucky*, 319-58; Lowell H. Harrison, *Civil War in Kentucky*, esp. 80-106; Cole, *Civil War*, 279; and Cross, "Civil War Comes to 'Egypt,'" 160-98. The centrality of the community as the fundamental unit of the Civil War experience is stressed persuasively in Paludan, *"People's Contest,"* 3-33. Mitchell, *Vacant Chair*, emphasizes the role that images of home and family shaped the Union soldier's approach to service. Lincoln's strategic thinking is best discussed in Neely, *Last Best Hope*, esp. 59-92.

46. See especially Clark, *Kentucky*, 126-29, 141, and *History of Kentucky*, 319-58; Lee, *Brief History of Kentucky*, 67-80; Harrison, *Civil War in Kentucky*, 80-106.

47. Thompson, *Breckinridge County*, 82, 84; Collins, *History of Kentucky*, 2:146-50, "Crittenden County," 241; Dew, "Owensboro," 700; Bryant, "Brandenburg," 113, "Smithland," 832, and "Union County," 908; Livingston County Historical Society, *Livingston County*, 1:39; Federal Writers Project, *Union County*, 156; Lee, *Brief History of Kentucky*, 545; and Heady, *Union County*, 13.

48. Clinton, "Social and Educational History," 37-38; Dew, *Shaping Our Society*, 23-32; Hodges, *Fearful Times*, 5-6, 10-13, 25-28, 74, 80. Hodges offers a rare study of a Kentucky community's experience during the war. Most references focus on military service and generally demean African Americans, especially their service in the Union army. Hodges's work is guilty of this, too.

49. Cited in Arnett, *Annals and Scandals*, 54. See also Starling, *Henderson County*, 193-238, 315-28; Federal Writers Project, *Henderson*, 37-43.

50. [Boulware,] *Daviess County*, 158-78; Potter, *Owensboro and Daviess County*, 81-85; Dew and Dew, *Owensboro*, 42-64.

51. Robertson, *Paducah*, 29-65, and "Paducah," 120-29; Neuman, *Story of Paducah*, 128-40; Long, "Paducah Affair," 269-74.

52. See Lucas, *Slavery to Segregation*, 146-209; and Howard, *Black Liberation*, 29-176. See also *Owensboro Messenger and Inquirer*, September 7, 1992. For an introduction to experiences in Evansville, see Bigham, *Fair Trial*, 16-24.

53. Henderson's population was not listed in the 1860 census. It was 1,775 in 1850 and 4,171 in 1870. Owensboro's population rose from 2,308 to 3,437 in the 1860s, and Paducah grew from a population of 4,590 to 6,866. In 1880, value of manufactures was lower than $100,000 in five Kentucky couunties. Ewan had capitalization of less than $125,000. By contrast, on the north shore, only Hardin produced less than $100,000 in goods, and just four counties in Illinois and Indiana had less than $165,000 in manufacturing capital. See U.S., 10th Census, 1880, *Compendium,* part 1: 696-700, 704-6, 761-62, 764-67, 772-77, part 2: 960-61, 963-65, 971-73; U.S., 10th Census, 1880, *Statistics,* 130-59, 189-95.

54. See, e.g., *EDJ,* May 8 and September 10, 1867, as well as Snepp, *Channels of Trade,* 332-39. For a discussion of the war's economic impact on Kentucky, see Thomas D. Clark, "Kentucky: A Historical Overview," in Kleber, *Kentucky Encyclopedia,* xxv-xxvi.

55. Starling, *Henderson County,* 329-32; *An Illustrated Historical Atlas of Henderson and Union Counties;* Dew and Dew, *Owensboro,* 65-80; and Robertson, *Paducah,* 66-84, 100-108; [Boulware,] *Daviess County,* 335-58.

56. Miller, "Steamboats," 359-81; Jackson, "Civil War Newburgh," 167-84; Hodges, *Fearful Times,* 10, 24; Thornbrough, *Civil War Era,* 337, 418-19. After the war, Paducah paid the Evansville packet company $30,000 for damages to the *Samuel Orr* (Robertson, *Paducah,* 66-67).

57. De La Hunt, *Perry County,* 258-87; Goodspeed, *Warrick, Spencer, and Perry Counties,* 676-82; *EDJ,* December 9, 1864, and January 26 and February 28, 1865.

58. Snepp, *Channels of Trade,* 365-70, 379-81; Conrod, "Limited Growth," 203; *EDJ,* July 14, 1863, and September 29 and October 19 and 30, 1865; Iglehart, *Vanderburgh County,* 96-98. Snepp, 337-40, offers a synopsis of the military activities affecting the city.

59. Schockel, "Manufactural Evansville," 234-38; Brant and Fuller, *Vanderburgh County,* 213-15; *EP,* August 29, 1995; *EDJ,* October 3, 1866.

60. Gilbert, *Evansville,* 1:125-26, 128-32; Snepp, *Channels of Trade,* 369; *EDJ,* December 10, 1862; Schockel, "Manufactural Evansville," 28, 64-65, 106-14, 207-10, 217-18.

61. Quoted in Pitkin, "When Cairo Was Saved," 305. See Lansden, *City of Cairo,* 128-37; Federal Writers Project, *Cairo Guide,* 34-39; Stover, *Illinois Central Railroad,* 85-107; Merrill, "Cairo, Illinois," 242-56. Control of the flotilla passed to the navy in October 1862, and David Dixon Porter was named commander of the Mississippi Squadron and given responsibility for the Mississippi and its tributaries north of Vicksburg. Porter, who had an office in Cairo, planned the Vicksburg campaign there with Grant. See Merrill, 254, 256. The overwhelming support of the Union, shown by the huge numbers of men from "Egypt" who served in the Union army, most of them Democrats, is ably documented in Cross, "Civil War Comes to 'Egypt,'" 160-69. Major General John A. Logan's leadership was a major factor. Metropolis's support for the Union—and its wartime shift to the Republican Party—is traceable to the efforts of attorney Green B. Raum. See May, *Massac County,* 31-42.

62. Merrill, "Cairo, Illinois," 243, 252, 256; Perrin, *Alexander, Union, and Pulaski Counties,* 549-60; and Howard, *Illinois,* 302.

63. Paludan, *"People's Contest,"* 376 and 378.

64. Nevins, *War for the Union,* 392-94.

65. As noted earlier, only Daviess and McCracken Counties across the river compared favorably with the leading north shore counties. See U.S., 10th Census, 1880, *Compendium,* part 1: 696-700, 704-6, 761-62, 764-67, 772-77, part 2: 960-61, 963-65, 971-73.

66. *An Illustrated Historical Atlas of Spencer County, Indiana* (Chicago, 1879), 60-61.

67. U.S., 10th Census, 1880, *Census of Manufactures,* 211, 247, and Volume 19, *Social Statistics,* part 2: 443.

68. Cole, *Civil War,* 353. Perrin, *Alexander, Union, and Pulaski Counties,* 217-20, portrays the Civil War as a liability for Cairo. See also Federal Writers Project, *Cairo Guide,* 58-60, and Keiser, *Building for the Centuries,* 10-11, for accounts of Cairo's growth. Mark Twain's comments are in chapter 25 of *Life on the Mississippi* (New York, 1883).

69. Lansden, *City of Cairo,* 280-86; Cole, *Civil War,* 351-53; Conrod, "Limited Growth," 107-21; Keiser, *Building for the Centuries,* 10-11. Steamboat arrivals declined from 4,105 to 2,868 in 1886, rising above 3,800 only in 1873 and 1880. Tonnage also declined from 1,500,000 tons in 1872 to 1,100 in 1886.

70. Perrin, *Alexander, Union, and Pulaski Counties,* 167, 217-20.

71. See, e.g., ibid., 549-60; Keiser, *Building for the Centuries,* 10-12; May, *Massac County,* 80-88, 160-62; Pope County Historical Society, *Pope County,* 58-59; Goodspeed, *History of Gallatin, . . . Williamson Counties,* 92-148; Leonard, *Posey County.*

72. Goldfield and Brownell, *Urban America,* 15-18.

73. See, e.g., *EDJ,* May 28, 1865; July 21, 1866; May 8 and September 10, 1867, July 17 and November 7, 1868, and January 15, February 5, and July 15, 1869.

74. White, *Evansville,* 25-29, and Iglehart, *Vanderburgh County,* 243-46. Incomes reported to the Internal Revenue Assessor for 1865 are found in *EDJ,* July 18, 1866. Reitz's income was about $12,000, well behind Samuel Orr's $16,022 and Samuel Bayard's $12,535. David J. Mackey's $47,653 placed him fourth from the top. John Ingle Jr.'s income was about $6,200, and longtime attorney and reformer H.Q. Wheeler earned $8,455 in 1865.

75. Lipin, *Producers,* 85-87; *EDJ,* October 3, 1866, and July 16, 1869. Data for Evansville manufacturing is found in U.S., 10th Census, 1880, *Compendium,* part 2: 963-65.

76. White, *Evansville,* 84-86, 203-6; Brant and Fuller, *Vanderburgh County,* 147-64, 400-401. Ingle's death is noted in *EDJ,* October 5, 1875. Orr died in 1882. In the last tax assessment before the Civil War, Archer and Mackey Company owned property valued at $28,250—an impressive amount, but well below such notables as Robert Barnes and Charles Viele, who were each worth slightly over $75,000. The Bement and Viele wholesale firm was valued at another $65,000. See City of Evansville tax assessment roll for 1860, Willard Library. In the first postwar report of income to the federal government, printed in the *EDJ* of July 18, 1866, Mackey's $47,653 was only slightly below Viele's $50,441. See Klingler, *City Founded to Make Money,* 33-40.

77. Robert, *Evansville,* 42, 66. See also 9-11, 23, and 31-42. The work was published by the *EC.*

78. Brant and Fuller, *Vanderburgh County,* 207-12, 558-71; *EDJ,* November 19, 1866, January 21, 1868, and January 26, 1869; and Board of Trade, *Industries of Evansville.* The German daily commenced in 1864, and the *Courier*—Democratic in politics—in 1865. The largest bank, Evansville National, the former branch of the state banking system, was renamed Old National in 1883. W.J. Lowry was its president after the war, followed by Samuel Bayard. Its directors included John Gilbert, Robert K. Dunkerson, Mackey, and Heilman. The presidents of First National Bank (the former Canal Bank and later named National City) were H.Q. Wheeler, John S. Hopkins, John Ingle Jr., and Charles Viele, in order. John A. Reitz was a director. The Merchants National Bank, formed in 1865 by Reitz, Gilbert, and wholesale baron C.R. Bement, lasted until 1885. Bement was presi-

dent. Samuel Orr was the first president of the German National Bank (1873), whose incorporators included Reitz, Bayard, and Dunkerson; Reitz succeeded him in 1883. The Citizens National Bank (1873) had S.P. Gillette as president. Lesser-known merchants and industrialists predominated, many of whom were German Americans, such as L. Lowenthal and F.W. Cook. See also U.S., 10th Census, 1880, *Report on the Social Statistics of Cities,* vol. 2: *The Southern and Western States* (Washington, 1887), 437-43.

79. Lipin, *Producers,* 94, 107-8; *EDJ,* October 23, 1865. Lipin's work, although offering valuable detail on the Evansville economy of the mid to late nineteenth century (see esp. 112-78) is driven by producerist theory—that the republican ideal of self-reliant, autonomous workers was assaulted by market capitalism, thus creating class consciousness and conflict. Ideology prevails—a sort of cookie-cutter approach that subordinates fact to theory. Hence Germans are treated as a fairly homogeneous group, "less artisanal" (110) than their New Albany counterparts, and well along "the road to proletarianization" (111). They are also portrayed as Democratic in politics and heavily Catholic in religious affiliation. The fact that many Germans—employers and workers—were Evangelicals and Republicans is overlooked, as is the fact that about half of the workers in 1880 had no German roots.

80. See Lipin, *Producers,* 81-82, 87-88; City of Evansville tax assessment roll for 1860; *EDJ,* July 18, 1866, and July 9, 1869. Lipin uses $20,000 as a criterion for 1870 in order to adjust for wartime inflation.

81. *EDJ,* August 10, 1855; Brant and Fuller, *Vanderburgh County,* 207-12.

82. Ambler, *Transportation,* 264-94.

8. Government, Society, and Culture

1. U.S., 10th Census, 1880, *Compendium,* 1536-38, 1543-46, 1596-1607, and Volume 7: *Report on Valuation, Taxation, and Public Indebtedness* (Washington, 1884), 760, 817-40.

2. Dew, "County Fever," 14, 16-17.

3. Clark, *History of Kentucky,* 16-18; Ireland, *County in Kentucky History,* 28-36, 54-83; Share, *Cities in the Commonwealth,* 44-65; Goldfield, *Cotton Fields and Skyscrapers,* 80-132; J. Allen Singleton, "Highway Development," in Kleber, *Kentucky Encyclopedia,* 429-30. For a review of late-nineteenth-century politics see Tapp and Klotter, *Kentucky.* This study, unfortunately, contains scant reference to events in western Kentucky.

4. Madison, *Indiana Way,* 193-215. This work reflects the pioneering studies of midwestern politics by Melvyn Hammarberg, Richard Jensen, and Paul Kleppner. For discussion of Democrats' appeal to wage earners, see Lipin, *Producers,* 147-78. For southern Illinois's penchant for provincial and petty politics, see Tenney, "Future of Southern Illinois," 172-78, and Brownell, *Other Illinois,* 3-5, 14-15, 254-61.

5. Madison, *Indiana Way,* 215, 218. This is based on Hyneman, Hofstetter, O'Connor, *Voting in Indiana.*

6. Shirley Postwood, "Blacks and the Republican Party in Alexander and Pulaski Counties, 1870-1900," paper delivered at the Organization of American Historians, Washington, D.C., March 31, 1995; Carrier, *Illinois,* May, *Massac County,* 99-101; Goodspeed, *Gallatin, . . . Williamson Counties,* 103-48; Goodspeed, *Warrick, Spencer, and Perry Counties,* 299-306, 608-11; *Evansville Revised Ordinances, 1901,* 440-65.

7. Goldfield and Brownell, *Urban America,* 166-97; Monkkonen, *America Becomes Urban,* 89-126, 141-43; and Rosenberg, *Cholera Years,* 5-6.

8. Madison, *Indiana Way,* 176.

9. Thornbrough, *Civil War Era,* 562. Unfortunately, the major state histories of this era in Illinois and Kentucky do not examine urban powers and services. Share's *Cities in the Commonwealth* offers a broad discussion of the matter.

10. Madison, *Indiana Way,* 176; Evansville Common Council minutes, August 18, 1865, March 19, 1866, and July 13, 1874 (Vanderburgh County Archives, Willard Library); *Revised Ordinances of the City of Evansville, Indiana* (Evansville, 1901), 56-58.

11. Thornbrough, *Civil War Era,* 569; U.S., 10th Census, 1880, *Report on the Social Statistics of Cities,* vol. 2: *The Southern and Western States* (Washington, 1887), 440; and Brant and Fuller, *History of Vanderburgh County,* 184-206. Only Fort Wayne and Evansville had municipal water systems. New Albany boasted the largest area of macadamized streets, but in 1880 only twenty-seven miles were paved. That was second only to Indianapolis's forty-five, and well above Fort Wayne's seven. The most catastrophic fire to date was reported in the *EDJ* of July 10-11, 1867. A conflagration in a chair factory near Market and John streets destroyed the factory and several nearby buildings. Willard Carpenter's nearby mansion was afire several times.

12. Thornbrough, *Civil War Era,* 569-71; Brant and Fuller, *Vanderburgh County,* 184-206; *EDJ,* January 19, 1864. See also *EDJ* February 22 and 27, 1868, and October 9, 1871, the latter of which provided the first schedule of lamp lighting and extinguishing.

13. Evansville Town Board, minute book 1841-1847, city clerk's office, City of Evansville. See, e.g., ordinances of January 29, 1842 and January 28, 1843. An abstract of this record was prepared by a former student, Rebecca G. Williams, in December 1980, and is on file in special collections at the University of Southern Indiana library. Editorial commentary on the menace of hogs is especially pointed in *EDJ,* June 19 and 28, 1872. Hogs devoured dead horses and other castaway flesh and made wallows even in respectable districts near the Episcopal Church. See Elliott A. Riggs's vivid account of "A Hog Drive to Evansville, 1879," *Ohio Valley Folk Research Project,* n.s., no. 46 (1960): 1-6.

14. Thornbrough, *Civil War Era,* 571-72; *EWJ,* July 18, 1860; *EDJ,* November 3, 1860, March 28, 1862, October 24, 1863, and February 26, 1865. *Report on the Social Statistics of Cities,* 2:441, noted that Evansville had an extensive system of sewers, but totals were not furnished the Census Bureau; municipal cleansing is reviewed on 2:442. The first sewers were constructed on Division Street in 1854. See *EDJ,* December 14, 1872, for a review of infrastructure improvements since 1860.

15. *EDJ,* August 24, 1866, March 20 and November 27, 1867, December 8 and 9, 1868, and June 7, 1869. See also Thornbrough, *Civil War Era,* 572-73.

16. U.S., 10th Census, 1880, *Social Statistics of Cities,* 2:441-42; *EDJ,* September 16, 1869. The politicizing of the health department remained a perennial problem in Evansville, reaching its apogee under Mayor Manson Reichert in the 1940s. See, for instance, *EC,* November 15, 1943.

17. Thornbrough, *Civil War Era,* 573-74; U.S., 10th Census, 1880, *Social Statistics of Cities,* 2:440; *EDJ,* April 12, May 31, June 5-6, 1866, December 8 and 11, 1867, and February 1, October 25, and November 20, 1869. A history of street railways is provided in *EJN,* May 1, 1921.

18. Elliott, *Evansville,* 223; Thornbrough, *Civil War Era,* 581-82.

19. Brant and Fuller, *Vanderburgh County*, 305-6.

20. White, *Evansville*, 379-82, and *EDJ*, February 1, 1868, and May 10, 1871. See also Thornbrough, *Civil War Era*, 583.

21. Brant and Fuller, *Vanderburgh County*, 200-205; U.S., 10th Census, 1880, *Social Statistics of Cities*, 2:440-41; *EDJ*, April 5, 1865, September 8 and 13, 1868, and May 18, 1869.

22. Leonard, *Posey County*, 92-93; Goodspeed, *History of Posey County*, 374, 376; *Rockport-Spencer County Sesquicentennial*, 20-22; De La Hunt, *Perry County*, 314-16; Griffing, *Atlas of Harrison County*.

23. Lansden, *City of Cairo*, 102-27, 157-63, 261-79; Federal Writers Project, *Cairo Guide*, 40-45, 58-60.

24. Lansden, *City of Cairo*, 63-95, and Lantz, *Community in Search of Itself*, 88-110, 132-45. In 1876, the trustees sold their interests to a new group, the Cairo Trust Property, in which Taylor was dominant. This group dominated the city for twenty years.

25. May, *Massac County*, 160-62, 179-92; Page, *Massac County*, 284-87; Hardin County Historical and Genealogical Society, *Hardin County*, 8-24; Goodspeed, *Gallatin*, . . . *Williamson Counties*, 92-148.

26. O'Malley, *Union County*, 790-98; Federal Writers Project, *Union County*, 168-71.

27. Starling, *Henderson County*, 276-77, 502-9; Arnett, *Annals and Scandals*, 332-37, 345-48; Federal Writers Project, *Henderson*, 57-59. For a discussion of New South town services, see Ayers, *Promise of the New South*, 81-103.

28. *History of Owensboro* (1883), 101-5, 321-35, and 423-24; Dew, *Owensboro*, 99-105. See also *Owensboro Messenger and Inquirer*, May 13, 1992.

29. Neuman, *Story of Paducah*, 61-73, 89-92, 164-67; Robertson, "Paducah," 129-36.

30. Federal Writers Project, *Henderson*, 94-98; *An Illustrated Historical Atlas of Henderson and Union Counties;* Dannheiser, *Henderson County*, 7-55; U.S., 9th Census, 1870, *Population Schedules of Henderson County*, National Archives microfilm M593, roll 469, *Kentucky*, 78-150. An overview of city and county government is found in Starling, *Henderson County*, 100-103, 255-60, 292, 301-2, 313, 315, and 329. The four governors were Lazarus Powell, John Brown, Augustus Stanley, and A.B. Chandler. The senators were Stanley, Chandler, Powell, and Archibald Dixon. The first mayor, Edward S. Ayres, was a popular riverboat captain who died after two weeks in office. See *Owensboro Monitor*, April 25, 1866.

31. U.S., 9th Census, 1870, *Population Schedules of Daviess County*, 257-300; Potter, *Owensboro and Daviess County*, 56-61; [Boulware,] *Daviess County*, 94-157, 336-57, and 429-507; Collins, *History of Kentucky*, 2:151-56; Clark, *History of Kentucky*, 429; and Tapp and Klotter, *Kentucky*, 24, 27.

32. Robertson, *Paducah*, 66-84; McCracken County Genealogical Society, *History and Families*, 19, 22-23.

33. *EDJ*, October 12, 1870, April 11, 1871; Brant and Fuller, *Vanderburgh County*, 147-86; Lipin, *Producers*, 120-66.

34. Brant and Fuller, *Vanderburgh County*, 69; *Evansville Revised Ordinances, 1901*, 440-65.

35. Ayers, *Promise of the New South*, 55-56.

36. Goodspeed, *Posey County*, 464-543. See also Leffel, *Posey County*, 189-94, 236, 273, and McConnell, *Posey County*, 89-151.

37. Hodges, *Fearful Times*, 34-82; McManaway, *1870 Census of Hancock County*, 1-26; Phillips and Watkins, *Hancock County*, 99-116.

38. *Biographical Review of Johnson, Massac, Pope, and Hardin Counties*, 457, 477, and 558-59.

39. Lansden, *City of Cairo*, xiii-xv, 190-207, 231-39; Perrin, *Alexander, Union, and Pulaski Counties*, 3-56.

40. *An Illustrated Historical Atlas of Henderson and Union Counties*, 24. The birthplaces and dates of settlement of some were not identified. Hence the actual totals may be higher or lower than those cited in the text. See also U.S., 9th Census, 1870, *Population Schedules of Henderson County*, 78-150.

41. U.S., 9th Census, 1870, *Population Schedules of Daviess County*, National Archives microfilm M593, roll 458, *Kentucky*, 257-300; *An Illustrated Historical Atlas of Daviess County, Kentucky* (N.p., 1876); *History of Daviess County* (Chicago, 1883), 354-56, 429-507. In 1870, many of the wealthy, as measured by real and personal property, were farmers. Among nonfarmers, the most notable were distiller Thomas Monarch, with property valued at $33,000; attorney George H. Williams, with $50,000; tobacco dealer Benjamin Bransford, with $100,000; stock dealer James C. Rudd, with $100,000; lawyer Richard Taylor, with $37,000; Senator Thomas McCreery, with $28,500; banker Bailey Tyler, with $31,000; and attorney William Sweeney, with $70,000.

42. The problem with studying Paducah's elite at this time is the paucity of county and town histories. Hence a sense of who ruled, and how, is difficult to determine. None of the works since Neuman's history in the 1920s explores this theme.

43. White, *Evansville*. Brant and Fuller, *Vanderburgh County*, published sixteen years later, included fifty major figures, a fifth of whom were postwar arrivals (147-86). Lipin, *Producers*, 110-11, asserts that the elite was becoming less unified as the workers were moving toward greater homogeneity. That fairly unsophisticated and ideology-driven observation overlooks religious and social divergence among workers, the persistence of powerful families in powerful roles, and the various means by which the elite adapted to change—e.g., through intermarriage.

44. Brant and Fuller, *Vanderburgh County*, 147-86; *EDJ*, March 20, 1895, and September 14, 1898; *EP*, February 5, 1915, and November 11, 1916; *Biographical Cyclopedia*, esp. 86.

45. Brant and Fuller, *Vanderburgh County*, 207-12; Iglehart, *Vanderburgh County*, 208-14; White, *Evansville*, 80-81; and *Biographical Cyclopedia*, 43-75, 107-11.

46. The various local histories noted in the text have been cited earlier. They are not to be confused with the historical atlases and county histories published by Chicago's Lake or Goodspeed firms after 1876 which followed a common pattern of organization and usually had a prominent local resident as compiler or writer of major portions of the manuscript, such as the Interstate Publishing Company of Chicago's 1883 history of Daviess County, in which W.W. Boulware (435-36) was identified as the local historian. Shawneetown had its first city directory in 1872, Mount Vernon in 1882, Owensboro in 1882, and Henderson in 1899. Only Evansville's appeared annually after its inception. Paducah had only a few issues by 1890.

There is some risk in using these early local histories as indices of community leadership, as they were driven by commercial and sometimes political concerns. But one senses in all of them an antiquarian desire for accuracy and comprehensiveness, and they are our only record, in most cases, of the towns' elites.

47. Lipin, *Producers*, 87-88, 94-95. Lipin unfortunately overlooks the fact that much housing was also erected in this period for skilled and white-collar workers in the near downtown as well as on the north and west sides.

48. *EDJ*, July 17, 1867, and April 10, 14, and 25, 1868.

49. *EDJ*, December 4, 1868, and July 9, 1869.

50. Lipin, *Producers*, 98-105.

51. Blacks' residential patterns are described in Bigham, *Fair Trial*, 21-36. See also Carrier, *Illinois*, 128. Unfortunately, little discussion of African Americans exists in the studies of these Illinois settlements and counties, and even that tends to be negative. See, e.g., Perrin, *Alexander, Union, and Pulaski Counties*, 163. A notable exception is Lansden, *City of Cairo*, which places the burden on hostile and unhelpful whites (146-47). A history of urban blacks in the state is much needed. On black migration, see Trotter, *Great Migration*, especially the concluding essay by Trotter on 147-52.

52. *An Illustrated Historical Atlas of Henderson and Union Counties*. See also Blue and Hazelwood, *Henderson County*, 41-137.

53. Dew, *Owensboro*, 92-95; Potter, *Owensboro and Daviess County*, unpaginated map; *Owensboro Messenger and Inquirer*, September 21, 1992; Neuman, *Story of Paducah*, 89-92; Robertson, *Paducah, 1830-1980*, 16.

54. Robertson, "Paducah," 129-36, offers some examples of the Germans' impact on Paducah. The *EDJ* of June 4 and 8, and September 5 and 9, 1870, vividly illustrates Germans' effect on Evansville—stories about the election of officers in the Central Turnverein, the sending of local musical groups to a massive Sangerfest in Cincinnati, and the celebrations (as well as charitable activities) associated with the Prussians' victory over the French. See also Bigham, *Reflections*, 6-8, 14-16.

55. Ayers, *Promise of the New South*, 136, 140, 141, 156-57. His chapter on race relations, 1880-1910 (132-59), is the most cogent account of this issue the author has read. See also Lucas, *Slavery to Segregation*, 209, and Lucas's review of social conditions, 268-91. Wright, *In Pursuit of Equality*, 3-4, counts thirteen lynchings in Logan County alone between 1880 and 1910.

56. Collins, *History of Kentucky*, 1:246a; Howard, *Black Liberation*, 140-41. See also Lucas, *Slavery to Segregation*, 142-45.

57. Howard, *Black Liberation*, 179, 255-57, 266.

58. Lucas, *Slavery to Segregation*, 235, 248, 255-57, 262, 266-67. See also *Daviess County* (1883), 367, and Hayes, *Sixty Years of Owensboro*, 237-60, 370. In 1883, per capita spending for Owensboro black pupils was $1.30, as compared with $12.00 for whites. Statewide spending had risen to only $2.25 by 1891.

59. Thornbrough, *Civil War Era*, 482; Tingley, *Structuring of a State*, 291-92; Lansden, *City of Cairo*, 261-79; May, *Massac County*, 99-101; *Rockport Democrat*, October 26, November 1, 15, and 20, and December 27, 1895, and December 21, 1900.

60. U.S., 8th Census, 1860, *Statistics of the Population of the United States* (Washington, 1866), 371-400.

61. See, e.g., Marty, *Pilgrims*, 227.

62. Brant and Fuller, *Vanderburgh County*, 269-304. See also Bigham, *Fair Trial*, 74-76.

63. See, e.g., *EDJ*, July 19, 1853, November 12 and 24, 1859, December 1, 1859, February 21, 1860, September 28, 1860, December 1, 1860, June 30, 1865, August 3 and 13, 1866, July 25, 1867, and January 12, 1869. *Israelite* of August 10, 1866 carried the story about Evansville. See also *Sunday Courier and Press*, October 12, 1947.

64. *EDJ*, December 26, 1853, February 17, 1855, June 15, 1859, June 14 through July 18, 1860. The YMCA opened a large new structure at Fourth and Sycamore in 1891. See *The Advance* 5 (January 1891): 18-25. This was the local Y's periodical. A YWCA was organized in 1911.

65. *EDJ*, September 17, 1866, July 25, 1867, and August 12, 1870; minutes of the Evansville School Board, book 1, 58-60, book 2, 145, 147, 157-59, and 175; Iglehart, *Vanderburgh County*, 163-207; Lipin, *Producers*, 118-20, 124; *Industries of Evansville* (1880), 42, 50-51; *Revised Ordinances of the City of Evansville, 1901*, 466-71. German instruction at the first grade level began in the fall of 1886. All this was changed in April 1918, when elementary training in German ended, and German instruction was curtailed.

66. U.S., 9th Census, 1870, vol., *Population*, 408-13; U.S., 10th Census, 1880, *Compendium*, part 2: 1645-53. According to the 1880 census, 22.2 percent of Kentuckians age ten and above could read, and 29.9 percent could not write. Illinois's percentages were 4.3 and 6.4, respectively, and Indiana's were 4.8 and 7.5. U.S., 12th Census, 1900, *Population* (Washington, 1902), 2:361, 401, 440, 470-76; Clark, "Public Education," *Kentucky Encyclopedia*, 745-46.

67. Federal Writers Project, *Henderson*, 13-20, 60-68; H. Thornton Bennett, *Henderson City Directory* (Evansville, 1900), 8-12, 19-20.

68. *Daviess County* (1883), 303-4, 359-408, and Neuman, *Story of Paducah*, 169-98.

69. Clinton, "Social and Educational History," 38-50. See also Briggs, *Early History of West Point*, 33-44, 93-102; Livingston County Historical Society, *Livingston County, Kentucky*, 1:39-51; Bryant, "Meade County," in Kleber, *Kentucky Encyclopedia*, 623; Federal Writers Project, *Union County*, 156-67.

70. See, e.g., Page, *Massac County*, 100-127; May, *Massac County*, 107-12, 179-87; Pope County Historical Society, *Pope County, Illinois*, 40-56; *Johnson, Massac, Pope, and Hardin Counties*, 117-222; Hardin County Historical and Genealogical Society, *Hardin County*, 28-38; Goodspeed, *Posey County*, 271-76; Leffel, *Posey County*, 122-46; Goodspeed, *Warrick, Spencer, and Perry Counties*, 629-45, 710-20; Fortune, *Warrick*, 171-73; *An Illustrated Historical Atlas of Warrick County, Indiana* (Philadelphia, 1880), 4, 46-51; *An Illustrated Historical Atlas of Spencer County, Indiana*, 60-61; *Tell City News*, centennial supplement, August 8, 1958, 17.

71. Reported in Botkin, *Mississippi River Folklore*, 467-68. See also Dew, *Shaping Our Society*, 15-21.

72. Cited in *Steamboatin' Days: Folk Songs of the Mississippi Packet Era*, ed. Mary Wheeler (Baton Rouge, La., 1944), 43-46.

73. Dew, *Shaping Our Society*, 9-15; Neuman, *Story of Paducah*, 99-112; Botkin, *Treasury of Mississippi River Folklore*, 118-19; Briggs, "Entertainment and Amusement in Cairo." The *Quickstep*'s owners, e.g., offered an upriver excursion leaving Cairo July 2, 1872, for eight dollars round-trip. The attraction was an "illumination" at Evansville's Artesian Spring Park (*EDJ*, June 26, 1872).

74. Dreiser, *Dawn*, 119-20.

75. A solid history of the game is Seymour, *Baseball*, 3-74. Riess, *City Games*, 33-48, captures its demography, not its elan.

76. Seymour, *Baseball*, 1:9, 41-44. Gilbert, *City of Evansville*, 1:106-10, credits Charlie Wentz, agent of the Adams Express Company, with introducing the national rules in Evansville in 1866.

77. See, e.g., *EDJ*, June 17, July 17 and 24, 1865, May 4, 1866, April 13, July 9, and August 5, 6, and 13, 1867. Also note Cole, *Civil War*, 447.

78. "Baseball in Cairo: A Footnote to Illinois History," *JISHS* 33 (June 1940): 234-37.

79. *EDJ*, October 2, 23, and 28, 1868, May 30, June 2 and 13, and August 8, 1868, June 12 and July 20, 1869, and September 10 and 12, 1870; Cole, *Civil War*, 447.

80. *EDJ*, June 12 and 18, July 16, and September 4, 1869; July 9 and September 10, 12, and 26, 1869; April 15 and 19, June 20, and October 9, 1871; April 9, May 22 and 30, June 17 and 29, July 1 and 4, August 9, 17, 19, 22, 26, 28, and 31, 1872; Gilbert, *City of Evansville*, 1:109-10.

81. Sutherland, *Expansion of Everyday Life*, 239-45; Ireland, *County in Kentucky History*, 19-27.

82. *Crittenden Press*, November 12, 1900. See also Livingston County Historical Society, *Livingston County History*, 1:16-22, and Sutherland, *Expansion of Everyday Life*, 236-39 and 258-62.

83. Sutherland, *Expansion of Everyday Life*, 249. The best brief account of vaudeville's appeal is found in Barth, *City People*, 192-228. Discussion of the emerging "low" and "high" cultures is found in Levine, *Unpredictable Past*, 139-71.

84. Potter, *Owensboro and Daviess County*, 189-214; Neuman, *Story of Paducah*, 99-112; Federal Writers Project, *Union County*, 156-67.

85. Stallings, "Drama in Southern Illinois," 190-202.

86. Federal Writers Project, *Cairo Guide*, 58-60; Keiser, *Building for the Centuries*, 17; and Iglehart, *Vanderburgh County*, 91-94.

87. *EDJ*, September 2, 1869; Hayes, *After Sixty Years*, 75-76; Potter, *Owensboro and Daviess County*, 189-214; *Tell City News*, August 8, 1958.

9. Patterns of Communities' Growth and Development

1. See, e.g., Goldfield and Brownell, *Urban America*, 16-18; Mohl, *Making of Urban America*, 73-74.

2. Jakle, "Ohio Valley Revisited," 42-43.

3. Thwaites, *On the Storied Ohio*, 223-95. Thwaites's travels are also recounted in an essay by Reid, "Pilgrims," 24-33.

4. Jakle, "Ohio Valley Revisited," 56-60.

5. On the English-Leavenworth fracas, see Schnellenberg, *Conflict between Communities*, 27-29.

6. Jones, *Ohio River*, 112-56.

7. For a discussion of the process whereby towns become cities, see Ayers, *Promise of the New South*, 20, 55-56, 453n. 36, 467n. 1. Much of this reflects Blumin, "When Villages Become Towns," 54-68. For definitions, see U.S., 13th Census, 1910, *Population*, 1:73-77; U.S., 14th Census, 1920, *Population* (Washington, 1921), 1:62-75; U.S., 15th Census, 1930, *Population* (Washington, 1931), 2:16-19; U.S., 16th Census, 1940, *Population* (Washington, 1943), vol. 2, 2:842; and U.S., 17th Census, 1950, *Population* (Washington, 1953), vol. 2, 13:xiv-xv. The term *standard metropolitan area* was introduced in 1950. When Evansville became part of a metropolitan district, it had more than the requisite 50,000 in the central city and 100,000 in the surrounding area, where there were at least 150 residents

per square mile. Census data for 1920 is found in U.S., 14th Census, 1920, *Population*, part 1: 197-204, 207-9, 222-25.

8. Phillips, *Indiana in Transition*, esp. 366-67; Keiser, *Building for the Centuries*, 10-11; Conrod, "Limited Growth," 82; and Still, *Urban America*, 210-11. U.S., 14th Census, 1920, vol. 3, *Population 1920* (Washington, 1922), 251-79, 289-311, 368-86; U.S, 14th Census, 1920, *Abstract of the Fourteenth Census of the United States 1920* (Washington, 1923), 154-56, 158-59.

9. U.S., 14th Census, 1920, *Population*, 3:296.

10. For migration patterns, especially after 1915, see Trotter, *Great Migration*, 1-21. Population data are cited in Bigham, *Fair Trial*, 20, 108.

11. U.S., 12th Census, 1900, *Population*, 1:499-501, 504-5, 535-37, 540-41; U.S., 14th Census, 1920, *Population*, 3: 251-79, 289-311, 368-86.

12. See, for example, Wright, *In Pursuit of Equality*, 1-14.

13. Chudacoff and Smith, *Evolution of American Urban Society*, 78-79, 113, 118-22.

14. Bigham, *Fair Trial*, 103-19.

15. A description of the Evansville economy in this period is found in Milliman and Pinnell, "Economic Redevelopment," 242-43. See also Federal Writers Project, *Cairo Guide*, 58-60; "Henderson," in Kleber, *Kentucky Encyclopedia*, 423; Burleigh, *Look at Newburgh*, 79-89; Leffel, *Posey County*, 107-8; McCracken County Genealogical Society, *History and Families*, 30-36; and Potter, *Owensboro and Daviess County*, 108-10. Most of the interurbans and street railways eventually came under the control of what by 1921 would be known as the Southern Indiana Gas and Electric Company of Evansville. Interurban service by rail generally ended in the 1920s and was followed by bus service. "Trollies" came to an end in the early 1930s. They, too, were replaced by buses. The ES&N was originally steam-powered. It also connected to Boonville and carried a great deal of freight, especially coal. Its records are in special collections at the University of Southern Indiana library. Articles of incorporation for the Evansville and Eastern, later E&OV, are found in the Vanderburgh County recorder's office, miscellaneous record E (1904), 308-9. This company's founders were two businessmen each from Evansville, Newburgh, and Rockport. Monkkonen, *America Becomes Urban*, 175-81, argues persuasively that improvement of city streets preceded automobiles, rather than the other way around, because late-nineteenth-century city leaders envisioned paved streets, among other things, as means of facilitating mass transit. Most of the paved roads in 1914 were located in cities.

16. Hercules Manufacturing Company, *Hercules Story*.

17. See, e.g., Courier Company, *Great Flood of '37*, 2; Federal Writers Project, *Union County*, 156-67; Livingston County Historical Society, *Livingston County History*, 1:39-42.

10. Making a Living

1. The effects of land mismanagement are shown persuasively in Clinton, "Social and Educational History," 16-22, and Hall, *Hardin County*, 30-57. Changes in southern Illinois agriculture (in this case, Union County in the interior) are described effectively in Adams, *Transformation*. Generally the patterns were a decline of kin-neighbor networks of production and the rise of mechanized, individualized production, and a change in social relations between men and women, owners and workers, and the like. The number of farms declined from a high of 2,400 in 1910 to 600 in the early 1980s. The greatest

drop occurred after 1945. Hall does not include the Ohio River or regional development in her study. The value of agricultural products in Alexander County in 1920 was $1.7 million, while manufactures were valued at $14 million; Vanderburgh's crops were worth $3.6 million and its manufactures $55 million. The leading county in value of agricultural goods was Daviess, with $8.2 million. Its manufactures were valued at $13 million. U.S., 14th Census, 1920, *Agriculture* (Washington, 1922), part 1: 323-434, and *Manufactures 1919* (Washington, 1923), 210-11, 374-75, 480-82.

2. For characteristics of industrial cities, see Mohl, *Making of Urban America*, 73-74. Teaford discusses industrial cities in the Middle West in *Cities of the Heartland*, esp. 48-71.

3. R.L. Polk and Company, *Kentucky Gazeteer and Business Directory for 1895-1896*, reprinted as *Kentucky Places and People* (Utica, Ky., 1983[?]), 14, 18, 19, 37, and 291. See also 41, 47, 297, and 303, which offer similar examples from Tolu, Chenault, Stephensport, and Concordia.

4. See, e.g., Ayers, *Promise of the New South*, 81-103. According to the *Kentucky State Gazeteer*, the following lacked rail connections: Chenault (Breckinridge County), Skillman Landing (Hancock County), Battletown, Concordia, and Wolf Creek (Meade County), and all of the river settlements in Crittenden and Livingston County. Indiana river communities without railroads included those downriver from Harrison County to Evansville and Mount Vernon except Cannelton, Tell City, and Rockport. Most Ohio River settlements in Illinois—with the exception of Cairo, Mound City, Metropolis, Bridgeport, Golconda, Rosiclare, and Shawneetown—also lacked rail ties.

5. Goldfield, *Cotton Fields and Skyscrapers*, 80-132, and Ayers, *Promise of the New South*, 55-56. See also Rabinowitz, *First New South*, 5-71, passim.

6. Leffel, *Posey County*, 189-95, 210-373; Posey County Historical Society, *Posey County, Indiana*, 11, 182-87. Despite its being on the National Register, the IOOF building was razed in 1996 to make way for a more "modern" bank facility.

7. Newman, *Ohio River Navigation*, 1; Page, *Massac County*, 90-98, 284-89; May, *Massac County*, 148-62, 192-95, and *History Papers of Massac County*, 58-60; Stover, *Illinois Central Railroad*, 196-97.

8. Baertich, *Troy*, 201-24; Taylor, *Indiana*, 228-29.

9. Ayers, *Promise of the New South*, 113-17; De La Hunt, *Perry County*, 258-67; Goodspeed, *Warrick, Spencer, and Perry Counties*, 645-68; Cannelton Sewer Pipe Company, files MS 5484, Indiana Historical Society. See also Zoll, *Perry County*, 391-465.

10. De La Hunt, *Perry County*, 89-93, 341-54; Goodspeed, *Warrick, Spencer, and Perry Counties*, 629-45; *Tell City News*, centennial edition, August 8, 1959, 20-43. Hame was the wooden device to which draft animals were attached so that they could pull wagons. Increasing costs of labor and timber hurt this community, but furniture making remained the town's mainstay for decades. In November 1996, the bankrupt Tell City Chair Company ceased operations after 131 years.

11. Goodspeed, *Warrick, Spencer, and Perry Counties*, 293, 326-54; *Rockport-Spencer County Sesquicentennial*, 4-9, 17-21; *EDJ*, January 16, 1873. Most goods were shipped by flatboat. In 1919-20, Spencer's agricultural goods were valued at $5.5 million and its manufactures at $2.2 million. See U.S., 14th Census, 1920, *Agriculture*, part 1: 323-434, and *Manufactures 1919*, 310-11, 374-75, 480-82. These sources are also used for agricultural and manufacturing data in subsequent citations in this chapter.

12. Perrin, *Alexander, Union, and Pulaski Counties,* 549-80; Allen, *Southern Illinois,* 291-93. In 1919 and 1920, Pulaski's agricultural goods were valued at $2.1 million and its manufactures at $2.4 million.

13. U.S., 10th Census, 1880, *Population Schedules of Breckinridge County,* National Archives microfilm T9, roll 405, *Kentucky,* 63-84, and U.S., 14th Census, 1920, *Population Schedules of Breckinridge County,* National Archives microfilm T625, roll 561, *Kentucky,* 66-81. See also Federal Writers Project, *Kentucky,* 404.

14. O'Malley, *Union County,* 113-99, 429-44; Federal Writers Project, *Union County,* 73-76, 95-112, and 160-67.

15. Goodspeed, *Gallatin, . . . Williamson Counties,* 92-102; Gallatin County Historical Society, *History and Families,* 8-22. In 1919 and 1920, Gallatin County's agricultural products were valued at $3.1 million and its manufactures at only $220,000. Nearby Union County produced $5 million worth of agricultural goods and $380,000 in manufactures.

16. Katterjohn, *Warrick,* 21, 30, 37-39; Burleigh, *Look at Newburgh,* 32-66, 79-89. In 1919 and 1920, Warrick County had just $100,000 in manufactures and $4.6 million in agricultural products.

17. Pope County Historical Society, *Pope County,* 18, 28-30, 30-31, 40-46, 58-59, 72.

18. Hall, *Hardin County,* 14, 30-57; Hardin County Historical and Genealogical Society, *Hardin County,* 8-24. Mining around Rosiclare commenced in the early 1870s, supported by wealthy eastern investors. Evansville firms were also involved, including Reitz and Haney, which built boilers. Smelting the ore was preferred, but apparently the means of doing it was problematic (*EDJ,* May 22, 1872).

19. House, *Report on the Internal Commerce of the United States,* 50th Cong., 1st sess., 1888, H. Doc. 6, 492. Census data for the five largest cities is found in U.S., 14th Census, 1920, *Population,* 1:197-2004, 207-9, 222-25.

20. Clark, introduction to *Kentucky Encyclopedia,* xxvi-xxx.

21. Tingley, *Structuring of a State,* 1-71. Also see Howard, *Illinois,* 331-41, and Keiser, *Building for the Centuries,* 182-83. As if to underscore the insignificance of the state's lower counties, Tingley's index contains no reference to the Ohio River.

22. Phillips, *Indiana in Transition,* 148-60, 190-97, 224-29, 267-70, 274-75, 318-19, and 386-407.

23. Conrod, "Limited Growth," 105-7, 109. See Mark Twain, *Life on the Mississippi* (New York, 1883), chap. 25. Much of the statistical evidence cited here came from the 1888 federal report on inland commerce.

24. Lansden, *City of Cairo,* 280. See also Lansden, 220-30; Conrod, "Limited Growth," 111-14; and Stover, *Illinois Central Railroad,* 202-5, 295-97.

25. Abdy, *On the Ohio,* 41; Lansden, *City of Cairo,* esp. 120-27, 138-67, and 231-39. Also see Lantz, *Community in Search of Itself,* 132-45.

26. Abdy, *On the Ohio,* 74-102. See also Conrod, "Limited Growth," 246-47.

27. Conrod, "Limited Growth," 247-48; Neuman, *Story of Paducah,* 87-98; Robertson, "Paducah," in Kleber, *Kentucky Encyclopedia,* 594; Wells, *Architecture of Paducah and McCracken County,* 18-20, 25-30.

28. Abdy, *On the Ohio,* 49-74. See also Conrod, "Limited Growth," 248; Robertson, *Paducah,* 100-108; Stover, *Illinois Central Railroad,* 202, 220-30; Neuman, *Story of Paducah,* 144-51.

29. Conrod, "Limited Growth," 249.

30. O'Malley, *Union County,* 433-38; Dannheiser, *Henderson County,* 182-85; Greene, *Green River Country,* 127-46.

31. House, *Report on the Internal Commerce of the United States* (1888), 395-99, 492-93; Phillips, *Indiana in Transition,* 255-56; Hilton and Due, *Electric Interurban Railways,* 256-57; Schockel, "Manufactural Evansville," 15; and Conrod, "Limited Growth," 204-9.

32. Conrod, "Limited Growth," 209-10, 212, 213.

33. Dannheiser, *Henderson County,* 337-66, and Merrill, "Henderson," in Kleber, *Kentucky Encyclopedia,* 423. The L&N, led by Milton H. Smith, gained control of the former Evansville, Henderson, and Nashville in the late 1870s and also acquired control over the line between Evansville and St. Louis. The line purchased all of the stock in the Henderson Bridge Company, and its directors saw to it that a bridge was completed (1885) over the Ohio at Henderson, thus giving the railroad a major northwest-southeast connection. The L&N, which in the mid-1880s shifted its southern tracks to a standard gauge, also secured control of the Ohio and Nashville and subsequently built a road that expanded east-west rail access to the coal fields south of Henderson. By 1898, it also formed an arrangement with the Evansville and Terre Haute and the Chicago and Eastern Illinois that cut passenger travel time between Chicago and Nashville to sixteen hours. The Ohio Valley Railroad, opened from Henderson to Princeton, Kentucky, in 1891, eventually reached Hopkinsville. This line, eventually controlled by the Illinois Central, which in 1904 was given permission to use the river bridge, offered enormous benefit to those seeking to expand the area's coal trade. See Klein, *L&N Railroad,* 182, 186, 191, 218, 291-93, and 336, and Arnett, *Annals and Scandals,* 121-29. Because of the small size of the city of Henderson, census data was provided only for the county; hence conclusions about the city's economy are inferred from county data. See U.S., 14th Census, 1920, *Agriculture,* part 1: 323-434, and *Manufactures 1919,* 480-82.

34. *Kentucky Gazeteer and Business Directory, 1895-1896,* 114-17; Bennett, *Henderson City Directory,* 18-19, 176-99; Starling, *Henderson County,* 508-22; Arnett, *Annals and Scandals,* 169-77; Dannheiser, *Henderson County,* 219-29.

35. Federal Writers Project, *Henderson,* 57-59; Federal Writers Project, *Union County,* 60-67, 156-57; Dew, *Owensboro,* 81-98; Hayes, *Sixty Years of Owensboro,* 121-25. Ayers, *Promise of the New South,* 106-7, offers a brief introduction to the cigarette phenomenon. Arnett, *Annals and Scandals,* 135, 142, points out another aspect of the rise of the tobacco trust. The first farmers' organization in the county was a chapter of the Agricultural Wheel, which introduced cooperative purchasing and marketing. Night riding and violence followed in the early twentieth century due to the ineffectiveness of this method in the face of low prices and market controls provided by huge corporate entities. See also Ayers, 214-48, for a discussion of southern farmers' alliances, and Tracy A. Campbell, "Black Patch War," in Kleber, *Kentucky Encyclopedia,* 84-85, and *Politics of Despair,* which unfortunately does not include discussion of counties downriver from Hardin.

36. For information on banks and newspapers, see *Henderson Directory for 1899-1900,* 14-15, 17. Manufacturing data is found in U.S., 12th Census, 1900, *Abstract,* 354-81; U.S., 13th Census, 1910, *Manufactures,* 323-24; U.S., 14th Census, 1920, *Manufactures 1919,* 327, 330-31, 370-71, 378, 383, 385, 409, 484, 486, 489, 504-5.

37. Lee A. Dew, "Henderson, Kentucky, and the Fight for Equitable Freight Rates, 1906-1918," *RKHS* 76 (January 1978): 34-44. See also King and Thurman, *Henderson's River Book,* 48.

38. Arnett, *Annals and Scandals,* 169-77; Federal Writers Project, *Henderson,* 57-59; and Merrill, "Henderson," 423.

39. *Henderson Directory for 1899-1900,* 14-15, and Starling, *Henderson County,* 511-14, 522.

40. Conrod, "Limited Growth," 117-23; Comeaux, "Impact of Transportation Activities," 91-93; Colby, *Pilot Study of Southern Illinois,* 40-41. For census data for the period from 1900 to 1928, see U.S., 14th Census, 1920, *Agriculture,* part 1: 323-434, and *Manufactures 1919,* 310-11, 320-23, 327, 330-31, 374-75, 383-85, 409, 480-82, 484-90, 504-5.

41. Conrod, "Limited Growth," 123, 125. Also note Lantz, *Community in Search of Itself,* 41-67.

42. Hayes, *Sixty Years of Owensboro,* 117-25, 132-35; Potter, *Owensboro and Daviess County,* 210-12; *Kentucky Gazeteer and Business Directory, 1895-1896,* 246-50; Lee A. Dew, "Coal Mining in Daviess County in the Nineteenth Century," *Daviess County Historical Quarterly* 5 (April 1987): 27-37; Klein, *L&N Railroad,* 153-54, 182, 191, 277, 335, 398. For census data for the period from 1900 to 1920, see footnote 40 above.

43. *Daviess County* 358; Potter, *Owensboro and Daviess County,* 178-79.

44. Hayes, *Sixty Years of Owensboro,* 117-25; Dew, "Industry and Agriculture," 80-91, and "Owensboro and Elsewhere," 74-82.

45. Dew, "Industry and Agriculture," 80-91; Dew, *Owensboro,* 105-16; and *Owensboro Daily Messenger,* April 28, 1901.

46. Hayes, *Sixty Years of Owensboro,* 121-25, and Dew, "Owensboro," 700-701. Value of manufactures in Owensboro was $3.5 million in 1900, $4.1 million in 1914, and rose to $8.6 million in 1919. The number of wage earners dropped from 1,582 in 1900 to 1,000 in 1914 and rose in 1919 to 1,380. See. U.S., 14th Census, 1920, *Manufacture 1919,* 327, 330-31, 370-71, 378, 383, 385, 409, 484, 486, 489, 504-5.

47. Potter, *Owensboro and Daviess County,* 122-30. See also *Daviess County* (1883), 336-57, 429-507, and U.S., 12th Census, 1900, *Population Schedules of Daviess County,* National Archives microfilm T623, rolls 517-18, *Kentucky,* 44-355, passim; Emerson and Williams, *Owensboro Directory, 1882-1883* (Louisville, 1882), 268-77.

48. Clark-Elwell Company, *City Directory of Owensboro,* 12-16. For data on wages, see census sources cited in note 46 above.

49. Potter, *Owensboro and Daviess County,* 165-76.

50. *Kentucky Gazeteer and Business Directory, 1895-1896,* 251; McCracken County Genealogical Society, *History and Families of McCracken County,* 172-73. See also Neuman, *Story of Paducah,* 113-26.

51. Robertson, "Paducah," esp. 130-36, and Neuman, *Story of Paducah,* 113-26. Also note Battle, Perrin, Kniffin, *Kentucky,* 2:96.

52. Conrod, "Limited Growth," 248-57; Neuman, *Story of Paducah,* 113-26; Robertson, *Paducah, 1830-1980,* 100-108; Wells, *Architecture of Paducah and McCracken County,* 25-30. Census data is found in U.S., 14th Census, 19920, *Manufactures 1919,* 327, 330-31, 370-71, 378, 385, 409, 484, 489, 504-5, 480-82.

53. Abdy, *On the Ohio,* 135, 139, 141-42, and 144.

54. Agricultural and manufacturing data are found in U.S., 14th Census, 1920, *Agriculture,* part 1:323-434; *Manufactures 1919,* 310-11, 327, 330-31, 370-71, 374-75, 378, 383, 385, 409, 480-82, 484, 486, 489, 504-5.

55. U.S., 14th Census, 1920, *Population*, 264-68.

56. Schockel, "Manufactural Evansville," 207-10. Alfred D. Chandler describes the rise of corporate integration and the production of consumer goods in *Strategy and Structure* (Cambridge, Mass., 1982). Cooper's *Once a Cigar Maker*, effectively recounts the evolution of the workforce in cigar factories. Women came to outnumber their male counterparts after 1910, developed their own assertive and militant traditions, and asserted that work culture was not the exclusive province of male craft unionists. Oral history materials in the University of Southern Indiana library assisted Professor Cooper's research. Discussions of Evansville workers are found on 178, 281, and 295.

57. Milliman and Pinnell, "Economic Redevelopment," 242-43; *EP*, March 1, 1919; *EJN*, June 26, 1920.

58. Phillips, *Indiana in Transition*, 364; Conrod, "Limited Growth," 228-32.

59. Schockel, "Manufactural Evansville," 125-30; Milliman and Pinnell, "Economic Redevelopment," 243-45; Conrod, "Limited Growth," 233; and Hercules Manufacturing Company, *Hercules Story*, 1-9. Sunbeam Electrical Manufacturing Company began making electric refrigerators in 1937; it merged with Seeger Refrigerator Company in the mid-1940s. By the late 1940s, Evansville called itself the refrigerator capital of the world.

60. Simplicity motor car brochure for 1907, in the author's collection; Milliman and Pinnell, "Economic Redevelopment for Evansville, Indiana," 243-44. Chrysler ceased operations in 1959, consolidating manufacturing in St. Louis.

61. Conrod, "Limited Growth," 234.

62. Articles of association, October 21, 1915, Vanderburgh County Recorder's Office. Cotton production did not end when the mill closed. Lincoln Mills broke ground for a large facility at the intersection of the Illinois Central and the Belt Line in October 1902 and was still in operation in 1920.

63. Conrod, "Limited Growth," 235, 237. On p. 239, he notes the long-term dangers of the city's dependence of manufacturing, especially of two consumer durables, and of its limited trading area, given the strength of rail and road connections to the north in Indiana and Illinois. Social, cultural, and political factors, though, are not considered seriously in this study. U.S., 14th Census, 1920, *Manufactures 1919*, 320-23, 327, 330-31, 383-85, 484-90.

64. Conrod, "Limited Growth," 236. Socialists' appeals were evident, e.g., in *EC*, October 25 through November 7, 1917. Occupational statistics are found in census records cited in note 63 above.

65. Iglehart, *Vanderburgh County*, 208-14.

66. Phillips, *Indiana in Transition*, 236-48; Brant and Fuller, *Vanderburgh County*, 400-402; Gilbert, *City of Evansville*, 1:190-98; Klein, *L&N Railroad*, 154-59, 247, 290-93, 310, 317, 336-37. As a result of reorganization of the C&EI, the "Big Four" acquired the coal-carrying Evansville, Indianapolis, and Terre Haute and created an Evansville division in 1921 (Phillips, 243).

67. Hulbert, *Ohio River*, 162-63, 359. River improvements are discussed in Havighurst, *River to the West*, 254-60.

68. Hulbert, *Ohio River*, 163, and Ohio Valley Improvement Association, *Official Program and History*. The Evansville celebration, at the McCurdy Hotel, was reported in the *EC* of October 24, 1929. Leland L. Johnson discusses construction of the locks and dams in *The Ohio River Division, U.S. Army Corps of Engineers: The History of a Central Com-*

mand (Cincinnati, 1992), 47-118. Johnson offers a briefer account in "Engineering the Ohio," in Reid, *Always a River,* 180-209.

69. See, e.g., *EJN,* October 12, 1903, June 26, 1904, April 28, 1912, October 24, 1917, and November 23, 1930, and *EC,* October 24, 1929. The *Hopkins* was constructed at Sewickley, Pennsylvania, in 1880, and was in the Cairo/Paducah service until 1915, when it became a showboat. Two years, it was destroyed by fire.

70. See Hunter, *Steamboats,* esp. 332, 418-519, passim.

71. Ambler, *Transportation,* 347-63.

72. Briggs, *Early History of West Point,* 71-92.

73. See, e.g., Robert A. Harper, "River Junction Communities," 364-70, and Havighurst, *River to the West,* 208-9. Jakle, "Ohio Valley Revisited," 57-60, appears to support this view. Compare Ambler, *Transportation,* 264-94, and Bigham, "River of Opportunity," 157-59.

74. Wayne E. Fuller, *RFD: The Changing Face of Rural America* (1964), cited in Gray, *Indiana History,* 225, 227, and 228.

75. Briggs, *Early History of West Point,* 40-41, 45-46; Neuman, *Story of Paducah,* 113-26; Potter, *Owensboro and Daviess County,* 178-79. See also Hardin County Historical and Genealogical Society, *Hardin County,* 8-24, and Fohs Hall Community Arts Foundation, *Crittenden County,* 421-26.

76. See, e.g., Glaab and Brown, *Urban America,* 268-73. For definitions, see U.S., 13th Census, 1910, *Population,* 1:73-77; U.S., 14th Census, 1920, *Population* (Washington, 1923), 1:62-75; U.S., 15th Census, 1930, *Population* (Washington, 1933), 2:16-19; U.S., 16th Census, 1940, *Population* (Washington, 1943), 2:842; U.S., 17th Census, 1950, *Population* (Washington, 1953), 13:xiv-xv.

77. Briggs, *Early History of West Point,* 45-48. West Point was tied more effectively with Louisville by a number of occurrences besides the expansion of Camp Knox and the state road system. This included a bridge across the Salt River in 1914 and bus service beginning in the early 1920s.

78. Elliott, *Evansville,* 233; Potter, *Owensboro and Daviess County,* 210-12; Neuman, *Story of Paducah,* 238-44; Gilbert, *City of Evansville,* 1:400-406; and Vanderburgh County Recorder's Office, articles of association, book 1, 291-94. As earlier, sloganeering was effective when linked with a realistic and coherent understanding of the city's future. Gilbert's map on 401 showed Evansville in 1910 as the center of a coal, oil, gas, tobacco, and grain belt extending to Cairo on the west, Terre Haute on the north, Hawesville on the east, and Hopkinsville on the south. Given the city's economic reach, this was an accurate picture and an apt reason for the city's slogan.

79. Brant and Fuller, *Vanderburgh County,* 173; Gilbert, *City of Evansville,* 1:416; *EJN,* January 21 and February 28, 1909, and June 30, 1912; Vanderburgh County, articles of incorporation, 1:291-94.

80. For the persistence of button manufacturing, see Briggs, *Early History of West Point,* 71-92, and Holzborg and Preflatish, *Crawford County,* 41.

11. Living Together: Society and Culture

1. Chudacoff and Smith, *Evolution of American Urban Society,* 205. For governmental and social change in these years, see 151-204.

2. Barth, *City People,* 232-33. See also Green, *Uncertainty of Everyday Life,* 17-18.

3. See, e.g., Bulleit, *Illustrated Atlas and History of Harrison County*; and Federal Writers Project, *Union County*, 168-71; Fohs Hall Community Arts Foundation, *Crittenden County*, 12-14.

4. Hardin County Historical and Genealogical Society, *Hardin County*, 8-24; Federal Writers Project, *Union County*, 160-67; Thompson, *Breckinridge County*, 27-32.

5. Clinton, "Social and Educational History," 49-57; May, *Massac County*, 179-87; Leonard, *Posey County*, 74-75, 260; Leffel, *Posey County*, 89-96.

6. Lansden, *City of Cairo*, 120-287; Federal Writers Project, *Cairo Guide*, 58-62; Lantz, *Community in Search of Itself*, 88-110, 132-45; Teaford, "City Government," 172.

7. Phillips, *Indiana in Transition*, 382-85. For an account of the Evansville city manager campaign, see the *EP*, May 3–June 21, 1921. Also note Hayes, *Sixty Years of Owensboro*, 52, 58-59, and Robertson, "Paducah," 101, 136.

8. For a review of Bosse's career, see, e.g., *EC*, April 4, 1922. For patterns of black voting, see Bigham, *Fair Trial*, 87-102, 194-214.

9. For accounts of Henderson, Owensboro, and Paducah see Dannheiser, *Henderson County*, 7-55; *Owensboro Messenger and Inquirer*, May 29, 1924; Hayes, *Sixty Years of Owensboro*, 101-16; Robertson, *Paducah*, 66-84; Neuman, *Story of Paducah*, 61-85; and McCracken County Genealogical Society, *History and Families of McCracken County*, 19, 22-23. For Evansville, see *Evansville Revised Ordinances 1901*, iii-vii.

10. See, e.g., Bigham, *Fair Trial*, 194-214. Evansville's Albion Fellows Bacon, wife of a prominent merchant, achieved prominence in combatting slum tenements in her town and then in lobbying successfully for the state's first comprehensive housing law (1913) applying to all incorporated cities in Indiana (Phillips, *Indiana in Transition*, 487).

11. Federal Writers Project, *Henderson*, 51-52; Arnett, *Annals and Scandals*, 121-29; Ayers, *Promise of the New South*, 72-73; *Henderson City Directory 1899-1900*, 6-8; *EP*, December 21, 1995. Henderson city commissioners were elected at large, with the one receiving the most votes serving four years as mayor. The other two held two-year terms; one was responsible for public finance and public property and the other for public safety and public works. The commissioners had legislative as well as executive authority. The only other elected officials were county judges and members of the board of education.

12. Heflin, "Owensboro City Railroad," 18-24; Potter, *Owensboro and Daviess County*, 108-10; and Hayes, *Sixty Years of Owensboro*, 52, 58-59, 60, and 83-84. The Evansville Railways Company acquired the Owensboro line in 1913. Service ended in April 1934. See also *Owensboro City Directory, 1920*, 12-16.

13. Neuman, *Story of Paducah*, 61-83, and McCracken County Genealogical Society, *History and Families*, 30-36.

14. Phillips, *Indiana in Transition*, 379-81; *EDJ*, June 28, 1895; *EJN*, May 21-November 3, 1912 (for a review of a major phase of the merger process), June 16, 1913, and June 1, 1914. For an example of conflict over the awarding of a contract—in this case, asphalt—see *EJN*, August 19, 1913. A review of city government powers is found in *Evansville Revised Ordinances 1901*, 1-75. The most substantial enhancement was in public health and safety. In October 1891, the common council authorized the Evansville Street Railway Company to construct lines that radiated from Second and Main streets to Howell on the southwest, to St. Joseph Cemetery on the northwest, to the city limits along Washington and Jefferson Avenues to the southeast and east, and to Oak Hill Cemetery, the northern boundary of the city. See *Evansville Revised Ordinances 1901*, 314-26.

15. Phillips, *Indiana in Transition*, 383.

16. *Evansville Journal,* January 8 and March 22, 1901; *EJN,* December 10, 1910. See also Bigham, *Album,* 60-63 and 110-11. For discussion of a proposed parkway system, see *EJN,* October 1, 1905, and February 4, 1906. For debates on riverside land use, see the *EP,* especially October 13-14, 1909, which disclosed collusion between proposed developers of a sand and gravel site and prominent city officials. A city council member was secretary-treasurer of the company, and the gas and electric company's general manager was a major stockholder. The council had recently decided to lease the land at $1.11 a day.

17. Phillips, *Indiana in Transition,* 469-70; *Evansville Revised Ordinances 1901,* 1-75; *EDJ,* March 10, 1893, and June 28, 1895; *Henderson City Directory 1899-1900,* 6-8; Arnett, *Annals and Scandals,* 348-50. A list of city offices in 1914 is found in the *Annual Report of the Departments of the Municipal Government, City of Evansville, for the Fiscal Year Ending December 31, 1914* (Evansville, 1915), 3-4.

18. Mortality rates in U.S., 12th Census, 1900, *Vital Statistics* (Washington, 1902), 2:12-15, are provided only for these two cities.

19. Lansden, *City of Cairo,* 148-56; Phillips, *Indiana in Transition,* 476-78; McCracken County Genealogical Society, *History and Families of McCracken County,* 335; Arnett, *Annals and Scandals,* 348-50; *Henderson City Directory 1899-1900,* 5-7; Potter, *Owensboro and Daviess County,* 108-10; Hayes, *Sixty Years of Owensboro,* 217-35.

20. *EP,* November 8 and 18, 1922; Phillips, *Indiana in Transition,* 482-88, 494-502; Hayes, *Sixty Years of Owensboro,* 80-82. Such women's organizations were a primary means whereby the nineteenth-century strictures on the powers and duties of women were greatly weakened. See, e.g., Evans, *Born for Liberty,* 142-74.

21. Wright, *In Pursuit of Equality,* 58-59.

22. Lucas, *Slavery to Segregation,* 327.

23. Ayers, *Promise of the New South,* 139-46; Wright, *In Pursuit of Equality,* 71-79.

24. Wright, *In Pursuit of Equality,* 43; Ayers, *Promise of the New South,* 146-59.

25. Wright, *In Pursuit of Equality,* 6-19.

26. Robertson, *Paducah,* 129.

27. Wright, *In Pursuit of Equality,* 54-56, 58, 102-3, 106-7; U.S., 12th Census, 1900, *Vital Statistics,* 2:470-76.

28. Wright, *In Pursuit of Equality,* 108-15; Dannheiser, *Henderson County,* 245-47.

29. Wright, *In Pursuit of Equality,* 133-34.

30. See, e.g., *Hardin County, Illinois,* 8-24.

31. Wright, *In Pursuit of Equality,* 37-42.

32. Ayers, *Promise of the New South,* 154-57. See also Grantham, *South in Modern America,* 20-22. Race relations in Kentucky after 1890 are discussed in Wright, *In Pursuit of Equality,* 43-102.

33. Lansden, *City of Cairo,* 138-47. See also Bigham, *Fair Trial,* 104-6, 120-35; Tingley, *Structuring of a State,* 291-92; Page, *Massac County,* 41; May, *Massac County,* 25-29.

34. Wright, *In Pursuit of Equality,* 76-86 (quote on 79); Clinton, "A Social and Educational History of Hancock County," 49-50; Hayes, *Sixty Years of Owensboro,* 370-77. Joel Williamson, in *William Faulkner and Southern History* (New York, 1993), 161-63, portrays the public, sensationalistic lynchings between 1890 and about 1915 as a distinctive phase of regional history brought on by anxieties about "black brutes" and the need to enforce Jim Crow. The decline of this form of activity after the war resulted from the discovery of new enemies of southern culture—Jews and Communists—as well as the stabilization in race relations.

35. Wright, *In Pursuit of Equality*, 84-102.

36. Lansden, *City of Cairo*, 138-47; *Daviess County* (1883), 359-408; Hayes, *After Sixty Years*, 75-76, 151-235, passim.

37. Starling, *Henderson County*, 817-22; Dannheiser, *Henderson County*, 219-29; Federal Writers Program, *Henderson*, 60-68; *Henderson City Directory 1899-1900*, 14-15, 18-19; Neuman, *Story of Paducah*, 169-98, 224-33.

38. For a detailed study of the anti-German events of the spring of 1918, see *EP*, April 6-May 20, 1918. The *Demokrat's* last issue was April 28, 1918. For an account of the potential devastation posed by the Trading with the Enemy Act for a German American business, see my "Charles Leich and Company of Evansville: A Note on the Dilemma of German Americans during World War I," *IMH* 70 (June 1974): 95-121. The best recent account of the Klan in Indiana is Moore, *Citizen Klansmen*. Early traces of the Hooded Order in Evansville are seen in *EP*, June 24 and September 20-23, 1921.

39. See, e.g., Chudacoff and Smith, *Evolution of American Urban Society*, 79-107. Also see U.S., 11th Census, 1890, *Statistics of the Population of the United States* (Washington, 1895), 2:703-4, and U.S., 14th Census, 1920, *Population* (Washington, 1922), 2:1290-92.

40. For a description of the city's neighborhoods and architectural history, see Historic Landmarks Foundation of Indiana, *Vanderburgh County Interim Report: Indiana Historic Sites and Structures Inventory* (Indianapolis, 1994), xiv-xv, xviii-xl.

41. Thomas D. Clark and Terry Birdwhistell, "Sullivan Law," in Kleber, *Kentucky Encyclopedia*, 860. See also Clark, "Public Education," in Kleber, *Kentucky Encyclopedia*, 746.

42. Clinton, "Social and Educational History," 50-57; Livingston County Historical Society, *Livingston County, Kentucky*, 1:39-51.

43. Phillips, *Indiana in Transition*, 388-89, 391, 393-400. By 1920, 4,800 one-room schools remained in Indiana, despite the fact that almost 4,000 had been abandoned since 1890. Although Indiana ranked fourth in the number of pupils in high school per thousand in 1917, three-quarters were enrolled in schools with fewer than 100 students. Indiana also had "almost the worst record among the states for short academic terms in four-year high schools." In 1917-1918, only 26 percent of its high schools had terms of more than 160 days, compared with 89 percent in the nation (ibid., 395).

44. U.S., 14th Census, 1920, *Population* (Washington, 1922), 3:244, 246, 251, 252-58, 262-68, 282, 284, 289-311, 364-86. U.S., 12th Census, 1900, *Population*, 2:388-401.

45. Bennett Directory Company, *Evansville City Directory* (Evansville, 1920), 28. Another public high school, named for Benjamin Bosse, would open in the affluent east side in 1925. A Catholic high school, named by Reitz to memorialize his parents, opened nearby a year later.

46. U.S., 14th Census, 1920, *Population* (Washington, 1923), 2:1094, and 3:244-386. For persons age ten and older, the overall illiteracy rates in Kentucky's lower Ohio counties ranged from 4.6 percent in McCracken to 10.4 percent in Breckinridge. Rastes for Hernderson, Owensboro, Hardin, and Pulaski were, respectively, 7.4, 5.7, and 6.4. Across the river, only Alexander, Hardin, and Pulaski counties in Illinois had rates approximately equal to Kentucky.

47. Neuman, *Story of Paducah*, 154-61; McCracken County Genealogical Society, *History and Families of McCracken County*, 344; *Daviess County* (1883), 197-206; Hayes, *Sixty Years of Owensboro*, 261-74; Lansden, *City of Cairo*, 163-67; and Arnett, *Annals and Scandals*, 293-97.

48. Daniel J. Leab, "Movies," in *The Reader's Companion to American History*, ed.

Eric Foner and John A. Garraty (Boston, 1991), 755. See also Chudacoff and Smith, *Evolution of American Urban Society,* 217-21.

49. Dew, *Shaping Our Society,* 15-21; May, *History Papers,* 58, 60-61, 64-65; Briggs, *Early History of West Point,* 33-58.

50. Seymour, *Baseball,* 1:345-48.

51. De La Hunt, *Perry County,* 336-40; *Rockport-Spencer County Sesquicentennial,* 7-21; Arnett, *Annals and Scandals,* 98-100; Neuman, *Story of Paducah,* 154-61; Taylor, *Indiana: A New Historical Guide,* 245-46; Hayes, *After Sixty Years,* 280-342; Lipin, *Producers,* 279n. 45. Willard Library received some funding from the city council. The Evansville public library system had its own taxing authority.

52. Hayes, *Sixty Years of Owensboro,* 217-35; Bolin, *Ohio Valley History,* 78-84; Neuman, *Story of Paducah,* 228-29; McCracken County Genealogical Society, *History and Families,* 306-8.

53. Historic Landmarks Foundation of Indiana, *Vanderburgh County Interim Report,* xxvii, 77, 269; *Architecture of Paducah and McCracken County,* 28-29; Neuman, *Story of Paducah,* 238-44.

Conclusion

1. U.S., 15th Census, 1930, *Population* (Washington, 1931), 1:280-306, 329-48; 431-51; U.S., 17th Census, 1950, *Population* (Washington, 1953), vol. 2, 13:9-23, 14:9-23, and 17:6-14.

2. A vivid reminder of the Ohio's significance in the tri-state area is found in a special feature on the river in Evansville, *Sunday Courier and Press,* August 21, 1955.

Bibliography

Abbott, Carl. "The Plank Road Enthusiasm in the Antebellum Middle West." *Indiana Magazine of History* 67 (June 1971): 95-116.
———. *Boosters and Businessmen: Popular Economic Thought and Urban Growth in the Antebellum Middle West.* Westport, Conn., 1981.
Abdy, Harry Bennett. *On the Ohio.* New York, 1919.
Adams, Edwin. *History of Warrick County, Indiana.* Evansville, 1868.
Adams, Jane. *The Transformation of Rural Life: Southern Illinois, 1890-1990.* Chapel Hill, N.C., 1994.
Allen, John W. *Legends and Lore of Southern Illinois.* Carbondale, Ill., 1963.
Allen, William B. *A History of Kentucky, Embracing Gleanings, Reminiscences . . .* Louisville, 1872; reprint, Green County Historical Society, 1967.
Ambler, Charles Henry. *A History of Transportation in the Ohio Valley.* Glendale, Calif., 1932.
Arbuckle, Robert D. "Ohiopiomingo: The 'Mythical' Kentucky Settlement That Was Not a Myth." *Register of the Kentucky Historical Society* 70 (October 1972): 318-24.
Arnett, Maralee. *The Annals and Scandals of Henderson County, Kentucky.* Corydon, Ky., 1976.
Ayers, Edward L. *The Promise of the New South: Life after Reconstruction.* New York, 1992.
Baertich, Frank. *History of Troy, Indiana.* Utica, Ky., 1983.
Ballard-Carlisle Historical-Genealogical Society. *Ballard and Carlisle Counties History,* vol. 1. Wickliffe, Ky., 1993.
Barge, William D., and Norman W. Caldwell. "Illinois Place Names." *Journal of the Illinois State Historical Society* 29 (October 1936): 189-311.
Barnhart, John D. *Valley of Democracy: The Frontier versus the Plantation in the Ohio Valley, 1775-1818.* Bloomington, Ind., 1953.
———. "The Impact of the Civil War on Indiana." *Indiana Magazine of History* 57 (September 1961): 183-224.
Barnhart, John D., and Dorothy L. Riker. *Indiana to 1816: The Colonial Period.* Indianapolis, 1971.
Barth, Gunther. *City People: The Rise of Modern City Culture in Nineteenth-Century America.* New York, 1980.
Battle, J.H., W.H. Perrin, and G.C. Kniffin. *Kentucky: A History of the State,* vol. 2: *Histories and Biographies of Ballard, Calloway, Fulton, Graves, Hickman, McCracken, and Marshall Counties, Kentucky.* Louisville, 1885.
Bennett, H. Thornton. *Henderson City Directory.* Evansville, 1900.

Bennett Directory Company. *Evansville City Directory.* Evansville, 1920.

Bennett, Pamela J., and Shirley S. McCord, eds. *Progress after Statehood: A Book of Readings.* Indianapolis, 1974.

Bernhard, Karl, duke of Saxe-Weimar-Eisenach. *Travels through North America, during the Years 1825 and 1826.* Weimar, 1828.

Bigham, Darrel E. "Charles Leich and Company of Evansville: A Note on the Dilemma of German Americans during World War I." *Indiana Magazine of History* 70 (June 1974): 95-121.

———. *Reflections on a Heritage: The German Americans in Southwestern Indiana.* Evansville, 1980.

———. *We Ask Only a Fair Trial: A History of the Black Community of Evansville, Indiana.* Bloomington, Ind., 1987.

———. *An Evansville Album: Perspectives on a River City, 1812-1988.* Bloomington, Ind., 1988.

———. "River of Opportunity: Economic Consequences of the Ohio." In *Always a River: The Ohio River and the American Experience,* ed. Robert L. Reid. Bloomington, Ind., 1991.

Biographical Cyclopedia of Vanderburgh County, Indiana. Evansville, 1897.

Biographical History of Eminent and Self-Made Men of the State of Indiana. Cincinnati, 1880.

Biographical Review of Johnson, Massac, Pope, and Hardin Counties, Illinois. Chicago, 1893.

Birdsall, Stephen S., and John W. Florin. *Regional Landscapes of the United States and Canada.* 3d ed. New York, 1985.

Birkbeck, Morris. *Letters from Illinois.* 1818; reprint, New York, 1970.

Blue, James Lincoln, and Donald Lee Hazelwood, comps. *Henderson County, Kentucky, 1880 Census.* Mount Vernon, Ind., 1995.

Blumin, Stuart M. *The Urban Threshold: Growth and Change in a Nineteenth-Century American Community.* Chicago, 1976.

———. "When Villages Become Towns: The Historical Context of Town Formation." In *The Pursuit of Urban History,* ed. Derek Fraser and Anthony Sutcliffe, 54-68. London, 1983.

Bodnar, John. *The Transplanted: A History of Immigrants in Urban America.* Bloomington, Ind., 1985.

Boggess, Arthur Clinton. *The Settlement of Illinois, 1778-1830,* vol. 5. Chicago Historical Society Collection. Chicago, 1908.

Bogle, Victor M. "Railroad Building in Indiana, 1850-1855." *Indiana Magazine of History* 58 (September 1962): 221-31.

Bolin, Daniel Lynn. *Ohio Valley History: West Point to Lewisport, a Bibliography . . .* New Orleans, ca. 1976.

Botkin, Benjamin Albert. *Treasury of Mississippi River Folklore.* New York, 1955.

[Boulware, W.W.] *History of Daviess County, Kentucky.* Chicago, 1883; reprint, Evansville, Ind., 1966.

Brant and Fuller. *History of Vanderburgh County.* Madison, Wisc., 1889.

Braudel, Fernand. *The History of France,* vol. 1: *History and Environment.* New York, 1988.

Briggs, Harold E. "Entertainment and Amusement in Cairo, 1848-1858." *Journal of the Illinois State Historical Society* 47 (autumn 1954): 232-51.

Briggs, Richard Arthur. *The Early History of West Point, Hardin County, Kentucky.* Louisville, 1955; reprint, Utica, Ky., 1983.

Brownell, Baker. *The Other Illinois.* New York, 1958.

Buck, Solon. *Illinois in 1818.* Springfield, Ill., 1917.

Buley, R. Carlyle. *The Old Northwest: The Pioneer Period, 1815-1840.* 2 vols. 1950; reprint, Bloomington, Ind., 1978.

Bulleit, G.A., comp. *Illustrated Atlas and History of Harrison County, Indiana.* Corydon, Ind., 1906.

Burleigh, William R., ed. *A Bicentennial Look at Newburgh.* Newburgh, Ind., 1976.

Caldwell, Norman W. "Fort Massac: The American Frontier Post, 1778-1806." *Journal of the Illinois State Historical Society* 43 (winter 1950): 265-81,

———. "Fort Massac since 1805." *Journal of the Illinois State Historical Society* 44 (spring 1951): 47-72.

Campbell, Tracy A. *The Politics of Despair: Power and Resistance in the Tobacco Wars.* Lexington, Ky., 1993.

Cannelton Sewer Pipe Company. Files MS 5484. Indiana Historical Society.

Carrier, Lois A. *Illinois: Crossroads of a Continent.* Urbana, Ill., 1993.

Chandler, Alfred D. *Strategy and Structure.* Cambridge, Mass., 1982.

Chark-Elwell Company. *City Directory of Owensboro, Kentucky.* Champaign, Ill., 1920.

Chinn, George Morgan. *Kentucky: Settlement and Statehood, 1750-1800.* Frankfort, Ky., 1975.

Chudacoff, Howard P., and Judith E. Smith. *The Evolution of American Urban Society.* 4th ed. Englewood Cliffs, N.J., 1994.

Clark, Thomas D. *The Kentucky.* New York, 1942.

———. *Kentucky: Land of Contrast.* New York, 1968.

———. *Historic Maps of Kentucky.* Lexington, 1979.

———. *A History of Kentucky.* 6th ed. Ashland, Ky., 1992.

Colby, Charles C. *Pilot Study of Southern Illinois.* Carbondale, Ill., 1956.

Cole, Arthur C. "Baseball in Cairo: A Footnote to Illinois History." *Journal of the Illinois State Historical Society* 33 (June 1940): 234-37.

———. *The Era of the Civil War, 1848-1870,* vol. 3 of *Sesquicentennial History of Illinois.* 1919; reprint, Urbana, 1987.

Collins, Lewis. *History of Kentucky.* 1874; reprint, Berea, Ky., 1976.

Collot, Victor. *A Journey in North America,* vol. 1. Translated by J. Christian Bay. Paris, 1826; reprint, Firenze, Italy, 1924. Available at the Indiana Historical Society Library.

Comeaux, Malcolm L. "Impact of Transportation Activities upon the Historical Development of Cairo, Illinois." M.A. thesis, Southern Illinois University, 1966.

Conclin, George. *A New River Guide, or a Gazeteer of All the Towns on the Western Waters.* Cincinnati, 1848.

Conkin, Paul K. *The Uneasy Center: Reformed Christianity in Antebellum America.* Chapel Hill, N.C., 1995.

Conrod, Charles Edward. "Limited Growth of Cities in the Lower Ohio Valley." Ph.D. diss., Northwestern University, 1976.

Cooper, Patricia A. *Once a Cigar Maker: Men, Women, and Work Culture in American Cigar Factories, 1900-1919.* Urbana, Ill., 1987.

Courier Company. *The Great Flood of '37.* Evansville, 1987.

Cramer, Zadok. *The Navigator*. Pittsburgh, 1802, 1811, 1814.

Cronon, William. *Nature's Metropolis: Chicago and the Great West*. New York, 1991.

Cross, Jasper W. "The Civil War Comes to 'Egypt,'" *Journal of the Illinois State Historical Society* 44 (summer 1951): 160-98.

Cumings, Samuel. *The Western Pilot, Containing Charts of the Ohio River, and of the Mississippi . . . Description of the Towns on Their Banks, Tributary Streams, etc. . . . *Cincinnati, 1825.

Dannheiser, Frieda J., ed. *The History of Henderson County, Kentucky*. Henderson, 1980.

De La Hunt, Thomas James. *Perry County: A History*. 1915; reprint, Owensboro, Ky., 1980.

De Bow, J.D.B. *Statistical View of the United States . . . Being a Compendium of the Seventh Census*. Washington, 1854.

————. *Mortality Statistics of the 7th Census*. Washington, 1855.

Dew, Lee A. "Henderson, Kentucky, and the Fight for Equitable Freight Rates, 1906-1918." *Register of the Kentucky Historical Society* 76 (January 1978): 34-44.

————. "Owensboro's Dream of Glory: A Railroad to Russellville." *Filson Club Quarterly* 52 (January 1978): 26-27. Reprinted in *Daviess County Historical Quarterly* 9 (July/October 1991): 63-71, 86-94.

————. "The Whig Party in Daviess County." *Daviess County Historical Quarterly* 1 (winter 1983): 15-21.

————. "Coal Mining in Daviess County in the Nineteenth Century." *Daviess County Historical Quarterly* 5 (April 1987): 27-37.

————. "Owensboro's River Trade, 1870." *Daviess County Historical Quarterly* 6 (April 1988): 27-37.

————. *Shaping Our Society: Transportation and the Development of the Society and Culture of Hancock County*. Hawesville, Ky., 1989.

————. "Industry and Agriculture: Owensboro and Daviess County in the First Decade of the Twentieth Century." *Daviess County Historical Quarterly* 11 (October 1993): 80-91.

————. "Owensboro and Elsewhere." *Daviess County Historical Quarterly* 12 (October 1994): 74-82.

————. "County Fever." *Kentucky Humanities* (summer/fall 1995): 14-17.

Dew, Lee A. and Aloma W. Dew. *Owensboro: The City on the Yellow Banks*. Bowling Green, Ky., 1988.

Dickens, Charles. *American Notes*. New York, 1842.

————. *The Works of Charles Dickens in Thirty Volumes*. New York, 1900.

————. *Martin Chuzzlewit*. New Oxford Illustrated Dickens. New York, 1968.

Doyle, Don H. *The Social Order of a Frontier Community: Jacksonville, Illinois, 1825-1870*. Urbana, Ill., 1978.

Drake, Charles D., ed. *Pioneer Life in Kentucky: A Series of Reminiscential Letters from Daniel Drake M.D. of Cincinnati to His Children*. Cincinnati, 1870.

Dreiser, Theodore. *Dawn: A History of Myself*. New York, 1931.

Dyson, John P. "The Naming of Paducah." *Register of the Kentucky Historical Society* 92 (spring 1994): 149-74.

Echeverria, Durand, ed. "General Collot's Plan for a Reconnaissance of the Ohio and Mississippi Valleys." *William and Mary Quarterly*, 3d ser., 9 (October 1952): 512-20.

Elkins, Stanley, and Eric McKitrick. *The Age of Federalism: The Early American Republic, 1788-1800*. New York, 1993.

Elliott, Joseph P. *A History of Evansville and Vanderburgh County, Indiana.* Evansville, 1897.

Emerson and Williams. *Owensboro Directory, 1882-1883.* Louisville, 1882.

Esarey, Logan. *The Indiana Home.* 1947; reprint, Bloomington, Ind., 1976.

Eslinger, Ellen. "The Shape of Slavery on the Kentucky Frontier, 1775-1800." Register of the Kentucky Historical Society 92 (winter 1992): 1-23.

Etcheson, Nicole. *The Emerging Midwest: Upland Southerners and the Political Culture of the Old Northwest, 1787-1861.* Bloomington, Ind., 1996.

Evans, Sara M. *Born for Liberty: A History of Women in America.* New York, 1989.

Evansville. *Annual Report of the Departments of the Municipal Government, City of Evansville, for the Fiscal Year Ending December 31, 1914.* Evansville, 1915.

Evansville. Tax assessment book for 1860. Vanderburgh County Archives, Willard Library.

Evansville City Council. *Revised Ordinances of the City of Evansville.* Evansville, 1901.

Evansville Common Council. Minutes, August 18, 1865, March 19, 1866, and July 13, 1874. Vanderburgh County Archives, Willard Library.

Evansville Town Board. Minute book 1841-1847. Office of the City Clerk, Evansville.

Fatout, Paul. *Indiana Canals.* West Lafayette, Ind., 1972.

Federal Writers Project, Works Progress Administration. *Cairo Guide.* Nappanee, Ind., 1938.

———. *Illinois: A Descriptive and Historical Guide.* Chicago, 1939.

———. *Kentucky: A Guide to the Bluegrass State.* New York, 1939.

———. *Henderson: A Guide to Audubon's Home Town in Kentucky.* Northport, N.Y., 1941.

———. *Union County, Past and Present.* Louisville, 1941; reprint, Evansville, 1972.

Ferguson, William. *America by River and Rail.* London, 1856.

Fischer, David Hackett. *Albion's Seed: Four British Folkways in America.* New York, 1989.

Flint, Timothy. *Recollections of the Last Ten Years . . .* Boston, 1826.

Fohs Hall Community Arts Foundation. *Crittenden County, Kentucky.* Marion, Ky., 1991.

Ford, Nancy H., comp. *Hancock County, Kentucky 1850 Census.* Owensboro, Ky., 1974.

Fortune, Will, ed. *Warrick and Its Prominent People.* Evansville, 1881.

Foster, John W. *A Report of the Board of Trade for Evansville, Indiana, for 1867.* Evansville, 1868.

Fraser, Kathryn M. "Fort Jefferson: George Rogers Clark's Fort at the Mouth of the Ohio River, 1780-1781." *Register of the Kentucky Historical Society* 81 (winter 1983): 1-24.

Freehling, William W. *Reintegrating American History: Slavery and the Civil War.* New York, 1994.

Funk, Arville L. *Historical Almanac of Harrison County, Indiana.* Corydon, Ind., 1974.

Gallatin County Historical Society. *History and Families of Gallatin County, Illinois.* Paducah, 1988.

Gilbert, Frank M. *History of the City of Evansville and Vanderburg [sic] County, Indiana,* vol. 1. Chicago, 1910.

Glaab, Charles N., and A. Theodore Brown. *A History of Urban America.* 3rd ed. New York, 1983.

Goldfield, David R. *Cotton Fields and Skyscrapers: Southern City and Region, 1607-1890.* Baton Rouge, La., 1982.

Goldfield, David R., and Blaine A. Brownell. *Urban America: From Downtown to No Town.* Boston, 1979.

Goodspeed Company. *History of Warrick, Spencer, and Perry Counties, Indiana.* Chicago, 1885; reprint, Evansville, 1973.

———. *History of Posey County, Indiana.* Chicago, 1886.

———. *History of Gallatin, Saline, Hamilton, Franklin, and Williamson Counties, Illinois*. Chicago, 1887; reprint, Evansville, Ind., 1971.

Grantham, Dewey W. *The South in Modern America: A Region at Odds*. New York, 1994.

Gray, Ralph D. *Transportation and the Early Nation*. Indianapolis, 1982.

———, ed. *Indiana History: A Book of Readings*. Bloomington, Ind., 1994.

Green, Harvey. *The Uncertainty of Everyday Life, 1915-1945*. New York, 1992.

Greene, W.P., ed. *The Green River Country from Bowling Green to Evansville: Its Traffic, Its Resources, Its Towns*. Evansville, 1898.

Griffin, Frederick P., comp. *History of Corydon and Harrison County, Indiana: A Scrapbook of Newspaper Clippings*. 2 vols. Paoli, Ind., 1991.

Griffing, B.N. *Atlas of Harrison County, Indiana*. Philadelphia, 1882.

Hall, James. *Letters from the West*. London, 1828.

Hall, Ruby Franklin. *History of Hardin County, Illinois*. Carbondale, Ill., 1970.

"Hancock County Tax Records." *Forgotten Pathways* 7 (fall 1991 and spring 1992): 17-21, 31-36, 42-47, 62-64.

Hardin County Historical and Genealogical Society. *Hardin County, Illinois*. Paducah, 1987.

Harper, Robert A. "River Junction Communities in the Lower Ohio Valley: A Study of Functional Change." *Journal of Geography* 59 (November 1960): 364-70.

Harshbarger, Marilyn. "A Study of the Philanthropic Contributions of the John Augustus Reitz Family." On file in special collections at the University of Southern Indiana library.

Hartley, Joseph R. *Economic Effects of Ohio River Transportation*. Bloomington, Ind., 1957.

Hatch, Nathan O. *The Democratization of American Christianity*. New Haven, Conn., 1989.

Havighurst, Walter J. *River to the West: Three Centuries of the Ohio*. New York, 1970.

Hawkins, Hubert H., ed. *Indiana's Road to Statehood: A Documentary Record*. Indianapolis, 1969.

Heady, Peyton. *Union County in the Civil War*. Morganfield, Ky., 1985.

Heflin, Sheila E. Brown. "The Owensboro City Railroad." *National Railway Bulletin* 44 (November 4, 1979): 18-24

Hercules Manufacturing Company. *The Hercules Picture Story*. Henderson, Ky., 1987.

Hilton, George W., and John F. Due. *The Electric Interurban Railways in America*. Stanford, Calif., 1960.

Historic Landmarks Foundation of Indiana. *Vanderburgh County Interim Report: Indiana Historic Sites and Structures Inventory*. Indianapolis, 1994.

Hodges, Glenn. *Fearful Times: A History of the Civil War Years in Hancock County, Kentucky*. Owensboro, Ky., 1986.

Holzborg, Janice, and Carol Preflatish, comp. *A Commemorative History of Crawford County, 1818-1993: 175 Years Old*. N.p., 1993.

Hopkins, John S. "A Short Biographical Sketch of John Stuart Hopkins." October 22, 1881. Copy in author's possession.

Horsman, Reginald. "The Collapse of the Ohio River Barrier: Conflict and Negotiation in the Old Northwest, 1763-1787." In *Pathways to the Old Northwest: An Observance of the Bicentennial of the Northwest Ordinance*. Indianapolis, 1988.

House, *Report on the Internal Commerce of the United States*. 50th Cong., 1st sess., 1888, H. Doc. 6, 492.

Howard, Robert P. *Illinois: A History of the Prairie State*. Grand Rapids, Mich., 1972.

Howard, Victor B. *Black Liberation in Kentucky: Emancipation and Freedom, 1862-1884.* Lexington, Ky., 1983.

Huff, Paul. "The Steamboat Trades of Owensboro in the 1870s." *Daviess County Historical Quarterly* 3 (April 1985): 27-36.

Hulbert, Archer B. *The Ohio River: A Course of Empire.* New York, 1906.

Hunter, Louis C. *Steamboats on the Western Waters: An Economic and Technological History.* Cambridge, Mass., 1949.

Hyneman, Charles S., C. Richard Hofstetter, and Patrick F. O'Connor. *Voting in Indiana: A Century of Persistence and Change.* Bloomington, Ind., 1979.

Iglehart, John E., ed. *An Account of Vanderburgh County from Its Organization,* vol. 3 of Logan Esarey, *A History of Indiana from Its Exploration to 1922.* Dayton, Ohio, 1923.

Illinois in 1837: With a Map. Philadelphia, 1837.

Illustrated Historical Atlas of Daviess County, Kentucky (N.p., 1876);

Illustrated Historical Atlas of Henderson and Union Counties, Kentucky. Philadelphia, 1880; reprint, Evansville, 1969.

Illustrated Historical Atlas of Spencer County, Indiana. Chicago, 1879.

Illustrated Historical Atlas of Warrick County, Indiana. Philadelphia, 1880.

Ireland, Robert M. *The County in Kentucky History.* Lexington, Ky., 1976.

Jackson, Adah. "Glimpses of Civil War Newburgh." *Indiana Magazine of History* 41 (June 1945): 167-84.

Jakle, John A. *Images of the Ohio Valley: A Historical Geography of Travel, 1740 to 1860.* New York, 1977.

———. "The Ohio Valley Revisited: Images from Nicholas Cresswell and Reuben Gold Thwaites." In *Always a River: The Ohio River and the American Experience,* ed. Robert L. Reid. Bloomington, Ind., 1991.

———. "Toward a Geographical History of Indiana: Landscape and Place in the Historical Imagination." *Indiana Magazine of History* 89 (September 1993): 177-209

James, U.P. *James's River Guide.* Cincinnati, 1856.

Jensen, Richard J. *Illinois: A Bicentennial History.* New York, 1978.

Jett, Oswald. *Hancock County, Kentucky, When It Was Frontier Country.* Utica, Ky., 1986.

Johnson, Leland L. "Engineering the Ohio." In *Always a River: The Ohio River and the American Experience,* ed. Robert L. Reid, 180-209. Bloomington, Ind., 1991.

———. *The Ohio River Division, U.S. Army Corps of Engineers: The History of a Central Command.* Cincinnati, 1992.

Jones, R.R., comp. *The Ohio River: Charts, Drawings, and Description of Features Affecting Navigation.* Washington, 1916.

Katterjohn, Monte N. *History of Warrick and Its Prominent People from the Earliest Time to the Present.* Boonville, Ind., 1909.

Keiser, John H. *Building for the Centuries: Illinois 1865 to 1898.* Urbana, Ill., 1977.

Kellar, James H. *An Introduction to the Prehistory of Indiana.* Indianapolis, 1983.

Kentucky Heritage Commission. *Survey of Historic Sites in Kentucky: Ballard County.* Frankfort, 1978.

King, Gail, and Susan Thurman. *Henderson's River Book.* Henderson, Ky., 1991.

Kleber, Albert. "The Naming of Troy, Indiana." *Indiana Magazine of History* 44 (1948): 178-80.

Kleber, John E., ed. *Kentucky Encyclopedia.* Lexington, Ky., 1992.

Klein, Maury. *History of the L&N Railroad.* New York, 1972.

Klingler, Ed. *How a City Founded to Make Money Made It: The Economic and Business History of Evansville.* Evansville, ca. 1977.

Kreipke, Martha. "The Falls of the Ohio and the Development of the Ohio River Trade, 1810-1860." *Filson Club Quarterly* 54 (April 1980): 197.

Kyte, George W. "A Spy on the Western Waters: The Military Intelligence Mission of General Collot in 1796." *Mississippi Valley Historical Review* 34 (December 1947): 427-42

Lansden, John McMurray. *A History of the City of Cairo.* 1910; reprint, Carbondale, 1976.

Lantz, Herman R. *A Community in Search of Itself: A Case History of Cairo, Illinois.* Carbondale, Ill., 1972.

Lawler, Lucille. *Gallatin County: Gateway to Illinois.* Crossville, Ill., 1968.

Leab, Daniel J. "Movies." In *The Reader's Companion to American History,* ed. Eric Foner and John A. Garraty. Boston, 1991.

Lee, Lloyd G. *A Brief History of Kentucky and Its Counties.* Berea, Ky., 1981.

Leffel, John C., ed. *History of Posey County, Indiana.* Chicago, 1913.

Leonard, W.P. *History and Directory of Posey County, Indiana.* Evansville, 1882.

Levine, Lawrence W. *The Unpredictable Past: Explorations in American Cultural History.* New York, 1993.

Lindley, Harlow, ed. *Indiana as Seen by Early Travelers: A Collection of Reprints from Books of Travel, Letters, and Diaries prior to 1830.* Indianapolis, 1916.

Lipin, Lawrence M. *Producers, Proletarians, and Politicians: Workers and Party Politics in Evansville and New Albany, Indiana, 1850-87.* Urbana, Ill., 1994.

Lippincott, Isaac. *A History of Manufactures in the Ohio Valley to 1860.* New York, 1973.

Livingston County Historical Society. *Livingston County History.* Paducah, 1989.

Lohmann, Karl B. *Cities and Towns of Illinois: A Handbook of Community Facts.* Urbana, Ill., 1951.

Long, E.B. "The Paducah Affair: Bloodless Action That Altered the Civil War in the Mississippi Valley." *Register of the Kentucky Historical Society* 70 (October 1972): 269-74.

Lucas, Marion B. *From Slavery to Segregation, 1760-1891.,* vol. 1 of *A History of Blacks in Kentucky.* Frankfort, Ky., 1992.

McClure, Daniel E. *Two Centuries of Elizabethtown and Hardin County, Kentucky.* Elizabethtown, Ky., 1979.

McConnell, Darlene Ann, comp. *Posey County, Indiana, 1870 Federal Census.* Mount Vernon, Ind., 1987.

McCracken County Genealogical Society. *History and Families of McCracken County, Kentucky.* Paducah, 1989.

McCutchan, Kenneth P. *At the Bend of the River: The Story of Evansville.* Woodland Hills, Calif., 1982.

McManaway, Robert, comp. *1870 Census of Hancock County.* Utica, Ky., 1982.

McPherson, James. *Ordeal by Fire: The Civil War and Reconstruction.* 2d ed. New York, 1992.

Madison, James H. "Businessmen and the Business Community in Indianapolis, 1820-1860." Ph.D. diss., Indiana University, 1972.

————. *The Indiana Way: A State History.* Bloomington, Ind., 1986.

Mahoney, Timothy R. *River Towns in the Great West: The Structure of Provincial Urbanization in the American Midwest, 1820-1870.* New York, 1990.

Marty, Martin E. *Pilgrims in Their Own Land: Five Hundred Years of Religion in America.* New York, 1984.

May, George W. *History of Massac County, Illinois.* Galesburg, Ill., 1955.

———. *History Papers of Massac County, Illinois.* Paducah, 1990.

Merrill, James M. "Cairo, Illinois: Strategic Civil War River Port." *Journal of the Illinois State Historical Society* 76 (winter 1983): 242-56.

Miller, Mitford M. "Evansville Steamboats during the Civil War." *Indiana Magazine of History* 37 (December 1941): 359-81.

———, comp. "Evansville Steamboat Clippings, 1848-1875." Willard Library, Evansville.

Milliman, J.W., and W.G. Pinnell. "Economic Redevelopment for Evansville, Indiana: A Case Study of a Depressed City." In *Community Economic Development Efforts: Five Case Studies.* Committee for Economic Development, suppl. paper no. 18. New York, 1964.

Mitchell, Reid. *The Vacant Chair: The Northern Soldier Leaves Home.* New York, 1993.

Mohl, Raymond A., ed. *The Making of Urban America.* Wilmington, Dela., 1988.

Monkkonen, Eric H. *America Becomes Urban: The Development of United States Cities and Towns, 1780-1980.* Berkeley, Calif., 1988.

Moore, Leonard J. *Citizen Klansmen: The Ku Klux Klan in Indiana, 1921-1928.* Chapel Hill, N.C., 1991.

Neely, Mark E. Jr. *The Last Best Hope on Earth: Abraham Lincoln and the Promise of America.* Cambridge, Mass., 1993.

Nevins, Allan. *The War for the Union: The Improvised War, 1861-1862,* vol. 5 of *The Ordeal of the Union.* New York, 1959.

———. *The War for the Union: The Organized War to Victory, 1864-1865,* vol. 8 of *The Ordeal of the Union.* New York, 1971.

Neuman, Fred G. *The Story of Paducah.* Paducah, Ky., 1927.

Newman, Charles W., comp. *Ohio River Navigation Past Present Future.* Cincinnati, 1979.

O'Malley, Charles J. *History of Union County, Kentucky.* 1886; reprint, Evansville, 1969.

Ohio Valley Improvement Association. *Official Program and History: Dedicatory Celebration of the Completion of the Nine Foot State from Pittsburgh to Cairo, October 19-23, 1929.* N.p., [1929].

Our Towns. Louisville, 1992.

Page, O.J. *History of Massac County, Illinois.* Metropolis [?], ca. 1900.

Paludan, Philip Shaw. *"A People's Contest": The Union and the Civil War, 1861-1865.* New York, 1988.

Pease, Theodore C. *The Frontier State, 1818-1848,* vol. 2 of *The Centennial History of Illinois.* 1918; reprint, Urbana, Ill., 1987.

Peck, John Mason. *A Guide for Emigrants, Containing Sketches of Illinois, Missouri, and the Adjacent Parts.* Boston, 1836.

Perrin, William Henry, ed. *History of Alexander, Union, and Pulaski Counties, Illinois.* Chicago, 1883; reprint, Utica, Ky., 1987.

Phillips, Claribel, and Dorothy Watkins, comp. *Hancock County, Kentucky, 1880 Federal Census.* Lewisport, Ky., 1991.

Phillips, Clifton J. *Indiana in Transition: The Emergence of an Industrial Commonwealth, 1880-1920.* Indianapolis, 1968.

Pitkin, William A. "When Cairo Was Saved for the Union." *Journal of the Illinois State Historical Society* 51 (autumn 1988): 305.

Pleasant, Hazen Hayes. *A History of Crawford County, Indiana.* 1926; reprint, Evansville, Ind., 1966.

Polk and Company. *Kentucky Gazeteer and Business Directory for 1895-1896,* reprinted as *Kentucky Places and People.* Utica, Ky., 1983[?].

Pope County Historical Society. *Pope County, Illinois.* Paducah, 1986.

Posey County Historical Society. *Posey County, Indiana: 175th Anniversary History, 1814-1989.* Paducah, 1989.

Postwood, Shirley. "Blacks and the Republican Party in Alexander and Pulaski Counties, 1870-1900." Paper delivered at the Organization of American Historians, Washington, D.C., March 31, 1995.

Potter, Hugh O. "Owensboro's Original Proprietor." *Register of the Kentucky Historical Society* 69 (January 1971): 1-16.

———, ed. *History of Owensboro and Daviess County, Kentucky.* Owensboro, 1974.

Rabinowitz, Howard N. *The First New South, 1865-1920.* Arlington Heights, Ill., 1992.

Raboteau, Albert J. *Slave Religion: The "Invisible Institution" in the Antebellum South.* New York, 1978.

Rawlyk, George A. "The 'Rising French Empire' in the Ohio Valley and the Old Northwest: The Dreaded Juncture of the French Settlements in Canada with Those of Louisiana." In *Contest for Empire, 1500-1775: Proceedings of an Indiana American Revolution Bicentennial Celebration,* ed. John B. Elliott. Indianapolis, 1975.

Reid, Robert L. "Pilgrims on the Ohio: The River Journey and Photographs of Reuben Gold Thwaites." *Traces of Indiana and Midwestern History* 8 (winter 1996): 24-33.

Revised Ordinances of the City of Evansville, Indiana. Evansville, 1901.

Rice, Otis K. *Frontier Kentucky.* 1975; reprint, Lexington, 1993.

Ridenour, George L. *Early Times in Meade County, Kentucky.* Louisville, 1929.

Riess, Steven A. *City Games: The Evolution of American Urban Society and the Rise of Sports.* Urbana, Ill., 1989.

Riggs, Elliott A. "A Hog Drive to Evansville, 1879." *Ohio Valley Folk Research Project,* n.s., no. 46 (1960): 1-6.

Rishel, Joseph F., ed. *American Cities and Towns: Historical Perspectives.* Pittsburgh, 1992.

Robert, Charles E. *Evansville: Her Commerce and Manufactures. A Descriptive Work of the Business Metropolis of Indiana.* Evansville, 1874.

———. "Paducah: Origins to Second Class." *Register of the Kentucky Historical Society* 66 (April 1968): 108.

Robertson, John E.L. *Paducah, 1830-1980: A Sesquicentennial History.* Paducah, 1980.

Robinson, Michael C. *History of Navigation in the Ohio River Basin.* Fort Belvoir, Va., 1983.

Rohrbough, Malcolm J. *The Land Office Business: The Settlement and Administration of American Public Lands, 1789-1837.* New York, 1969.

———. *Trans-Appalachian Frontier: People, Societies, and Institutions, 1775-1850.* New York, 1978.

Roose, William H. *Indiana's Birthplace: A History of Harrison County, Indiana.* Rev. ed. Chicago, 1966.

Rose, Gregory S. "Hoosier Origins: The Nativity of Indiana's Native-Born Population in 1850." *Indiana Magazine of History* 81 (September 1985): 201-32.

———. "The Distribution of Indiana's Ethnic and Racial Minorities in 1850." *Indiana Magazine of History* 87 (September 1991): 224-60.

Rosenberg, Charles E. *The Cholera Years: The United States in 1832, 1849, and 1866.* Chicago, 1987.

Ross, Frank E. "The Fur Trade of the Ohio Valley." *Indiana Magazine of History* 34 (December 1938): 417-43.

Rudolph, L.C. *Hoosier Zion: The Presbyterians in Early Indiana.* New Haven, 1963.

————. *Hoosier Faiths: A History of Indiana's Churches and Religious Groups.* Bloomington, Ind., 1995.

Savage, James P. Jr. "Do-It-Yourself Books for Illinois Immigrants." *Journal of the Illinois State Historical Society* 62 (spring 1964): 39.

Schlereth, Thomas. "Regional Culture Studies and American Culture Studies." In *Sense of Place: American Regional Cultures,* ed. Barbara Allen and Thomas J. Schlereth. Lexington, Ky., 1990.

Schnellenberg, James A. *Conflict between Communities: American County Seat Wars.* New York, 1987.

Schockel, Bernard. "Manufactural Evansville, 1820-1933." Ph.D. diss., University of Chicago, 1947.

Schultz, Stanley K. *Constructing Urban Culture: American Cities and City Planning, 1800-1920.* Philadelphia, 1989.

Sellers, Charles G. *The Market Revolution: Jacksonian America, 1815-1846.* New York, 1991.

Seymour, Harold. *Baseball,* vol. 1: *The Early Years.* New York, 1960.

Share, Allen J. *Cities in the Commonwealth: Two Centuries of Urban Life in Kentucky.* Lexington, Ky., 1982.

Shockley, Ernest V. "County Seats and County Seat Wars." *Indiana Magazine of History* 10 (March 1914): 1-46.

Simpson, George B., comp. *Caseyville River Merchant Trade and Sale Records for 1854 and 1855 and the Tradewater Valley Farmers, Planters, and Miners.* Sturgis, Ky., 1988.

Sims, Shelly, comp. *Meade County, Kentucky 1850 Census.* Vine Grove, Ky., 1984.

Smelser, Marshall. "Material Customs in the Territory of Illinois." *Journal of the Illinois State Historical Society* 29 (April 1936): 40-41.

Sneed, Glenn J. *Ghost Towns of Southern Illinois.* Royalton, Ill., 1977.

Snepp, Daniel W. *Evansville's Channels of Trade and the Secession Movement, 1850-1865.* Indiana Historical Society Publications, vol. 8, no. 7. Indianapolis, 1928.

Sprague, Stuart Seely. "Town Making in the Era of Good Feelings: Kentucky, 1814-1820." *Register of the Kentucky Historical Society* 72 (October 1974): 337, 340.

Stallings, Roy. "The Drama in Southern Illinois (1865-1900)." *Journal of the Illinois State Historical Society* 28 (June 1940): 190-202.

Starke, Aubrey. "The Indigenous Iron Industry of Illinois." *Journal of the Illinois State Historical Society* 27 (January 1935): 432-33.

Starling, Edmund L. *The History of Henderson County, Kentucky.* Henderson, 1887.

Still, Bayard. *Urban America: A History with Documents.* Boston, 1974.

Stover, John F. *History of the Illinois Central Railroad.* New York, 1975.

Stroble, Paul E., Jr. *High on the Okaw's Western Bank: Vandalia, Illinois, 1819-1839.* Urbana, Ill., 1992.

Sutherland, Daniel E. *The Expansion of Everyday Life, 1860-1876.* New York, 1989.

Sutton, Robert P., ed. *The Prairie State: A Documentary History of Illinois,* vol. 1: *Colonial Years to 1860.* Grand Rapids, Mich., 1976.

Tapp, Hambleton, and James C. Klotter. *Kentucky: Decades of Discord, 1865-1900.* Frankfort, Ky., 1979.

Taylor, George Rogers. *The Transportation Revolution, 1815-1860.* New York, 1951.

Taylor, Robert M., Jr., ed. *Indiana: A New Historical Guide.* Indianapolis, 1989.

Teaford, Jon C. "City Government." In *The Reader's Companion to American History,* ed. Eric Foner and John A. Garraty. Boston, 1991.

————. *Cities of the Heartland: The Rise and Fall of the Industrial Midwest.* Bloomington, Ind., 1993.

Tell City Chair Company. Centennial pamphlet. N.p., 1965[?]. Stored in Indiana Historical Society Library.

Tell City News. Centennial supplement, August 8, 1958.

Tenney, Charles D. "The Future of Southern Illinois." *Journal of the Illinois State Historical Society* 57 (summer 1964): 172-78.

Thomas, Emory. *Robert E. Lee: A Biography.* New York, 1995.

Thompson, Bill. *History and Legend of Breckinridge County.* Utica, Ky., 1976.

Thornbrough, Emma Lou. *The Negro in Indiana: A Study of a Minority.* Indianapolis, 1957.

————. *Indiana in the Civil War Era, 1850-1880.* Indianapolis, 1965.

Thurston, John Gates. *A Journal of a Trip to Illinois in 1836.* Mount Pleasant, Mich., 1971.

Thwaites, Reuben Gold. *On the Storied Ohio.* 1903; reprint, New York, 1975. Originally titled *Afloat on the Ohio* (1897).

————, ed. *Early Western Travels, 1748-1846.* Cleveland, 1905.

Tingley, Donald F. *The Structuring of a State: The History of Illinois, 1899 to 1928.* Urbana, Ill., 1980.

Tocqueville, Alexis de. *Democracy in America.* Edited by J.P. Mayer. Garden City, N.Y., 1969.

Torrey, Kate Douglas. "Visions of a Western Lowell: Cannelton, Indiana, 1847-1851." *Indiana Magazine of History* 73 (December 1977): 276-304.

Trail, Robert. "Livingston County, Kentucky—Stepping Stone to Illinois." *Register of the Kentucky Historical Society* 69 (July 1971): 239-72.

Trollope, Mrs. [Frances M.]. *Domestic Manners of the Americans.* London and New York, 1832.

Trotter, Joe William Jr., ed. *The Great Migration in Historical Perspective: New Dimensions of Race, Class, and Gender.* Bloomington, Ind., 1991.

Twain, Mark. *Life on the Mississippi.* New York, 1883.

Upp, John. *Sketches of Western Adventure Comprising a Biographical Narrative of the Life of Jacob Upp . . .* Henderson, Ky., 1851.

United States. 4th Census, 1820, *Population Schedules of Vanderburgh County,* National Archives microfilm M33, roll 14, *Indiana.*

————. 5th Census, 1830, *Population Schedules of Vanderburgh County,* National Archives microfilm M19, roll 32, *Indiana.*

————. 6th Census, 1840. *Compendium of the Enumeration of the Inhabitants and Statistics of the United States.* Washington, 1841.

————. 6th Census, 1840, *Population Schedules of Vanderburgh County,* National Archives microfilm 704, roll 96, *Indiana.*

————. 7th Census, 1850. *Seventh Census: Embracing a Statistical View of Each of the States and Territories.* Washington, 1853.

―――. 7th Census, 1850, *Population Schedules of Daviess County,* National Archives microfilm M432, roll 198, *Kentucky.*

―――. 7th Census, 1850, *Population Schedules of Vanderburgh County,* National Archives microfilm M432, roll 176, *Indiana.*

―――. 8th Census, 1860. *Statistics of the Population of the United States.* Washington, 1864.

―――. 8th Census, 1860. *Manufactures of the United States in 1860.* Washington, 1864.

―――. 8th Census, 1860. *Slave Schedules, Kentucky,* National Archives microfilm M653, roll 402, *Daviess County;* roll 403, *Henderson County;* roll 404, *Union County.*

―――. 9th Census, 1870. *Statistics of the Population of the United States,* vol. 1. Washington, 1872.

―――. 9th Census, 1870. *Population Schedules of Daviess County,* National Archives microfilm M593, roll 458, *Kentucky.*

―――. 9th Census, 1870. *Population Schedules of Henderson County,* National Archives microfilm M593, roll 469, *Kentucky.*

―――. 10th Census, 1880. *Statistics of the Population of the United States.* Washington, 1883.

―――. 10th Census, 1880. *Report on the Agencies of Transportation in the United States.* Washington, 1883.

―――. 10th Census, 1880. *Report on the Social Statistics of Cities,* vol. 2: *The Southern and Western States.* Washington, 1887.

―――. 10th Census, 1880. *Census of Manufactures.* Washington, 1883.

―――. 10th Census, 1880. *Compendium of the 10th Census (year ending June 1, 1880).* Washington, 1883.

―――. 10th Census, 1880. *Population Schedules of Breckinridge County,* National Archives microfilm T9, roll 405, *Kentucky.*

―――. 11th Census, 1890. *Statistics of the Population of the United States.* Washington, 1895.

―――. 12th Census, 1900. *Population,* vols. 1 and 2. Washington, 1901-2.

―――. 12th Census, 1900. *Vital Statistics.* Washington, 1902.

―――. 12th Census, 1900. *Abstract.* Washington, 1903.

―――. 12th Census, 1900, *Population Schedules of Daviess County,* National Archives microfilm T623, rolls 517-18, *Kentucky.*

―――. 13th Census, 1910. *Population,* vol. 1. Washington, 1912.

―――. 13th Census, 1910. *Manufactures.* Washington, 1912.

―――. 14th Census, 1920. *Population,* vols. 1-4. Washington, 1921-1923.

―――. 14th Census, 1920. *Agriculture.* Washington, 1922.

―――. 14th Census, 1920. *Manufactures 1919.* Washington, 1923.

―――. 14th Census, 1920. *Population Schedules of Breckinridge County,* National Archives microfilm T625, roll 561, *Kentucky.*

―――. 15th Census, 1930. *Population,* vols. 1 and 2. Washington, 1931-1933.

―――. 16th Census, 1940. *Population,* vol. 2. Washington, 1943.

―――. 17th Census, 1950. *Population,* vol. 2. Washington, 1953.

―――. House of Representatives. *Report on the Internal Commerce of the United States.* Document 6. 50th Congress, first sess., 1888.

Vanderburgh County Commissioners. Record books A and E. Special collections at the University of Southern Indiana library.

Vanderburgh County Historical Society. Minutes, September 1879 to January 1884, transcribed in 1933.

Vanderburgh County Recorder's Office. Articles of association, book 1.

Wade, Richard C. *The Urban Frontier, 1790-1830.* Cambridge, Mass., 1957.

Waldrep, Christopher. "An Interloper in the Oligarchy: Livingston County's County Seat Controversy, 1806-1809." *Register of the Kentucky Historical Society* 78 (spring 1980): 115-22.

Walker, Francis A. *Compendium of the Ninth Census (year ending June 1, 1870).* Washington, 1872.

Watts, William Courtney. *Chronicles of a Kentucky Settlement.* New York, 1897.

Weisenburger, Francis P. "The Urbanization of the Middle West: Town and Village in the Pioneer Period." *Indiana Magazine of History* 41 (March 1945): 19-30.

Wells, Camille. *Architecture of Paducah and McCracken County.* Paducah, 1981.

Wheeler, Mary, ed. *Steamboatin' Days: Folk Songs of the Mississippi Packet Era.* Baton Rouge, La., 1944.

White, Edward. *Evansville and Its Men of Mark.* Evansville, 1873.

Whittlesey, Charles. *Fugitive Essays upon Interesting and Useful Subjects Relating to the Early History of Ohio, Its Geology and Agriculture . . . A Dissertation upon the Antiquity of the Material Universe, Being a Reprint from Various Periodicals of the Day.* Hudson, Ohio, 1852.

Wiebe, Robert H. *The Opening of American Society: From the Adoption of the Constitution to the Eve of Disunion.* New York, 1984.

————. *Self-Rule: A Cultural History of American Democracy.* Chicago, 1995.

Wilhelm, Hubert G.H. "Settlement and Selected Landscape Imprints in the Ohio Valley." In *Always a River: The Ohio River and the American Experience,* ed. Robert L. Reid, 72-81. Bloomington, Ind., 1991.

Wormer, Maxine E., transcriber. *Pope County, Illinois: 1850 Census.* Thomson, Ill., 1973.

Wright, George C. *In Pursuit of Equality, 1890-1980,* vol. 2 of *A History of Blacks in Kentucky.* Frankfort, 1992.

Zoll, Yvonne D., comp. *Perry County, Indiana, 1900 Federal Census.* Owensboro, 1982.

Index

Page numbers in italics refer to maps or tables.